T0230079

Lecture Notes in Computer Science   653

Edited by G. Goos and J. Hartmanis

Advisory Board: W. Brauer   D. Gries   J. Stoer

A. Bensoussan   J.-P. Verjus (Eds.)

Future Tendencies in Computer Science, Control and Applied Mathematics

International Conference
on the Occasion of the 25th Anniversary of INRIA
Paris, France, December 8-11, 1992
Proceedings

Springer-Verlag

Berlin Heidelberg New York
London Paris Tokyo
Hong Kong Barcelona
Budapest

Series Editors

Gerhard Goos
Universität Karlsruhe
Postfach 69 80
Vincenz-Priessnitz-Straße 1
W-7500 Karlsruhe, FRG

Juris Hartmanis
Cornell University
Department of Computer Science
4130 Upson Hall
Ithaca, NY 14853, USA

Volume Editors

Alain Bensoussan
INRIA, Domaine de Voluceau Rocquencourt, B. P. 105
F-78153 Le Chesnay, France

Jean-Pierre Verjus
INPG, 46 av. Félix Viallet
F-38031 Grenoble, France

CR Subject Classification (1991): D, F, G, H, I, C, J.6

ISBN 3-540-56320-2 Springer-Verlag Berlin Heidelberg New York
ISBN 0-387-56320-2 Springer-Verlag New York Berlin Heidelberg

© Springer-Verlag Berlin Heidelberg 1992
Printed in Germany

Typesetting: Camera ready by author/editor
Printing and binding: Druckhaus Beltz, Hemsbach/Bergstr.
45/3140-543210 - Printed on acid-free paper

Foreword

The *International Conference on Research in Computer Science and Control* organised by INRIA on December 8–11, 1992, was an exceptional event.

To celebrate its 25th anniversary, INRIA wanted to bring together a large number of the world's leading specialists in information technology who are particularly active in the fields covered by the Institute's research programmes.

Although INRIA's six research programmes present a real unity, they nonetheless cover a wide diversity of subjects. In response to INRIA's demand, the invited speakers agreed to give presentations focusing on the major advances and outlook of their particular field. This, owing to the increasing interpenetration of the topics, has been of considerable interest for the whole scientific community.

The challenges now facing computer scientists come from the technological advances which, today, allow us to foresee real changes of scale, such as the number of processors that will be interconnected in the near future in a massively parallel machine or in a distributed system, and, at the same time, to anticipate the requirements of other disciplines and major applications, including those which concern the general public.

Among these, scientific computing remains both the oldest and one of the most motivating fields for today's and tomorrow's computer science developments.

This tendency was clearly expressed in the opening address given by Professor J.-L. Lions, who evoked the permanent evolution of applied mathematics, a subject which remains the unavoidable basis for all computing and modelling activities.

The lectures by Professors F. Brezzi, R. Glowinski, T.J.R. Hughes, and A. Jameson illustrate the advances in scientific computing in the major fields of application, notably those of aeronautics and space.
The size and scale of the computer programs that must be developed in order to solve the problems referred to above necessitate the use of vectorial supercomputers and, more and more, massively parallel machines.

These modular, expandable architectures are being simultaneously studied in research centres (see the article by Professor C.L. Seitz) and developed in industry. The potential benefits of high-performance computation are considerable and have mobilized major research programmes in the U.S.A. (the HPCC programme), in Europe (the HPCN) and in Japan. The issues raised by the implementation of these new architectures and computer systems are similar to those of distributed networked systems. In the latter case it is more a question of cooperative processing than intensive computation. The library of the future (see the article by Professor J.H. Saltzer) is one of the applications that will require considerable resources not only in terms of computational power and memory (via dedicated – probably massively parallel – servers, managing large information bases), but also in terms of communication. The storage, transfer and manipulation of multimedia data are adding a new dimension – although raising new issues – to the development of communication and more generally distributed systems.

In step with these two evolutions in architecture, it is necessary to adapt or reconsider the knowledge, tools and methods required to tackle problems related to algorithms (see the articles by Professors F.P. Preparata and M.O. Rabin), programming languages and software engineering, protocols and communication software (see the article, by Professor R. Sethi), reliability, security and protection (see the article by Professor B. Randell), and the management of large multimedia information bases (see the article by Professor J.D. Ullman). All research efforts in these areas call for further fundamental studies on the complexity or the theory of languages and their semantics (see the articles by Professors R.L. Constable, Z. Manna, G.D. Plotkin).

Whatever the computer does, it works in partnership with the user, the degree of interaction varying according to the requested application. Communication may be via a number of means and could involve vision, sound, gesture or touch, or a combination of any or all of these (see the article by Professor J.M. Carroll).

Classical data processing techniques and methods mainly make use of the possibilities that the computer offers for symbolic manipulations. What is known as artificial intelligence is currently extending these possibilities, using our knowledge of human cognitive processes. These methods are based on a body of knowledge that researchers are attempting to represent in large knowledge bases (see the article by Professor R.J. Brachman), in decision support models (see the article by Professor J. de Kleer), as well as in new learning modes, some of them being based on an analogy with the functioning of the brain (see the article by Professor E. Wong). Although not directly stemming from AI, the probabilistic approach represents another means of widening the symbolic and deterministic possibilities of algorithmic development (see the article by Professor M.O. Rabin).

These new techniques also have the power to tackle difficult problems encountered in image processing, artificial vision and robotics, where they may be combined with more traditional techniques to form an extremely powerful union (see the articles by Professors P. Varaiya, R.W. Brockett, J.M. Brady, and J.J. Koenderink as well as the article by Dr. Netravali on the technological challenges of HDTV).

These fields are also very close to control and signal processing, which are themselves sources of many delicate mathematical problems (see the article by Professors H.J. Sussmann and W.H. Fleming) and subjects which are rich both from the point of view of the issues they raise (see the article by Professor A.S. Willsky) and from their numerical aspects (for example, the use of neural computing; see the article by Professor E. Wong).

We hope that this very brief overview gives not only an indication of the density and dimensions of the subjects, but also of the united outlook and approach to computer science and control experienced by INRIA.

We would like to express our gratitude to Professor Hubert Curien, Minister of Research and Space, who gave his sponsorship to the Conference and delivered the inaugural address during the opening session.

Our gratitude is also directed to all the contributors whose efforts have provided INRIA with the most valuable anniversary present. With the exception of Professor Lions, all these contributions come from outside France, which we trust will be considered as a token of our thanks to all the members of the international scientific community who have, over the last 25 years, shown their friendship for the Institute.

It should, of course, not be forgotten that the French themselves (from both INRIA and from various French research laboratories) have played an extremely active role in this conference, firstly acting as moderators in presenting the field covered by each session, as well as during the ten *Specialized Workshops* bringing together French and foreign researchers.

Our particular thanks are due to Therese Bricheteau, who was in charge of this conference, and to all those who, with her, have actively contributed to make this event a great success.

We also would like to extend our thanks to the publisher *Springer-Verlag*, who accepted to publish these proceedings in the *Lecture Notes in Computer Science* series.

Our goal of creating a concentration as rich as possible of Computer Science from December 8th to December 11th 1992 has clearly been achieved: INRIA deserves this *event* for its 25th anniversary.

Alain Bensoussan   Jean-Pierre Verjus

Invited Speakers

Karl Johan Åström

Ronald J. Brachman

J. Michael Brady

Franco Brezzi

Roger W. Brockett

John M. Carroll

Robert L. Constable

Wendell H . Fleming

Thomas J.R. Hughes

Jan J. Koenderink

Jacques-Louis Lions

Zohar Manna

Arun N. Netravali

Franco P. Preparata

Brian Randell

Jerome H. Saltzer   Charles L. Seitz   Ravi Sethi

Hector J. Sussmann   Jeffrey D. Ullman   Pravin Varaiya

Alan S. Willsky   Eugene Wong

Table of Contents

II. Symbolic Computation, Programming, and Software Engineering

III. Artificial Intelligence, Cognitive Systems, and Man-Machine Communication

IV. Robotics, Image and Vision

V. Signal Processing, Control and Manufacturing Automation

VI. Scientific Computing, Numerical Software, and Computer Aided Engineering

Inaugural Conference

World Mathematical Year 2.000 and Computer Sciences

J.L. Lions

Collège de France

1   WMY 2.000

The year 2.000 has been declared, at Rio de Janeiro, on May 6th 1992, the World Mathematical Year : WMY 2.000.
The declaration has been made by IMU (International Mathematical Union), with the sponsorship of Unesco (Prof. F. Mayor), the 3rd World Academy of Sciences (Prof. A. Salam), the Minister of Research and Space of France (Prof. H. Curien), the State Secretary for Science and Technology of Brazil (Prof. H. Jaguaribe) and the Federal Councellor of Switzerland (Exc. Flavio Cotti).
The declaration ceremony took place at IMPA (Instituto de Matematica Pura ed Aplicata) in Rio ; a research center of worldwide repute, with the participation of Prof. C. Chagas, representing the 3rd World Academy of Sciences and former President of the Pontifical Academy, of the Brazilian Academy of Sciences (Prof.I. Vargas), of Prof. A. Marzollo (representing Unesco).
IMU was represented by its executive board[1].

WMY 2.000 has the ambition to contribute in a significant way to the three following goals :

(I) *The Challenges of the 21st Century, in Pure and Applied Mathematics.*
What are they ?   What is the situation with respect to the main problems as stated by D. Hilbert in his conference at the ICM Paris 1900 (International Congress of Mathematicians) ? A first presentation of what is envisioned for this goal will be given at ICM Zürich 1994 by the *Turn of the Century Committee*[2], a Committee whose constitution was decided by the General Assembly of IMU at Kobe, August 1990, at the proposal of the American Mathematical Society.

(II) *Mathematics (Pure and Applied) are one of the keys to the Development.*
Therefore most of the countries which are members of Unesco should achieve, by the end of this century, a *Mathematical Level* making it possible for them to

---

[1] See page 16
[2] Members of this Committee are V.I. Arnold, F. Hirzebruch, L. Lovasz, B. Mazur, S. Mizohata, G.D. Mostow, J. Palis Jr (Chairman), J. Tits, W. Thurston, S. Varadhan.

enter IMU[3].
In order to achieve this goal, actions are under preparation in close cooperation with Unesco concerning *Education and Information*.

Several initiatives are going to be presented by the two main commissions of IMU :
ICMI : International Commission on Mathematical Instruction[4].
CDE : Commission on Development and Exchange[5]
One of the key issues, for developed and less developed countries as well, concerns *Networks and the Library of the Year 2.000*.
Ideas of the type of those presented in the lecture of Prof. J.H. Saltzer in this Conference are going to be extremely useful in this context.

(III) *The Image of Mathematics (Pure and Applied).*
In order to achieve the above goals one needs a good image and a clear presentation of what Mathematics (Pure and Applied) are about. This is "the image of Mathematics" in Information Society. This goal is the simplest to state. Achieving it is another matter. WMY 2.000 will try to contribute to this goal, in close cooperation with the corresponding initiatives already taken in several countries. ∎

Making the declaration at *IMPA*, Rio de Janeiro, in 1992, was very significant for (among others !) the following reasons :
(i) 1992 is the one hundreth anniversary of the publication of the "Leçons de Mécanique céleste" by H. Poincaré.
(ii) 1992 is the year of the Rio de Janeiro Congress on Environment and of the International Space Year (on the occasion of the 500th anniversary of Ch.COLOMB discovery). ∎

The Executive Committee of IMU wishes to make further steps in the direction of *Industrial Mathematics* (in cooperation and at the initiative of CICIAM[6]), of *Computer Sciences, Decision and Control, Operations Research*.

The present meeting, on the occasion of the 25th anniversary of INRIA, seems to be an excellent opportunity to ask the audience for ideas and proposals along these lines, and also an opportunity to try myself a very small step towards goal (I) of WMY 2.000.

---

[3] In 1992 IMU has 50 members (Members of IMU are countries).

[4] See page 16

[5] See page 16

[6] Committee of the International Conference on Industrial and Applied Mathematics, Chairman: Professor W. Gear

2 Some trends and problems in System Sciences

It goes without saying that what follows does not pretend, by any means, at being exhaustive. Among other things, stochastic aspects are not considered here (except a few hints) and many further questions in the field of "Applied Mathematics" are to be found in other lectures of this meeting. ∎

In a somewhat vague and fuzzy sense, the "leading concept" of the problems to be presented (briefly) below, is a remark made by N. Wiener in a letter to J. von Neumann, dated January 1945[7]. N. Wiener reports that he and Pitts are working on "*the problem of transition from the computing machine to the control machine*". ∎

2.1 "One cannot go faster than nature"

In a recent note[8], Dahleh, Peirce, and Rabitz present ideas on the control of molecular dynamics. They report that "typically interesting dynamical events will occur on the ultra-fast time scales 10^{-9} to $10^{-15}s$., eliminating the possibility of simultaneously monitoring the evolution of the molecular state and feeding back that information to redirect the driving field". They proceed by noting that, under these circumstances : "it will not be possible to have observation of the system on a real time scale, open loop controllers will be needed and this places enormous demand on the correctness of the theoretically designed fields for laboratory implementation", the fields being here optical fields to produce "a molecular pair of scissors".

Put in fuzzy terms, I shall summarize by saying, "One cannot go faster than nature". The dynamical systems on the fastest time scales (whatever that means) will *never* be controlled on line, by whatever "machine" we can think of.

It seems to me that the challenge mentioned in[8] loc cit, is basic. (Is not fusion control in a somewhat similar situation ?)

2.2 "One can (possibly) go at the same pace as nature"

One can dream of controlling a system S by a "brother" system S^* of the same family, therefore with similar time scales than S. What we have in mind here is the *control of chaos* and, in particular, *synchronization*.

We refer here to the recent papers of E. Ott, C. Grebogi and J.A. Yorke "Controlling Chaos"[9], W.L. Ditto, S.N. Raused and M.L. Spano "Experimental Control of Chaos"[10] and to the works of M. Gorman[11], L.Pecora, N.Velarde. A very large number of important applications seem to open up in these directions. Let

---

[7]Source : W. Aspray - The origins of John von Neumann's Theory of Automata in *the Legacy of John von Neumann*, AMS, vol. 50, (1990), p. 289-309, footnote 36.

[8]M. Dahleh, A.P. Peirce, M. Rabitz - Design Challenges for Control of Molecular Dynamics. IEEE Control Systems April 1992, p. 93-94.

[9]Physical Review Letters, 64 (11), (March 1990), p. 1196-1199.

[10]Ibid. 65 (26), (December 1990), p. 3211-3214.

[11]Dep. of Physics, University of Houston. I thank him very much for his precious indications.

us notice that "synchronization" is (somewhat) related to the idea of observers, a classical idea in the framework of System Sciences and Control.

2.3 "Climate is simpler to control than to predict"

This phrase has been reported to me by Prof. Dvoretsky[12] as being said by John von Neumann.

Von Neumann mentioned in Nature, 1955[13] that it *could* be possible to act on climate in a very significant way (for instance by modifying the albedo on the ice caps). He hastens to say that it is not because this would be "simple" (?) that it should be made !!

Challenge : how to control systems which are only partially and imperfectly modeled ? (I return to that below).

2.4 Control of turbulence - or "when you don't understand it, control it"

Controlling turbulence is a classical topic - if not completely well defined. Let me mention here some *very particular* questions *related* to the general problem. Let us consider the Navier Stokes equations :

$$(1) \quad \begin{cases} \dfrac{\partial y}{\partial t} + y \bigtriangledown y - \mu \Delta y = - \bigtriangledown p \\ \\ div \, y = 0 \end{cases}$$

in a domain $\Omega \subset \mathbb{R}^3$. The initial velocity field is given

$$(2) \quad y|_{t=0} = y^0.$$

The control is applied on a part Γ_1 of the boundary Γ of Ω, i.e.

$$(3) \quad \begin{cases} y = v \text{ on } \Gamma_1 \times (0, T) \\ \\ y = 0 \text{ on } (\Gamma/\Gamma_1) \times (0, T). \end{cases}$$

In (3) $v = \{v_1, v_2, v_3\}$ can depend on x and t, with some other constraints. Of course one should have (following from $div \, y = 0$ and Stokes formula)

$$(4) \quad \int_{\Gamma_1} v\nu \, d\Gamma_1 = 0, \quad \forall t$$

where ν stands for the unit normal to Γ, directed (to fix ideas) towards the exterior of Ω.

---

[12] On the occasion of a presentation of "Mathematics and Climate" made at the Israel Academy of Sciences, Jerusalem, (1989).

[13] Can we survive Technology - Nature - 1955 - Collected works of J. von Neumann, Pergamon, 1962, vol. VI.

In order not to have *regularity* difficulties, assume that the boundary Γ is very smooth, that Γ_1 is a "nice" subset of Γ and that $v(x,t)$ is as smooth as we like.

We can find a weak solution of (1) (2) (3). Let $y(x,t;v)$ be a solution[14] and let $E(\Gamma_1,T;y^0)$ be the set described, in a suitable space, say E[15], by all possible $y(x,T;v)$, where T is given and when v spans the set of all smooth vector fields satisfying (4).

Conjecture. Given Γ_1, arbitrarily "small" and given T arbitrarily small, given y^0 arbitrarily in, say, a L^2 space,

$$\text{the set } E(\Gamma_1,T;y^0) \text{ is dense in } E.$$

In other words, we conjecture[16] *approximate controllability*. We conjecture this density property to be true even when v_3, say, is *zero* (what about the case when v_2 and v_3 are zero ?). ∎

Of course this question is only slightly related to the "control of turbulence" but one can consider several similar questions and related conjectures for other models than Navier Stokes, such as Thermo-hydrodynamics :
Challenge : how to "control" Benard Rolls ? ∎

One step further would be along the lines of 2.3. above. In a series of papers (to be followed by a book), R.Temam, S. Wang and myself, we are pursuing the goal of having physically sound and significant *global models* of the coupled Ocean - Atmosphere System of Planet Earth[17] and *to prove* for these systems *existence theorems*[18]. Then *conceptual* problems of *control of climate* can be considered in a *precise* (if not realistic ...) setting. ∎

These questions lead in a natural way to two families of problems. The first one is theoretical. Can one envision a *classification of non-linear P.D.E's of evolution according to their controllability* ?

---

[14] Uniqueness is not known. This is a big challenge, open since the fundamental work of J. Leray, J.M.P.A. 12, (1933), p. 1-82, 13 (1934), p. 331-418, Acta. Math. 63 (1934), p. 193-248.

[15] cf. for instance J.L. Lions - Quelques méthodes de résolution des problèmes aux limites non linéaires - Paris, Dunod, 1969.

[16] J.L. Lions
Are there connections between turbulence and controllability ? In Proceedings INRIA Conf. on Analysis and Optimization of Systems - Springer Verlag - Lecture Notes in Control and Information Sciences - 144, (1990).

[17] J.L. Lions, R. Teman, S. Wang. In Nonlinearity (1992), Modelling and Scientific Computing (1993), Coupled Atmosphere Ocean Equations, (to appear).

[18] Curiously enough, this program does not seem to have been attempted before. It is of course the key for defining in a non ambiguous manner *stable approximation schemes*. Uniqueness seems to be out of reach ??

This question is already extremely difficult for *ordinary* differential equations[19]. It seems hopeless for PDE's except if, as it is natural, we restrict the question to "*physically relevant*" systems of non-linear PDE's[20]. ∎

Another family of questions related to the above conjecture(s) is concerned with the *numerical aspects* of it.[21].

A general (and vague) question is the following : Is it possible to give "convincing numerical evidence" of approximate controllability ? How can one "numerically prove" that a set is *dense* ?

A number of systematic numerical algorithms in situations where controllability is known (exact ot approximate) are presented in[21] loc. cit. cf. already[22]. ∎

2.5 More imaginative control design

The following question seems less difficult than the ones alluded to before, but is it ?

Optimum design (or control design) is control theory where the control variable is a (geometrical) domain Ω. We have then to consider mappings

$$(5) \qquad\qquad \Omega \to J(\Omega)$$

and to try to find[23], $\inf_{\Omega} J(\Omega)$, with constraints on Ω.

There are many constraints. One should be able to actually build Ω_0 (if Ω_0 is "the" optimal design) depending on technology available, feasibility, transport, cost etc.

Moreover there are in general *several cost functions* $J(\Omega)$ so that one has to look for *multicriteria* problems.

We confine ourselves here to (5).

There is no simple structure (and in particular *differentiable* structure) on the set of all Ω's. And one should be able to allow in the course of the computations for changes in the topology of Ω.

This is not at all a simple matter. An idea has been introduced by F. Murat andL.Tartar[24] and seems very interesting. One *begins* with a very complicated open set Ω_1, containing many "holes", the "holes" being "more or less empty" and one proceeds in iterative steps. If the grid of holes is fine enough and if, on the other hand, one allows some semi-empty holes to become holes, one can

---

[19] We refer in particular to the work of Sontag and of H. Sussman.

[20] For linear PDE's cf. D.L. Russel, SIAM Review (1978), J.L. Lions, SIAM Review (1988) and R.M.A., Masson, vol. 1 and 2, 1988, and E. Zuazua, C. Bardos, J. Lebeau, J. Rauch and Tataru (to appear).

[21] cf. R. Glowinski and J.L. Lions, Acta Numerica, 1993.

[22] R. Glowinski, C. Li, J.L. Lions, Japan Journal of Applied Mathematics (1990).

[23] cf. also A. Jameson lecture in this Conference.

[24] cf. more or less published works of F. Murat and L. Tartar and F. Murat (Personal communication).

obtain (theoretically) in the limit *any topology*. Some techniques of *homogenization* are used by these authors in this context. ∎

A related topic is "*real time control design*". Suppose we have a functional of the form

$$J(t; \Omega)$$

so that

$$\inf_{\Omega} J(t; \Omega)$$

may have an optimal solution Ω_0 depending on t, i.e.

$$\Omega_0 = \Omega_0(t).$$

How to find $\Omega_0(t)$ in real time ?

Examples :
  . variable geometry in hypersonic planes ;
  . control by vibrational devices ;
  . stealthiness.
These questions naturally lead to the following one :

2.6   Reverse Engineering from living systems

"Variable geometry" in "real time" immediately leads to the classical question : how do fishes and birds "control" their "trajectory" ? Indeed a classical question since Leonardo da Vinci !
And one returns here to the question of Norbert Wiener concerning "the problem of transition from the computing machine to the control machine".

2.7   More on Asymptotics

Let us consider the return on earth of a space plane. It will meet, on its return, first a plasma, with a number of (more or less precisely modelled) chemical reactions, to enter next in a denser and denser atmosphere.

From a conceptual view point it is "the D. Hilbert program in action" (with Chemistry added to it). One begins with the Boltzmann equations and one proceeds with the various models which can be deduced - at least formally - by asymptotic methods.
Program : can one prove the validity of these asymptotic expansions ?
Now that global existence for Boltzmann equations has been obtained[25], achieving the D. Hilbert program does not seem completely out of reach[26].

---

[25] R. di Perna and P.L. Lions - Annals of Maths, (1989).
[26] A number of works are in progress along these lines.

It should be possible to deduce from all that better and better numerical algorithms, improving the already very good existing ones. ■

In a different context, the "planet earth modelling", already alluded to above, leads to systems of non linear P.D.E.'s where *very many different scales are present*, both in space and in time. How to use this to our profit, by simplification of the models and, more importantly, *by obtaining new models* in a rigourous fashion ? We shall try to begin such a program in the work already mentioned of R. Temam, S. Wang and the Author.

Can one use the observations concerning the fractal dimension of the coast line to obtain better boundary conditions at the interface liquid ocean / solid earth ?[27]

Modelling vegetation is (apparently) another case in point. One faces there a very *inhomogeneous* situation. Homogenization theory has already been applied there for the interpretation of measurements.

2.8 Interfaces

Interfaces lead to a very large number of questions concerning *modelling* (Analysis and Control will come later). Let us give some examples of what we have in mind.

Mushy regions
If one looks at a space image of the "interface" - at any given time - between liquid ocean / solid ocean, one sees an "interface" which is not well defined and with an extremely complicated structure.
Examples of these "mushy" regions abound. They arise in metal processing (steel, copper, aluminium, ...) at the interface between solid and liquid state. They also arise in many geologically related processes.
From a mathematical view point, these problems belong to the family of *free surface problems*. ■

These are related to apparently completely different topics, namely "Optimal Stopping Times" and "Impulse Control"[28]. The analogy (in short) is as follows : in the state space where the process takes place - the evolution of a stock of goods for instance - the regions where we should place orders or where we should not are separated by an "interface".
It is this "economic" interface which is connected with the "free surfaces" of, say, physics.
Now, we can think of defining *"fuzzy stopping times"*, or *"fuzzy impulse control*

---

[27] L. Tartar Personal Communication.
[28] cf. A. Bensoussan and J.L. Lions - *Temps d'arrêt optimaux*. Paris, Dunod, 1978.
Contrôle Impulsionnel et Inéquations Quasi Variationnelles. Paris, Dunod, 1982.

times" etc... These are, for instance, times where we more and more seriously consider placing orders. Can we in this way make precise an analogy with mushy regions ? (The next question being: is this going to be useful... ?). ∎

Another family of problems where interface questions do arise concerns *Flexible Structures.*

These are structures (of the type of large space structures or of flexible robots) which consist of several (many) sub-structures, all these sub-structures having *different* properties :
- parts are rigid, other parts are flexible,
- some parts are of dimension 3, others are of dimension 2 or 1[29]
- materials are different (including composite materials).

The interfaces between these various components are the *junctions.*

How can one model the boundary conditions at these interfaces, depending on the manner in which these structures are joined together ?

Very interesting asymptotic methods[30] have been proposed, in particular, by Ph.Ciarlet[31] and E. Sanchez-Palencia[32].

Other, more direct, methods are proposed and studied by J. Lagnese and W.Leugering[33]. Related question : how to adequately model molding processes for instance ?
Experiments are difficult for structures to be built, and used (i.e. stabilized) in a micro-gravity environment. Adaptive methods of control seem to be necessary to use in this context[34].

2.9 Real time validation

The example just alluded to of a situation where information keeps coming as the "process" is already (almost) in use, belongs to a very large family of somewhat similar situations.

A classical case is the one of *meteorology.* Assuming that one has chosen a reasonably significant model for short or medium range (in time) predictions, one never disposes of a complete data for the initial conditions and for the boundary conditions. But, on the other hand, information keeps flowing from space (meteorological satellites) and from the ground. How to make best possible use of these information is the so called *assimilation theory*, introduced

---

[29] Of course this is an idealization of a situation where the width in one (resp. 2) direction(s) is "small".

[30] This topic could as well have been presented in 2.7. above.

[31] Books published at Masson. cf. also a book by Le Dret, 1990 - 1993.

[32] Book to be published.

[33] J. Lagnese and W. Leugering - Various works to appear.

[34] cf. the work of K.J. Aström and his group.

and used every day by meteorologists. There are (at the time of writing this paper) two methods.   ■

In one method one uses filtering, and more precisely the extended Kalman filter. "Extended" because one keeps using the *linearized* state equation at the time of the computation, the state equations being non linear. Cf. the exposition made by R.Daley[35].   ■

In a second method one uses *optimal control*[36]. One introduces a "distance" between "the" state corresponding to an initial condition y^0 (which is *partially known*) and the "real" state - more precisely with the "real" observations of the state. Minimizing this functional (and making a long story very short ...) provides the "good" initial conditions for the computation to give the "good" answer. One uses there the methods of Lagrange multipliers, adjoint state - and one ends with a "two point boundary value problems". Satisfactory results are reported along these lines cf. R. Daley, loc. cit. and[37].   ■

The challenge
In the "Global Change Programs"[38] more and more phenomena are going to be taken into account on a well documented basis. In other words : *the models are growing*.

Parallel to that, of course, the amount of data is going to grow in *enormous proportions*, since more Earth Observing satellites are going to be flown, more ground and ocean data will be obtained.

The challenge is then quite obvious : *"how to assimilate in real time all these data ?"* (fortunately "real time" has different meanings depending on the different subsystems - but if we disconnect too much, how is the *global* aspect to be taken care of ?).   ■

Real time validation also arises in the modelling of accidents, where a "crash" model may be needed to initiate the best possible decisions. In that case, with the evolution of the situation, the *model* itself will change.   ■

2.10   P.D.E's in infinite dimensions

From a general theoretical point of view, the real time optimal control (or decision) is given through the solution of the Hamilton-Jacobi-Bellman (H.J.B.) equation.

---

[35] R. Daley - Atmosphere Data Analysis - Cambridge University Press, 1991.

[36] This method can be applied to *every* identification problem.

[37] Clermont Ferrand - Data Assimilation Symposium, organized by F.X. Le Dimet and O. Talagrand, in the framework of WMO (World Meteorological Organization).

[38] IGBP (International Geosphere Biosphere Program) and WCRP (World Climate Research Program) jointly sponsored by ICSU (International Council of Scientific Unions) and by WMO (World Meteorological Organization).

The catch is that this H.J.B. equation will be, in the examples we have indicated so far[39], a *non linear* PDE *with an infinite number of variables*.
Is this hopeless ?   ■

It seems that, from a theoretical view point, good notions of "solutions" have appeared with the so called "viscosity solutions"[40].
What can be done from the numerical view point ?
Can one use ideas of the type of those introduced by L. Lovasz[41] in a completely different context (to compute integrals in large dimensions) ?

2.11   What is an island ?

The examples we have just mentioned are of somewhat "global" nature. Many other examples of a similar trend can be mentioned. Connection with the environment in all industrial processes (emissions, wastes, etc...) is such an example. The management with 0 stock, 0 defect, 0 delay imposes a global approach.

At the same time this global approach, if pushed too far, can lead to the impossibility of doing anything.

Subsystems have to be defined again ![42]

The argument may look strange and awkward. We *started* from subsystems. We observed that some (more and more) of these subsystems are tied together, so as to give a system. We now want to return to subsystems *but they are not necessarily the same.*

We have now, at least, three parameters of flexibility. First we have the choice[43] of the region, of the domain we want to study. In other words we have the choice of the geographical variable. Second, we have the choice of the time horizon. Third, we have the choice of the components of the state we want to study with particular care.

In environment, examples abound. The Mediterranean region is a subsystem. The monsoon is another one. El Niño is a famous other example.

Cloud Physics is another example (at what scale ?).   ■

---

[39]Notice that a one dimensional state equation with a *time delay* leads *also* to the same situation.

[40]H. Crandall and P.L. Lions - Various works since 1989.

[41]L. Lovasz - Lecture in Rio de Janeiro - May 1992.

[42]One can observe a somewhat similar question in Geopolitics.

[43]To be taken on (hopefully) a rational scientific basis.

Once a subsystem is chosen, methods to define appropriate boundary conditions on, for instance, the artificial boundaries, do exist.

Are there methods to *define* adequate *subsystems* for large set of non linear PDE's ?

An obvious idea is to use spectral decomposition. The ideas of attractors may enter in this family of questions, as does the theory of slow manifolds introduced in meteorology. For the connections between inertial manifolds and slow manifolds, we refer to R. Temam[44].

Another idea is to use the statistical methods and, more precisely, Principal Component Analysis, for defining adequate Inertial Manifolds[45].

2.12 Analysis and control of systems with incomplete data

We have given many examples of systems where available data are *not* complete, not sufficient to (uniquely) define the solution of the model. They abound in a large variety of situations: experiments impossible or dangerous (such as in Medicine) or too costly etc...

Traditional methods to extract the "best" possible information out of such situations, and to act accordingly, rely on Probalistic and Statistical methods. They are not considered here.
Other methods rely on optimal control theory such as sentinels[46/47]. They aim at finding relevant information we are interested in, without attempting to compute things of no interest.
How to do that in real time is an open question.   ■

How to control such systems, imperfectly defined, is still another topic. An idea is to use "low regret policies" or "low regret controls" : we wish to define and to study controls which cannot make the situation worse (no regret) or which can at worse make it slightly worse (low regret) and which *may* improve the situation. This is related to Pareto control and to Pareto sets[48].

The somewhat related question of the study of Pareto sets in *real time* seems to be very interesting[49].
On these matters, we have introduced in[48] "controllability against adversity".

[44] R. Temam - Attractors and Slow Manifolds, in Mathematics, Climate and Environment - Proceedings of the El Escorial Summer Course, J.I. Diaz and J.L. Lions ed. - Masson, 1993.
[45] I. Titi - (to appear).
[46] J.L. Lions - Sentinelles dans les systèmes distribués - Masson RMA, 1992.
[47] J.P. Kernevez - Sentinelles et Environnement - Masson R.M.A., 1993.
[48] J.L. Lions - Contrôle à moindres regrets. Lectures at Collège de France, (1992-1993).
[49] V.P. Maslow - Private communication - (1990).

3   Where are the Great Integrators ?

We have listed above a number of technical questions, without attempting nor having the capacity for an exhaustive presentation. Some topics are conspicuously absent : *wavelets*, by now already classical ; *particle methods* which appear so promising[50] ; *image analysis*, etc...

In parallel to these technical questions, another one seems to arise, of a more "organizational" type.

Going from "subsystems" to "systems", and after due analysis, implementing "controls" for such "composite" systems are two important trends. It means *"integration"*.

We have more and more to consider the "system" consisting of : "computer + transmission + workstation + access to data + software"[51] in connection with "real world systems"[52/53].

An immediate question arises : who is "in Charge" for doing (attempting) such an Integration ? *Where are the Great Integrators ?* They are going to play an essential role.
Is not INRIA going to play an eminent role among the Great Integrators ?

---

[50] We wish to mention here the very interesting initiative taken by G. Laval and P.A. Raviart in the framework of CNRS.

[51] P. Caseau - Private Communication, a CADAS report and E.D.F. reports (1991-1992).

[52] Such as those presented in all the examples I have indicated.

[53] We also refer to the work of A. Bensoussan.

International Mathematical Union (IMU)
Union Mathématique Internationale (UMI)
Executive Board 1991-1994

Professors   James Arthur, Mathematics, University of Toronto (Canada), Member
John Coates, Mathematics, University of Cambridge (U.K.), Vice-President
Albrecht Dold, Inst. de Mathematics, University of Heidelberg (Germany), Member
Ludwig D. Faddeev, LOMI, St. Petersbourg and Moscow (CEI), Former President
Hikosaburo Komatsu, Mathematics, Faculty of Sciences, Tokyo (Japan), Member
J.L. Lions, Collège de France, Paris (France), President
Laszlo Lovasz, Loránd Eötvös, University of Budapest (Hungary), Members
David Mumford, Harvard University, Maths., Cambridge (U.SA.), Vice-President
Jacob Palis Jr., IMPA, Rio de Janeiro (Brazil), Secretary
Edward Zehnder, ETH-Zentrum, Zürich (Switzerland), Member

International Commission on Mathematical Instruction (ICMI)
Commission Internationale pour l'enseignement des Mathématiques (CIEM)
Executive Board 1991-1994

Professors   Yuri L. Ershov, Rector, University of Novosibirsk (C.E.I), Member
Miguel de Guzman, University of Complutense, Madrid (Spain), President
Jeremy Kilpatrick, Dept. Math. Ed., University of Georgia (USA), Vice-President
Lee Peng-Yee, National University of Singapore (Singapore), Vice-President
Eduard Luna, p.t. Barry University, Miami Shores (USA), Member
Mmogens Niss, IMFUFA, University of Roskilde (Denmark), Secretary
Anna Sierpinska, Inst. of Mathematics, Ac. Sci. of Poland, Warsaw (Poland), Member

Ex-officio :   Jean-Pierre Kahane, University Paris-Sud, Orsay (France), Former President
J.H. van Lint, Rector Magnif. Techn. Univ. of Eindhoven (NL), repr. IMU/ICSU-CTS
J.L. Lions, Collège de France, Paris (France), President IMU
Jacob Palis Jr., IMPA, Rio de Janeiro (Brazil), Secretary IMU

Commission on Development and Exchange (CDE)
Commission pour le Développement et les Echanges
Executive Board 1991-1994

Professors   Pierre Berard, Inst. Fourier, University of Grenoble, (France), Secretary
Cesar Camacho, IMPA, Rio de Janeiro (Brazil), Member
Alberto Grunbaum, University of California, Berkeley (USA), Member
Aderemi O. Kuku, University of Ibadan (Nigeria), Member
J. Mawhin, Inst. of Mathematics, University of Louvain (Belgium), Member
M.S. Naraimhan, TIFR, Bombay (India) and ICTP, Trieste, (Italy), Chairman
T. Ochiai, Faculty of Sciences, University of Tokyo, (Japan), Member
Pier Luigi Papini, University of Bologna (Italy), Member
Wu Wetsün, Academia Sinica, Inst. Systems Sciences Beijing (China), Member

Ex-officio :   J.L. Lions, Collège de France, Paris, President IMU
Jacob Palis Jr., IMPA, Rio de Janeiro, (Brazil), Secretary IMU

I. Parallel Processing, Databases, Networks, and Distributed Systems

Dependable Parallel Computing by Randomization

(Abstract)

by

Michael O. Rabin

Hebrew University of Jerusalem

Harvard University, Cambridge, MA

An idealized model of parallel computations involves n virtual processors $V_1, \cdots, V_n$ addressing a shared memory and working in *synchrony*. These processors execute a program P in parallel instructions where in the $\pi - th$ parallel instruction $V_i, 1 \le i \le n$, executes $x_i := f_i(y_i, z_i)$ involving some program variables x_i, y_i, z_i and an operation (function) f_i.

In real parallel computers involving real processors $P_i, \cdots, P_n$, the assumption that these processors execute in complete synchrony is unrealistic, and an attempt to impose such synchrony either by hardware or operating-system constructs would be inefficient and costly. A special case of asynchrony is the possibility that processors may fail which can be interpreted as a processor becoming infinitely slow.

Thus it is a fundamentally important question whether a synchronous parallel execution of a program P on an idealized computer can be simulated on a realistic asynchronous computer. In a series of papers Rabin, in cooperation with Aumann, Kedem, and Palem, have solved this problem in a manner which also promises to be of practical significance. These results are the first of their kind and represent a breakthrough in this field.

Given a parallel program P written for an n-processor synchronous computer, a compilation process is defined in [KPRR 92] and [AR 92] which produces a compiled program $T(P)$. This program $T(P)$ will simulate the execution of P on any asynchronous n-processor computer in a manner which is: i. Correct. ii. Continually progressive. iii. Efficient. Three constructs play a role in this simulation. Replicated variables ensure that tardy processors do not "clobber", by overwriting, a correct value of a variable. A program-implemented shared phase-clock, which is read by the processors in order to know what program simulation phase they are in. An All-Done Array which is used to indicate that a parallel instruction execution is completed. All the above constructs use randomization. In fact, it has been proved that such a simulation is not possible by deterministic algorithms.

The constructions of [KPRR 92] and [AR 92] simulate a parallel step involving n instruction executions by the individual processors, by $n \log^3 n$ and $n \log^2 n$ instructions, respectively, of the asynchronous computer. While these results are of theoretical significance, the $\log^2 n$ blow-up factor is too large from the practical point of view. In more recent work Aumann, Kedem, Palem, and Rabin have addressed this issue. They considered programs P for data processing tasks such as on-line transaction processing or large queries against a data base. In such computations, the program variables are "large objects" such as records, pages, or rows of a relational data base. This makes it possible to use Rabin's Information Dispersal Algorithm (IDA) [Rab 89], rather than replication, for representing the variables in memory. This does away with the $\log n$ multiplicative overhead factor inherent to the simulations in [KPRR 92, AR 92]. The final result is that for large objects a parallel step involving w machine instructions can be simulated on the asynchronous machine be $w \cdot \log^* n$ processor instructions. Her $\log^* n$ denotes the number of iterations of the log function (natural log) required to get from n to a value less than 2. For example, $\log^* 1000 = 3$. Thus the overhead is within a very practical range. The use of IDA also ensures that the computation is resilient with respect to memory faults as well as to processor failures.

An intriguing aspect of this research into asynchrony are the possible implications to the study of neural systems. Even though the study of artificial neural nets usually postulates synchrony, it stands to reason that in the living neural systems the individual neurons, especially those comprising different interacting centers, are not driven by an overall "clock". It would be interesting to see if the methodology for coping with asynchrony has a counterpart in living systems. In particular, Aumann and Rabin are conducting a study of certain biological pace-makers which seem to employ randomization in their structure. This connection will also be discussed in the present lecture.

Bibliography

1. [Rab 89] M.O. Rabin. Efficient Dispersal of Information for Security, Load Balancing, and Fault Tolerance, *Jour. of Assoc. for Comp. Machinery*, vol. 38 (1989), pp. 335-348.

2. [KPRR 92] Z.M. Kedem, K.V. Palem, M.O. Rabin and A. Raghunathan. Efficient Program Transformation for Resilient Computation via Randomization. *Proceedings of the Annual ACM Symposium on the Theory of Computing, (STOC)*, (1992), pp. 306-318.

3. [AR 92] Y. Aumann and M.O. Rabin. Fast PRAM Simulation on Fully Asynchronous Parallel Systems, to appear in *Proceedings of Foundation of Computer Science (FOCS)*, October 1992.

System Dependability

Brian Randell

Dept. of Computing Science
University of Newcastle upon Tyne

Abstract. The paper starts with a brief account of how and why, at about the time of the birth of what is now INRIA, the author and his colleagues became interested in the subject now known as system dependability. The main body of the paper summarizes the work over the last three years of the ESPRIT Basic Research project on Predictably Dependable Computing Systems (PDCS). This is a long term collaborative research activity, centred on the problems (i) of producing quantitative methods for measuring and predicting the dependability of complex software/hardware systems, (ii) of incorporating such methods into the design process, and (iii) of developing appropriate architectures and components as bases for designing predictably dependable systems. A further section of the paper then describes, in somewhat more detail, one of the current activities within PDCS. This is work being carried out by the author in collaboration with an INRIA colleague, Dr. Jean-Charles Fabre, on a unified approach to providing both reliability and security termed Object-Oriented Fragmented Data Processing (OOFDP).

1. Introduction

Twenty-five years ago my personal research interests were focussed on system design methodology in the area of complex multiprocessing operating systems. I was then at the IBM T.J. Watson Research Center, where I and my colleagues were aiming to aid system designers by providing means of predicting the likely impact of their various design decisions on the ultimate performance of the overall final system. The approach we developed was based on expressing the system design as a simulation program. Such a program would evolve and grow vastly more detailed as the design process progressed and hence its careful structuring would be of paramount importance. It was these twin issues of system structuring and design decision-making, though both motivated mainly by performance considerations, that were uppermost in my mind when I received an invitation to the first NATO Software Engineering Conference, held at Garmisch in 1968.

The impact of this conference, particularly on many of the attendees, was immense. For example, both Edsger Dijkstra and I have since gone on record as to how the discussions at this conference on the "software crisis", and the potential for software-induced catastrophes, strongly influenced our thinking and our subsequent research activities. In Dijkstra's case the discussions led him into an immensely fruitful long term study of the problems of producing high quality programs. In my own case, following my move to Newcastle soon after the Garmisch Conference, they led me to consider the then very novel, and still somewhat controversial, idea, of software fault tolerance. Suffice it to say that our respective choices of research problems suitably reflect our respective skills at program design and verification.

It will thus soon be twenty-five years since my research interests, though continuing to involve a strong concern with issues of system structuring, switched rather abruptly to an aspect of the topic that (thanks incidentally to a French colleague, of whom more anon) I now know as *system dependability*. However this is not intended as a historical talk, summarizing developments in system dependability over the entire twenty-five year period. Rather, I will concentrate largely on recent work on the subject undertaken in connection with the ESPRIT Basic Research Project entitled PDCS (Predictably Dependable Computing Systems) that I have the honour of leading.

2. Computing Systems

The title of our project, with its emphasis on "computing systems", implies that it is not concerned solely with either hardware or software. Indeed for many years I - not alone of course - have held the view that the conceptual differences between hardware and software design were small, and indeed diminishing as VLSI technology makes possible the implementation of ever more complex logical designs on a single chip.

I thus always react negatively to discussions which imply that, for example, software design practices are developing more slowly than hardware design practices, that software is especially prone to design faults, or even that software designers are less professional than hardware designers, when the differences really concern relative complexity. For obvious practical reasons, the more complex algorithms involved in providing a system's required functionality will normally be implemented in software rather than hardware. And, though there is no well accepted measure of the complexity of a logical design, even by such inadequate means as "lines of code", "number of transistors, etc.", it is clear that the complexity of the software in most large scale computing systems is several orders of magnitude greater than that of the hardware.

Such differences in complexity, far more than cultural or technical differences, are the root cause of the differing practices that are followed by the hardware and software design communities. And it was in fact a debate about these differing practices at a meeting a few years ago of the IFIP Working Group 10.4 on System Dependability and Fault Tolerance which in part led me to formulate, with some colleagues, a programme of long term research which has since become the PDCS project.

This particular IFIP Working Group meeting was the occasion of a number of very interesting presentations on the role of predictive evaluation in hardware design. These presentations brought home to me the extent to which the computer industry's hardware designers routinely made, and had their further decision making guided by, predictions as to the likely ultimate reliability, availability and performance of their systems.

A number of different techniques were involved, from simple rules of thumb, through stochastic models, to complex simulations. However, it became clear during the discussions following the presentations that these techniques were being increasingly challenged by the ever-growing complexity of the logical designs that the hardware designers were being called upon to produce, and that none took account of the possibility of residual design faults.

Nevertheless, within these limitations, the skilled deployment of these techniques enabled the hardware design process to be much more of an engineering process than was, or indeed is, the case with most if not all software engineering. (Parenthetically, let me mention that my involvement in the 1968 NATO Software Engineering conference - whose title was an expression of an aspiration, rather than a reality - made me extremely cynical regarding the vast mass of software activity that was suddenly re-labelled Software Engineering in the early 1970s. I have retained much of this cynicism to this day.)

Given this situation regarding the predictive evaluation of hardware designs, it was evident to me and my colleagues that it would be a very worthwhile although extremely challenging task to try to extend the scope of logical design evaluation techniques and tools (i) to deal with the much greater complexity levels that were characteristic of software sub-systems, and hence of complex computing systems as a whole, and (ii) if possible to allow for the all-too-real likelihood that residual design faults would exist at such complexity levels, despite all attempts to prevent this. Moreover, we felt that such techniques and tools were best investigated within an overall design and system framework - just as in reality, if they were to be useful, they would need to be deployed as an integral part of an overall system engineering design process.

3. System Dependability

Turning back to much earlier work for a moment, when I and colleagues at Newcastle became interested in the possibility of achieving useful degrees of design fault tolerance, we found that one of the problems facing us was the inadequacy for our purposes of the concepts and terminology that hardware reliability engineers were then using.

In the 1970s hardware engineers took various particular types of fault (stuck-at-zero, stuck-at-one, etc.) which might occur within a system as the starting point for their definitions of terms such as system reliability and system availability. But given not just the absence of any useful categorization of design faults, but also the realization that in many cases the actual identification of some particular aspect of a complex system design as being *the* fault might well be quite subjective, we felt in need of a more general set of concepts and definitions. And of course we wanted these definitions to be properly recursive, so that we could adequately discuss problems that might occur either within or between system components at any level of a system.

The alternative approach that we developed took as its starting point the notion of *failure*, whether of a system or a system component, to provide its intended services. Depending on circumstances, the failures of interest could concern differing aspects of the services - e.g. the average real-time response achieved, the likelihood of producing the required results, the ability to avoid causing failures which could be catastrophic to the system's environment, the degree to which deliberate security intrusions can be prevented, etc. The ensuing generality of our definitions of terms thus led us to start using the term "reliability" in a much broader sense than was perhaps desirable, or acceptable to others; it was our French colleague, Dr. Jean-Claude Laprie of LAAS-CNRS, who came to our linguistic and conceptual rescue by proposing the use of the term "dependability" instead.

Dependability is defined as the trustworthiness of a computer system such that reliance can justifiably be placed on the service it delivers [15; 39]. Dependability thus includes as special cases such properties as reliability, integrity, privacy, safety, security, etc., and provides a very convenient means of subsuming these various concerns within a single conceptual framework. It also provides means of addressing the problem that what a user usually needs from a system is an appropriate balance of several such properties.

The problem of producing a fully adequate set of system dependability concepts and terminology, appropriate for all the ways in which "things could go wrong", and all approaches to trying to prevent or cope with this situation, turned out to be much more difficult and complicated than I imagined at the outset. Indeed it is a problem that has engaged the efforts of various groups of colleagues, mainly under Dr. Jean-Claude Laprie's leadership, in the IFIP Working Group, and the PDCS project, and has recently culminated (I hesitate to say terminated), in the publication of a five-language book. I will start by summarizing some basic definitions from this book [39]:

A system **failure** occurs when the delivered service no longer complies with the **specification**, the latter being an agreed description of the system's expected function and/or service. An **error** is that part of the system state which is liable to lead to subsequent failure: an error affecting the service is an indication that a failure occurs or had occurred. The adjudged or hypothesized cause of an error is a **fault**.

A failure occurs when an error "passes through" the system-user interface and affects the service delivered by the system - a system of course being composed of components which are themselves systems. Thus the manifestation of failures, faults and errors follows a "fundamental chain":

$$\ldots \rightarrow \ \text{failure} \ \rightarrow \ \text{fault} \ \rightarrow \ \text{error} \ \rightarrow \ \text{failure} \ \rightarrow \ \text{fault} \ \rightarrow \ \ldots$$

Faults and their sources are extremely diverse; they can be classified in various different ways. One can distinguish **accidental faults**, which appear or are created fortuitously, from **intentional faults**, which are created deliberately, presumably malevolently. One can, sometimes somewhat arbitrarily, classify faults as being **physical faults**, which are due to adverse physical phenomena, and **human-made faults**, which result from human imperfections. With respect to a system boundary, one can distinguish **internal faults**, which are those parts of the state of a system which when invoked by the computation activity will produce an error, from **external faults**, which result from interference or interaction with its physical or human environment. Depending on when a fault was created, it can be termed a **design fault**, i.e. one that arises during the development of the system or of its operating and maintenance procedures, or an **operational fault**, which appears during actual use of the system. And depending on the nature of the conditions which govern the presence of the fault, it can be classed as a **permanent** or a **temporary fault**.

The methods involved in developing a dependable computing system can be classed into:

- **fault prevention**: how to prevent fault occurrence or introduction;

- **fault tolerance**; how to provide a service complying with the specification in spite of faults;

- **fault removal**; how to reduce the presence (number, seriousness) of faults;

- **fault forecasting**: how to estimate the present number, the future incidence, and the consequence of faults."

These four means for dependability all feature in the work of PDCS, though we put comparatively little stress on the first, fault prevention. This is not to imply that we view this topic as being of less importance than the other three; rather it is that virtually all research related to system design and construction is of relevance to fault prevention, even when not undertaken with this as an explicit aim. However the point I would stress is that combined utilization of all four means is normally needed if a high level of dependability is required - preferably at each step in the design and implementation process.

4. The PDCS Project

The above comments make it clear that dependability is very much a *systems issue*, since virtually all aspects of a computing system, and of the means by which it was specified, designed and constructed, can affect the system's overall dependability. Users gain little satisfaction from being assured that particular system components are functioning faultlessly or that particular parts of the design process have been carried out absolutely correctly if the overall *system* does not provide a level of dependability commensurate with the level of dependence that they have to place on it.

Moreover, realistic dependability prediction and assessment normally have to involve careful calculation of probabilities and risks, rather than naive belief in certainties. Thus they should, if at all possible, be based on stochastic models and well-established statistics, rather than simplistic assumptions, whether about the functioning of system hardware components, or the care with which system design processes have been carried out.

These were the views which Jean-Claude Laprie and I shared when we initiated the planning of what became the PDCS project, a project whose membership is drawn largely from the European contingent on IFIP WG 10.4. However, it also includes various other leading European researchers with the complementary skills and interests that we felt were needed to make a suitably broad attack on the overall problem of achieving predictable dependability for complex computing systems.

The project started in 1989, and had a first phase which we now term PDCS1 that ran for three years. The institutions and principal investigators that were involved in PDCS1 were:

Centre for Software Reliability, The City University, London, UK (Bev Littlewood)

IEI del CNR, Pisa, Italy (Lorenzo Strigini)

Institut fur Algorithm und Kognitiv Systeme, Universität Karlsruhe, Karlsruhe, Federal Republic of Germany (Tom Beth)

LAAS-CNRS, Toulouse, France (Jean-Claude Laprie)

Computing Laboratory, The University of Newcastle upon Tyne, Newcastle upon Tyne, UK (Brian Randell)

LRI, Université Paris-Sud, Paris, France (Marie-Claude Gaudel)

Institut fur Technische Informatik, Technische Universität Wien, Vienna, Austria (Herman Kopetz)

Department of Computer Science, The University of York, York, UK (John McDermid)

The second phase, PDCS2, has just started, with almost the same set of institutions involved, though not all as full partners, and with one additional full partner, namely Chalmers Technical University, Göteborg.

In view of what I have already said, it should be clear that the single most important characteristic of our work is the stress we have, and are continuing to, put on the necessity of taking a "systems engineering" approach, aimed at achieving well-coordinated progress towards:

(i)   developing effective techniques for establishing realistic dependability requirements, and so producing dependability specifications against which the system design process and its resultant products can be assessed;

(ii) producing quantitative methods for measuring and predicting the dependability of complex software/hardware systems, allowing for the possible presence of design and deliberate faults as well as operational faults;

(iii) incorporating such methods more fully into the design process, and all its means of attempting to prevent, remove and tolerate faults, so as to make the process much more controlled and capable of allowing design decisions (and decisions concerning the actual deployment of the system) to be based on meaningful analyses of risks and quantified likely benefits; and, ultimately

(iv)   producing an effective design support environment populated both with the tools necessary to facilitate practical use of such techniques and methods, and with ready-to-use families of system components with known dependability characteristics.

An important characteristic of the goal we thus set ourselves was, and remains, to facilitate increased use of quantitative assessments of system dependability. Clearly there will be limits to the extent that many process and product characteristics can be meaningfully and accurately quantified. Nevertheless, we feel that a degree of concentration on techniques which will help lay the foundations of increased use of quantitative methods is fully justified. Indeed, as I have implied already, our view is that increased effective use of quantitative methods is a prerequisite to turning the activity of constructing large computer-based systems into a true engineering discipline.

The PDCS group's ultimate long term objective, a design support environment which is well-populated with tools and ready-made components, and which fully supports the notion of predictably dependable design of large distributed real-time computing systems, is of course extremely ambitious, and not something one would expect to achieve within the time span of a single project, but it nevertheless provides a good long-term focus for our work.

At the outset of the PDCS1 project we concluded a detailed review of the state-of-the-art with the comments: "although much research has been, and is continuing to be, undertaken on the multi-faceted problem of system dependability of complex hardware/software systems, comparatively little progress has been made on drawing all the relevant research threads together. For example, there are to date few links between work on fault prevention and fault forecasting - links which might greatly facilitate the tasks of (i) deciding what levels of effort should be expended, in a major system development project, on what types and methods of fault avoidance and fault tolerance, and (ii) predicting the probable outcome. Similarly, there are inadequate links between research activities aimed at different facets of dependability, such as reliability and security. "

Many of the topics which the PDCS Project has worked on, and in many cases is still actively pursuing, are therefore particularly "integrative" in nature. These include:

*   the very notion of design environments for fault-tolerant systems which incorporate dependability evaluation tools in order to assist design choices

*   a fault tolerance approach to object-oriented system security using the fragmentation/redundancy/scattering technique

- the derivation of optimal test strategies mixing deterministic and statistical testing

- the validation (wrt both fault removal and fault forecasting) of fault-tolerant systems via fault injection

- the assessment of the effect of different system environments on the reliability of a software system" via two approaches: discrete-time reliability growth models and explanatory variables

- an attempt to develop a cost-based model of operational security similar to the time-based model for reliability that is universal for reliability

- work on extending the current limitations to the reliability evaluation of safety-critical software, via a combination of information relating to the product, its production process, and past experience on similar products.

Clearly, there is insufficient time for me to provide adequate descriptions of all of these and our various other activities (work on which has resulted in, or contributed to, over a hundred publications in refereed journals and international conferences over the last three years).

Instead, after summarizing the project's work under the four headings: Fault Prevention, Fault Tolerance, Fault Removal, and Fault Forecasting, I will concentrate on just one topic. I have three reasons for the particular choice I have made. First, it is an example of Anglo-French cooperation, second the French contribution is led by an INRIA Researcher based at LAAS, Dr. Jean-Charles Fabre, and finally it is the research topic within PDCS in which I am currently most involved. It concerns the provision of reliability *and* security via a single unified mechanism, and takes advantage of object-oriented system structuring - something that, for all its current trendiness, I have remained sympathetic to ever since the original Simula Common Base Language report was published, twenty-five years ago. Clearly this is a vintage year for Silver Jubilees!

5. An Overview of Work to Date in PDCS

This overview is based on sections of a report on PDCS1 - like this report it is structured according to the four principal means involved in achieving dependable systems: fault prevention, fault tolerance, fault removal and fault forecasting.

5.1. Fault Prevention

Any computer system that meets its requirements is dependable only to the extent that those requirements represent the user's needs; yet *requirements analysis and specification* is still one of the more neglected areas of computer science. Most system failures can be attributed to subtle design faults introduced because of a mismatch of assumptions and requirements relevant to various different system aspects. Work in the ESPRIT ORDIT project has produced a methodological framework for understanding the process of elicitation, modelling and re-presentation back to the user of organizational requirements (i.e. requirements which affect the design of the whole surrounding socio-technical system and not just the design of the computer system). In PDCS1 we have used this framework to look at some issues of determining security policies [25] and as a basis of the meaning of the terms "safety" and "security" [14]. We have also examined the process by which non-functional requirements are transformed into functional requirements.

Work on *real time object models and notations* has been oriented towards providing a framework for specifying, analyzing and implementing real-time systems. Work in PDCS1 has focused on foundational issues, establishing classes of timeliness requirements and ways of classifying architectures. The classification has centred on ideas of timing grids which enable architectures to be characterised, and bounds to be placed on certain temporal characteristics, e.g. carrying out 'synchronised' actions at physically different nodes in a distributed system. Foundational work was also undertaken in producing (formally based) object models for defining and reasoning about architectures, although this has not yet reached a stage suitable for publication.

Timeliness analysis is a central issue to PDCS. In real-time systems, the intended result must be produced within a specified time interval after the occurrence of a stimulus. Considerable work in a number of areas has been performed recently by PDCS [71] and a number of other projects [35; 54; 62; 71]. For example, we have analyzed the diverse effects which determine the maximum execution time of a simple application, the control of a rolling ball, in the very restricted execution environment given by the MARS architecture.

5.2. Fault Tolerance

Advances in our understanding of *fault tolerance strategies, architectures and notations* have been made in PDCS1, including: (i) classifying existing architectures for combined hardware and software fault tolerance [40]; (ii) generalizing the notion of adjudication in redundant systems [24]; (iii) proposing design rules for the composition of subsystems employing different fault tolerance strategies [64]. In PDCS1 two description languages have been defined and investigated [7; 10], based on a data-flow model, suitable both for describing fault-tolerant schemes in application software and as intermediate languages to be supported by a fault-tolerant interpretation layer. A design notation for a wide class of fault-tolerant software structures is proposed in [17], and an approach to fault-tolerant design based on system-level diagnosis theory has been introduced [72].

The application of formal methods to program development has already made it possible in certain cases to refine a program specification into the text of a program which is guaranteed to satisfy the specification. It is now possible to study the use of such techniques for fault-tolerant programs. In PDCS1, a method has been explored for obtaining diversity in redundant variants of a software component, while preserving consistency with a formal specification [31].

The production of a *design support environment* populated by a number of ready-to-use tools will be fundamental to the design of predictably dependable computing systems in practice. In PDCS1 several significant advances have been made with regard to such tools, in particular by the definition and implementation of SoRel from LAAS, a tool for quantitative dependability evaluation and by the development at Vienna of a tool set for the MARS Design System (MARDS), which is a prototype design environment for real-time systems.

Reaching agreement is an essential problem in distributed fault-tolerant systems. Examples are agreement on data (reliable broadcast)[6; 22], time (clock synchronization), and component state (membership) [21; 37] in spite of different kinds of failures in the components and in the communication system. In PDCS1 we have worked on the problem of distributed clock synchronization and the distributed membership problem, and have also investigated the problems of a monitoring service for improving the availability of distributed systems and the security aspects.

Several solutions have been proposed to the problem of *tolerance of accidental and intentional operational faults*: classical solutions based on data replication and ciphering, information dispersal for files [55], and alternate routings for communications [36]. A novel solution is Fragmentation-Redundancy-Scattering (FRS) [29], the principle of which is to split sensitive information into fragments, to add redundancy to them, and finally to scatter them over a distributed system. Any isolated fragment does not by itself provide any significant information. Availability and integrity are obtained through redundancy of fragments, and confidentiality is ensured due to the absence of logical relation between the fragments. This is the basis of the work on object-oriented fragmented data processing [56] described in more detail below.

5.3. Fault Removal

Regarding work on *testing in the value domain*, software test criteria proposed in the literature as guides for determining input test cases relate to the structure or to the function of the software, defining respectively structural and functional testing. Using these criteria, the methods for generating the test cases can be either deterministic or probabilistic. In the first case test data are predetermined by selection in accordance with chosen criteria. In the second case test inputs are generated according to a probability distribution on the input domain; both the distribution and the number of input data items being determined according to the chosen criteria. Work in PDCS1 concentrated upon examination of the fault revealing power of software statistical testing [65]. This involves the notion of statistical test quality with respect to one or several criteria, and a new ordering relation to compare the stringency of different criteria with regard to random test data. We defined an original testing method, *structural statistical testing*, and the partial ordering of fifteen current structural criteria is shown in [66]. Experiments were conducted on industrial software (four real programs) from the nuclear field [69]. These indicated that the power of structural statistical testing — i.e. of random test data generated according to an appropriate distribution defined so that the program structure is properly scanned — to reveal faults is higher than that of deterministic test data, or of random data generated from a uniform distribution over the input domain. The efficiency of the mixed testing strategy combining deterministic and random test inputs [65] was confirmed by these experiments. Another experiment was conducted [33] on a software product, in which statistical testing was found to be superior to deterministic testing. Surprisingly, there was some evidence that this superiority of statistical testing was more pronounced for the more elusive (smaller rate) faults than for others.

Concerning *testing in the time domain*, within PDCS1 we have developed the notions of event-triggered (ET) and time-triggered (TT) systems [38]. These characterize two different system architectures where ET systems observe (internal and external) events and react to them by initiating appropriate actions, whereas TT systems initiate all their actions only at predefined points in time. TT systems are especially attractive for implementing real-time applications, because they allow design of the temporal behaviour of the system. In ET systems, many decisions affecting the temporal behaviour must be taken at run-time (e.g. scheduling) or are left to "chance" (e.g. ordering of messages). Our preliminary analysis of the problems of testing real-time systems has shown that TT systems offer a number of specific advantages which considerably ease the testing of such systems, especially with respect to repeatability and controllability of test runs. Based on these system properties, we have developed a test methodology for the MARS architecture [59]. This test methodology includes the definition of several test phases, each with a distinct and well-defined purpose, the design of test beds to facilitate test execution, and the proposal of a number of test tools.

As dependability of fault-tolerant systems is conditioned to a large extent by the efficiency of the fault tolerance algorithms and mechanisms, testing of fault tolerance is to be considered as an integral part of the validation of fault-tolerant systems. Fault injection constitutes an invaluable means towards this end by providing inputs for exercising fault tolerance. Up to now — except for the work related to the validation of fault tolerant protocols recently reported in [26] — most fault injection studies have focused on the fault forecasting objective. Previous experiments carried out on actual fault tolerant systems [2] have shown that the data gathered during experiments aimed at fault forecasting can be used in practice in a feedback loop so as to influence the design and implementation of fault tolerance algorithms and mechanisms: i.e. these experiments contribute to fault removal. Preliminary studies carried out in PDCS1 [5] concerning the refinement of the fault injection input and output attributes introduced in [4] have shown that the elaboration of such a test sequence can be obtained from the definition of structural and behavioural simulation models of fault tolerance that serve as bases for the application of the results of the test theory.

5.4. Fault Forecasting

Several important advances have been made in *reliability and availability modelling* in PDCS1. The position now is that we understand fairly well how to obtain reasonably accurate reliability growth predictions in a wide class of circumstances. More importantly, we have techniques that allow us to know in a particular context whether the answers are ones that we should trust. All this has come about through the invention and validation of techniques such as u-plots, prequential likelihood, etc. for the analysis of predictive accuracy [44]. These techniques have allowed us to demonstrate that new non-parametric models, with much weaker underlying assumptions than conventional models, can perform with comparable accuracy in many situations [11; 12]. They have also allowed us to develop a powerful and general new technique of dynamic model recalibration, which can improve the accuracy of certain models in particular circumstances, often with dramatic effect [13].

Other important results obtained in PDCS1 widen the scope of the models. We have generalized (i) the classical, hardware oriented, reliability and availability theory to incorporate software as well, and (ii) the software reliability growth theory, to incorporate hardware as well [41]. We are now able to model multi-component systems taking into account reliability growth of their components thanks to the "transformation approach" where the (classical) Markov model of a system in stable reliability is transformed into another Markov model which incorporates reliability growth thanks to some properties of our hyperexponential model [42]. This approach has been applied to model fault-tolerant software architectures in presence of reliability growth: we have shown that unreliability is strongly dependent on reliability growth factors of the different components [34]. Tools have been developed to facilitate the use of these new techniques: SoRel (for software reliability analysis and prediction) and a tool for reliability prediction and recalibration.

Concerning *statistical testing of software*, previous work has focused on the quantitative assessment of reliability. Two different approaches have been proposed depending on whether the evaluation is deduced from a zero-failure test experiment [50; 52], or from failure records during the test phase [17]. The applicability of the second approach is restricted to non-critical software as it involves observed failures without fault fixing. We have therefore put a particular emphasis on the evaluation from a zero-failure experiment for which we propose the use of simple Markov models — both in continuous and discrete time — to quantify the test duration required to ensure a target reliability or availability objective with a given confidence level [67; 68].

We now have a good general understanding of how to evaluate reliability when relatively modest levels are needed. When it comes to *evaluation for ultra-high dependability*, however, the difficulties seem very severe. In PDCS1 we have begun to investigate these limits to evaluation in a formal way [46]. We have shown that none of the various approaches alone is able to assure ultra-high dependability. For example, current models are limited to evaluating reliability levels of approximately the order of 10^{-4} failures per hour. However, it remains to be seen how much we can increase our confidence when we combine information from disparate sources, e.g. formal verification using discrete domain models, operational testing, knowledge of fault-tolerant architecture, etc. [43].

Several modelling studies of system behaviour in the presence of faults were carried out in PDCS1. These included pipelines of TMR nodes [27], high speed data networks [51] and multiprocessor systems with arbitrary failure modes [16]. A number of interesting results were obtained, and in one case a new numerical solution methodology was employed. Because of their generality, Markov and semi-Markov models are able to represent complex interactions among system components (e.g. state dependent failure rate, complex repair policy). Their main limitation of is the inability to handle many states, and much further work is needed on *large state space modelling*. For realistic models, the state space requirements often exceed the memory and CPU capabilities that can be expected from computing systems, even in the foreseeable future. Approximations, for instance state space truncation, can be applied to cope with this state space explosion, but the numerical errors introduced are difficult to quantify, especially if the dependability measures of interest are related to rare events (i.e. faults in the present case). We have recently started the study of a new technique to evaluate the eigenvector system of large (possibly infinite) Markov chains [18; 19; 20], which allows both steady-state and transient system characteristics to be evaluated and so can be applied to determine measures of availability.

Since *coverage evaluation by fault injection* gives *conditional* dependability measures (i.e., conditioned on the occurrence of a fault), models incorporating the fault occurrence process are also needed in order to enable the evaluation of dependability measures. For this purpose, we have defined [1; 4] an experimental evaluation method aimed at bridging the gap between (i) the analytical modeling approaches used for the representation of the fault occurrence process (e.g. Monte Carlo simulations, closed-form expressions, Markov chains) and (ii) the experimental measures obtained by fault injection approaches characterizing the error processing and fault treatment provided by the fault tolerance algorithms and mechanisms. Two fault injection systems, which we have developed outside of PDCS1, are now available: one uses heavy-ion radiation to inject transient faults into integrated circuits [32] and has been applied to evaluating watchdog error detection schemes, the second is a pin-level injection system, called MESSALINE that has been applied to the validation of two fault-tolerant systems [2; 3].

In PDCS1 we have started work on *security modelling* with the intention of obtaining operational measures of security. Although there are many important ways in which the reliability metaphor applies to security (such as the inevitability of a stochastic approach), some of these similarities tend to operate at a high conceptual level and for practical application there are some important differences which need to be recognized [45]. For example, it seems that the choice of variable to represent the role played by time in the reliability models needs to be chosen with great care in security: a variable that captures the notion of effort expended, not necessarily in time, seems essential. In addition, the importance of different viewpoints needs to be emphasized in security, since it is unlikely that these will coincide even in the case when each observer has a large amount of information.

6. Object-Oriented Fragmented Data Processing

Reliability/availability and security, though attributes of the generic concept of dependability, are often considered separately because the techniques used to achieve them are usually perceived as being mutually antagonistic. Firstly, *reliability* and *availability* are generally achieved by incorporating mechanisms for tolerating any faults (especially accidental faults) that occur, or that remain despite attempts at fault prevention during the system design process. These techniques will of necessity involve space and/or time redundancy; they can easily take advantage of a distributed computing architecture by means of replicated computation using sets of untrusted (or fallible) processors. Secondly, *security features* are generally achieved by means of fault prevention mechanisms (w.r.t. intentional faults, such as intrusions) whereby critical applications are implemented using physically and/or logically protected computers; such protection is usually based on the *TCB* (Trusted Computing Base) or *NTCB* (Network Trusted Computing Base) concepts.

6.1. Fragmented Data Processing

The technique termed "Fragmented Data Processing" (FDP) [23; 30; 70] is an approach to the *combined* provision of overall system security (in the sense of data and processing confidentiality) and reliability in distributed systems. It can provide each of the users of a distributed system with an individual set of processing and storage resources which are to a great extent protected not only from the effects of hardware and software faults but also of so-called "intrusions". By this term we mean (presumably) deliberate attempts by other (possibly unauthorized) users of the system to gain information from, or modify, or deny access to, the user's resources. For example, such attempts could even involve tampering physically with the hardware, or inserting "Trojan Horse" software.

The FDP approach, and the original Fragmentation-Redundancy-Scattering (FRS) scheme [29] on which it is based, are strongly related to conventional fault tolerance techniques. FDP achieves high reliability/availability and security for critical applications by arranging that their execution depends merely on (i) the correct execution of a majority of a set of copies of each of a number of program fragments, and (ii) the reliable storage of a majority of a set of copies of each of a number of data fragments; such fragments are widely distributed across a number of computers in a distributed computing system so as to impede intruders and to tolerate faults, and are defined so as to ensure that an isolated fragment is not significant, due to the lack of information it would provide to a potential intruder.

In effect, fragmentation and scattering is just a form of encryption, though one whose overheads are quite modest, and whose use fits well with general fault tolerance provisions (replication and voting) that are aimed at providing high reliability and availability despite the presence of hardware and software faults. Indeed, the crucial point about FDP is that the services it provides depend not on the integrity of any individual software or hardware components (which would imply the existence of "single points of failure"), but rather on majority voting by members of various sets of components. It simply presumes that such majorities exist (thus assuming a limit on the number of simultaneous faults) and in particular that voting is not being invalidated by either accidental or deliberate collusion between voters.

More specifically, systems employing FDP are, from the point of view of each user, divided into two sets of resources, namely a "trusted" (and it is hoped trustworthy) set and an "untrusted" set. Typically, the untrusted resources form a shared set of processing and storage servers, which users access from their individually trusted personal workstations, and it is in these terms that the technique will be described here.

Two major implemented examples of the application of the original FDP scheme have been completed, both using the DELTA-4 distributed system [53]. These are respectively an archiving system [58] and a user authorization service [9; 23]. These both involved explicit implementation of the fragmentation and scattering mechanisms by the application programmer.

6.2. Object-Oriented FDP and its Implementation

Although FDP was not originally based on the use of object-oriented programming, the object-oriented model gives a reasonably straightforward method of implementing FDP which involves arranging that objects are split into fragments consisting of the subsidiary objects of which they were originally composed. This is done by defining and providing an implementation of the appropriate class characteristic and then choosing which classes of object should inherit this characteristic. Thus just as Arjuna [63] allows all objects of a class to be declared as recoverable, so the objects of a given class could be declared to be "Secured" by being fragmented and scattered. By such means the user can exercise control over the granularity of fragmentation without being involved in the actual implementation of the FDP mechanisms.

Declaring a given class to be "Secured" will of course mean arranging for this class to inherit a set of facilities defined in an appropriate class declaration. These characteristics will, for example (i) ensure that when objects of this given class are created, their constituent sub-objects will be scattered, and (ii) provide each object with any necessary information, such as a "key", needed to control the fragmentation and scattering and the means by which the object's operations access its scattered sub-objects. Some such keys might be used only at compile and generation time, and then deliberately discarded (i.e. for what can be termed "static" fragmentation and scattering). Others are likely to be retained within, or associated with, objects at run time (e.g. for "dynamic" fragmentation and scattering, in which sub-object names are computed when the sub-objects are invoked). The keys themselves need to be protected - for example using the notion of a threshold scheme [60].

An object which has been declared to inherit the characteristic "secured" would thus be largely empty, apart from the information necessary for accessing its now remote subsidiary objects, and the code (or a reference to the code) for the various operations (methods). The fact that the subsidiary objects were allocated, in many cases, to separate machines would involve overheads, but would also provide significant potential parallelism for achieving a speeding-up of the original object's methods. (There already exist a number of techniques (under various different names) which are somewhat akin to fragmentation and scattering, aimed at exploiting parallelism for performance purposes rather than at providing security. These include, at the hardware level, so-called "disk striping" and, in object-based programming, the object fragmentation provisions of the SOS system at INRIA [48; 61].)

The actual means by which such forms of fragmentation and scattering can be achieved, e.g. the methods for placing, and later accessing remote subsidiary objects, will depend on the strategy that is being provided to users for handling distribution problems. For example, the programming of the class "secured" might be based on the use of a simple, but rather inflexible, facility of a single virtual name space (e.g. [8]), whose implementation embodies and hides the distribution policies which are in use. Another alternative is the facility provided in SOS for declaring and implementing shared distributed objects (termed "fragmented objects" in SOS) out of elementary objects which are located on different computers. (Clearly, with such an approach the distribution policies remain under user program control.)

6.3. An Electronic Diary Example

Object-oriented fragmented data processing (OOFDP) has to date been investigated using several detailed examples. The first was in fact based on part of the specification of the user authorization service [9; 23] provided in the DELTA-4 distributed system [53]. A fuller account of this first example to be found in [57].

More recently an example based on a distributed Electronic-Diary has been designed using Eiffel [49] tools and implemented on top of the DELTA-4 Support Environment (DELTASE). The summary given here is based on a fuller account provided in [28].

The electronic diary service is described by a small set of classes. These show how the information related to a meeting is composed of a given topic, a group of people attending, a venue and time/date information. Any two or more of such items are considered as constituting confidential information. Otherwise, any person attending is defined by several identification items and can be considered as being public information.

Some of the object classes (and their component objects) forming the E-Diary application object are shown in Figure 1, where an asterisk indicates the possibility of there being several components of a given object class.

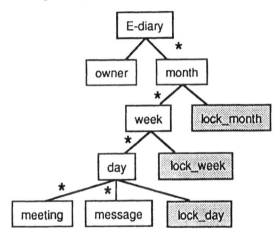

Figure 1: The E-Diary object composition hierarchy

The object hierarchy represented in Figure 1 for the E-diary service is as follows: the **E-Diary** is composed of several **month** objects and is owned by a given user (**owner**). Each month is composed of a number of weeks and can be locked (**lock_month**) for a given reason (holidays, for instance). Each week is composed of a number of days and can also be locked (**lock_week**) for a given reason (travel abroad, for instance). Any day is composed of a list of **meetings**, a list of **messages** (note pad) and can be also locked for a given reason (**lock_day**). Any lock set to true implies that no meeting can be allocated in the month, week or day, respectively. The E-Diary is considered as a persistent object and can thus be activated (from persistent storage) after being created. It offers several services to the owner: create, modify, move, delete a meeting, put, release a message in the note pad of a given day, and lock a month, a week, or a day for a given reason.

The object which is of interest in the hierarchy shown above is the meeting object which contains confidential information; the composition hierarchy of this object is presented in Figure 2. A **meeting** is composed of a persons list (**P-list**), a **venue, time** and **topic**. The P-list can be implemented in various different ways, possibly using the Eiffel predefined class list (of **persons**). Person is composed of three sub-objects in our example: **name, address** and **position**.

The object hierarchies presented in Figure 1 and 2 illustrate (in a form similar to Eiffel browser output) the various components in the design of the E-Diary object down to elementary objects (i.e. a combination of Eiffel elementary objects such as integers, booleans, strings...). Some of the elementary objects represented by grey boxes are confidential leaves of the tree that it is assumed for present purposes cannot be usefully decomposed into smaller objects; for instance the topic is a string that is ciphered to ensure confidentiality as soon as it is entered by the user in the system. The same is true for lock objects which correspond to a boolean value and a string that indicates the locking reason.

An example is given below of the effects that can be achieved by arranging that the characteristic "secured" be inherited by a given object class, say the meeting class that was shown in Figure 1. In this and the next figure, the various objects are labelled with numbers indicating the different (sets of) computers they have been allocated to. These numbers have been chosen based on the simplistic rule that the immediate sub-objects of any fragmented object, and the object itself, are allocated to different (sets of) computers, depending on which class(es) of objects have been defined to inherit the characteristic "Secured". Inheritance of the "secured" characteristic is denoted by "Secured: ObjectClass" in the figures.

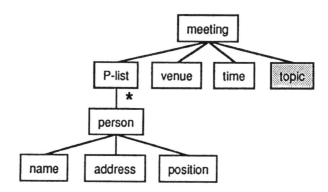

Figure 2: The Meeting object composition hierarchy

Site number 1 represents the user site where the owner is able to execute management operations (in particular input/output operations) and where all the meeting descriptors are located when FDP is not used. In this first case the characteristic "secured" is attached to the *meeting* class. This solution leads to processing (and perhaps storing) *Person list, venue, time* and *topic* at distinct sites as shown in Figure 3. (The fragmentation and scattering of the P-list objects is discussed later.)

In this case, site 1 is responsible for the management of *meeting* objects. Considering just *P-list* objects, all the *person* objects that appear in the meeting will be managed (and perhaps stored) at the same site (say site 2). An intruder located at site 2 is unable to find out about the *topic* of the meeting (even in its enciphered form) ; the confidentiality of the relation (*person list, topic*) is thus preserved by sites 2 and 5. Similarly, an intruder located at site 5 is able to obtain the (enciphered) topic of the meeting but is unable to find out the list of persons attending.

Secured: meeting

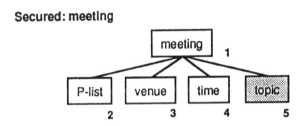

Figure 3: "Secured" meeting descriptors

The characteristic "secured" could however be attached not just to the meetings but also inherited by the *P-list* object as in Figure 4.

This solution provides a complete fragmentation and scattering of *person* objects belonging to the *P-list*. An intruder located at any of sites 6 to 9 is unable to get the P-list information (the list of persons attending the same meeting). At site 2, the P-list object is a collection of references to *person* objects: these references are produced by a naming facility based on one-way functions similar to those used in the archiving system described in [23].

Secured: meeting, P-list

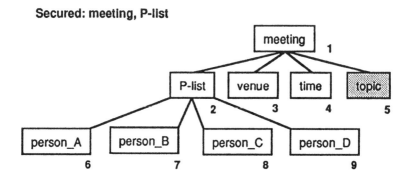

Figure 4: Secured meetings and P-list by inheritance

This last solution is the basis of the current implementation of E-Diary on the DELTA-4 platform. DELTA-4 [53] does not provide an object-oriented layer but provides a run time support for objects as a collection of servers responsible for object management; a server is defined by an interface composed of a set of operations described using an Interface Definition Language and operation activation from the clients is transparent. In our implementation a server is associated with an Eiffel class and is responsible for the management of object instances of this class. For a given class several servers can be created on several sites, such as *person* servers in the above example. The Eiffel design presented in this section has been mapped onto DELTA-4 by hand. The complete application including more objects and more confidentiality constraints (including operator interface, ciphering and naming functions) is currently running using scattering and replication (with majority voting) on a set of Unix workstations at LAAS, using the DELTASE layer and the DELTA-4 error processing protocols, based on DELTA-4's Multicast Communication System.

6.4. An Initial Assessment

Experiments such as the above indicate to us that FDP, in common with certain other approaches to security so far explored mainly in the database world, can derive significant benefits from being viewed and used in conjunction with a suitable object-oriented structuring scheme. Indeed, its provision as an independently inheritable characteristic alongside the use of several forms of inheritable reliability characteristics (such as "stable" and "atomic") that have already been devised elsewhere, such as in the Arjuna Project, seems perfectly feasible. However, one particularly attractive feature of the FDP technique is that it would seem to have the potential of being simultaneously beneficial not just to security and reliability but also, because of its exploitation of parallelism, to performance - characteristics which are normally mutually antagonistic!

Detailed experimental investigations are however now needed to determine the likely actual cost/effectiveness of OOFDP, as compared both to the FDP that has already been implemented in DELTA-4, and to any other approaches to the joint provision of reliability and security.

7. Concluding Remarks

One of the great difficulties about system dependability is also one of its greatest attractions as a research area. This is the fact that, as mentioned earlier, virtually every aspect of a system and the way in which it is developed is potentially relevant to the system's eventual dependability. Thus, since Newcastle took up the topic nearly twenty-five years ago our work has, at different times, concentrated on programming languages, processor and memory architectures, networking protocols, distributed systems, etc. (A much longer list of topics are covered by the expertise of the PDCS community as a whole.) Another "attraction" of the research topic is that as improved levels of system dependability are achieved, all too often one finds levels of user dependence and of required system functionality increasing correspondingly, so putting further demands on the system dependability research community. This I suppose is perhaps my main excuse for having remained involved in the topic for as long as INRIA has existed - a claim I do not expect to be invited, or even able, to repeat at INRIA's golden jubilee! However I have much appreciated this chance to help celebrate the Silver Jubilee.

8. Acknowledgements

Self-evidently, the work I have discussed in this paper has been largely carried out by my colleagues, whose texts I have also drawn on extensively - it is a pleasure to acknowledge the debt I owe to them all. The work of PDCS is supported by the CEC's ESPRIT Programme.

9. References

1.   J. Arlat. Dependability Validation by means of Fault Injection — Method, Implementation, Application. National Polytechnic Institute, Toulouse, France, 1990. Also published as LAAS Report RR 90-399 (in French)

2.   J. Arlat, M. Aguera, L. Amat, Y. Crouzet, J.C. Fabre, J.C. Laprie, E. Martins and D. Powell, "Fault Injection for Dependability Validation — A Methodology and Some Applications," IEEE Trans. Software Eng., Special Section on Experimental Computer Science, vol. 16, pp.166-182, 1990.

3.   J. Arlat, M. Aguera, Y. Crouzet, J.C. Fabre, E. Martins and D. Powell, "Experimental Evaluation of the Fault Tolerance of an Atomic Multicast Protocol," IEEE Trans Reliability, Special Issue on Experimental Evaluation of Computer Reliability, vol. 39, no. 4, pp.455-467, 1990.

4.   J. Arlat, Y. Crouzet and J.C. Laprie. "Fault-Injection for Dependability Validation of Fault-Tolerant Computing Systems," in Proc. 19th IEEE Int. Symp. Fault-Tolerant Computing (FTCS-19), pp. 348-355, Chicago, IL, USA, 1989.

5.   J. Arlat, Y. Crouzet and J.C. Laprie. "Fault-Injection for the Experimental Validation of Fault Tolerance," in Second Year Report, Volume 3, Chapter 1, Section III, PDCS, 1991. (To appear in Proc. Esprit Conference, (CEC-DGXIII), Brussels, Belgium, November 25-29, 1991.)

6.   O. Babaoglu, "Streets of Byzantium: Network architectures for fast reliable broadcasts," IEEE Trans. on Software Engineering, vol. SE-11, no. 6, pp.546-554, 1985.

7.   O. Babaoglu, L. Alivisi, A. Amoroso and R. Davoli. "Paralex: An Environment for Reliable Parallel Programming in Distributed Systems," in PDCS 2nd year Report, PDCS, 1991.

8.   E.H. Bal and A.S. Tanenbaum. "Distributed programming with shared data," in Proc. of the ICCL, pp. 82-91, Miami, FL, IEEE, Computer Society Press, 1988.

9.   L. Blain and Y. Deswarte. "An intrusion-tolerant security server for an open distributed system," in Proc. of the European Symposium in Computer Security (ESORICS 90), pp. 97-104, Toulouse (France), AFCET, ISBN 2-9036778-9, 1990.

10.   A. Bondavalli and L. Simoncini. "Failure classification with respect to detection," in Proc. 2nd Workshop on Future Trends of Distributed Computing Systems in the 90s, pp. 47-53, Cairo, IEEE, 1990.

11.   S. Brocklehurst. A Non-Parametric Approach to Software Reliability Modelling, PDCS Technical Report No. 4, PDCS, 1989.

12. S. Brocklehurst. A Multi-Model Approach to the Analysis of Software Failure Data, PDCS, 1992. (in preparation)

13. S. Brocklehurst, P.Y. Chan, B. Littlewood and J. Snell, "Recalibrating Software Reliability Models," IEEE Transactions on Software Engineering, vol. 16, no. 4, pp.458-470, 1990.

14. A. Burns, J.A. McDermid and J.E. Dobson, "On the Meaning of Safety and Security," Computer Journal, vol. 34, no. 1,1992.

15. W.C. Carter. "A Time for Reflection," in Proc. 12th IEEE Int. Symp. on Fault-Tolerant Computing (FTCS-12), pp. 41, Santa Monica, CA, 1982.

16. R. Chakka and I. Mitrani. "Multiprocessor Systems with General Breakdowns and Repairs," in Proc. Sigmetrics - Performance '92, Newport, RI, 1992.

17. C.-K. Cho. Quality Programming: Developing and Testing Software with Statistical Quality Control, John Wiley and Sons, Inc., 1987.

18. P.-J. Courtois and P. Semal, "Bounds for the Positive Eigenvectors of Non-Negative Matrices and for their Approximations by Decomposition," J. ACM, vol. 31, no. 4, pp.804-825, 1984.

19. P.-J. Courtois and P. Semal, "Computable Bounds for Conditional Steady-State Probabilities in Large Markov Chains and Queueing Models," IEEE Trans SAC, vol. 4, no. 6, pp.926-937, 1986.

20. P.-J. Courtois and P. Semal. "Bounds for Transient Characteristics of Markov Chains with Large State Spaces," in Proc. First Int. Conf. on Numerical Solutions of Markov Chains, Raleigh, NC, USA, 1990.

21. F. Cristian. "Agreeing on Who is Present and Who is Absent in a Synchronous Distributed System," in Proc. IEEE Int. Symp. on Fault-Tolerant Computing (FTCS-18), pp. 206-211, Tokyo, Japan, 1988.

22. F. Cristian, H. Aghili, R. Strong and D. Dolev. "Atomic Broadcast: From simple message diffusion to Byzantine agreement," in Proc. 15th IEEE Int. Symp. on Fault-Tolerant Computing (FTCS-15), pp. 200-206, Ann Arbor, Michigan, 1985.

23. Y. Deswarte, L. Blain and J.C. Fabre. "Intrusion Tolerance in Distributed Computing Systems," in Proc. 1991 IEEE Symposium on Research in Security and Privacy, Oakland, California, 1991.

24. F. Di Giandomenico and L. Strigini. "Adjudicators for Diverse-Redundant Components," in Proc. 9th Symposium of Reliable Distributed Systems, pp. 114-123, Huntsville, Alabama, IEEE, 1990.

25. J.E. Dobson and J.A. McDermid. An Investigation into Modelling and Categorisation of Non-Functional Requirements, YCS 141, University of York, 1990.

26. K. Echtle and Y. Chen. "Evaluation of Deterministic Fault Injection for Fault-Tolerant Protocol Testing," in Proc. 21st IEEE Int. Symp. Fault-Tolerant Computing (FTCS-21), pp. 418-425, Montréal, Québec, Canada, 1991.

27. P. Ezhilchelvan, I. Mitrani and S.K. Shrivastava, "A Performance Evaluation Study of Pipeline TMR Systems," IEEE Transactions on Parallel and Distributed Systems, vol. 1, no. 4, pp.442-456, 1990.

28. J.C. Fabre and B. Randell. "An Object-Oriented View of Fragmented Data Processing for Fault and Intrusion Tolerance in Distributed Systems," in Proc. ESORICS'92, Toulouse, 1992.

29. J.-M. Fray, Y. Deswarte and D. Powell. "Intrusion Tolerance Using Fine-Grain Fragmentation-Scattering," in Proc. IEEE Symp. on Security and Privacy, pp. 194-201, Oakland CA, USA, IEEE, 1986.

30. J.M. Fray and J.C. Fabre. "Fragmented Data Processing: an Approach to Secure and Reliable Processing in Distributed Computing Systems," in Proc. 1st IFIP Int. Working Conf. on Dependable Computing for Critical Applications, pp. 131-137, Santa Barbara, California, 1989.

31. M. Gaschignard and M.C. Gaudel. "Diversification from Algebraic Specification," in PDCS Project First Year Report, ESPRIT Project 3092, 1990.

32. U. Gunneflo, J. Karlsson and J. Torin. "Evaluation of Error Detection Schemes using Fault Injection by Heavy Ion Radiation," in Proc. 19th IEEE Int. Symp. Fault-Tolerant Computing, pp. 340-347, Chicago, IL, 1989.

33. A. Jassim, B. Littlewood, P. Mellor and D. Lazenby. Random testing compared with structural testing, City University, 1990.

34. K. Kanoun, M. Kaaniche, C. Beounes, J.C. Laprie and J. Arlat. "Reliability Growth of Fault-Tolerant Software," in PDCS 2nd year Report, 2 Chapter 2 Part 3, PDCS, 1991.

35. E. Kligerman and A. Stoyenko, "Real-Time Euclid: A Language for Reliable Real-Time Systems," IEEE Trans. on Software Engineering, vol. SE-12, no. 9, pp. 941-949, 1986.

36. Y. Koga, E. Fukushima and K. Yoshihara. "Error recoverable and securable data communication for computer network," in Proc. 12th IEEE Int. Symp. on Fault-Tolerant Computing (FTCS-12), pp. 183-186, Santa Monica, 1982.

37. H. Kopetz, G. Grünsteidl and J. Reisinger. "Fault-Tolerant Membership Service in a Synchronous Distributed Real-Time System," in Dependable Computing for Critical Applications, ed. A. Avizienis and J. C. Laprie, pp.411-429, Springer-Verlag, 1991.

38. H. Kopetz and K. Kim. "Temporal Uncertainties in Interactions among Real-Time Objects," in Proc. 9th Symposium on Reliable Distributed Systems, pp. 165-174, Huntsville, AL, USA, IEEE Computer Society Press, 1990.

39. J.C. Laprie, (Ed.). Dependability: basic concepts and terminology - in English, French, German, German and Japanese, Vienna, Springer-Verlag, 1992, 265p. p.

40. J.C. Laprie, J. Arlat, C. Beounes and K. Kanoun, "Definition and Analysis of Hardware-and-Software Fault-Tolerant Architectures," IEEE Computer (Special Issue on Fault Tolerant Systems), vol. 23, no. 7, pp.39-51, 1990.

41. J.C. Laprie and K. Kanoun. "X-ware Dependability Modelling and Evaluation," in PDCS 2nd year Report, 2 Chapter 2 Part 1, PDCS, 1991.

42. J.C. Laprie, K. Kanoun, C. Beounes and M. Kaaniche, "The KAT -- Knowledge-Action-Transformation -- Approach to the Modeling and Evaluation of Reliability and Availability Growth," IEEE Trans. on Software Engineering, no. April,1991.

43. J.C. Laprie and B. Littlewood. "Quantitative Assessment of Safety-Critical Software: Why and How?," in Int. Conf. on Probabilistic Safety Assessment and Management, Beverley Hills, 1991. (Presented, but not in Proceedings.)

44. B. Littlewood. "Modelling growth in software reliability," in Software Reliability Handbook, ed. P. Rook, 1990.

45. B. Littlewood, S. Brocklehurst, N.E. Fenton, P. Mellor, S. Page, D. Wright, J.E. Dobson, J.A. McDermid and D. Gollman. Towards Operational Measures for Computer Security, Second Year Report, Volume 3, PDCS Project, 1991.

46. B. Littlewood and L. Strigini. "Validating Ultra-High Dependability for Software-Based Systems," in PDCS 2nd year Report, PDCS, 1991.

47. C. Liu. "A General Framework for Software Fault Tolerance," in PDCS 2nd year Report, PDCS, 1991.

48. M. Makpangou, Y. Gourhant, J.-P.L. Narzul and M. Shapiro. Structuring Distributed Applications as Fragmented Objects, Research Report 1404, INRIA, Rocquencourt, France, 1991.

49. B. Meyer, "Eiffel: Programming for Reusability and Extendibility," ACM SIGPLAN, vol. 22, no. 2, pp.85-94, 1987.

50. D.R. Miller. "The Role of Statistical Modeling and Inference in Software Quality Assurance," in Software Certification, ed. B. d. Neumann, pp.135-152, Elsevier Applied Sciences, UK, 1989.

51. D. Mitra and I. Mitrani. "Asymptotic Optimality of the Go-Back-n Protocol in High Speed Data Networks with Small Buffers," in Proc. 4th Int. Conf. on Data Communication Systems and Their Performance, Barcelona, 1990.

52. D.L. Parnas, A.J.v. Schouwen and S.P. Kwan, "Evaluation of Safety-Critical Software," Communications of the ACM, vol. 33, no. 6, pp.636-648, 1990.

53. D. Powell. "Delta4: A Generic Architecture for Dependable Distributed Computing," in Research Reports ESPRIT (Vol. 1), Springer-Verlag, 1991.

54. P. Puschner and C. Koza, "Calculating the Maximum Execution Time of Real-Time Programs," Real-Time Systems, vol. 1, no. 2, pp.159-176, 1989.

55. M.O. Rabin, "Efficient Dispersal of Information for Security, Load Balancing and Fault-Tolerance," Journal of the ACM, vol. 36, no. 2, pp.335-348, 1989.

56. B. Randell and J.C. Fabre. "Fault and Intrusion Tolerance in Object-Oriented Systems," in Proc. Int. Workshop on Object-Orientation in Operating Systems, pp. 180-184, Palo Alto, CA, IEEE Technical Committee on Operating Systems and Application Environments (TCOS), 1991.

57. B. Randell and J.C. Fabre. FDP techniques in Object-Oriented Systems, Research Report N°91.114 (Also TR 337, Computing Laboratory, University of Newcastle upon Tyne, 1991.), LAAS, Toulouse, France, 1991.

58. P.G. Ranéa, Y. Deswarte, J.M. Fray and D. Powell. "The Security Approach in DELTA-4," in Proc. of the European Telematics Conference (EUTECO-88) on Research into Networks and distributed Applications, pp. 455-466, Vienna, Austria, North-Holland, 1988.

59. W. Schütz. "Real-Time Simulation in the Distributed Real-Time System MARS," in Proc. 1990 European Simulation Multiconference, pp. 51-57, Nuremberg, Germany, The Society for Computer Simulation International, 1990.

60. A. Shamir, "How to Share a Secret," Comm. ACM, vol. 22, no. 11, pp.612-613, 1979.

61. M. Shapiro, Y. Gourhant, S. Halbert, L. Mosseri, M. Ruffin and C. Valot, "SOS: An Object-Oriented Operating System - Assessment and perspectives," Computing Systems, vol. 2, no. 4, pp.287-338, 1989.

62. A.C. Shaw, "Reasoning About Time in Higher-Level Language Software," IEEE Trans. on Software Engineering, vol. SE-15, pp.875-889, 1989.

63. S.K. Shrivastava, G.N. Dixon and G.D. Parrington, "An Overview of the Arjuna Distributed Programming System," IEEE Software, vol. 8, no. 1, pp.66-73, 1991.

64. L. Strigini and F. Di Giandomenico. "Flexible schemes for application-level fault tolerance," in Proc. 10th Symposium on Reliable Distributed Systems, pp. 86-95, Pisa, Italy, IEEE, 1991.

65. P. Thévenod-Fosse. "Software validation by means of statistical testing: retrospect and future direction," in Proc. 1st Int. Working Conference on Dependable Computing for Critical Applications., pp. 23-50, Santa Barbara, USA, Springer-Verlag, 1989. (Dependable Computing and Fault-Tolerant Systems,Vol. 4, 1991.)

66. P. Thévenod-Fosse. "On the Efficiency of Statistical Testing with respect to Software Structural Test Criteria," in Proc. IFIP Working Conference on Approving Software Products, pp. 29-42, Garmisch-Partenkirchen, FRG, North Holland, 1990.

67. P. Thévenod-Fosse and H. Waeselynck. On Software Dependability Evaluation from a Statistical Testing Approach, 90.235, LAAS, Toulouse, France, 1990. PDCS Report No. 28

68. P. Thévenod-Fosse and H. Waeselynck, "An Investigation of Statistical Software Testing," J. of Software Testing, Verification and Reliability, vol. 1, no. 2, pp.5-25, 1991. (PDCS Report No. 46)

69. P. Thévenod-Fosse, H. Waeselynck and Y. Crouzet. "An Experimental Study on Software Structural Testing: Deterministic versus random input generation," in Proc. 21st IEEE Int. Symp. on Fault-Tolerant Computing (FTCS-21), Montreal, 1991.

70. G. Trouessin, J.C. Fabre and Y. Deswarte. "Reliable Processing of Confidential Information," in Proc. of the 7th Int. Conf. on Computer Security, IFIP/SEC'91, Brighton, UK, 1991.

71. A. Vrchoticky and P. Puschner. "On the Feasibility of Response Time Predictions - An Experimental Evaluation," in Second Year Report, 2, PDCS, 1991.

72. J. Xu. "Fault Tolerance Based on System Diagnosis Techniques," in PDCS Project Second Year Report, ESPRIT Project 3092, 1991.

Technology, Networks, and the Library of the Year 2000

Jerome H. Saltzer

Massachusetts Institute of Technology
Cambridge, Massachusetts

Abstract: An under–appreciated revolution in the technology of on–line storage, display, and communications will, by the year 2000, make it economically possible to place the entire contents of a library on–line, in image form, accessible from computer workstations located anywhere, with a hardware storage cost comparable to one year's operational budget of that library. In this paper we describe a vision in which one can look at any book, journal, paper, thesis, or report in the library without leaving the office, and can follow citations by pointing; the item selected pops up immediately in an adjacent window. To bring this vision to reality, research with special attention to issues of modularity and scale will be needed, on applying the client/server model, on linking data, and on the implications of storage that must persist for decades.

1 Overview

The idea that computer technology could somehow be useful in libraries has been around for decades, and inspired and visionary proposals have never been in short supply.[1] Unfortunately, until very recently these ideas were interesting but academic, because the computer technology that was available was simply not capable enough to do the job.

The theme of this paper is that accumulated computer technology changes of the last decade, together with those expected in the next, finally make possible some of the ideas proposed at the dawn of the computer age. In fact, the rate of technology change has been so great that it will soon be commonplace to store page images, a possibility that seems hard to envision even today.

This paper has three main purposes:

- To describe a new vision of the high–technology electronic library.
- To examine the driving technologies.
- To identify the system engineering challenges.

Our overall approach is from a computer systems design perspective. That is, we consider a real application that would stress current systems technology, and then look at the stressed points for guidance on what systems problems need research.

---

1. For examples, see Vannevar Bush, 1945; John Kemeny et al., 1962; J. C. R. Licklider, 1965; J. Francis Reintjes 1984; Edward Feigenbaum, 1986.

2 The Vision

2.1 What, exactly, is a library?

The library is one of several closely related—even overlapping—information–rich applications that are being created or revolutionized by advancing computer and communication technology. These applications include:

- the library;
- news gathering and dissemination;
- on–line bulletin boards and discussion groups;
- electronic mail;
- personal files and databases;
- scientific, engineering, and business data banks;
- electronically assisted publishing;
- government & business reports;
- collaborative work.

The boundaries separating these several areas in some cases are appropriate, while in others they are artificial and only loosely related to technological realities. Many of these boundaries will be the subject of battles over the next decade, as people stake out revenue streams and novel ideas enter the arena. However, even though we can be certain that some boundaries will move, it isn't plausible to try to innovate across the whole area and at the same time within each area. Instead, we suggest that these various information–intensive fields will proceed by a process of successive approximation, with individual areas first working under the assumption that each will maintain roughly its traditional interfaces with the others. Then, as adjacent areas become comfortable with new paradigms, they will explore pair–wise negotiation of the boundaries that separate them. (There is no reason to believe that this approach is the *best* way to proceed, just that this is the way things will probably work out in practice.)

2.2 The Library's defining properties

Even if we aren't certain where the edges of the future library may lie, we need to locate its center. We therefore take as the defining properties of the future electronic library the following more or less traditional characteristics. The materials of a library are:

- *Selective.* A publisher or editor selects things to make available and a librarian or curator chooses ("collects") from among these published items. This selectivity characteristic distinguishes the library from, say, a public bulletin board, to which anyone can contribute without review, and the ultimate reader must perform all selection.
- *Archival.* The contents of the library are expected to persist for time periods measured in decades, and a user can depend on again finding things that were found there once before.

- *Shared.* The collection is used by many people. The activity of collecting is thus a shared and centralized one, and there are generally specialists (reference librarians) who stand ready to help users find things in the collection.

2.3 Technology and collections

The traditional concept of a library collection involves both the physical books and the catalog that lists those books. As our first observation about the impact of technology, we may note that in an electronic library these two parts can, and probably will, become much more independent. In an electronic library, the physical collection comprises a set of bits in computer storage that represent the words or page images of books, reports, and journals. The catalog is a set of references to those bits, organized in ways to make it easy to find things. The interesting opportunity is that, thanks to communications networks, the catalog (which we should now call the "logical collection") can refer not only to things in the local physical collection but also to things in the physical collections of other libraries. That opportunity carries significant implications.

In an electronic world, an item can be collected simply by including it in the catalog; if any other library anywhere in the network already has the item in its physical collection, it is not necessary for this library to acquire another physical copy of the file of bits that represent the item. Instead, it can simply place in its catalog a cross–reference to the physical copy in the other library. Communications thus make it possible to share physical collections, and one can even imagine future electronic libraries that consist exclusively of logical collections, a kind of space–age inter–library loan system.

Several interesting consequences flow from this single observation. One might expect to see new kinds of specialization in which some libraries concentrate on building up very large physical collections, while others instead focus on creating catalogs for specialized audiences. Publishers will be very interested in understanding how such sharing of physical copies will affect their revenue streams, and they may conclude that they should use copyright to restrict placement of their own publications to physical collections over which they have some control.

2.4 How Computers might help

Noticing the potential for separation of physical and logical collections has caused us to digress slightly from the first question we should have asked: how can computer technology help in a library? Traditional views of how computers might be useful in libraries concentrate on one of two quite different concepts, and advances in computing technology prompt us to propose that a third is now feasible:

1. *Discovery of relevant documents* ("Search" or "Information Retrieval"). For over thirty years, computer scientists have strongly focused on tools to help people discover things because of the potential both for finding things that would otherwise be missed and for saving time. Study has ranged from simple database queries ("find papers by Einstein") to knowledge–based measures of document "relatedness" ("show me documents like this one") and concepts with a distinct flavor of artificial intelligence ("find Broadway plays

that use plots from Shakespeare.") Progress has been slow, for several reasons. Probably the prime one is that "relevance" has proven to be an elusive concept. A second reason is that information retrieval ideas are hard to test—it takes a lot of effort to acquire a large enough body of on–line material with which to practice. A review of current research in information retrieval was recently published in *Science* magazine.[2]

Despite this limited progress, over–optimistic computer people have occasionally announced that they have just developed exactly the retrieval technology needed for the library of the future. The natural result of this series of premature announcements has been that librarians have learned to be very wary of the claims of computer people.

The second traditional use of computing in the library is

2. *Back office automation.* Behind the scenes in a library are several record–keeping and organizing activities that are quite amenable to computer support: acquisition (ordering books), preparing catalogue records, circulation (keeping track of checked–out books), overdue notices, serials control, and inter–library loans. Librarians have usually embraced this form of automation with enthusiasm, because it reduces drudgery and releases time for the intellectual aspects of librarianship. One side–effect of use of computers to input, edit, and review catalogue records has been the creation of on–line catalogs and, more recently, making those on–line catalogs available to library patrons. There are now more than 100 research library catalogs available on the internet.

The relevance of changing technology to libraries is that there has quietly emerged a third, new way in which computer technology can be useful in a library:

3. *Storage, browsing, and identification.* The computer system can be used as a bulk storage and browsing device, enhancing the speed and ease of access to a very large body of material. One way that access can be eased is by navigation: moving from one work to another by following citations. We can think of storage, browsing, and navigation as extensions of traditional cataloguing activities along two dimensions—to include the documents themselves, and to catalog their entire contents, for example in a full–text index.

Browsing and navigation involve *identification* of documents from their citations, a concept distinct from discovery (the traditional computer science interest mentioned earlier). Identification and discovery can be viewed as being at the opposite ends of a spectrum; on the one hand we have a more or less complete description of a desired document, as found in a citation, while at the other extreme we have only a vague inquiry in mind, not knowing whether or not anything in the library satisfies the inquiry. Once this identification/discovery spectrum is in mind, it is apparent that tools such as full–text search fall somewhere in the middle and are likely to be among the first available in practical systems.

In these terms, we can now more specifically identify the opportunity: if modern technology can support storage, browsing, and identification at an attractive price, a very

---

2. Gerald Salton, 1991.

useful system can be constructed, even without the potential enhancement of advanced discovery tools. The market for such a system could be vast—every communication–capable desktop workstation and personal computer in the world is a potential client for some form of this service. And the existence of such a system (particularly the large resulting collection of on–line books, journals, and reports) would speed up the rate of research on better discovery tools. So a bootstrapping opportunity is apparent; all we have to do is convince ourselves that the technology is capable of storage, browsing, and identification.

2.5 The Vision

Pulling these observations together leads to the following two–component vision of the future electronic library:

1. Anyone with a communication–capable desktop workstation or personal computer can browse through any book, paper, newspaper, technical report, or manuscript without actually visiting the library.

The primary implication of this first component is that the full text of all documents is on–line, in image form.

2. While reading a document, if one notices an interesting–looking reference or citation, one should be able to point to that citation, press a button, and expect the cited document to appear immediately in an adjacent window.

The primary implication of the second component is that there be a robust mechanism of connecting references with physical documents, thereby giving the library the feel of a hypertext system.

Note that this vision does not propose to replace books, but rather to augment them. We assume that there will still be a way to obtain a paper copy of the book for detailed study. The primary goal of the envisioned system is to allow the library user to browse the book to ensure that it is of interest, before going to the trouble of calling it from the stacks. Anyone who has found it necessary to go beyond the reference collection in a large research library and call books from compact stacks, closed stacks, or repository storage will immediately recognize the potential for saving huge quantities of time, both for library staff and for themselves.

3   The Four Advancing Technologies

Four technologies are driving the opportunity to create an electronic library:

- High–resolution desktop displays.
- Megabyte/second data communication rates.
- Client/Server architecture.
- Large capacity storage.

We explore each in turn.

3.1 High–resolution desktop displays

Displays commonly seen today are not very comfortable to use in reading scanned images. However, it turns out that they are just below a critical psycho-optical threshold, above which they become quite acceptable for browsing and perhaps even for extended reading. The change required to cross that acceptance threshold is the addition of shades of grey—at least eight levels. Since this feature can usually be implemented by simply adding random–access memory to the display controller, it is already standard on many high–end desktop workstations, and it is likely to become a standard feature of virtually all computer displays. Thus we can expect that usable display technology for the electronic library will be widely available well before the library itself will be on–line.

3.2 Higher data communication speeds

Megabyte per second data communication speeds are gradually becoming available over community–sized distances such as from the office to the nearest library, and Megabit per second data communications from there to more distant major libraries. Thus data communications, both campus–sized and nationwide, now or soon will permit moving a page image from library storage to a display workstation in about a human reaction time, again at reasonable cost. There is both bad news and good news associated with this change in data communication technology. The bad news is that, because of the very large installed base of older, slower, communication equipment, it will probably take quite some time for these higher speeds to become widely available, for example, to residential locations. As a result, the range of locations from which an electronic library will initially be usable may be limited. The good news is that the technology and economic improvements that have become available are so dramatic that entrepreneurs are looking to devise ways to bypass the traditional telephone-based data communication installations, using techniques such as radio and cable. One would expect the good news eventually to overcome the bad news; the only question is when. Since we are looking toward a time that is nearly ten years away, there is hope that the available technology will be in place.

3.3 Client/Server architecture

The client/server model, an organizing method in which a network links multiple computers each separately dedicated to distinct functions, has proven very effective in large–scale systems such as Project Athena[3]. The client/server model has matured to the point where it is directly applicable, and it looks like it may provide exactly the right modularity tool for dealing with several problems that traditionally inhibit technological progress in the library. Of the four advancing technologies, applying this one appears, perhaps, to be the easiest: it is an off–the–shelf technology that provides natural solutions to several problems: ubiquity, competition, cooperation, stability, modularity, performance, and so on. A later section of this paper describes these problems and explores the research aspects of verifying this claim.

---

3. George A. Champine, 1991.

3.4 Large capacity storage

If there is a single technological advance that is most strongly driving the opportunity to build an electronic library, it must be the rapid decrease in cost of magnetic disk storage. Today's (1992) two-Gigabyte disk costs about $2500. It is instructive to examine the rate at which that technology has been changing. Figure one shows the size, in bytes, of the high-end, $2500, 5.25-inch "Winchester" hard disk drive over the last ten years. The slope of the line in that figure is astonishing—note the logarithmic scale on the left—the number of bits available for this price has been doubling every year for the entire decade.[4]

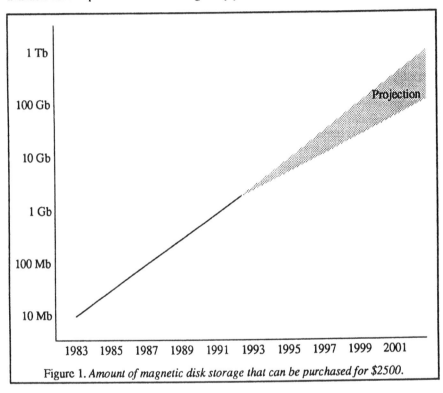

Figure 1. *Amount of magnetic disk storage that can be purchased for $2500.*

Going into the laboratory to find out whether or not this rate of cost improvement can be sustained, one learns that a primary constituent of the slope has been improvement in magnetic areal density (MAD), or number of bits per unit area. MAD has been climbing 40% per year for as long as anyone can recall, and current progress suggests that it will continue to rise at that rate for at least another decade. The greater slope (100% per year) for products in the field apparently came about because early disks did not attempt to approach the MAD limit. More recent designs have begun to narrow the gap, but at the

4. Based on street prices for 5.25-inch hard disks as appearing in advertisements in popular magazines over the period.

same time, arm positioning technology borrowed from the world of optical storage is beginning to show up in magnetic disks; this and other innovations may allow the slope to continue at the higher rate for a little longer. Based on these observations, we can with some confidence predict that disk cost over the next decade will track somewhere within the shaded area of the figure, and the bottom edge of the shaded area represents the minimum improvement that one might expect to see.

The bottom line is that there have been at least two factors of ten improvement since 1983, and two more factors of ten will probably accumulate by 2002, perhaps as early as 1999. The cumulative impact of these four orders of magnitude is that all prior assumptions about what is feasible to do with disk storage must be revisited; 100 Gigabytes of magnetic disk storage will cost about $2500 at the turn of the century.[5]

Probably the biggest impact of this cost improvement is that it will soon be economically attractive to store scanned page images in on–line disk storage.

If one scans a typical book in monochrome at 120 pixels/cm, one obtains about 300 Megabytes of raw data, or after compression, about 30 Megabytes.[6] Other resolutions should scale, after compression, with the square of the log, so doubling the resolution might add 20% to the bit count. For comparison, the character content of the same book would be about 1.2 Megabytes, about one twenty–fifth as much[7]. This ratio will be of some importance in choosing appropriate technology for indexing.

At 30 Megabytes per book, one of today's two-Gigabyte disk drives would hold the page images of about 66 books, at a cost of $40 per book and occupying a storage volume of 400 cm^3 per book, about one third of the space occupied by the book itself. By the end of the decade the equivalent disk drive should hold 3300 books, at a cost of 80 cents per book, and the space required will be less than 1% of the space occupied by the book.

For a library the size of M. I. T., which currently has about two million books, an array of six hundred such disk drives, costing about $1.5 million and occupying the space of a single small office, would suffice—about 60 Terabytes of storage. The U. S. Library of

---

5. Although much attention has been focused on the potential of optical storage, both read–only and write–once, the mechanical engineering of optical media happens to be driven by the requirements of the entertainment industry rather than the computer business. As a result, even though writable optical storage costs about one tenth that of magnetic disk, its performance in one critical area—its access time—is three orders of magnitude worse. This devastating performance difference makes it difficult to apply optical storage outside of a few very special applications.

6. This calculation assumes a 23 x 30 cm book of 400 pages. Such a book would have an average of about 450 cm^2/page of printed area and a total of 180,000 cm^2 of printed area to be scanned. Using the suggested scanning resolution would produce about 1800 data bytes/cm^2, or 300 Megabytes for a book. The group IV FAX compression algorithm, when applied to text, normally achieves about a ten to one compression ratio. Assuming that most books are dominated by text (images such as photographs do not compress so well) the average book would yield about 30 Megabytes.

7. Assuming 70 characters per line and 40 lines per page gives 2800 characters per page or about 1.2 Megabytes per book.

Congress holds about 90 million works of various types and collects another 30,000 per day[8]. Those works probably are on average somewhat smaller than the book on which we based our estimate, but if we assume they are all that size the Library would require about 2.7 Petabytes to start and an additional 225 Terabytes each year.[9] Putting scanned images on magnetic disk, in ten years, storage for the entire Library of Congress will fit on one floor of a small office building and the storage equipment will cost $60 million.

We can interpolate between these two cases to conclude that for most libraries, in a space much smaller than the present library and at a cost in the ballpark of one year's budget, the purchase of magnetic disk storage to contain scanned images of every document is feasible. Put another way, by the year 2000, storage of scanned images will seem so reasonable that it will be difficult to avoid.[10] Note, however, that this observation applies exclusively to the cost of the storage media; it does not offer any help in figuring out how to go about getting all those books, journals, and reports scanned; the cost of scanning, which is potentially quite labor–intensive, is another matter. Images of future publications may be materializable from the machine representations that were used in their preparation, but scanning of existing materials will probably not make much progress until it is forced by conservation requirements or storage space costs.

4   The Research Challenges

So much for the driving technologies. Availability of those technologies only enables the solution; creating a workable system involves tackling many interesting engineering problems. At the highest level, workable engineering of a system is a grand challenge: finding the proper modularity, finding techniques that simplify operations and maintenance, finding algorithms that allow working at very large scales. At the next level down, there seem to be three major problems, plus a list of more modest ones. The three major ones are:

- applying client/server design
- how to represent links
- persistent storage

---

8. From Michael R. Lawrence, *Memory and Imagination: New Pathways to the Library of Congress*, [Los Angeles: KQED: 1990]

9. One of the secrets of keeping up with the computer business is that one needs to learn a new metric prefix each decade. *Tera–* is beginning to show up as a common prefix just now, and *Peta–* will be with us by the end of the decade. If you want to keep one step ahead, *Exabytes* will be the unit of discourse in 2010.

10. Again, to check on the corresponding situation with optical storage, off–line CD ROMS can put 20 scanned books in a jewel box and thus already with today's technology apparently take up much less space than the books themselves. But jewel box storage is off–line, so we are discussing a very different kind of system. On–line storage would require a "jukebox," which brings the volume requirement to about one–tenth that of the book. Unfortunately the severe performance penalty that comes with jukeboxes makes the idea feasible only for rarely used materials, or with a complex and relatively expensive system of staging to magnetic disk.

4.1 Applying the client/server model

Although the client/server model appears to be well adapted to solving several obvious problems of applying technology to the library, each of these obvious examples needs to be verified in the field:

- *Hardware ownership.* Traditionally, the presentation device (for example, the display of a public access catalog of a library) has been owned by the library, so library budgets limit the range of locations and ubiquity of those displays. But with a client/server model, the presentation device can equally well be a workstation or personal computer that is owned by the customer. Thus ubiquity of access points can be achieved without the need for extravagant capital budgets.
- *Third–party sources.* With the client/server model, presentation management, customizing, and inquiry state all become the responsibility of the program that runs on the customer's workstation. Improvements in these areas can thus go on somewhat independently of the library itself, and can be the subject of third party competition. Network protocol standards can assure stable interfaces in the face of evolution of both user facilities and searching systems.
- *Function separation.* With a client/server model, one can easily and naturally separate indexing and search systems (the logical collection mentioned above) from storage devices (the physical collection.) This separation brings both the administrative benefit of decoupling physical from logical collections, thereby permitting sharing of physical collections, and also the performance benefit of allowing bulk storage to take place on a large, slow, cheap system without impeding search speed. Similarly, the circulation management system, which needs fast response, has traditionally operated in the same computer as the bibliographic search program, which soaks up lots of computing capability and degrades response to other activities. With the client/server model, one can separate these functions and place each on an appropriately configured computer.
- *Modular evolution.* Modularity also simplifies change. In traditional, monolithic library systems, any change is a big deal; the effort involved in changing everything at once inhibits needed change. But client/server components plug together like a hi-fi system, allowing modular replacement of any obsolescent component without replacing whole system. One would expect modular replacement to be the key way of achieving the system longevity requirement of a library.
- *Parallel inquiry.* One can make multiple, parallel inquiries to several search services, for example, to the local library, to the Library of Congress, and to a Books–in–Print server, so that the system can respond, "We have identified the thing you asked for, but we don't have it in the local library." Traditional catalog systems cannot distinguish between the two outcomes "Cannot identify the thing you asked for" and "This library doesn't have that item." They return the single response "Search failed," even though the appropriate thing to do next may be completely different in the two cases.
- *Reconciling alternative methods.* Libraries do bibliographic cataloguing of books, while for–fee services do the same service for journal articles, and the two worlds use independent, different, search methods. Similarly, different collections may call for different search techniques. These alternative views can be reconciled with a

client/server model that encompasses multiple collections with distinct search engines.

- *Cooperation.* Traditionally, inter–library cooperation is done at arms–length, yet much of any collection duplicates other collections. The client/server model makes inter–library cooperation technically straightforward.
- *Unregistered collections.* If one wants to extend a search to unregistered private collections, the client/server model again provides a natural mechanism.

Each of these concerns appears superficially to be well addressed with a client/server model, but field experience with real designs is needed to see if it actually works. As with all modularity proposals, the challenge is not just a matter of cutting the system into modules, it is finding the *right* cuts.

4.2 Links

The second area of research interest is links. A link is the cross–reference that allows one data object to mention another one, perhaps stored elsewhere in the network. In a library system, links potentially appear everywhere:

- Many papers, reports, and books contain explicit references to other papers, reports, and books.
- Some books are bibliographic reference works that consist of nothing but links, together with descriptions of their content and perhaps opinions as to their value.
- A user's request for "other things by this author" is actually an inquiry about an implicit work consisting of a list of works by the author; the user has asked about the links in that implicit work.
- Similarly, a request for "other things in this journal" follows links from its table of contents.
- A request for "other things catalogued as being on the same subject" invokes links provided by the librarian in preparing a traditional card catalogue.

Most research on distributed systems has been on a program–oriented model of cooperation (remote procedure call), in which one machine asks another to run a program. Links call for a different model of cooperation in which one machine needs to maintain over a long time references to data stored by the other. They require a carefully engineered blend of direct reference (for performance) and stand–offishness (for insulation against failures, change, and lack of cooperation). Links appear to involve, but are not limited to, the rendezvous provided by naming services.

The mechanics of links seem superficially to be straightforward. Given a citation, one needs to be able to locate the object cited by identifying it, what library holds it, and some method of obtaining it. The systems challenge is how to represent links, considering that the target of a link may be on the same machine, on a machine elsewhere running the same program, on a machine elsewhere running the same program but administered by someone else, on a machine elsewhere running a different program that is alleged to meet the same specification, or on a machine elsewhere running a different model of the universe.

A more extensive discussion of the research problems surrounding links appeared on the agenda of a recent SIGOPS European workshop.[11]

4.3 Persistence

A third research challenge is persistence—managing archival storage with a time horizon measured in decades, rather than years. Most experience in computer file system design is with data that is expected to persist with a lifetime of at most a few years. The occasional data set that must last longer may be handled as a special case. But the storage system for an electronic library must be designed for data that will virtually all be kept around for fifty years or more. Current systems aren't designed to handle data that is meant to be retained for times that are one or two orders of magnitude greater than the lifetime of storage media, data compression techniques, forward error correction techniques, and representation standards. Several observations come to mind.

At about the time the system reaches its storage capacity, one should expect that the disks that the system started with will be on the verge of becoming obsolete. But the proper goal is to preserve the information, not the disks, so part of the system design must be a component, similar in spirit to backup in time–sharing systems, that automatically moves data from obsolescent storage devices to newer technology without getting in anyone's way. This technology refresh component may well be running in the background much of the time, and its correct operation is critical to the success of the system. A carefully designed ceremony is required to copy the data, to ensure that it all gets copied and the new copy hasn't been corrupted by the copying process itself. Because copying will undoubtedly be a long–running job, it must be coordinated with updates and additions that are going on at the same time.

A similar concern arises surrounding using data compression to reduce disk space. Is it safe to compress data? How does one read data that was compressed 75 years ago, using techniques, algorithms, and programming languages that have long been superseded and then forgotten? One possibility is to try to store the compression algorithm with the data. But this possibility leaves one wondering how to devise a timeless description of the algorithm. Another, perhaps more plausible, answer is to decompress and recompress the data, using the latest compression technology, whenever the disks are being replaced, as part of the data copying procedure. If this kind of technology refresh procedure is used, it would seem advisable to avoid using the non–reversible (lossy) compression algorithms that have been suggested for moving video. Over the course of 50 years, one may have to decompress and recompress with newer standards five or ten times; losses from incompletely reversible algorithms would be expected to accumulate in the form of increasing degradation.

An almost identical argument about occasionally refreshing the technology applies to the use of forward error correction, or coding, to insure that data will be readable despite occasional media errors, but with an extra edge. In order to replace forward error correction coding it is necessary to remove the old coding, so while the data is being copied, it is

---

11. J. H. Saltzer, 1992.

unprotected and vulnerable to undetected errors. Thus a very carefully designed copying ceremony is required.

Finally, a threat that looms larger when decades are involved is media loss through disaster—fire, hurricane, earthquake, civil disturbance, flood, war, or whatever. For reliability, there must be more than one copy of the data, but traditional backup methods involving full and incremental copies made to tape do not appear to scale up well in size and they are notoriously complex and error–prone. In addition, the kinds of disaster listed suggest that the copies should not be in the same room, building, or city. One hypothesis is that one can approach the necessary reliability with geographically separated multiple copies, plus a change log that allows recovery from mistakes in updating. Of course if the data is replicated at multiple sites, then the previous discussion of forward error coding should be revisited. Perhaps error detection will suffice, and after a new copy, with new error–correcting codes, compression algorithm, and disk technology, is made at one site it can be compared with the older copy at another site to insure that nothing went wrong while the data was unprotected. Yet another aspect is that for information that isn't regularly used (e.g., the least–used 50% of a library's collection,) trade–offs among the number of copies, reliability, and geographical dispersion need to be explored; the best parameters may be quite different from those applicable to frequently–used materials.

Persistence, replication, backup, technology refresh, and the interactions among them in the electronic library application were explored briefly in two recent workshop papers.[12]

4.4 Other Research problems

There are quite a number of other interesting problems raised by the prospect of the electronic library. Some of them are specific to the library application, while others probably apply to any application that is enabled by the same four technology advances.

1. *Caching and replication.* The opportunity to share part or all of a physical collection among several libraries opens a question of when to share and when to collect a copy of a document. One might expect that more than one library should collect a physical copy of any particular document for reliability. Those libraries that find that their own users frequently use a document might collect a copy, either temporarily or permanently, to improve availability or to reduce communications costs. Finally, a library might collect a copy because it is not satisfied with the administrative arrangements and assurances that surround the copies already collected under other administrations. The trade–offs and balances among these three pressures are quite interesting and some field experience will be needed.

2. *Administration.* The administrative aspect of deciding when to collect a physical copy calls attention to a cluster of other political and administrative problems involved in negotiating the transition from the traditional paper–based library to the electronic version. First, one must maintain production continuity. Second, the cost of hardware is continually changing, generally in the downward direction. Although lower costs generally improve the

---

12. J. H. Saltzer, 1991 and J. H. Saltzer, January, 1991.

situation, they also present a dilemma of when to buy in. Third, the prospect of sharing physical collections, and the prospect of very effective access from the office or home both threaten to disrupt traditional revenue flows that have been negotiated among authors, publishers, booksellers, libraries, and users. (This concern usually shows up in discussions labelled "copyright" or "intellectual property protection.") More deeply, the concern for revenue flows may affect the fundamental structure of a library as a resource shared by a community. In an academic community, for example, there is a tradition that once a scholar has been admitted to the community, he or she can carry out library research without limit, which means without a fee proportional to usage. But for-fee information search services are already changing this tradition, in ways that may act to inhibit scholarly research. It seems likely that a scholar will behave differently when a meter is ticking, as compared to when one is not. Finally, new modes of organizational cooperation need to be worked out. Different organizations will be the natural providers of different physical collections, logical collections, and indexing services. New relations of inter-dependence among players must be worked out.

3. *Reference support*. One important function of a traditional library is that of the reference librarian, who helps users find their way through the collection. The corresponding concept in an electronic library is probably that a reference librarian works with a user remotely, using "collaborative work" techniques. The exact techniques, as well as the effectiveness, of remote reference help, remain to be discovered.

4. *Representation*. The question here is how to represent documents in storage. There appear to be many possibilities, for example, bit-maps representing scanned images, ASCII, PostScript, SGML, FAX Group IV, etc., but the requirement of storing the data for decades seems to reduce the field drastically, to forms that are simple and self-describing. It is possible that the right thing to do is to collect scanned images and minimally-tagged ASCII for every document, on the basis that those are the only representations likely to survive for a long time. A sub-problem is cross-representation coordination: how to identify a scanned image with the corresponding ASCII representation of the text. For example, how does one relate a mouse click on a displayed image to the corresponding words in the ASCII form?

5. *Variant copies*. When large numbers of documents go on-line, the need for coordination of variant copies will become pressing. It may be common that the local system has an old copy of something, while some remote system has an up-to-date copy but is currently out of touch or not available. The user interface, as well as the underlying storage and search systems, need to provide semantics to deal with this situation gracefully. To the extent that the information is textual and will be examined by a person, it may be reasonable to go interactive and offer the user an opportunity to choose, especially if well-thought out defaults are part of the design. An interesting related question is how one discovers that two things from different collections are actually the same object, or a minor variation of one another.

6. *Large RAM*. As mentioned earlier, the space occupied by the scanned images of the pages of a book is about twenty-five times as great as the space occupied by the corresponding ASCII text. We can draw another interesting observation from that ratio by

comparing the cost of magnetic disk with that of random access memory (RAM). Specifically, we notice that the cost of RAM has followed a similar trend line to that of magnetic disk, and will probably continue to do so for the rest of the decade. Taking current street prices of $25 per Megabyte for RAM and $1 per Gigabyte for magnetic disk, we note that the cost of RAM is about twenty–five times as great as that of magnetic disk.

The somewhat startling implication is that if we can afford to place scanned images on magnetic disk, we can also afford to place full–text indexes of the contents of those images in RAM. Evidence that such an implication is reasonable abounds; today's personal computers are being delivered with eight Megabytes of RAM, and desktop workstations can be configured with as much as 0.5 Gbyte of RAM already.

Large RAM indexes provide another interesting subject for research; most research on full–text indexing is based on strategies intended to minimize the number of disk arm movements; completely different algorithms may be appropriate when the index for a large collection can reside permanently in random access memory.

7. *User interface.* A major challenge in a library system is to provide the user with a simple, intuitive model of what is going on, especially if multiple collections are being searched.

8. *Resale architecture.* The client/server model opens another opportunity, that a value–added reseller can repackage and offer to the public alternative access paths to library collections. The terms and conditions, as well as the technical aspects, under which such value–added services might be offered will require considerable thought.

Even the most casual reader will quickly think of several things to add to this laundry list of research problems.

5 Conclusion

In summary, we have claimed that advances in computer technology (especially in magnetic disk storage) will make a library of scanned page images with full–text search feasible within the decade. Networking will make it possible to share physical collections, and introduce the option of creating logical collections for purpose of searching and indexing. Networking will also make every desktop workstation and personal computer a potential access point for the electronic library. However, the availability of the technology is only one part; bringing it together involves many challenging tasks of system engineering, including getting the modularity right, arranging for an orderly transition from traditional methods, and identifying solutions that scale up in size in a satisfactory way. There are quite a number of research problems that need to be explored before an electronic library will actually be feasible.

5.1 Acknowledgement

Work on this subject began during a sabbatical at the University of Cambridge, and the author is grateful for extensive discussions there with Roger Needham, Karen Sparck–

Jones, Sam Motherwell, and many graduate students. Work continued during temporary assignments at the Digital Equipment Corporation Systems Research Center, where discussions with Paul McJones, John Detreville, Michael Burrows, John Ellis, Chuck Thacker, and Andrew Birrell were very helpful. At M. I. T., discussions with Gregory Anderson, Tom Owens, Mitchell Charity, David Clark, and David Gifford provided many ideas. Finally, over the course of the last two years, legions of librarians made extensive contributions by patiently explaining to me how their collections are organized in ways that are different from all other collections. Research support was kindly provided through grants from Digital Equipment Corporation and the IBM Corporation. Finally, because they had a significant influence on the thinking behind this paper, several otherwise uncited sources appear in the bibliography that follows.

Bibliography

Arms, Caroline R., ed. *Campus Strategies for Libraries and Electronic Information.* [Bedford, Massachusetts: Digital Press: 1990] ISBN 1-55558-036-X.

The Bibliothèque de France: a Library for the XXIst Century. [Paris: Etablissement Public De La Bibliothèque de France: October, 1990].

Brindley, Lynne J. "Libraries and the wired-up campus: the future role of the library in academic information handling," *British Library Research and Development Report 5980* (August, 1988).

Bush, Vannevar. "As we may think," *Atlantic Monthly 176,*1 (July, 1945) pp 101–108.

Champine, George A. *M. I. T. Project Athena: A Model for Distributed Campus Computing.* [Bedford, Mass.: Digital Press: 1991].

Dertouzos, Michael L. "Building the information marketplace," *Technology Review 94,* 1 (January, 1991) pp 29-40.

Evans, Nancy H., Troll, Denise A., Kibbey, Mark H., Michalak, Thomas J., and Arms, William Y. "The vision of the electronic library," *Carnegie Mellon University Mercury Technical Report Series 1* (1989).

Feigenbaum, E. A. "The library of the future," lecture given to mark the opening of Aston University's new Computing Suite, Manchester, England, November 11, 1986.

Kemeny, John G., Fano, Robert M., and King, Gilbert W. "A library for 2000 A. D.," *Management and the Computer of the Future.* Martin Greenberger, ed. [New York: The M. I. T. Press and John Wiley & Sons, Inc.: 1962] pp 134–178.

Licklider, J. C. R. *Libraries of the future.* [Cambridge, Mass.: M. I. T. Press: 1965].

Lynch, Clifford A. "Image retrieval, display, and reproduction," *Proceedings of the 9th National Online Meeting,* (May, 1988), pp 227-232.

Lynch, Clifford A. "Information retrieval as a network application," *Library Hi Tech 32*, 4 (1990) pp 57-72.

Reintjes, J. Francis. "Application of Modern Technologies to Interlibrary Resource-Sharing Networks," *Journal of the American Society for Information Science 35*, 1 (January 1984), pp 45-52.

Salton, Gerard. "Developments in automatic text retrieval," *Science 253*, 5023 (August 30, 1991) pp 974-980.

Saltzer, J. H. "Fault–tolerance in very large archive systems," *Operating Systems Review 25*, 1 (January, 1991), pp 81–82.

Saltzer, J. H. "File system indexing, and backup," in *Operating Systems for the 90's and Beyond, Lecture Notes in Computer Science 563*. Arthur Karshmer and Juergen Nehmer, eds., [New York: Springer–Verlag,: 1991] pp 13–19.

Saltzer, J. H. "Needed: A systematic structuring paradigm for distributed data," to appear in ACM SIGOPS 5th European Workshop, September 21-23, 1992, Le Mont Saint–Michel, France.

Tilburg University. *The New Library and the Development of Innovative Information Services at Tilburg University.* [The Netherlands: Tilburg University Press: 1989] ISBN [90-361-9662-0.

Mosaic C:
An Experimental Fine-Grain Multicomputer

Charles L. Seitz

Computer Science 256-80
California Institute of Technology
Pasadena, CA 91125

Abstract. Commercial medium-grain multicomputers aimed at ultra-supercomputer performance are pursuing a less profitable scaling track than fine-grain multicomputers. The Caltech Mosaic C is an experimental, fine-grain multicomputer that employs single-chip nodes and advanced packaging technology to demonstrate the performance/cost advantages of the fine-grain-multicomputer architecture. Each Mosaic node includes 64KB of memory, an 11MIPS processor, a packet interface, and a router. The nodes are tied together with a 60MBytes/s, two-dimensional, routing-mesh network. The compilation-based programming system allows fine-grain, reactive-process, message-passing programs to be expressed in an extension of C++, and the runtime system performs automatic, distributed management of system resources. Mosaic components and programming tools have already been used by another project to implement the 400Mbits/s ATOMIC local-area network, and a 16K-node machine is under construction at Caltech to explore the programmability and application span of the architecture for large-scale computing problems.

1. Background and Rationale for the Experiment

1.1 Opening Perspective

Highly concurrent and highly parallel computers emerged from the laboratory into commercial practice during the second half of the 1980s. The development of these machines has been a quest to achieve performance that is at the extreme permitted by current technology, that is *scalable* both with machine size and with advances in microelectronics technology, and that is more economical than the high-clock-speed approach taken by vector supercomputers.

The first generation of highly concurrent computers offered a fraction of the performance of contemporary vector supercomputers, albeit at a smaller fraction of their cost. As expected, their performance and memory capacity has escalated in step with advances in microelectronics technology, particularly the single-chip processor and memory technologies that have also fueled the advances in personal and workstation computers. There are now many economically important applications, principally in science and engineering, for which second-generation, highly concurrent computers offer a modest multiple of the performance of vector supercomputers of comparable cost. The upcoming third generation of concurrent ultra-supercomputers that have been announced but not yet delivered, such as a

\$55M, 4096-node, 300Gflops, Intel Paragon multicomputer, or a \$120M, 4096-node, 500Gflops Thinking Machines CM-5 multicomputer, will simply be extensions of this trend.

Yet, are these behemoths the important part of the future of highly concurrent computing? If so, it is a narrow future, indeed. Perhaps our world society may be able to afford to build, operate, and program a few hundred or a few thousand ultra-supercomputers for demanding and important applications. The mainstream of computing, however, will continue to be the tens or hundreds of millions of personal and workstation computers, and the even larger number of computers that control our tools, vehicles, and telecommunications. The physical characteristics of microelectronics technology suggest that there is a fundamental advantage in performance/cost in using concurrent machines for those computations that have concurrent formulations, and the finer the "granularity" of concurrent execution, the larger the advantage. Thus, there should be a substantial advantage in applying concurrency to the mainstream of computing, but what is an appropriate architecture for small, programmable, concurrent machines?

1.2 Multicomputers

The architecture that has thus far been dominant [1, 2] for building highly concurrent supercomputers is the multicomputer, an ensemble of computing *nodes* connected by a message-passing network (figure 1). Each node of a multicomputer is a computer, including read-write memory, a read-only memory for bootstrap and initialization, one or more instruction-interpreting processors, and an interface to the message-passing network. The network connects the nodes in a regular topology such as a hypercube or mesh, so that message packets can be routed algorithmically (without reference to routing tables) from any node to any other node.

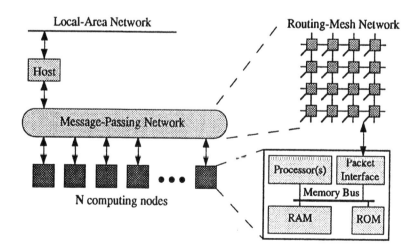

Figure 1: Logical and physical structure of a multicomputer.

The computational model is a simple abstraction of the structure of a multicomputer. By expressing a computation in terms of *processes* rather than nodes, and in terms of *messages* directed to processes rather than data transfers through channels, the details of the nodes and network are hidden, and the computation is represented in a way that allows it to be mapped easily onto different machines. Indeed, programming systems such as the Cosmic Environment [8] allow a concurrent program to be executed either on a multicomputer, or on a collection of network-connected UNIX workstations, or with processes distributed across both the multicomputer nodes and the workstations.

Each process is an *instance* of a defining program that can be expressed in any of the usual imperative programming notations, such as C, FORTRAN, or Pascal. In addition to the usual assignment, conditional, and iteration statements, the program that defines a process may contain statements for sending and receiving messages, and for creating new processes. The multiprogramming operating system on each node schedules, manages resources for, and handles message and process-creation operations for multiple processes per node. All processes are potentially concurrent, whether by residing on different nodes or by being interleaved in execution on a single node. Process execution and message transport take place concurrently. There is an arbitrary interval between when a message is sent and when it is available at its destination; however, message order is preserved between pairs of communicating processes.

Multicomputer application programs are *explicitly concurrent* programs, and may be based on different algorithms than sequential programs for the same applications. Highly regular applications (*eg,* matrix computations) commonly employ numerous processes instantiated from a single program, with each process dealing with one part (*eg,* a submatrix). Less regular or more complex applications (*eg,* compiling a program) may formulate the computation so that programs specialized to particular functions may be instantiated as they are required. Although most application programs are still written directly in terms of processes and messages, high-level programming systems that support other abstractions are becoming available, and offer advantages for particular applications.

A more detailed exposition of my thoughts about multicomputer architecture, design, and programming can be found in [9].

1.3 Granularity

The term "granularity," although used loosely, refers to the size either of the processes or the computing elements that perform a computation.

Consider a computation that can be performed by N concurrent processes, in which the division of effort is nearly equal, and the communication between processes is sparse relative to their computational demands. It is evident that such a computation can be performed nearly N times faster with N copies of a given computing element than with one. Although the computing time is reduced by N, the cost of the computation is the same, because the *cost per operation* is determined by the given computing element. Equivalently, one may say that it costs the same to use one element for time T as it does to use N elements for time $\frac{T}{N}$.

If we fix the time T, how might we reduce the overall cost of the computation? If the computation is again performed with N concurrent computing elements, each element is required to be only $\frac{1}{N}$th as fast as before. It happens that the *cost per operation* of operations that need to be performed only $\frac{1}{N}$th as fast may decrease as rapidly as $\frac{1}{N}$. The silicon area for the logic that performs the operation may decrease as rapidly as $\frac{1}{N^2}$, but the computation uses this area N times longer, resulting in $\frac{1}{N}$th the cost per operation.

This relationship is observed in VLSI-complexity results that show that, for members of a broad class of computations that are limited by the internal communication across their physical bisections, for silicon area A, and for latency T, AT^2 is bound by a problem-dependent function of the technology and problem size. Here, AT is the cost per operation, and AT varies as $\frac{1}{T}$. The same relationship is observed in certain electronic circuits that expose the limiting tradeoffs between the energy (the usual physical metric of cost) and time required to perform an operation. Finally, this phenomenon of diminishing returns in performance with cost is commonly seen in system design and engineering, particularly toward the limits of performance. As noted in the example below, these relationships between the cost per operation and the latency apply only over certain ranges and under certain conditions. See section 1 of [10] and *op cit* for details.

The *formulation* of a concurrent computation may also exhibit different granularities. For example, the multiplication of two $n \times n$ matrices requires n^3 constituent operations, accumulating multiplies. One may perform this computation concurrently with $\frac{n}{k} \times \frac{n}{k}$ ($1 \le k \le n$, and k divides n) processes, each of which stores and performs the computations associated with a $k \times k$ submatrix. The parameter k controls the granularity. If there is one process for each of N computing elements, $N = \frac{n^2}{k^2}$. The base case $k = n$ is the maximum-grain, sequential implementation, for which $N = 1$. The case $k = 1$ is the minimum-grain, maximally concurrent formulation, for which $N = n^2$.

Would it then be possible in practice to achieve an n^2-fold speedup? Generally not, at least on the commercial multicomputers, for this reason: In order to distribute the matrix-multiplication computation, each submatrix must be communicated to $\frac{n}{k}$ other nodes; this communication is ordinarily done in a systematic pipelined or systolic [4] fashion. Each operand (matrix element) received participates in k operations. Communicating an operand uses network and memory bandwidth, and requires time. Even if the time required to convey the operand were comparable to time required to perform a single operation, and generally it is greater, it would be necessary that $k \gg 1$ to make the time required for interprocess communication much less than the time required for the node computations. N is accordingly limited to be much, much less than n^2.

Would it be possible to design a concurrent engine to provide an n^2-fold decrease in the cost of the computation? Again, generally not, at least for the interesting case in which n is large, but for a different reason. The silicon area A required to perform a multiplication operation cannot be reduced below a certain minimum no matter how slow the multiplier circuit is allowed to operate. The AT^2 results apply only to relatively fast multiplier circuits.

However, in the broad, middle range, we can exploit concurrency to achieve reductions either in the computing time or cost, or in some combination of the two, and within this range the gains increase with N.

1.4 Multicomputer Scaling Tracks

The Cosmic Cube is an experimental multicomputer that my students, staff, and I designed, built, and programmed in the early 1980s. The Cosmic Cube nodes included 128KB of primary memory, an Intel 8086/8087 processor, and interfaces to binary n-cube (hypercube) channels. These nodes were implemented with 84 chips on a 23cm×33cm circuit board. We built a 4-node prototype in early 1982, and a 64-node, binary 6-cube machine in 1983. In a January 1985 paper [7] about the Cosmic Cube, I wrote that: "The Cosmic Cube nodes were designed as a simulation in hardware of the nodes we expect to be able to integrate onto one or two chips about five years hence. Future machines of thousands of nodes are feasible ..." In other words, we built the Cosmic Cubes as vehicles for testing our ideas about the programming systems and application programming for this class of scalable, message-passing, concurrent computers.

The Mosaic C multicomputer closely fulfills the prediction in this 1985 paper. The first Mosaic multicomputers, with processor, packet interface, and router on one chip, and with 128KB of memory on separate chips (that could as easily have been a single chip), were demonstrated in 1990. The first Mosaic based on single-chip nodes, which include 64KB of memory, was demonstrated in 1991. The evolution from the Cosmic Cube to the Mosaic is an example of one type of *scaling track*, in which advances in technology are employed to re-implement nodes of a similar logical complexity, but faster, smaller, lower power, and less expensive. Such is the progress in microelectronics over the past decade that the Mosaic nodes are ≈60 times faster, use ≈20 times less power, are ≈100 times smaller, and are (in constant dollars) ≈25 times less expensive to manufacture than the Cosmic Cube nodes. Because the nodes are less expensive, one can use more of them, and thus achieve the gains that result from scaling N together with the gains in node performance, *eg*, the Mosaic C is ≈60×25 = ≈1500 times more cost-effective than the Cosmic Cube.

However, the Cosmic Cube turned out also to be the archetype of the medium-grain, commercial multicomputers, and the origin of a different scaling track. Instead of using advances in technology to shrink the physical size and cost of the nodes, the commercial-multicomputer scaling track has maintained approximately the same physical size and cost for the nodes, and used advances in technology to increase the complexity of the nodes. One of the advantages of this approach is that the nodes, because they have been similar in complexity to personal and workstation computers, have been able to employ the same commodity processor, memory, and software technology.

In fact, the trend has been to somewhat enlarge the size and increase the cost of the nodes. For example, in the evolution from the 1985 Intel iPSC/1 (512KB, i80286, $N \leq 128$) to the 1987 Intel iPSC/2 (4MB, i80386, $N \leq 128$) to the 1989 Intel iPSC/860 (8MB, i80860, $N \leq 128$) to the 1991 Intel Delta prototype (16MB, i80860, $N = 512^+$), the size and cost of the nodes has approximately doubled. The slight increase in N in typical installations is due entirely to the architecture proving itself, so that people are willing to buy larger, more costly configurations. The node complexity, which is determined principally by the memory, has increased by ≈ 32 times, and the integer performance by ≈ 40 times. Other than the vast improvement in floating-point performance achieved by the i80860 processor, the Intel Delta is only about 20 times more cost-effective than the iPSC/1. It is evident that this constant-node-cost scaling track, although easier in terms of technology and programming, is less profitable in performance/cost than the constant-node-complexity scaling track.

Together with larger node memories, multicomputers are acquiring larger, more cumbersome, operating systems. Intel, for example, reports that they intend to use a version of Mach as the node operating system for their announced Paragon system. One of the difficulties of writing efficient programs for commercial multicomputers is that these machines require the equivalent of several *hundred* instructions to send and receive even a very short message. This "software overhead" in the operating system is not only the principal component of the message latency, it consumes cycles that would otherwise be used for the application program. The matrix-multiplication example in the previous section illustrates that efficient application programs may need to conserve message-system bandwidth by employing messages that are large enough to provide many operations per operand. These large messages are also required to amortize the software overhead over a large number of operands.

In principle, concurrent programs formulated at a fine granularity, *ie,* with relatively small processes and messages, have advantages for execution even on medium-grain multicomputers. A large number of processes per node allows statistical load balancing between nodes (by the law of large numbers), and the queueing of incoming messages for many processes hides the message-network latency. In practice, however, fine-grain concurrent programs are woefully inefficient on the commercial, medium-grain multicomputers due to the software overhead of sending and receiving messages. Fine-grain multicomputers, which must of necessity execute relatively fine-grain concurrent programs, require both high message bandwidth and very low software overhead for sending and receiving messages.

2. Mosaic C

In the first part of this paper, I have tried to outline some of the reasons why fine-grain multicomputers appeared to me to have very attractive properties. However, as Edsger W. Dijkstra once taught me in another context (self-timed systems), even good ideas require more than an argument of their expected, good properties; to have an impact, they require an existence proof or constructive demonstration. In addition, new computer architectures and their programming systems raise many questions of design, programmability, and application span that cannot be explored adequately without "doing the experiment." The Mosaic C is that existence proof, constructive demonstration, and experiment. This project has required several years, and the dedicated efforts of several of my students and staff, whom I shall mention in the following descriptions.

2.1 Mosaic C Node

The Mosaic C multicomputer node is a single 9.25mm×10.00mm chip fabricated in a 1.2μm-feature-size, two-level-metal, CMOS process. At 5V operation, the synchronous parts of the chip operate with large margins at a 30MHz clock rate, and the chip dissipates ≈0.5W. The tested but unpackaged cost of the silicon at the 40–50% yields typical of this chip is approximately $30/chip. The chip area is used approximately as follows (see figure 1 for a block diagram):

63% The 64KB *dynamic RAM* is organized as 32K 16-bit words. Memory cycles require only a single clock period; the memory bandwidth is, accordingly, 60MBytes/s. This dynamic memory is refreshed automatically by the processor in otherwise-unused cycles. Designer: Don Speck.

1% The *read-only memory* contains self-test, initialization, and bootstrap programs. Designer: Don Speck.

3% The 16-bit instruction-interpreting *processor* is programmed in C rather than assembly language, using the Gnu C compiler targeted to the Mosaic instruction set. Standard C benchmarks rate the processor at ≈11MIPS. Designers: Jakov Seizovic, Wen-King Su, Chuck Seitz.

3% The 16-bit *packet interface* handles the transfer of packets between the router and memory; performs reliable synchronization between the asynchronous, self-timed router and the synchronous memory; and forms the routing header of packets that are sent from the node. The packet interface is able to send or receive packets at a 30MHz 16-bit-word rate, which corresponds to the 60MBytes/s memory and router-channel bandwidths. Designer: Jakov Seizovic.

5% The two-dimensional, self-timed, mesh *router* implements the node's part of the message-passing network. The router's 8-bit-wide channels operate asynchronously, but at a rate somewhat in excess of 60MBytes/s. Designers: Chuck Seitz, Wen-King Su.

20% The *pad frame* for 136 connections to the package pins, most of which are used for the four bidirectional channels that connect to the north, south, east, and west neighbors; and the wiring between the router and the pad frame.

5% *Other wiring* between the parts listed above, internal power distribution, the clock driver, and unused area.

The most remarkable aspect of this breakdown is that about one quarter of the silicon-area budget – the packet interface, router, and pad frame – is devoted to communication. Very-large-scale-integration (VLSI) microelectronics is, indeed, a communication-limited medium. Experienced computer designers would not, however, find it remarkable that only 3% of the silicon area is used for the processor, or that 20 times more area is used for the memory than for the processor. These relationships are typical also of personal and workstation computers, but it would be possible to include a much larger processor without greatly increasing the overall chip area.

In addition to providing adequate memory and network bandwidth, the chip architecture provides a very general, programmable mechanism for low-overhead and low-latency handling of message packets. The instruction-interpreting processor and the packet interface share the same datapath, and operate in close concert. The memory addresses and limits for transfers between the packet interface and memory are processor registers. The processor also includes two program counters and two sets of general registers to allow zero-time context switching between user programs and message handling. Thus, for example, when the packet interface has received a complete packet, received the header of an packet, completed the sending of a packet, exhausted the allocated space for receiving packets, or any of several other events that could be selected, it can interrupt the processor by switching it instantly to the message-handling context. Instead of several hundred instructions to handle a packet, the Mosaic typically requires only about ten instructions. The number of clock cycles for the message-handling routines could be reduced to insignificance by placing them in hardware, but we chose this more general mechanism so that we could experiment with different message-handling strategies.

My students, staff, and I are well along with the design of the successor to the Mosaic C chip. The Mosaic T, which is targeted for a 0.8μm-feature-size, three-level-metal, CMOS process, and 50MHz, 3.3V, 0.5W operation, is being designed to come as close as we can to the following specifications: 128KBytes of single-clock-cycle internal memory in two banks of 16K×32, providing 400MBytes/s memory bandwidth; ≈40MIPS, 32-bit, RISC processor; 200MBytes/s channels; and provision for external, secondary, dRAM memory.

2.2 Message-Passing Network and Router

The two-dimensional, self-timed, mesh router implements a blocking form of cut-through routing that is sometimes referred to as "wormhole" routing. The flow-control unit (*flit*) is an 8-bit byte, and flits are conveyed in a queue discipline with a request and an acknowledge signal. Up to five packets may be traversing a single router concurrently. The head of a packet includes $\Delta x, \Delta y$ flits for deadlock-free, dimension-order routing, in which a packet is routed first in x and then in y. The head of a packet forms a path through the network in ≈30ns/router. If the packet encounters a channel that is already occupied, the packet is blocked in the network. The tail flit of the packet breaks the path. See section 3 of [9] for additional details of the flow control, choice of topology, freedom from deadlock, and engineering of these message-passing networks.

The choice of a two-dimensional mesh for the Mosaic was based on a 1989 engineering analysis; we had planned originally to use a three-dimensional mesh network. As illustrated in the closeup of a Mosaic array shown in figure 2, the mutual fit of the two-dimensional-mesh network and the circuit-board medium provides high packaging density, and allows the high-speed signals between the routers to be conveyed on short wires. The short wires between neighboring chips take little board area; in addition, they exhibit very low capacitance and inductance, so that the interchip communication can be accomplished at relatively high speed and low power. Subsequent, extensive simulations by Michael J. Pertel have demonstrated the optimality of the choice of a two-dimensional network [6], and of oblivious, dimension-order routing rather than any form of minimal, adaptive routing [5].

Figure 2: Closeup of a Mosaic array.

To offer a comparison with medium-grain multicomputers, the router in the Mosaic C chip is similar to an earlier router that we packaged by itself, in a pad frame, as a mesh-routing chip (MRC). These MRCs were provided to Intel for use in their one-of-a-kind Delta prototype, and to several other projects and companies. The Delta node, essentially an iPSC/860 node with a 30MBytes/s mesh-interface module replacing the 2.8MBytes/s iPSC/2 hypercube-routing module, is able to source or sink packets at less than half of the bandwidth available on an MRC channel. Such is the difference in attention to internode communication between medium- and fine-grain multicomputers that, whereas the Mosaic devotes 25% of its silicon-area budget to the router and pad frame, the Intel Delta devotes much less than 1%. Intel later developed a 16-bit-wide, 200MBytes/s "iMRC" under license from Caltech for use in the Intel Paragon multicomputer. This iMRC is still well under 1% of the silicon area of a Paragon node.

2.3 The Mosaic C 8×8 and Host-Interface Boards

Sixty-four Mosaic chips are packaged by tape-automated bonding (TAB) in an 8×8 array on the circuit board shown in figure 3. These boards, in turn, self-compose using stacking connectors to allow the construction of arbitrarily large, two-dimensional arrays of nodes. This style of packaging was meant to demonstrate some of the density, scaling, and testing advantages of mesh-connected systems, whether for multicomputers or for other architectures.

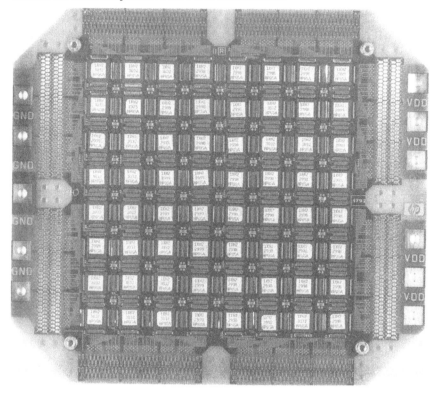

Figure 3: A Mosaic C 8×8 board.

TAB packaging achieves substantially lower cost, higher reliability, and higher density than conventional packaging. Instead of bonding chips into packages and packages onto boards, the chips are bonded directly onto boards. After inner-lead bonding, the chips are encapsulated and re-tested. The outer leads of this packaged part are then bonded onto the boards. The lead pitch is 250μm at both the inner and outer TAB leads, and the chip pitch is only 19mm.

Chips and boards are both tested automatically at their point of manufacture. In addition to developing the internal self-test code and the wafer-test programs, Wen-King Su developed a diagnostic board-test program that displays a graphical animation of the board test as the test proceeds from two corners to cover all of the nodes and all of the channels. The display allows the operator to determine the location of any faulty chips or connections.

A pilot-production run of four 8×8 boards allowed us to verify the complete design with a 256-node Mosaic C system, which is fully operational and very reliable.

The Mosaic chips and 8×8 boards are now in modest-scale production under a subcontract with Hewlett-Packard Company. After packaging the $30-cost Mosaic C chips onto 8×8 boards, the cost rises to about $75/node, or $4800/board. The first 256 boards from the production line will be used to build a 16,384-node, 128×128 machine that will have 1GByte of primary memory, and a peak instruction rate of ≈180GIPS.

Here is another comparison with between medium- and fine-grain multicomputer technology. Two stacked Mosaic 8×8 boards are about the same size, cost, and power as a single node of the Intel Delta. This 8×16 Mosaic array has half the primary memory of the 16MB Delta node. The instruction rate of the 8×16 Mosaic is ≈1400MIPS rather than the ≈20MIPS + ≈60 peak Mflops of the Delta node. The aggregate message bandwidth through the 96 edge channels of the 8×16 Mosaic is 5,760MBytes/s, in comparison with 30MBytes/s for the Delta node.

The Mosaic C processor, packet interface, and router were originally fabricated and the design refined using a 4.5mm×4.5mm "memoryless Mosaic" chip. These chips are used to built host-interface boards, such as the (Sun SPARCstation) Sbus board illustrated in figure 4. This 8.9cm×14.6cm (postcard-size) board contains a 2-node Mosaic; each node includes a 64K×16 external memory that can also be read and written by the workstation. Such boards were used at first to give us a head start on developing Mosaic programming tools, test programs, programming systems, and some early applications. The shared memory between the Mosaic and workstation simplifies "bootstrapping" and debugging, and allows Mosaic programs to be monitored by the workstation during their execution.

Figure 4: An Sbus Mosaic host-interface board.

Host-interface boards are also used to connect workstations and Mosaic arrays. In order to limit the number of pins in the memoryless Mosaic chips, only a subset of the routing channels is brought out to the pad frame; the other pins are used for the interface to the external memory. The subset consisting of eastbound-in, eastbound-out, northbound-in, and northbound-out allows the memoryless Mosaic chips and host-interface boards to be chained, as illustrated in figure 5; in addition, under the Mosaic's first-x-then-y dimension-order routing, any host-interface node can route packets directly to any array node, and any array node can route packets directly to any host-interface node.

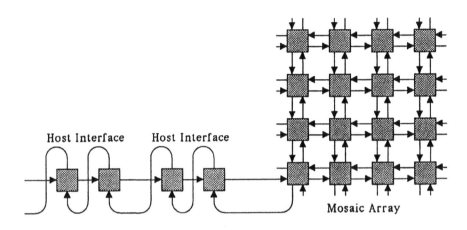

Figure 5: Standard connection of Mosaic host-interfaces and arrays.

Figure 5 also illustrates that, in addition to the Mosaic host-interface and array boards, complete Mosaic systems require cables that connect between host interfaces and arrays. The zero-slack (non-interference) protocol used between Mosaic nodes that are physically close also operates correctly over long cables, but the bandwidth is limited by the round-trip cable delay. Slack chips that convert between zero-slack and slack protocols have been developed, and allow the same 60MB/s bandwidth on long cables as is provided between Mosaic nodes that are physically close.

The host-interface boards and slack chips were designed by Wen-King Su.

2.4 Programming System

The programming system that we have developed for the Mosaic is based on the same message-passing, reactive-process [8, 9, 10, 12], computational model that we have used with earlier multicomputers: A process executes only in response to receiving a message, and may in execution send messages, create new processes, and modify its persistent variables before it either exits or becomes dormant in preparation for receiving another message. This model is implemented for the Mosaic in a way that supports fine-grain concurrency. Source programs are expressed in an object-oriented programming notation, a derivative of C++ called C+−. The Mosaic runtime system, which is written in C+−, provides automatic process placement and highly distributed management of system resources.

The C+− Programming System. C+− is an effort to achieve the advantages of a compilation-based programming system and of object-oriented programming in expressing and executing message-passing, reactive-process, concurrent programs. The only departure from the programming model used in our earlier systems is that, instead of a single entry point, processes have a fixed, compile-time-determined set of entry points, each of which can be enabled or disabled at run time. The effect of this slight departure is to restrict and streamline the dispatch of messages to the functions that process them.

C+− differs in implementation from earlier systems in requiring that the source program be expressed lexically together, such that the C+− compiler can perform checks that, in systems in which process definitions are separate programs, are performed at run time, if at all. Processes appear in the object code as functions that co-exist within a single address space; dynamic linking of processes as they are created obviates the need for address translation. This scheme avoids the overhead of "heavyweight," operating-system-style processes in providing system services, including message-sending operations, and in context switching for dispatching messages to functions.

Although C+− is a modest extension of C++, it is important to understand that the Mosaic does not profitably execute arbitrary C++ programs; rather, reactive-process programs can be expressed in C+− notation. C+− introduces a *process* concept into C++. The C+− **processdef** keyword parallels the C++ **class** keyword syntactically, including inheritance, overloading, and the full range of object-oriented features for controlling default behaviors. However, whereas invoking a function of an *object* created from a **class** has the immediate action characteristic of the semantics of sequential programming notations, invoking a function of a process created from a **processdef** has the delayed and independent action that is the usual characteristic of concurrent processes. A function of a process is invoked in the same way as a function of an object, *eg*, the statement *process reference->function name(argument list)* can be thought of as sending the argument list as a message to the specified process, together with a selector that indicates that the message is to be processed by a particular function of that process. Similarly, the C++ **new** is carried over intact into C+−, and returns a process reference.

Although C+− continues to develop with experience from its implementation and use, its expressivity has been more than adequate both for the Mosaic runtime system and for more typical application programs. Its efficiency on the Mosaic is extraordinary; the software overhead is only a few instructions per message. The C+− system is also portable: The C+− compiler is written in C++. All that is required to run compiled C+− programs on a given machine or under a given operating system is a small library of C+− functions that access to the communication capabilities of the system. The design and implementation of C+− is part of the PhD research of Jakov Seizovic, and will be described in detail in a forthcoming thesis [11].

The Mosaic Runtime System. In contrast with the other principal, but much less scalable, multiple-instruction, multiple-data (MIMD) concurrent architecture, the shared-memory multiprocessor, the memory of each multicomputer node is private to that node. All large memories are physically distributed, but, because the distributed nature of the memory of a multicomputer is visible to the programmer, multicomputers are referred to as *distributed-memory* machines. A fine-grain multicomputer partitions its memory and processing resources into smaller pieces than a medium-grain multicomputer, but is its memory actually "more distributed?" The individual, disjoint, address spaces are much smaller, but the barriers to communication between these memories are also much smaller. The goal of the Mosaic runtime system is not to provide the appearance of a large, single-address-space, shared memory from thousands of small memories, although it could easily do this; rather, it is a goal that is more ambitious and more appropriate to the computational model: The Mosaic runtime system exploits the communication capabilities of the Mosaic to provide fully distributed, automatic management of memory, processing, and communication resources for a myriad of small processes and messages.

For example, the node operating system or runtime system of a multicomputer maintains a node receive queue whose length fluctuates constantly as the node receives and consumes messages. Receive-queue overflow is a not-uncommon occurrence in medium-grain multicomputer programs, even though the space for the receive queue in an 8MByte node may be 1MByte or more. Although the aggregate memory of the machine may well have been adequate for the computation, receive-queue overflow results in an error message and the termination of the program. The programmer must then figure out how to redistribute the processes to better balance the memory utilization.

The problem of receive-queue overflow is much worse with fine-grain multicomputers, because the node memory is much smaller, and the message traffic is more intense. Imagine the disgust of a programmer whose application has encountered a receive-queue overflow when only a fraction of the overall memory was actually used, and who is faced with the task of figuring out how to redistribute thousands of processes to avoid this transient situation. The right solution, clearly, is to allow the runtime system to redistribute receive-queue overflows, processes, and code, and to manage all of these resources for the application program. Distributed resource management is required not only to ease some of the burdens of programming, but to make the system robust.

One of the unique properties of MADRE, the Mosaic runtime system, is that its message handling is accomplished without copying. The message-handling layer of MADRE is interrupt-driven, and runs in the message-handling sequence of the Mosaic processor. The arrival of a header consisting of the first several words of an incoming packet causes the message handling routines to allocate space appropriate to the type and size of the packet before the payload of the packet is allowed to continue into memory.

Above the message-handling layer, MADRE is a fine-grain, reactive-process program written in C+−. Each *component* runtime system is implemented as a set of fine-grain *kernel* processes resident on the node, and a set of additional, *remote* processes may reside on different nodes. The runtime system is simply a fine-grain concurrent program that manages a user computation. The operation that is most critical to MADRE's ability to distribute both runtime and user processes is process creation. Process placement is determined by a code module that can employ compile-time-determined information, randomization, and history to maintain an effective balance between localization of the message traffic and dispersion of concurrent processes. Of course, the default code module for process placement can be overloaded by applications requiring specialized process placement. The modularity of MADRE separates essential capabilities for message passing and process creation from optional features such as application-specific process-placement algorithms, receive-queue-overflow handling, other exception handling, code distribution, and termination detection. These optional features may, for example, be required in a prototype development environment, but not in an embedded-system application.

Although MADRE is written in C+−, it can support other programming notations and systems at the level of processes and messages. Currently, however, the MADRE system runs on Mosaic C nodes and supports user programs written in C+−. The design and implementation of the Mosaic runtime system, and of the distributed algorithms that it employs, are part of the PhD research of Nanette J. Boden, and will be described in detail in a forthcoming thesis [3].

2.5 The ATOMIC Local-Area Network

In August 1991, our project started supplying prototype Mosaic components and programming tools to a project lead by Danny Cohen at the University of Southern California Information Sciences Institute (USC/ISI). The goal of the ATOMIC (ATM over Mosaic) project was to build, demonstrate, and experiment with a high-bandwidth, local-area network (LAN) based on Mosaic components. From the standpoint of the people developing ATOMIC, the Mosaic host-interface boards (figure 4) are the interfaces from workstations to the network, which is constructed in the manner illustrated in figure 5. The multiwire slack cables are the communication medium, and the 8×8 boards (figure 3) are 16×16 switches capable of connecting different network segments by cut-through, store-and-forward, multicast, and multiple-path routing. From the standpoint of the Mosaic developers, ATOMIC is an early, embedded-system application of the Mosaic, *ie*, a system that is used, but not programmed, by its users.

Within a matter of weeks after receiving the prototype hardware, the ATOMIC team had a 400Mbits/s LAN with TCP/IP protocols running on top of a Mosaic transport layer, and, of course, all of the usual services (FTP, email, *etc*) running on top of TCP/IP. In the intervening year, the ATOMIC network at USC/ISI has conveyed more than 10^{15} bits without a single error, and, using the Mosaics themselves as generators, has set LAN speed records such as operating at more than 5Mpackets/s (for very short packets). The bottleneck in the network performance occurs, of course, in the interface to the workstation operating system. The developers of ATOMIC have been learning how to deal with such limitations; in addition, they use ATOMIC for multi-media communication, such as distributing digital video on the network along with TCP/IP packets.

3. Concluding Remarks

I believe that the commercial, medium-grain multicomputers aimed at ultra-supercomputer performance have adopted a relatively unprofitable scaling track, and are doomed to extinction. With their relatively modest numbers of nodes, they may, as Gordon Bell believes [2], be displaced over the next several years by shared-memory multiprocessors. For the loosely coupled computations on which they excel, ultra-super multicomputers will, in any case, be more economically implemented as networks of high-performance workstations connected by high-bandwidth, local-area networks such as ATOMIC.

The most profitable niche and scaling track for the multicomputer, a highly scalable and economical MIMD architecture, is the fine-grain multicomputer. The Mosaic C demonstrates many of the advantages of this architecture, but the major part of the Mosaic experiment — exploring the programmability and application span of this class of machine — lies ahead. If these experiments succeed, the Mosaic may be taken as the origin of two scaling tracks. (1) Single-chip nodes are a technologically attractive point in the design space of multicomputers. Constant-node-size scaling will result in single-chip nodes of increasing memory size, processing capability, and communication bandwidth, but in systems of larger N than are practical for shared-memory multiprocessors. (2) Constant-node-complexity scaling will, for example, allow a Mosaic 8×8 board (figure 3) to be implemented as a single chip, with about 20 times the performance per node, within less than ten years.

4. Acknowledgments

The research described in this report was sponsored by the Defense Advanced Research Projects Agency, and monitored by the Office of Naval Research. In addition to my coworkers who are mentioned in the text of this paper, let me acknowledge the very important contributions to the Mosaic project made by our operations manager, Arlene DesJardins, and by our coworkers at Hewlett-Packard Company, notably John Vietor (wafer fabrication), Kathleen Ryan (wafer testing), and Bill Hanna (packaging design).

5. References

1. Tom Alexander, "How to Stop Fearing and Start Loving the Parallel Computer," *NSF Mosaic*, pp. 2–11, Spring 1992, National Science Foundation.

2. Gordon Bell, "Ultracomputers: A Teraflop Before Its Time," *CACM*, 35(8): 26–47, August 1992.

3. Nanette J. Boden, "Runtime Systems for Fine-Grain Multicomputers," Caltech Computer Science PhD thesis forthcoming; publication expected December 1992.

4. H. T. Kung and Charles L. Leiserson, "Algorithms for VLSI Processor Arrays," Section 8.3 in *Introduction to VLSI Systems* by Carver A. Mead and Lynn A. Conway, Addison-Wesley, 1980.

5. Michael J. Pertel, "A Critique of Adaptive Routing," Caltech Computer Science Technical Report Caltech-CS-TR-92-06, 1992.

6. Michael J. Pertel, "The Optimal Dimension for Multicomputer Routing Networks," Caltech Computer Science Technical Report Caltech-CS-TR-92-09, 1992.

7. Charles L. Seitz, "The Cosmic Cube," *CACM*, 28(1): 22–33, January 1985.

8. Charles L. Seitz, Jakov Seizovic, Wen-King Su, "The C Programmer's Abbreviated Guide to Multicomputer Programming," Caltech Computer Science Technical Report Caltech-CS-TR-88-1, 1988.

9. Charles L. Seitz, "Multicomputers," Chapter five in *Developments in Concurrency and Communication*, edited by C. A. R. Hoare, Addison-Wesley, 1990.

10. Charles L. Seitz, "Concurrent Computation and Programming," Chapter one in *VLSI and Parallel Computation*, edited by Roberto Suaya and Graham Birtwistle, Morgan Kaufmann Publishers, 1990.

11. Jakov Seizovic, "The Architecture and Programming of a Fine-Grain Multicomputer," Caltech Computer Science PhD thesis forthcoming; publication expected June 1993.

12. Wen-King Su, "Reactive-Process Programming and Distributed Discrete-Event Simulation," Caltech Computer Science Technical Report Caltech-CS-TR-89-11, 1989.

3. *Reliable*; i.e., a database system must preserve data in the face of hardware and software errors.

4. *Sharable*; i.e., a database system must support simultaneous access to data by many users, and these accesses must appear "atomic," so they do not interact with one another in unexpected ways. Often, accesses are from sites remote from the data itself.

2.1 Early Systems

The earliest database management systems became products in the late 1960's. Systems such as IMS (see Ullman [1988] for a discussion of early DBMS's) were based on the "hierarchical model," that is, data organized as tree-structured records with pointers from one field to another, as needed. Others were built along the lines of the CODASYL [1971] "network" model, using flat files with many-one relationships between files.

The applications for which these systems were intended required all four of Bancilhon's properties. These applications included airline reservation systems, inventory systems, banking systems, and many other commercial systems. For example, the database for an airline reservation system surely involves massive amounts of data ("large"), records must continue to exist after a transaction that reserves a seat finishes ("persistent"), it is essential that records not be lost ("reliable"), and it is normal that many reservation operations are being performed at once, initiated at sites across the world, and that these transactions must be executed in an atomic way, so that, for example, we do not sell the last seat twice ("sharable").

2.2 Relational Systems

The first major change in DBMS technology came with the relational model of data. This model got rid of pointers as a concept for the user of the system, and instead invited the user to view data as relations, or sets of tuples, which are an abstraction of the flat file. The relational model is generally regarded as originating with a series of papers by Codd [1970, 1972a, 1972b], although many of the concepts used in this model actually had their origins in the 1960's (see the bibliographic notes of Ullman [1988] for a history of the subject.)

This new model had a profound effect on the way databases could be accessed. It pushed many computational details, such as the data structures used to support efficient access to the data, out of the database programming language ("query language"). Thus, it allowed the programmer to express queries and data manipulation in a language that was much higher-level than the languages associated with the earlier systems.

The result was that new classes of people could use databases in new ways. No longer was it necessary to be a professional programmer in order to get useful information from a database. People with limited training could learn to use a language like SQL (Astrahan and Chamberlin [1975]), which has become the de facto standard relational query language, or any of a number of other early languages that were based on high-level algebraic or logical constructs. For example, an airline reservation system is normally built by having professional programmers implement

New Frontiers in Database System Research

Jeffrey D. Ullman

Department of Computer Science, Stanford University
Stanford CA 94305

Abstract. After many years of development centered around business applications, database systems are now recognized as a key technology in many new application areas being addressed by Computer Science today. We shall mention some of these applications, and the general sorts of advances in technology needed to support these applications. For example, there is a need to deal with databases of progressively larger size, containing data of a wide variety of types, and there is a need to perform operations of nonstandard kinds on this data. There is a need to combine data from widely distributed databases and integrating this data to form a useful whole.

1 Introduction

This paper is an opportunity to reflect on various aspects of database research. In what follows, we should remember the distinction between a *database*, which is a repository of data intended to address a particular application, and a *database management system* (DBMS, or just "database system"), which is a software system designed to organize the data in a database, access ("query") the database, and manipulate (modify) the data of the database.

In successive sections, we shall consider

a)   The historical development of the database field that leads us to the present set of models and paradigms.

b)   The new problem directions that are driving the field.

c)   The influences that are changing the nature of the field.

d)   The role of theory in database system research.

2 Historical Perspective

Perhaps the best definition of a database system is taken from Bancilhon [1988], who gives four characteristics:

1.   *Large*; i.e., database systems must be capable of handling an amount of data that does not fit in main memory, and must access and manipulate this data efficiently.

2.   *Persistent*; i.e., a database system must support data whose existence continues independent of any process that may be using that data.

Work supported by NSF grant IRI-90-16358, ARO grant DAAL03-91-0177, and a gift of Mitsubishi Electric Corp.

procedures that allow clerks to do standard operations like booking a seat, ordering a special meal, and so on. That is probably the way it should be; we don't want clerks using the database in "creative" ways.

On the other hand, a middle-level manager of the airline might like to know something interesting and unusual from the database, for example, "on what routes has our percentage of filled seats dropped by 5% or more over the past month?" In nonrelational systems, it has been necessary for the manager either to be a skilled programmer or to call in a skilled programmer to write the query. It is likely, however, that the manager can learn to write such a query in SQL or a similar language without too much trouble. Thus, a relational interface to a database opens up new opportunities for using the data.

However, the relational model was not an immediate blessing. There is a general rule for programming languages that the higher the level, i.e., the less detail that must be supplied by the programmer, the harder it is to execute programs efficiently; this tradeoff is an important aspect of what Vaughan Pratt called the "competence/performance dichotomy" (Pratt [1977]). It took most of the decade of the 1970's for systems like System R (Astrahan et al. [1976]) and Ingres (Stonebraker, Wong, Kreps, and Held [1976]) to solve the optimization problems and develop into commercial systems capable of matching or in some cases outperforming the earlier systems.

It is interesting to note that optimization of relational query languages remains today the only clear example of how it is possible to optimize a very high-level language and produce competitive code. In comparison, attempts to optimize other very high-level languages, such as APL, have been much less successful. On the other hand, we should also bear in mind that SQL and other relational languages are just about the only widely used languages that are not Turing-complete; that is, it is not possible to express arbitrary computable functions in SQL. Perhaps the ability to optimize successfully (get "performance") is dependent on the limited "competence" of SQL and similar languages.

2.3 Importance of Classical DBMS's

Before going on to the future of database management systems, let us pause to remind ourselves of the vital role played by the database management systems in current use. They have addressed a very important class of problems, mostly commercial in nature. They do what they do extremely well, and there is a widespread market for the services and products of a number of companies operating in this arena. Nevertheless, the technologies involed have a limitation that prevents their direct adaptation to some of the newer problems that would appear superficially to require database technology. We shall discuss some of these problem areas in the next section.

3 New Applications for Database Management Systems

There is a clear vision of a large class of problems that we may fairly regard as "database" problems, and these problems suggest many new areas of research. A statement of the future for DBMS research was presented in the "Lagunita Report," Silberschatz, Stonebraker, and Ullman [1990], and this vision has been ratified and amplified by the recent report to the US Computer Science and Telecommunications Board: Hartmanis and Lin [1992]. These reports see two general directions:

1. *Ultra-Large Databases*, and

2. *Heterogeneous, Distributed Databases.*

3.1 Ultra-Large Databases

There is motivation from science, libraries, entertainment, and other sources, to construct databases of ever increasing size. To make matters more complex, the "data" stored therein is often not classical "record-oriented" data. Rather, the data often is in the form of signals, such as video signals.

EOSDIS. For example, NASA will soon put into orbit a collection of satellites that will, early in the next millenium, send down to earth about a third of a petabyte[2] of information per year. To make this data available to Earth Scientists, NASA is implementing EOSDIS (Earth-Observing Satellites Data and Information System). This system is intended to provide data not only from this series of satellites, but data from satellites of other nations and data gathered from non-satellite sources, all in a coherent, well integrated fashion. Data in unprecedented volumes is to be delivered to the desktop of researchers in a matter of minutes.

Scientific databases on the terabyte-petabyte scale in areas such as astrophysics, chemistry, and molecular biology either exist or will exist in the near future. Further, it is most certainly true that classified observation systems, which will operate on the scale of the EOSDIS database, are in place or soon to be in place.

Electronic Libraries. We can see in the near future that books and other forms of information such as videotape will be available electronically, from a single source across a high-speed network. The Stanford library has about 6 million books, and currently buys only 4% of all English-language books available. If we store a book in electronic source, e.g. TeX, it takes about 1-2 megabytes. Thus, the Stanford library represents about 10 terabytes of data, and if we estimate that there are 25 times as many English-language books available, we might store all English literature in a quarter of a petabyte.

However, the situation is much worse for a book that must be stored in image form, such as a volume that contains significant numbers of drawings or other aspects that require a more detailed representation, e.g., a book composed in a font that no longer exists and whose style adds to the value of the book. Proper representation of such a book requires about half a gigabyte per page.[3] Further, a study by the French National Library estimates that 5–10% of its collection requires such treatment.[4] If this estimate applied to the Stanford library alone, we would require about 200 gigabytes for a 400 page book, and we would find perhaps 500,000 such books, for a total of 100 petabytes.

But books aren't the only items that would go into an electronic repository. Television signals and images of various sorts could be handled in much the same

---

[2] Peta = 10^{15} if you're not yet used to thinking on this scale.

[3] Charles Bigelow, private communication, April, 1991.

[4] Witold Litwin, private communication, June, 1992.

way as electronic books. However, TV signal at reasonable resolution requires 35 megabytes per second, or 100 gigabytes for an hour program.

Data Mining Applications. Silberschatz, Stonebraker, and Ullman [1990] tells of a department store chain that stores a terabyte of recent sales information and allows its managers to query the data in ad-hoc ways to detect sales trends quickly. The effect of the system was a 3% increase in sales per unit floor area, which provides remarkable leverage to a company in a competitive market. Similarly, there are numerous financial companies concerned with predicting market performance by querying historical market data in an ad-hoc way. Tsur [1990] surveys other applications of a similar nature.

The common element in these problems is that investigators want to "mine" large amounts of data for interesting or significant patterns. The process is one of research, since we do not know in advance what questions are important. We thus need not only the ability to store volumes of data in the terabyte range, but the ability to query this data in a very high-level language efficiently, so non-programmers can get the answers they need quickly.

3.2 Heterogeneous, Distributed Databases

The second trend of great significance in the new generation of database systems is the need to integrate related databases to make them work as a whole. There are very important applications in manufacturing, specifically making systems such as design tools, simulators, and constructors (e.g., integrated circuit fabricators, milling machines) talk to one another in a common way. However, even some seemingly trivial problems are quite difficult. In a recent discussion concerning database integration at an aircraft company,[5] I was told that the company has 23 databases that involve "employees," and none of the definitions are the same. For example, the benefits department might include retirees, but not the payroll department; some databases include consultants or employees of the cafeteria subcontractors.

If we are to integrate these databases into a single view that allows us to deal with "employees," then we must describe and implement two-way translators between the unified view and each of the relevant databases. We must describe how data in each database is translated into facts about employees in the view, and we must describe how two translate queries about employees, posed on the view, into actions on the databases.

There has been significant progress on techniques for "interoperability" of databases, but much of the commercially viable work is at the system level, e.g., making two manufacturers' SQL systems talk to one another. The first steps toward integration on the logical level, that is, combining databases that talk about almost, but not quite the same concepts, are surveyed in Elmagarmid and Pu [1990] and Rusinkiewicz, Sheth, and Karabitis [1991]. Krishnamurthy, Litwin, and Kent [1991] discusses linguistic issues for logical interoperability.

A key concept in the construction of complex networks of interoperating databases is the "mediator" (Wiederhold [1991]). The idea is to supplement the databases with systems that are capable of talking to a few of the databases and also

---

[5] Randall Johnson, private communication, March, 1990.

communicating with users and other mediators in a common, or widely understood language. This same approach is receiving prominence in the artificial intelligence community as well, through the related concept of the "agent" (Shoham [1992]).

3.3 Research Areas for Ultra-Large Databases

There are two important observations we must make when we contemplate research on extending the size at which databases are usable.

1. Many significant characteristics of computer hardware have been doubling every 2-3 years, that is, improving by a factor of 10 in about 10 years. Examples include the number of instructions per second for a fixed cost, and the number of bits stored for a fixed cost.

2. A factor of 10 increase in a significant parameter is certain to produce a new set of problems that did not surface for the smaller systems.

Point (1) tempts us to imagine that all problems will simply go away in a reasonable period of time. But point (2) reminds us that there will always be new challenges if we are to take advantage of the technology improvements. The intuitive reason for (2) is that good designs always balance the bottlenecks, so that the throughput of each part of a system is close to what the other parts need.

As a simple example, when we read a track from a disk we need to pass the data through a channel and then process the data in some way. In a well tuned system, the channel can carry data at exactly the rate it passes under the reading head, and the processing, which is dependent on the processor speed, is just able to keep up with the flow of data. Ten years later, processor speed and storage density have each gone up by a factor of 10. We would like to feed data to the processor at 10 times the rate, but the disk is too slow. It will have approximately 3 times as many tracks, each with 3 times as many bits per track. If rotation speeds have not increased, we need to redesign the system so that three disks provide the data in parallel. Moreover, the channel rate may also influence what can be achieved; it may suddenly become a bottleneck if its speed has not increased by at least a factor of 3.

Thus, when we consider a research agenda for ultra-large databases, we should bear in mind that the actual problems are often technology-dependent and the availability of new kinds of devices, for example optical storage or communication, frequently determine where the bottlenecks lie. Here are some general areas that appear fruitful:

1. *Tertiary Storage.* When we get into the terabyte range, it is clear that with current technology, secondary storage (disks) is inadequate to hold the entire database. We need devices that involve physical movement of data-storage objects, such as "silos" of tape cassettes. These "tertiary" storage methods store orders of magnitude more data than secondary storage devices, but also involve many orders of magnitude more time to access a given item. How do we present the user of the database with the appearance of an on-line database? Interestingly, the same problem has been faced by computer architects for decades, and they have come up with a series of ideas — caches and virtual memory,

for example — that hide the slowness of secondary and even primary memory from the user. Do these lessons say anything to the database community?

2. *Data Compression.* When I give an hour lecture, a transcript of what I say fits easily into 25,000 bytes. The videotape of the class covers 100 gigabytes. Is there really 4 million times as much information in the image of the class than in the words spoken? More generally, how much can we compress typical data so that it can be retrieved and decompressed at the appropriate time, efficiently?

3. *Intelligent Access.* When we start storing data that is not record-oriented, it becomes harder to access data by content, which is the typical query in conventional database systems. For example, we are used to thinking about queries like "who are the employees in the Toy Department?" and answering this query with the aid of an index on Department. How do we instead handle a query about still images asking for an image of the heart with an enlarged left ventricle? Given a library of journal articles represented by ASCII text (not image, which would be much harder), how do we search them for information relevant to a specific research question?

4. *Making Use of Networks.* If the exponential growth in capacity mentioned above continues for a decade, I expect to find at Stanford 10,000 workstations, each with a 100 gigabyte disk. I expect these to be connected by a network with gigabit-per-second speed. If I were to borrow just 1% of that storage, I would have enough for a 10-terabyte database, and it would be "on-line," i.e., no tertiary storage would be necessary. That's enough to store the Stanford library in text format. If we did this on a worldwide scale, the capacity would be well above the petabyte range. How would we manage access to such a database? How would we make it resilient to local failures?

3.4 Research Areas for Heterogeneous, Distributed Databases

There are special problems connected with distributed databases of all sorts. For resilience in the face of failures, we may need to keep multiple copies, and we need to keep these copies consistent and/or reconcile them when a link between disconnected sites is reestablished. None of these issues relate specifically to the problems of heterogeneity and integration of related databases. Yet, as the number of sites involved grows by orders of magnitude, we expect that new solutions to old problems will become necessary, just as we believe will be the case for ultra-large databases.

I see the problem of logical interoperability — that is, integration of databases — as primarily a linguistic issue and a question of the development of the proper modeling tools. The questions are similar to those faced two decades ago concerning the tools for database description (e.g., entity-relationship diagrams; see Ullman [1988]) and the appropriate kinds of query languages to use. Now again, we need to develop models and notations sufficient to describe the meaning of the data being integrated, and we need to develop languages that are suitable for such tasks as:

1. Describing the mappings among data in various databases.

2. Serving as a language with which we can communicate with a mediator or agent.

As with the question of new query languages in general, we find two different, and somewhat incompatible approaches: logical and object-oriented. Two manifestos, one favoring the logical (i.e., extensions of relational systems), and the other favoring the object-oriented methodology have recently been promulgated: Stonebraker et al. [1990], and Atkinson et al. [1989], respectively. The author's views on the general issue have been expressed before (see Ullman [1991], e.g.); I favor the logical or deductive approach because it alone offers the very high-level programming that has made the relational model successful and that makes database access available to nonprogrammers.

However, this argument does not necessarily apply to integration problems. Integration of heterogeneous databases and implementation of mediators are not tasks lightly assigned to nonprogrammers. Further, the object-oriented paradigm, with its message-passing form of computation, matches very well with the client-server model of communication that pervades distributed systems today. Thus, let us simply propose that an extremely important area of research is to experiment with integration languages and tools. For this purpose, the logical approach and the object-oriented approach are complementary in an interesting way, as we discuss below.

The Logical Approach to Heterogeneity. Logical approaches are *data-centric*; the integration requires a description of the data, and the operations permissible then follow from the notation, as for example, relational systems support the same (relational algebra) operations on whatever data scheme one chooses. Logical languages therefore require us to write translators between the scheme of one database and the scheme of the unified view or another database. Having done so, the processing of queries on the unified database can be implemented straightforwardly by composing the query and the translators.

The Object-Oriented Approach to Heterogeneity. In contrast, object-oriented approaches are *operation-centric*. The most natural "object-oriented" way to integrate databases is to establish a unified view that supports a collection of methods. These methods are implemented by messages sent to the constituent databases. The messages are implemented at each database by whatever operations are deemed suitable to the designer. We never have to concern ourselves about what the data at a constituent database "means" or how it relates to data at other databases; it is sufficient to support the methods of the view.

4 Trends in Database Systems

Now, let us consider the future from another viewpoint: what are the forces that will influence the nature of the database system research field over the next decade? We see two important trends:

1. The monolithic view of what a database system is, as expressed by Bancilhon's four properties mentioned in Section 2, needs to change.

2.   As the scope of problems addressable by database system technology increases, the database field begins to look more like several other fields of Computer Science, and vice versa.

4.1 Divestiture of Database Capability

The four properties of database systems each imply a cost, sometimes a substantial cost. For example, the need to guarantee complete reliability means that a transaction, however small, cannot execute without at least one write operation to stable storage (i.e., disk). That write can increase by orders of magnitude the time required to execute a transaction. Similarly, sharing of data usually implies atomicity of transactions, with the attendant cost of locking or a similar scheme for assuring that transactions do not interfere with one another.

Yet there are many applications for which we can relax one or more of the requirements. For example, classical database technology has been found too slow to support computer-aided design systems for applications such as integrated circuit design. Orders-of-magnitude speedup is possible if we relax the requirement for absolute reliability and allow that a piece of a design being changed when the system crashes may become corrupted in limited ways. Similarly, data sharing in design systems is rarely at the level of small transactions. Rather, a design file is checked out by a designer, perhaps for a whole day, and locked to others. The methodology and cost of such limited sharing is radically different from what we require in, say, a banking system or airline reservation system.

Thus, a trend in database system design is to make components that address each of the capabilities of a general DBMS, and allow the user to assemble the appropriate software from a subset of these components. For example, this approach is present in the system EXODUS (Carey et al. [1986]) and DADAISM (Wiederhold et al. [1986]). An additional advantage of the componentizing of systems is that we can redesign components when necessary and install them in a complete system with minimum effort.

4.2 Relationship to AI

One of the most interesting phenomena is the way the artificial intelligence and database communities have each expanded their vision to include substantial portions of the other's interest. The traditional view is that AI people are interested in enhancing the capabilities of computers, but do not put efficiency issues foremost, especially in the context of what happens when the amount of information involved gets very large. Thus, many "AI systems" have rather small upper bounds on the amount of data with which they can deal. On the other hand, database systems have been perceived as robust, able to handle very large volumes of data, but largely unimaginative in their capabilities.

Over the past few years, there has been a drawing together of interests. Database researchers are becoming aware of the technologies of AI, and we can observe some quarters where database technology is penetrating the AI community. However, progress is uneven. A few observations may amplify these points.

Knowledge Bases. I was pleased to hear John McCarthy refer recently to the

Lenat CYC project as a "database for common-sense reasoning."[6] Indeed, if one examines the book Lenat and Guha [1990], one finds that they are indeed creating a deductive database of great size. At least at the time of the book, their computational methods were limited and inefficient compared to what is known in the deductive database community (see Ullman [1989], Bry [1989], Ross [1991], Kemp, Stukey, and Srivastava [1991], among many other works on the subject).

Nonmonotonic Reasoning. The problem of dealing properly with negative information, e.g., "X is a bachelor unless there exists Y such that $married(X, Y)$," was addressed by both the database and AI communities at about the same time. For example, McCarthy [1980] discusses "circumscription," which is a general way to describe the handling of negative information, and several papers in Gallaire and Minker [1978] address computational ways to handle negative information in database queries (this book is also heavily influenced by the AI community).

More recently, two rival approaches to nonmonotonic reasoning have come out of the two camps: *well-founded semantics* (Van Gelder, Ross, and Schimpf [1991]) and *stable-model semantics* (Gelfond and Lifschitz [1988]). Interestingly, both have their origins at a meeting of the "XP" group[7] in Oregon in 1987, attended by Allen Van Gelder and Vladimir Lifschitz. It is good to see that each community is beginning to become aware of the work of the other, even though the AI community tends to emphasize expressiveness, and the database community tends to emphasize efficiency.

Logical Languages for Representing Information. The AI community is beginning to experiment with logical languages for data representation, such as KIF (Knowledge Interchange Format); see Genesereth, Fikes et al. [1992]. They have had some interesting successes using KIF as a language for "agents" in a simulated manufacturing scenario. Sadly, this work is part of a larger project that has tried very hard to exclude the database community, even to the extent of canceling a planned talk at a recent SIGMOD conference.

On the other hand, the KIF group has been wrestling with a number of issues such as reasonable ways to deal with higher-order logics and interfacing with object-oriented systems, that have also been addressed in the database community with a good deal of success. For example, a group centered at INRIA has made significant progress on logical languages that exhibit object-oriented features, as typified by Abiteboul and Kanellakis [1989], and Grumbach and Vianu [1991]; see also the survey by Beeri [1992]. A group at Stony Brook has also addressed this problem and the problem of incorporating higher-order logics into a first-order logic framework: Chen, Kifer, and Warren [1989], Kifer and Lausen [1989], and Kifer and Wu [1989].

Rule-Based Reasoning. The use of "triggers" — rules that look asynchronously for conditions and cause certain actions — has been an important paradigm in AI systems for many years. Recently, we see attempts by the database community to incorporate this concept into DBMS's, and there has been an attendant consideration of efficiency issues. The survey by Sellis [1989] and some interesting theory

---

[6] John McCarthy, private communication, Aug., 1992.

[7] An irregular meeting of the author's former students and random others; the XP stands for "ex-Princeton."

on the subject by Ceri and Widom [1990] exemplify what is happening along these lines.

4.3 Relationship to Distributed Systems

In the near future there will be major increases in communication bandwidth and in the degree to which computers are networked to form part of a larger whole. Until recently, distributed systems research has centered on simple notions of what the distributed objects were, e.g., files and messages. Progress has reached the point where, on the Internet, we can imagine that we are dealing with a "world file system" with a single, worldwide name space.

The next step forward will involve the creation of a *world information system*, where databases everywhere are connected in a deeper sense. Not only will we be able to reach them by name, but their information will be integrated in the manner discussed in Section 3.2 to form larger units, accessible through mediators/agents that communicate both with users and with the relevant databases themselves.

The combination of database and distributed systems technologies will lead to a profound difference in the way we perceive the world of information. For example, there needs to be only one copy of any object in the world, except for purposes of reliability and efficiency of access. What will it mean to be a book publisher in such a world, where there is no need for paper copies, and any book can be called up on one's screen as desired? What will it mean to publish a newspaper or produce a movie? What new information resources will prove useful and commercially viable?

4.4 Relationship to Programming Languages

There has been a recent history of interchange between the database and programming language communities. The two major programming paradigms for new database systems, logical languages and object-oriented languages, arose from corresponding explorations in the programming language community. In the other direction, programming language research now includes "persistent" languages, which take one of the central properties of a DBMS and combines it with traditional programming language approaches.

5 Database Theory

Our vision of the future of database systems research cannot be complete without a discussion of the role of theory in the database community. While other communities, such as operating systems, graphics, programming languages, or AI, seem in general to be capable of assimilating theory and theoreticians, the same has been true only to a limited extent in the database field. For example, the history of the PODS conference, which was created only after repeated failure of the SIGMOD conference to open itself to theory, is well known, and Won Kim, the present SIGMOD chair deserves a great deal of credit for attempting to bring the two conferences together.

It is easy to recognize the mean-spirited putdown of theory in the "Laguna" report (Bernstein et al. [1989]). However, it is less easy to see the condescension toward theory in an article like Date [1992], with its seemingly friendly title "Theory is Practical!" Apparently, Date believed there was nothing useful in 20 years of database theory until he chanced upon a theorem of Ron Fagin that relates third and fifth normal form.

5.1 Problems with Theory

One can always point to particular theoretical papers, or even whole lines of theoretical development, that in retrospect were ill-advised and do not lead to any useful results. Worse, it is easy to point to phenomena where theoretical research seems to sidetrack itself, producing a long series of papers each of which addresses only problems posed by the previous paper, with no connection back to the real world. Many point to cases where the real problem seems to be abstracted away to such an extent that the results obtained only appear to be applicable.

5.2 The Case for Theory

Without trying to argue that the problems mentioned above are not real, let us outline the value that theory brings to a field, and to database systems in particular.

Concrete Contributions. Perhaps the least important reason for encouraging a theory is the instances where a particular paper proves, perhaps many years after its publication, to be the solution to a real-world problem. Shuky Sagiv tells me of a start-up company formed recently to develop software that supports instantiated views, and found the paper by Sagiv and Shmueli [1986] to be central to their work. It is gratifying to discover that some of the much-maligned work on logical database languages is now beginning to see the light of day in serious commercial implementations.

Demographic Impact. Theory has a way of attracting some of the brightest young students to a research field, because many look for the opportunity to show what they can do in individual research. It is interesting to note how many of the authors of Bernstein et al. [1989] wrote theoretical theses. A related phenomenon is that a theory for a subject supports the development of courses with satisfactory academic content. Such courses, in turn, popularize the field and disseminate its fundamental ideas to a wide audience.

Infrastructure. Vaughan Pratt is fond of saying that "good theory is invisible." For example, functional dependencies are not perceived as "theory"; they're just the way one thinks about the structure of relations. The same could be said for a number of other concepts from database theory: normal forms, serializability of schedules, joins, e.g., and the list is going to grow as the field matures. In general, when a theory has the desired impact, it becomes "invisible" as a theory and is regarded instead as an everyday tool of the field.

Thus, while it is too much to expect that every theoretical idea will prove to be influential and useful (just as only a small fraction of the lines of code ever written actually appear in useful systems), we look forward to a future where theory is accepted and welcomed as an important facet of database systems research. Indeed, as Computer Science matures, we should expect it to become more normal that a phase of theoretical development will precede the implementation phase in projects at the frontier.

6 Summary

The database field is changing rapidly. Databases are getting bigger and holding data of many new forms, and there is a need to integrate large numbers of databases distributed among distant sites. There is a consequent change in the dominant paradigms of the field, with considerable cross-fertilization with artificial intelligence, distributed systems, and programming languages.

References

Abiteboul, S. and P. C. Kanellakis [1989]. "Object identity as a query language primitive," *ACM SIGMOD International Conf. on Management of Data*, pp. 159–173.

Astrahan, M. M. and D. D. Chamberlin [1975]. "Implementation of a structured English query language," *Comm. ACM* 18:10, pp. 580–587.

Astrahan, M. M., et al. [1976]. "System R: a relational approach to data management," *ACM Trans. on Database Systems* 1:2, pp. 97–137.

Atkinson, M., F. Bancilhon, D. DeWitt, K. Dittrich, D. Maier, and S. Zdonik [1989]. "The object-oriented database system manifesto," *Proc. First Intl. Conf. on Deductive and Object-Oriented Databases*, Kyoto, pp. 40–57.

Bancilhon, F. [1988]. "Object-oriented database systems," *Proc. Seventh ACM Symposium on Principles of Database Systems*, pp. 152–162..

Beeri, C. [1992]. "New data models and languages — the challenge," *Proc. Eleventh ACM Symposium on Principles of Database Systems*, pp. 1–15.

Bernstein, P. A. et al. [1989]. "Future directions in DBMS research," *SIGMOD Record* 18:1, pp. 17–30.

Bry, F. [1989]. "Query evaluation in recursive databases: bottom-up and top-down reconciled," *Proc. First Intl. Conf. on Deductive and Object-Oriented Databases*, Kyoto, pp. 20–39.

Carey, M. J., D. J. DeWitt, D. Frank, G. Graefe, J. E. Richardson, E. J. Shekita, and M. Muralikrishna [1986]. "The architecture of the EXODUS extensible DBMS," *Proc. Intl. Workshop on Object-Oriented Database Systems*, Asilomar, CA., Sept., 1986.

Ceri, S. and J. Widom [1990]. "Deriving production rules for constraint maintainence," *Proc. International Conference on Very Large Data Bases*, pp. 566–577.

Chen, W., M. Kifer, and D. S. Warren [1989]. "HiLog: a first order semantics for higher order programming constructs," in *Second Intl. Workshop on Database Programming Languages*, Morgan-Kaufmann, San Mateo.

CODASYL [1971]. *CODASYL Data Base Task Group April 71 Report*, ACM, New York.

Codd, E. F. [1970]. "A relational model for large shared data banks," *Comm. ACM* 13:6, pp. 377–387.

Codd, E. F. [1972a]. "Further normalization of the data base relational model," in *Data Base Systems* (R. Rustin, ed.) Prentice-Hall, Englewood Cliffs, New Jersey.pp. 33–64.

Codd, E. F. [1972b]. "Relational completeness of data base sublanguages," *ibid.* pp. 65–98.

Date, C. J. [1992]. "Theory is Practical!," *Database Programming and Design* 5:9, pp. 21–22.

Elmagarmid, A. and C. Pu (eds.) [1990]. *ACM Computer Surveys* **22**:3.

Gallaire, H. and J. Minker [1978]. *Logic and Databases,* Plenum Press, New York.

Gelfond, M. and V. Lifschitz [1988]. "The stable model semantics for logic programming," *Proc. Fifth ICLP,* MIT Press, Cambridge MA, pp. 1070–1080.

Genesereth, M. R., R. E. Fikes et al. [1992]. "Knowledge interchange format version 3.0 reference manual," Logic-92-1, Stanford University Logic Group, June 1992.

Grumbach, S. and V. Vianu [1991]. "Tractable query languages for complex object databases," INRIA Rapport de Recherche 1573, Dec., 1991.

Hartmanis, J. and H. Lin (eds.) [1992]. *Computing the Future: A Broader Agenda for Computer Science and Engineering,* National Academy Press, Washington DC.

Kemp, D. B., P. J. Stuckey, and D. Srivastava [1991]. "Magic sets and bottom-up evaluation of well-founded models," *Intl. Conf. on Logic Programming,* pp. 337–350.

Kifer, M. and G. Lausen [1989]. "F-logic: a higher-order logic for reasoning about objects, inheritance, and schemes," *ACM SIGMOD International Conf. on Management of Data,* pp. 143–146.

Kifer, M. and J. Wu [1989]. "A logic for object-oriented programming," *Proc. Eighth ACM Symposium on Principles of Database Systems,* pp. 379–393.

Krishnamurthy, R., W. Litwin, and W. Kent [1991]. "Language features for interoperability of databases with schematic dependencies," *ACM SIGMOD International Conf. on Management of Data,* pp. 40–49.

Lenat, D. B. and R. V. Guha [1990]. *Building Large Knowledge-Based Systems,* Addison Wesley, Reading, Mass.

McCarthy, J. [1980]. "Circumscription — a form of non-monotonic reasoning," *Artificial Intelligence* 13:1-2, pp. 27–39.

Pratt, V. R. [1977]. "The competence/performance dichotomy in programming," *Proc. Fourth ACM Symposium on Principles of Programming Languages,* pp. 194–200.

Ross, K. A. [1991]. "On negation in HiLog," *Proc. Tenth ACM Symposium on Principles of Database Systems,* pp. 206–215.

Rusinkiewicz, A., A. Sheth, and G. Karabitis [1991]. "Specifying interdatabase dependencies in a multidatabase environment," *IEEE Computer,* Dec., 1991.

Sagiv, Y. and O. Shmueli [1986]. "The equivalence of solving queries and producing tree projections," *Proc. Fifth ACM Symposium on Principles of Database Systems*, pp. 160–172.

Sellis, T. [1989]. (ed.) *SIGMOD Record* 18:3, pp. 3–77.

Shoham, Y. [1992]. "Agent oriented programming, an overview and summary of recent research," *Proc. Workshop on Distributed AI*.

Silberschatz, A., M. Stonebraker, and J. D. Ullman (eds.) [1990]. "Database systems: achievements and opportunities," *Comm. ACM* 34:10, pp. 110–120.

Stonebraker, M. et al. [1990]. "Third-generation database system manifesto," *SIGMOD Record* 19:3, pp. 31–44.

Stonebraker, M., E. Wong, P. Kreps, and G. Held [1976]. "The design and implementation of INGRES," *ACM Trans. on Database Systems* 1:3, pp. 189–222.

Tsur, S. [1990]. "Applications of deductive database systems," IEEE COMPCON, Feb., 1990.

Ullman, J. D. [1988]. *Principles of Database and Knowledge-Base Systems* Vol. I: *Classical Database Systems*, Computer Science Press, New York.

Ullman, J. D. [1989]. *Principles of Database and Knowledge-Base Systems* Vol. II: *The New Technologies*, Computer Science Press, New York.

Ullman, J. D. [1991]. "A comparison between deductive and object-oriented database systems," *Proc. Second Intl. Conf. on Deductive and Object-Oriented Databases*, Munich, pp. 263–277.

Van Gelder, A., K. A. Ross, and J. S. Schlipf [1991]. "The well-founded semantics for general logic programs," *J. ACM* 38:3, pp. 620–650.

Wiederhold, G. [1991]. "Mediators in the architecture of future information systems," *IEEE Computer*, March, 1991.

Wiederhold, G. et al. [1986]. "Modularization of an ADA database system," *Advanced Database Symposium*, Information Processing Society of Japan, Tokyo, August 1986, pp. 135–142.

II. Symbolic Computation, Programming, and Software Engineering

Formal Theories and Software Systems: Fundamental Connections between Computer Science and Logic

Robert L. Constable*
Department of Computer Science
Cornell University
Ithaca, NY 14853
rc@cs.cornell.edu

September 22, 1992

Abstract

A formal Theory of Logics is sketched using concepts from a modern proof development system (like Nuprl, Coq or other such software systems). The Theory can be applied to understanding these software systems, and the application suggests a design principle called the *theories-as-systems notion*. Applications of the Theory to automated reasoning have led to an empirical study of the notion of *obvious inference*. Experimental results are cited to explain key constants of a scientific theory of *obvious inference*. The constants appear in what is called here the *deBruijn equation*.

1 Introduction

1.1 Historical Context

Computer Science and Logic have had a major impact on the intellectual life of the 20th Century. They reach into most branches of science, and the artifacts of Computer Science have transformed everyday life on much of the planet. Logic led the way,

---

*This research supported by NSF grant CCR-9244739 and ONR grant N00014-92J-1764.

starting, say, with the 1879 results of Frege [28], but even before then Babbage was dreaming of computing. From mid-20th-century onwards there has been an alignment of concerns between Logic and Computer Science (referred to hereafter as CS).

Frege showed us exactly how to formalize sentences, introducing propositional functions, predicates and quantifiers. Thus concepts needed to define what CS calls *formal specifications* were already in place by 1879. Russell introduced the idea of *types* to provide a consistent way of abstracting over propositions [60], and of course types have played a key role in programming languages since the beginning, as in (Algol60, Algol68, Pascal, Simula, ADA, Standard ML). By 1925 Hilbert defined the concept of a *formal system* and made clear the role of metamathematics in studying them. He also set an agenda for using formalism for precise reasoning. This turned out to be an agenda for using computers to check our work; Computer Science has followed this agenda trying out the ideas of program verification and computer assisted program development. Herbrand and Gentzen refined Hilbert's ideas to include forms of reasoning found in everyday mathematics, and they showed how to incorporate them into the theory of logic. All of these results have had an impact on the design of computer software.

Already by 1901 Brouwer forced us to look at the role of computation in mathematics, especially the large part it played in providing *meaning* to abstract mathematics. Out of this Herbrand isolated an idea of computability which Gödel connected to the notion of Turing computability. Church, Kleene, Rosser and Curry saw how this computability could be expressed at all the types needed to provide a foundation for mathematics, and they gave us a functional programming language paradigm (based on the λ calculus) going well beyond the primitive recursive functions of Dedekind (1888).

By 1930 Gödel had shown that the basic concepts of modern logic were more than formalisms for rigorously expressing mathematics and computation. They were the substance from which he crafted some of the most intriguing theorems of mathematics—his *incompleteness* theorems. These results revealed fundamental limits to the nature of formal knowledge and told us about the creative character of mathematical truth. Even without a quantitative theory of information or of computational complexity (both to come later, [46] for information, [35] for complexity), Gödel was able to discover laws that governed the architecture of formal knowledge. He also put in place the concepts and methods that would eventually enable computer scientists to pose some of their most compelling questions, e.g. does $P = NP$ [21, 51].

The above concepts provided the substance for another major principle, this time discovered independently by several people [22, 24, 36, 48] but often known as the *Curry-Howard isomorphism* or as the *propositions-as-types principle*. This principle can express some of Brouwer's deepest insights about the nature of proof as the instrument of mathematical truth. At their foundations, Brouwer believed that the distinction between logic and mathematics disappeared. This belief is reflected in the name of the principle, "propositions-as-types"; a meeting of the *propositions* of logic with the *types* of mathematics[1].

This principle enabled Per Martin-Löf [52, 58] and Jean-Yves Girard [29] to design two modern type theories which relate computability concepts to the basic structure of typed languages[2]. These theories have yielded logics for reasoning about functional programs that are very attractive to computer scientists [19, 41]. One of these originates at INRIA in a project led by G. Huet [42, 43]; it is called Coq. The other is called Nuprl, and it originated at Cornell [19]. The unification of two of the major concepts from Logic and CS has sparked hopes of a Unified Type Theory [18, 30] which might merge concurrent computation and the implicit calculus of names from logic into a unified picture of types and computations. Work of Abramsky [2] on Linear Logic and Milner on the pi-calculus [55] are encouraging signs in this endeavor.

1.2 Outline of This Paper

This paper offers some thoughts about the application of these modern type theories and their implementations to achieving two of the oldest goals of Logic. The first goal was articulated already by Leibniz [50] who hoped to use his logical calculus to assist in everyday reasoning. In Leibniz's own words "We can judge immediately whether propositions presented to us are proved, and that which others could hardly do with the greatest mental labor and good fortune, we can produce with the guidance of symbols alone... ". The advent of computers has quickened the pace of this work.

---

[1] This principle fits well with another called *proofs-as-programs*. The idea is that many programs can be understood well as the executable part of constructive proofs (lately even of certain classical proofs [57]). The idea is a natural expression of Kleene's realizability concepts [45] that were an attempt to relate Brouwer's ideas about constructivity to Turing computability. The connection to programming languages was made explicit in CS [17] and mathematics [9] and led directly to the development of software [19, 15].

[2] Douglas Howe [40] has shown that this principle can be used to simplify the presentation of Feferman's [26, 27] type theories and make it easier to relate them to those of Martin-Löf and Girard. Howe has implemented his version as a variant of Nuprl's logic.

Now there is an entire field of *automated reasoning* concerned with realizing Leibniz's dream.

Another goal of Logic has been to understand cognitive processes through their manifestation in reasoning. This theme is apparent even from the title of Boole's classical treatise, *The Laws of Thought*. Again the advent of computers has led to a deeper and more quantitative study here than was practiced before. Much of the field of Artificial Intelligence is occupied with questions of how computers can manage complex cognitive tasks.

These two goals intersect in the problem of providing effective computer support in automated reasoning. It has seemed to many of us that by narrowing the domain reasoning to mathematics (and programming) we gain in two ways. First, we can build on the discoveries of the talented mathematical logicians who came before. Second, because the subject of software reliability is useful to society (and becoming more critical every day), there will be funds to support the collection of the large amounts of data needed to explore the scientific theory. McCarthy saw society's interest in 1962 [54], and already because of it we have been able to acquire a great deal of experimental knowledge (often at great cost in human effort to master the incredibly tedious). I want to reflect briefly on two aspects of this knowledge. First I speculate about how well we can formalize the concept of proof in certain areas of mathematics and CS and in particular about how we treat the notion of an *obvious step of inference*. To do this I will sketch a particular theory of automated reasoning and then discuss various issues in the context of that theory. Second I will report on how we are in fact using this theory in managing the Nuprl system development. Experience here has led us to think of Nuprl as a formal theory and has led to the notion of *theories-as-systems*.

2 Formal Theories

2.1 A Theory of Logics

Here is a brief sketch of a formal theory about proofs and functions for constructing them. The proofs are built of *sequents* and *justifications*; *tactics* are one kind of justification. Sequents are a list of terms paired with a term, so to begin we need a section of the theory dealing with terms. (Formulas are a special case of terms.) Tactics are functions that build proofs, and we discuss them later.

1. Terms

Terms have a very simple structure, just $op(\overline{v}_1.t_1; \ldots; \overline{v}_n.t_n)$ where op is an operator name, $\overline{v}_i$ is a list of variables (called binding variables, whose *scope* is t_i) and t_i is a *subterm*. The $\overline{v}_i$ is optional; if it is empty then we write just t_i instead of $nil.t_i$.

The operators actually have structure which we will not have time to discuss here (see [3]).

If the list of pairs is empty, we display the operator simply as an element of *OpName*. Some of the *OpNames* for Nuprl are: (variable, U, int, list, nil, cons, list_ind, union, val, inr, decide, product, equal, spread, pair, function, lambda, apply, set, rec, rec_ind, IFam, IFName, OpName). The type is *open-ended* in that new names can be added at any time and everything we say in *the theory* remains valid. (So we do not say that the *only* operators are those listed here.)

Let *Var* be the type of variables. This is a discrete enumerable type.

A precise definition of the terms is now given inductively. If t denotes the type of terms, then it satisfies:

$$t = Op \times (Var\ list \times t)\ list.$$

In general if we have a definition of the form $t = F(t)$, we denote the recursive type being defined by $rec(t.\ F(t))$.

With this notation we define the terms as

Definition: $Term\ ==\ rec(t.\ Op \times (Var\ list \times t)\ list).$

Some standard terms of Nuprl include: apply(f;a), lambda(x.b), spread(p;u,v.t), pair(a;b) where x, u, v ϵ *Var* and f, a, b, p, t are terms.

We can define functions and predicates over *Term* by $Term - induction$, the induction principle that comes with every recursive type (see [19]). We write the combinator for it this way.

$$term\_ind(t; O, L, V.g)$$

where O is the operator and L is the list of pairs and V is the list of values of the function or predicate being defined on the subterm in L. The term g will usually do a case analysis on whether or not L (and hence V) are empty.

We can define the relation of subterm between terms this way. Let $subterm\ (t)$ be the propositional function $Term \rightarrow Prop$ which is true when the argument is a subterm of t. This is defined as

$$term\_ind(t; O, L, V.\ \lambda x.(x =< O, L > \ \lor \ \exists v\ on\ L.v(x)))$$

2. Substitution and α-equality

Using $term\_ind$ we can define the usual notions of α-equality, $=_\alpha$, free variables of a term t, $FV(t)$, and the substitution of a term s for the variable x in the term t, $t[s/x]$. All the basic theorems about the concepts can be proved by the induction principle given by $term\_ind$ via the propositions-as-types principle. For example, we can prove:

Theorem: If $t_1 =_\alpha t_2$ in Term and $x \epsilon FV(t_1)$ & $x \epsilon FV(t_2)$
then $t_1[a/x] =_\alpha t_2[a/x]$.

3. Libraries

All terms are manipulated in the *context* of other ones defined earlier. These contexts are organized by the notion of a *library* which is an assignment of addresses to terms and their definitions (as well as to proofs and tactics). Given a library L and an address a we might find at $L(a)$ a *definition* which is a pair of terms (the *definiendum* (or left-side) *definiens* (or right-side)).

Associated with libraries is the operation of *expansion* which is the replacement of a definiendum by its definiens. There are the relations D ExpandsTo D' and D FullyExpands to D'. To fully expand is to continue expanding until primitive concepts are reached.

4 Evaluation

An evaluation relation is defined on closed elements of Term; it is denoted t EvalsTo t'. This relation is defined from *evaluation fragments* which are supplied for each operator telling how it is to be evaluated. For this article, the EvalsTo relation is given explicitly for just one example

We say that *apply* $(f; a)$ *EvalsTo c*

provided that f EvalsTo lambda$(x.b)$ and

$b[a/x]$ *EvalsTo c*.

In this way the evaluation rules are provided for all terms. This introduces the notion of *computability* into the theory in a direct way.

We can prove these facts about this relation.

Theorem: $\forall t : Term.$ if $\exists t', t'' : Term.$ t Evals To t' and t Evals To t'' then $t' = t''$ in Term.

There are terms which do not evaluate, and there are terms which evaluate to terms t' with the property that subterms of t' do not evaluate.

A partial function on term, Val, is used to compute values when they exist. We have

Theorem: $\forall t : Term.$ $\exists t' : Term(t$ Evals To $t' \Rightarrow t' = Val(t)$ & $Val(t') = t')$.

5. Proofs

A *proof* will be a tree of sequents and justifications telling why one sequent follows from a list of others. The root of the tree is its *goal* or the theorem being proved. Proofs can be incomplete in that some sequents are unjustified. We think of the trees as being generated top down, from the goal to subgoals. This type represents the notion of a so-called sequent-style proof. The top down organization makes it resemble tableau proofs. Here are the relevant types.

Definition: $Sequent$ $==$ $(Var \times Term)$ $list \times Term$

$Justification$ $==$ $unit \mid PrimRule \mid Term \mid (Term \times int \times Library)$

We are using the notation $A|B$ for A and B types to denote their *disjoint union*. The type unit is just $\{1\}$, and the type $PrimRule$ is a list of all the primitive rule names for a particular logic. The library will develop a theory by including these rules. For the coretype theory of Nuprl there are about 75 rules. Now we can define the skeleton of a proof.

Definition: $PreProof$ $==$ $rec(p.$ $sequent \times Justification \times (p$ $list))$

To define actual proofs we need a predicate telling how justifications link sequents. This is called $IsAProof(p; n; L)$ where p is a $PreProof$, n is the level of
reflection allowed in p (a topic we won't have time to discuss), and L is a library.

6. Tactics

A tactic is a computable function which maps a sequent to a proof (or an exception condition). It works by trying to build a proof and reporting failure if it
cannot make progress.

Tactics are used to raise the level of a proof by suppressing detail. They are
also used to discovering simple proofs by informed search. The evaluation of a
tactic on a goal might generate hundreds of primitive rule steps. The collection
of tactics grows as we learn to identify patterns of reasoning. (Presently Nuprl
uses over 400 general purpose tactics organized into a hierarchy of progressively
higher level methods of proof.)

Here are some tactics that will appear in the sample proof.

Auto: this performs a number of "automatic" steps, including the
so-called *introduction steps* of a natural deduction proof such as introduction of a universal quantifier.

NSubsetInd: this performs induction on the subset of natural numbers
(defined to be $\{z : int \mid 0 \leq z\}$).

DTerm $'t'$ n: this "decomposes" a term in either the conclusion ($if\ n =$
0) or in the nth hypothesis ($if\ n > 0$), using the term t. If for example
the goal is an existential, $\exists x : N.\ P(x)$, then DTerm $'t'$ 0 will produce
the subgoal $P(t)$.

SupInf: this applies the sup-inf arithmetic decision procedure to the
conclusion (see [10, 62]).

Decide $'t'$: this does a case analysis on whether the term t considered
as a formula is true or not.

We present a complete sample proof done in Nuprl. The sequents as we know
from the definition have the form of a list of terms called *hypotheses* and a

conclusion. For display purposes the formulas in the list are numbered, and separated from the conclusion by $>>$. So a sequent looks like this.

$$1.\ F_1\ \ 2.\ F_2 \ldots n.F_n\ >> G$$

where F_i, G are terms. The top sequent, the goal of the proof, has no hypotheses; its conclusion G is

$$\forall i:\{8\ldots\}.\ \exists m:N.\exists n:N.\ (3*m\ +\ 5*n = i)$$

which says that for all numbers greater than or equal to 8, we can find m and n natural numbers such that the arithmetic relation holds (where $*$ is multiplication over N).

The first subgoal generated by the tactic rule Auto has the hypothesis 1. i : $\{8\ldots\}$. This is result of applying the primitive rule for introducing a universal quantifier, i.e. we examine an arbitrary value i.

The second subgoal is a sequent with three hypotheses, 1: $i:\mathbb{Z}$ 2. $0 < i$ 3. $8 = i$. We get these because the natural numbers are defined as a subset of the integers, $\mathbb{Z}$.

The step Decide $'n > 0'$ performs a case analysis on the induction hypothesis (hypothesis 5 in the previous sequent). The proof splits into two subproofs whose sequents have the forms

$$1.\ i:\mathbb{Z}\ \ 2.\ 8 < i\ \ 3.\ m:N\ \ 4.\ n:N\ \ 5.\ (3*m\ +\ 5*n = i-1)\ \ 6.\ 0 < n >> G$$
$$\text{and}$$
$$1.\ -\ 5.\ \text{the same}\ \ 6.\ \neg(0 < n) >> G.$$

One of these subproofs is done in one step, the other in two. All the hard work is being done by Auto which applies a basic arithmetic decision procedure called **arith**. This procedure checks the simple symbolic arithmetic needed to prove the results. (This procedure is a residue of the PL/CV system [15].)

Here is the complete proof. It is an element of the data type *Proof(L)* in a library *L* that contains the definitions of the quantifiers ($\forall, \exists$) and the natural numbers (N).

```
>> ∀i:{8...}. ∃m:N. ∃n:N. 3 * m + 5 * n = i
|
BY Auto
 \
  1. i: {8...}
  >> ∃m:N. ∃n:N. 3 * m + 5 * n = i
  |
  BY NSubsetInd 1
THEN Auto
  |\
  | 1. i: ℤ
  | 2. 0 < i
  | 3. 8 = i
  | >> ∃m:N. ∃n:N. 3 * m + 5 * n = i
  | |
  | BY DTerm '1' 0 THENM DTerm '1' 0 THEN Auto
   \
    1. i: ℤ
    2. 8 < i
    3. ∃m:N. ∃n:N. 3 * m + 5 * n = i - 1
    >> ∃m:N. ∃n:N. 3 * m + 5 * n = i
    |
    BY D 3 THEN D 4
     \
      3. m: N
      4. n: N
      5. 3 * m + 5 * n = i - 1
      >> ∃m:N. ∃n:N. 3 * m + 5 * n = i
      |
      BY Decide 'n > 0' THENA Auto
      |\
      | 6. n > 0
      | >> ∃m:N. ∃n:N. 3 * m + 5 * n = i
      | |
      | BY DTerm 'm + 2' 0 THENM DTerm 'n - 1' 0 THEN Auto
       \
        6. ¬n > 0
        >> ∃m:N. ∃n:N. 3 * m + 5 * n = i
        |
```

```
BY DTerm 'm - 3' 0 THENM DTerm 'n + 2' 0 THEN Auto
 \
   >> 0 ≤ m - 3
   |
   BY SupInf THEN Auto
```

2.2 Value of Formal Theories

Applied Logic

We use the word "theory" to refer to purely mathematical theories, such as *number theory*, as well as to empirical theories, such as quantum mechanics. What we have sketched above is a purely mathematical theory, but it is part of a theory about the nature of mathematical practice. As such it could be a component of a theory of cognition—both human and 'artificial'.

We know that many mathematical theories turn out to have applications in science and engineering. The above theory definitely has. It is applied in Computer Science and as such is from a branch of Applied Logic. It is applicable because the theory models aspects of computer systems. In this regard it is like the mathematics used in economics and statistics; we make a few assumptions about the behavior of natural systems, and then use the theory to deduce consequences or guide the design of artifacts. We will examine this role in section 3.

Logicians study formal theories, and formal theories are models of the theories we use in problem solving. What kinds of questions are usually asked of a theory T?

> Is it consistent? Is it true? Does it have models? Is it faithful? Does it express such and such concepts? Can it interpret another theory, T'? Does it explain certain phenomena (better than another theory)?

Let us consider some of these questions for the Theory of Logics sketched above. Is the theory consistent? It is based on a type theory which has been proven consistent relative to other theories (see [5]).

Does the theory have a model? The constructive type theories of Martin-Löf are accepted as meaningful, and they provide models. We also know that there are set theoretic models [39].

Does the theory allow us to express the methods used to automate reasoning? We have defined the tactic-oriented approach [19, 32, 33] directly. In this framework we can easily express decision procedures [19, 44, 61]. We can also speak of the methods of resolution theorem proving. We have been able to express the ideas of forward chaining inference, as from McAllester's Ontic for example [53] in this setting [12].

This last line of inquiry leads to an interesting question. Can this Theory of Logics account for the behavior of a software artifact such as Nuprl which attempts to express the methods of automated reasoning? We look at this next.

Empirical Theory of Automated Reasoning Tools

This theory gives a description of some of the components of Nuprl, an implemented proof development system, a real software artifact. We can ask whether this theory can *explain* how Nuprl works at some level and whether it can be used to support informal reasoning about it. These are questions that can be tested by experiment.

We have investigated this question to some extent. We have written down the informal explanations given to users of the system and checked whether they can be expressed in the Theory of Logics. So far we have been able to track the declarative content of these lessons [3].

2.3   A Theory of Obvious Inferences

A Scientific Theory of Proofs?

The subject of *automated reasoning* is concerned with using computers to help humans discover and write formal proofs. The enterprize depends on the existence of computers (and indeed its nature changes as the power of computers changes). There is a considerable body of knowledge built up in the area [23]. One branch of the field is most concerned with using machines to fill in the *routine steps* of a proof, expecting humans to provide the difficult steps and creative insights [19, 24, 33] We might say it is concerned with a "Theory of the Obvious".

Our current knowledge of this problem is based on the following judgements. First, there seems to be a coherent notion of what it means to give a *rigorous informal proof*. Admittedly this is a matter of mature judgement, but in particular areas of mathematics, there seems to be a consensus used in judging whether a result has been established. Standards vary from subject to subject and from setting to setting, but we can fix on the standards set in leading undergraduate textbooks as a benchmark for example.

Second, for a *textbook* on calculus or algebra (and similar subjects), there is wide agreement that we know how to formalize the mathematics. This is the result of years of work in mathematical logic [45] and in mathematics [11].

Third, deBruijn [24] observed that the expansion factor in going from a rigorous informal proof to a completely formal proof is bounded regardless of the level of the result. He claims that there is a linear relationship, i.e. there is a constant d_B such that:

size of formal proof $\leq d_B$ (size of rigorous proof)   for all *proofs* in the theory

We call this the *deBruijn equation*. The constant d_B, depends on the particular formal theory. DeBruijn had estimated this constant; we take it to be about 5,000 for conventional formal systems without computer assistance[3]. The proof checkers built for the Automath theories [25] were able to reduce the constant to 50 based on a fixed set of simple routines to expand definitions and check equalities. Our work supports a factor of 5,000.

Fourth, computer scientists believe that it is possible to reduce this constant nearly to 1 [16, 54] by employing the methods of computer science: a programming language designed for proof construction, data structures and algorithms tailored to the task some of which will be efficient decision procedures for arithmetic and equality. Data using these techniques suggests that the constant is below 5 for elementary parts of algebra.

Fifth, we advance here the judgement that the first four points can be expressed in the Theory of Logic sketched here because the computer science tools are elegantly expressible and the concept of formula and proof being used are already adequate representations of the informal concept. So we can state in the Theory certain conjectures which approximate the thesis underlying the computer science effort, call it the "$d_B \leq 1$ thesis".

Here is one way to approximately formulate the thesis. We introduce a new proof type, called *RealProof(L)*, where L is a library, in which the justification obvious is

---

[3]He estimated perhaps several hundred times 50 [25]. In this paper we take the 5,000 figure since it is close to our estimate.

allowed. It can be used only for steps that are obvious in a rigorous proof. It might of course be mistakenly invoked, but we know the intent. Now we allow books to be written using *RealProofs*. Suppose they are $Bk_i, \ldots, Bk_n$. We attempt to write a tactic, called Obvious, which expands every such rule into a correct formal proof of the goal in a uniform way. We require it to be reasonably fast in that proofs can be checked in only a small additional amount of time and generate no more than 5,000 primitive rule steps. So the precise statement we can make is that:

there is a tactic, Obvious, such that
$$RealProof\ (L(Bk_i)) \subseteq Proof(L(Bk_i) \cup \{Obvious\})\ i = 1, \ldots, n.$$

This means that for each book Bk_i in its library context, $L(Bk_i)$, each occurrence of obvious in the real proof is replaced by Obvious and hence belongs to Proof.

Proving the result in the Theory of Logic would suggest that we can make the even stronger claim that:

for any library L of calculus or algebra,
$$RealProof(L) \subseteq Proof\ (\hat{L}).$$

This would be done by exhibiting a specific tactic collection, $\mathcal{T}$, library $\hat{L}$. We could then add the "synthetic axiom" to the Theory of Logics saying that $\hat{L}$ with $\mathcal{T}$ is a theory of obvious inference for elementary algebra and analysis.

Adding this statement of *law* to the Theory of Logics would result in an empirical *Theory of Obvious Inference*. This theory could be studied for what it said about mathematical reasoning as well as for what it said about logic. If the law is true then the Obvious tactic will be quite interesting, and the scientific theory will deepen as we try to understand why it is true.

Theoretical Aspects

Consequences of Gödel's work tell us that we must be careful about framing a theory of obvious inference steps. We know that obvious cannot mean "obviously true" because such statements might not even be provable in the logic we are working in. So we have in mind a fixed theory in our library of formal theories, call it T. (T could be Nuprl or Coq for example.) We might want to say that a conclusion G is obvious iff it has a short proof *in* T. But even here we must be careful.

We know from results of Gödel [31] and more extensively from Hartmanis [34] that infinitely many long proofs of theorems in T can appear trivial in a stronger theory, T'.

Hartmanis says that in any formal theory there are trivial theorems with arbitrarily long proofs. So we want to insist that we call a conclusion G obvious only if it has a short proof *in* T (we might call such internally obvious facts *very obvious*). Based on insights from experiments, we propose that G is *obviously provable in* T iff there is a proof of it requiring fewer than 5,000 primitive rule steps and if G is considered obvious in RealProofs

The goal of a theory of obvious inference is to understand the structure of these 5,000 step subproofs so that the space of them can be organized for search by tactics or for a classification into large proof steps. That is, we are interested in a *proof theory in the large*. The creation and organization of tactics in theories such as Nuprl, Coq, and HOL are generating material for this enterprise. We already know that many of those steps are concerned with type checking (many of these we understand well enough not to run them [4]). Others correspond to steps of equality reasoning. Another large number correspond to providing high-level derived rules of inference (one might believe that informal reasoning uses 500 high-level rules each of which expands to 100 primitive proof steps, but we think this is *not* the case). There is much to learn before we really understand this large scale proof theory.

Although there is evidence that this Theory of Obvious Inference is correct as far as it goes, and although it might be accredited as a scientific theory (of information or of cognition or something else), it is only the beginning in an attempt to understand the full notion of RealProof. Such a theory should also be able to deal with the concept of *relativity obvious* proof in the following sense; one argues based on a given proof that another result is obvious *by the same method*. Does the formal Theory of Logics defined above enable us to express those properties of a proof that are abstracted in recognizing this kind of similarity? A lot of work is being done on this question now, especially in AI; the mechanism of *transformation tactics* in Nuprl captures some of the relevant properties.

Perfect Proofs and the Role of Computers

Our judgements about automated reasoning and our conjecture on automating the routine steps of a proof all hinge on experience gained in actually building proofs with mechanical assistance. At Cornell our experience is based on proving thousands of theorems with Nuprl. We have worked in elementary number theory [12, 38], algebra [44], real analysis [13], metamathematics [20], hardware [1, 8, 49], combinatorics

[57], programming language semantics [5, 37], automata theory [47], elementary programming [59], concurrency models [14], and abstract recursion theory [7]. We are expanding some of these efforts considerably [1, 41, 44] because our experience has been so rewarding.

The computer plays a central role in our conjecture as well because the tactic style of proof requires that a system expand the tactic call. The computer plows unflagging through the 5,000 extra steps needed to reduce a tactic to primitive rule applications. We might then ask in light of our conjecture whether the computer *must* be used or is it possible that there exists a formal system, of such expressiveness that all rule applications could be checked quickly and yet the loss factor is still 1 or less. This would be a formal system that defined a *perfect notion of formal proof*. If we cannot get $d_B \leq 1$ without computer aid, could we get $d_B \leq 2$? Just what is the necessary role of the computer in expressing a proof once we have found it?

We do know that the computer can already find a proof in many cases where $d_B \leq 1$ if we count as a proof step just the name of the tactic written as a justification. In our sample proof above there are only 8 justifications written at the top level. While each of these tactics corresponds to what we would write in an informal proof, they also generate many unseen subgoals dealing with type checking and equality. So the formal proof is much "bushier" than the informal one. If we leave out all of the searching done by the tactics and list only those that perform a definite step, then the tree of these provides the material from which a perfect proof might be constructed. If we understood the nature of the tactics well enough, we might be able to justify the highest level tactic calls without running them. This might lead to a notion of formal proof that could be used precisely by humans without the need of computer assistance in expressing the argument, only in finding it.

Gödel's Theorem

Suppose we accept the principle that the Theory of Obvious Inference is true for elementary number theory, say Rich Peano Arithmetic (RPA). So every rigorous proof is a formal proof. Then Formalism has succeeded to a large extent in this case despite Gödel's incompleteness theorem. Let us assume that the principle is true for proof theory as well. So we know, and can formally prove, that there is a true theorem about numbers that cannot be proved in Rich Peano Arithmetic. This does not contradict our experience at all. Likewise we know that some rigorous proofs about numbers will be longer in RPA than in other formal theories, but this is because the other theories are stronger. But the mathematical world in which we live is one of a large number of formal theories, a library of them. The library even contains a formal metatheory that tells us how we can properly extend many of the theories in it. None of this is contradictory and none of it tells us that there is no such thing as a Perfect Proof. It only tells us that life in the universe is more interesting with an open ended collection of many different formal systems, perhaps mutually inconsistent, than with only one theory. We might say that the *design consequences* of Gödel's theorem are in the structuring of libraries (they also appear in the design of reflexive proofs (see [4])).

3   Software Systems

3.1   The Nuprl System Implements the Theory of Logics

We say that a programming language can implement the Theory of Logics if it can define the data types and compute the defined functions (such as substitution and the tactics). Clearly any universal programming language can do this, some more easily than others. Lisp does it well, SML even better. The Nuprl system includes a typed functional programming language which bears strong resemblance to Standard ML [56]; so Nuprl can do it as well. The generated code would not be as efficient as for the other two languages, but the data type definitions would be exceptionally clear.

In fact, the Theory of Logics as defined in section 1 actually used Nuprl types and functions. So the mathematical definition in type theory is already a major part of the implementation of the theory. This is possible because Nuprl is simultaneously a mathematical language and an implemented computer system. So theories defined in it are known to be implementable. SML can serve in a similar way since its types are so rich. For example the SML of NJ compiler [6] is easy to read because it is written in SML itself. Nevertheless, Nuprl is able to define its theories even more naturally since its type structure is so expressive.

In addition to defining the core of the Theory of Logics, a good implementation will provide a user interface and input/output facilities. These can be built in Nuprl as well, but not as nicely. Also Nuprl has no imperative or concurrency constructs, so important features of possible implementations are not covered as Nuprl stands.

3.2 The Theory of Logics Defines the Core of Nuprl

The definitions of Term, Sequent, PreProof, Proof, and Tactic, etc. given in the Theory of Logics actually define the data types used to implement Nuprl in Lisp [19] and in SML. They are part of the system specification and of a design document and of a user's guide.

The properties we can prove about substitution and proof refinement will be properties of the Nuprl system. What is noteworthy here is that these documents are *formal.* They can be incorporated into a defining report and into an expository textbook to make them more rigorous and complete.

The formal definition of Nuprl in itself describes a large part of the implementation. This is a remarkable fact; we have *forced the software artifact* to be a mathematical object. This is nearly true of SML as well, except that it is not a logical theory; and some of its constructs, such as imperative types and equality types are not amenable to a clean mathematical treatment.

The fact that the formal theory of Nuprl is nearly the same as an implementation of Nuprl in itself, suggests an extension of the *proofs-as-programs* principle to the *theories-as-systems* principle. This idea makes sense on an intuitive level. A formal theory in Nuprl will be a collection of definitions and functions. The functions are computable and the theorems are their specifications. The software system is just the structured collection of functions from this theory.

In the case of the proofs-as-programs notion, we think of the program as the executable part of a proof. In the theories-as-systems principle, we think of the system as the executable part of a theory. Work in our project at Cornell is trying to determine whether this is a useful idea for software engineering as well as a valid theoretical observation. At least this is another concept from Logic with serious software *design consequences.* We are following these consequences and enjoying the journey.

Acknowledgements

I would like to thank Heidi Angus for preparing this manuscript so patiently and competently under deadline pressure. Also Heidi and I thank Elizabeth Maxwell for teaching her the typesetting skills. I would also like to thank Stuart Allen, Klara Kedem and Paul Jackson for helpful comments on drafts of this paper.

References

[1] M. Aagaard and M. Leeser. Verifying a logic synthesis tool in Nuprl. In G. Bochmann and D. Probst, editors, *Participants copy of Proceedings of Workshop on Computer-Aided Verification*, pages 72–83. Springer-Verlag, June 1992. To appear by Springer Verlag, 1993.

[2] S. Abramsky. Computational interpretations of linear logic. *TCS*, 1992. To appear.

[3] W. Aitken and R. C. Constable. Reflecting on Nuprl Lessons 1-4. Technical report, Cornell University, Computer Science Dept., 1992. To appear.

[4] S. Allen, R. Constable, D. Howe, and W. Aitken. The semantics of reflected proof. *Proc. of Fifth Symp. on Logic in Comp. Sci., IEEE*, pages 95–197, June 1990.

[5] S. F. Allen. A non-type-theoretic definition of Martin-Löf's types. *Proc. of Second Symp. on Logics in Computer Science, IEEE*, pages 215–224., June 1987.

[6] A. Appel. *Compiling with Continuations*. Cambridge University Press, 1992.

[7] D. Basin. An environment for automated reasoning about partial functions. In *9th International Conference on Automated Deduction*, pages 101–110. Springer-Verlag, NY, 1988.

[8] D. Basin, G. Brown, and M. Leeser. Formally Verified Synthesis of Combinational CMOS Circuits. *Integration: The International Journal of VLSI Design*, 11:235–250, 1991.

[9] E. Bishop. Mathematics as a Numerical Language. In *Intuitionism and Proof Theory.*, pages 53–71. North-Holland, NY, 1970.

[10] W. W. Bledsoe. A new method for proving certain Presburger formulas. *Fourth IJCAI*, September 1975. Tblisi, USSR.

[11] N. Bourbaki. *Elements of Mathematics, Algebra, Volume 1*. Addison-Wesley, Reading, MA, 1968.

[12] W. Chen. Tactic-based theorem proving and knowledge-based forward chaining. In D. Kapur, editor, *Eleventh International Conference on Automated Deduction*, pages 552–566. Springer-Verlag, June 1992.

[13] J. Chirimar and D. Howe. Implementing constructive real analysis: a preliminary report. In *Symposium on Constructivity in Computer Science*. Springer-Verlag, 1991. To appear.

[14] R. C. Cleaveland. *Type-Theoretic Models of Concurrency*. PhD thesis, Cornell University, 1987.

[15] R. Constable, S. Johnson, and C. Eichenlaub. *Introduction to the PL/CV2 Programming Logic, LNCS*, volume 135. Springer-Verlag, NY, 1982.

[16] R. Constable, T. Knoblock, and J. Bates. Writing programs that construct proofs. *J. Automated Reasoning*, 1(3):285–326, 1984.

[17] R. L. Constable. Constructive mathematics and automatic program writers. In *Proc. IFP Congr.*, pages 229–33, Ljubljana, 1971.

[18] R. L. Constable. Lectures on: Classical proofs as programs. *NATO ASI Series, Constructive Methods of Computing Science*, F, 1991.

[19] R. L. Constable et al. *Implementing Mathematics with the Nuprl Development System*. Prentice-Hall, NJ, 1986.

[20] R. L. Constable and D. J. Howe. Implementing metamathematics as an approach to automatic theorem proving. In R. Banerji, editor, *Formal Techniques in Artificial Intelligence: A Source Book*, pages 45–76. Elsevier Science Publishers (North-Holland), 1990.

[21] S. Cook. The complexity of theorem proving procedures. In *Proc. of the 3rd ACM Symposium on Theory of Computation*, pages 151–158. ACM, NY, 1971.

[22] H. Curry, R. Feys, and W. Craig. *Combinatory Logic, Vol. 1*. Amsterdam:North-Holland, 1968.

[23] M. Davis. The prehistory and early history of automated deduction. In *Automation of Reasoning 1*, pages 1–28. Springer-Verlag, NY, 1983.

[24] N. deBruijn. The mathematical language Automath, its usage and, some of its extensions. *Symp. on Automatic Demonstration, Lecture Notes in Math*, 125:29–61, 1968.

[25] N. deBruijn. A survey of the project Automath. In *To H.B. Curry: Essays in Combinatory Logic, Lambda Calculus, and Formalism.*, pages 589–606. Academic Press, 1980.

[26] S. Feferman. A language and axioms for explicit mathematics. In *Algebra and Logic, Lecture Notes in Mathematics*, pages 87–139. Springer-Verlag, 1975.

[27] S. Feferman. Polymorphic typed lambda-calculi in a type free axiomatic framework. *Contemporary Mathematics*, 106:101–135, 1990.

[28] G. Frege. Begriffsschrift, a formula language, modeled upon that for arithmetic for pure thought. In *From Frege to Godel: A Source Book in Mathematical Logic, 1879-1931*, pages 1–82. Harvard University Press, Cambridge, Mass., 1967.

[29] J.-Y. Girard. Une extension de l'interpretation de godel a l'analyse, et son application a l'elimination des coupures dans l'analyse et la theorie des types. In *2nd Scandinavian Logic Symp.*, pages 63–69. Springer-Verlag, NY, 1971.

[30] J.-Y. Girard. On the unity of logic. In *Proceedings of Computer and Systems Sciences, NATO Advanced Science Institute Series F*, 1991.

[31] K. Gödel. On intuitionistic arithmetic and number theory. In M. Davis, editor, *The Undecidable*, pages 75–81. Raven Press, 1965.

[32] M. Gordon. HOL: A machine oriented formalization of higher order logic. Technical Report 68, Cambridge University, 1985.

[33] M. Gordon, R. Milner, and C. Wadsworth. *Edinburgh LCF: a mechanized logic of computation*, volume 78 of *Lecture Notes in Computer Science*. Springer-Verlag, NY, 1979.

[34] J. Hartmanis. *Feasible Computations and Provable Complexity Properties*. SIAM, Philadelphia, PA, 1978.

[35] J. Hartmanis and R. Stearns. On the computational complexity of algorithms. *Transactions of the American Mathematics Society*, 117:285–306, 1965.

[36] W. Howard. The formulas-as-types notion of construction. In *To H.B. Curry: Essays on Combinatory Logic, Lambda-Calculus and Formalism*, pages 479–490. Academic Press, NY, 1980.

[37] D. Howe. The computational behaviour of Girard's paradox. *Proc. of Second Symp. on Logic in Comp. Sci., IEEE*, pages 205–214, June 1987.

[38] D. Howe. Implementing number theory: An experiment with Nuprl. *8th International Conference on Automated Deduction*, pages 404–415, July 1987.

[39] D. Howe. Equality in lazy computation systems. In *Proc. of Second Symp. on Logic in Comp. Sci.*, pages 198–203. IEEE Computer Society, June 1989.

[40] D. Howe. A simple type theory for reasoning about functional programs. pre print, 1992.

[41] D. Howe. Reasoning about functional programs in Nuprl. *Functional Programming, Concurrency, Simulation and Automated Reasoning, LNCS*, 1993. To appear.

[42] G. Huet. Theorem proving systems of the Formel project. In *Proc. of the 8th International Conference on Automated Deduction, Lecture Notes in Computer Science*, pages 687–688. Springer-Verlag, 1986.

[43] G. Huet. A uniform approach to type theory. In G. Huet, editor, *Logical Foundations of Functional Programming*, pages 337–398. Addison-Wesley, 1990.

[44] P. B. Jackson. Nuprl and its use in circuit design. In V. Stavridou, T. Melham, and R. Boute, editors, *Proceedings of the IFIP TC10/WG10.2 International Conference on Theorem Provers in Circuit Design: Theory, Practice and Experience*, pages 311–336. North-Holland, The Netherlands, June 1992.

[45] S. C. Kleene. *Introduction to Metamathematics*. D. Van Nostrand, Princeton, 1952.

[46] A. Kolmogorov. Three approaches to the concept of 'the amount of information'. *Probl. Inf. Tramsm.*, 1:1–7, 1965.

[47] C. Kreitz. Constructive automata theory implemented with the Nuprl proof development system. Technical Report TR 86-779, Cornell University, Ithaca, New York, September 1986.

[48] H. Lauchli. An abstract notion of realizability for which intuitionistic predicate calculus is complete. In *Intuitionism and Proof Theory.*, pages 227–34. North-Holland, Amsterdam, 1970.

[49] M. Leeser. Using Nuprl for the verification and synthesis of hardware. *Phil. Trans. R. Soc. Lond.*, 339:49–68, 1992.

[50] G. Leibniz. *Logical Papers: A Selection*. Clarendon Press, Oxford, 1966.

[51] L. Levin. Universal search problems. *Problemy Peredaci Informacii 9*, pages 115 116, 1073.

[52] P. Martin-Löf. Constructive mathematics and computer programming. In *Sixth International Congress for Logic, Methodology, and Philosophy of Science*, pages 153–75. North-Holland, Amsterdam, 1982.

[53] D. A. McAllester. *ONTIC: A Knowledge Representation System for Mathematics*. MIT Press, Cambrige, Mass., 1989.

[54] J. McCarthy. Computer programs for checking mathematical proofs. In *Proceedings of the Symposium in Pure Math, Recursive Function Theory, Vol V*, pages 219–228. AMS, Providence, RI, 1962.

[55] R. Milner, J. Parrow, and D. Walker. A calculus of mobile processes, part 1. Technical Report CSR-302-89, LFCS, University of Edinburgh, June 1989.

[56] R. Milner, M. Tofte, and R. Harper. *The Definition of Standard ML*. The MIT Press, 1991.

[57] C. Murthy. An evaluation semantics for classical proofs. In *LICS, '91*, pages 96–107, Amsterdam, The Netherlands, July 1991.

[58] B. Nordstrom, K. Petersson, and J. Smith. *Programming in Martin-Lof's Type Theory*. Oxford Sciences Publication, Oxford, 1990.

[59] C. Paulin-Mohring. Extracting $F_\omega's$ programs from proofs in the calculus of constructions. In *Proceedings of POPL*, 1989.

[60] B. Russell. Mathematical logic as based on a theory of types. *Am. J. Math.*, 30:222–62, 1908.

[61] N. Shankar. Towards mechanical metamathematics. *J. Automated Reasoning*, 1(4):407–434, 1985.

[62] R. Shostak. A practical decision procedure for arithmetic with function symbols. *JACM*, 26:351–360, 1979.

Time for Concurrency *

Zohar Manna †   Amir Pnueli ‡

Abstract. A hierarchy of models that capture realistic aspects of reactive and real-time systems is introduced. On the most abstract level, the *qualitative* (non-quantitative) model captures the temporal precedence aspect of time. A more refined model is that of *timed transition systems*, representing the metric aspects of time. The third and most detailed model is that of *hybrid systems*. This model allows the incorporation of *continuous* components into the studied reactive system.

Keywords: Temporal logic, real-time, specification, verification, hybrid systems, Statecharts, proof rules.

1   Introduction

As our ability to specify and develop programs for reactive systems increases, there is a growing interest in the representation of more realistic features of such systems in the formal models and languages used for their specification, verification, and development.

As is the case with the application of mathematics to other scientific and engineering disciplines, no single model can fully capture the physical phenomenon under study. This paper presents a hierarchy of three models for the specification and verification of reactive systems:

- A *qualitative* (non-quantitative) model that captures the *temporal precedence* aspect of time. This model can only identify that one event precedes the other but not by how much.

- A *real-time* model that captures the *metric* aspect of time. This model can measure the time elapsing between two events.

- A *hybrid system* model that allows the inclusion of *continuous* components in a reactive system. Such continuous components may cause continuous change in the values of some state variables according to some physical or control law.

*This research was supported in part by the National Science Foundation under grants CCR-89-11512 and CCR-89-13641, by the Defense Advanced Research Projects Agency under contract NAG2-703, by the United States Air Force Office of Scientific Research under contract AFOSR-90-0057, by the European Community ESPRIT Basic Research Action Project 6021 (REACT) and by the France-Israel project for cooperation in Computer Science.
†Department of Computer Science, Stanford University, Stanford, CA 94305
‡Department of Applied Mathematics and Computer Science, Weizmann Institute, Rehovot, Israel

This paper omits many details of the models and their verification. A fuller account of these missing elements is provided in [MP92].

2 The Qualitative Model

The qualitative model uses an abstract notion of time, based on the ordering of events during an observed computation. This is the main model used, for example, in [MP91].

2.1 Computational Model: Fair Transition System

The computational model for the qualitative level is that of *fair transition systems*. Such a system consists of the following components.

- $V = \{u_1, ..., u_n\}$: A finite set of *state variables*.

  We define a *state* s to be an interpretation of V, assigning to each variable $u \in V$ a value $s[u]$ over its domain. We denote by Σ the set of all states.

- Θ : The *initial condition*. This is an assertion characterizing all the *initial states*, i.e., states at which a computation of the program can start. It is required that Θ be satisfiable, i.e., there exists at least one state satisfying Θ.

- T : A finite set of *transitions*. Each transition $\tau \in T$ is a function $\tau : \Sigma \mapsto 2^\Sigma$, mapping each state $s \in \Sigma$ into a (possibly empty) set of τ-successor states $\tau(s) \subseteq \Sigma$.

  A transition τ is *enabled* on s iff $\tau(s) \neq \phi$. Otherwise τ is *disabled* on s.

  The function associated with a transition τ is represented by an assertion $\rho_\tau(V, V')$, called the *transition relation*, which relates a state $s \in \Sigma$ to its τ-successor $s' \in \tau(s)$ by referring to both unprimed and primed versions of the state variables. An unprimed version of a state variable refers to its value in s, while a primed version of the same variable refers to its value in s'. For example, the assertion $x' = x + 1$ states that the value of x in s' is greater by 1 than its value in s.

- $\mathcal{J} \subseteq T$: A set of *just* transitions (also called *weakly fair* transitions). Intuitively, the requirement of justice for $\tau \in \mathcal{J}$ disallows a computation in which τ is continually enabled beyond a certain point but taken only finitely many times.

- $\mathcal{C} \subseteq T$: A set of *compassionate* transitions (also called *strongly fair* transitions). Intuitively, the requirement of compassion for $\tau \in \mathcal{C}$ disallows a computation in which τ is enabled infinitely many times but taken only finitely many times.

The transition relation $\rho_\tau(V, V')$ identifies state s' as a *τ-successor* of state s if

$$\langle s, s' \rangle \models \rho_\tau(V, V'),$$

where $\langle s, s' \rangle$ is the joint interpretation which interprets $x \in V$ as $s[x]$, and interprets x' as $s'[x]$.

The enabledness of a transition τ can be expressed by the formula

$$En(\tau): \quad (\exists V')\rho_\tau(V, V'),$$

which is true in s iff s has some τ-successor. We require that every state $s \in \Sigma$ has at least one transition enabled on it.

Let S be a transition system for which the above components have been identified. We define a *computation* of S to be an infinite sequence of states $\sigma : s_0, s_1, s_2, ...$, satisfying the following requirements:

- *Initiation:* s_0 is initial, i.e., $s_0 \models \Theta$.

- *Consecution:*   For each $j = 0, 1, ...$, the state s_{j+1} is a τ-successor of the state s_j, i.e., $s_{j+1} \in \tau(s_j)$, for some $\tau \in \mathcal{T}$. In this case, we say that the transition τ is *taken* at position j in σ.

- *Justice:*   For each $\tau \in \mathcal{J}$ it is not the case that τ is continually enabled beyond some point in σ but taken at only finitely many positions in σ.

- *Compassion:*   For each $\tau \in \mathcal{C}$ it is not the case that τ is enabled on infinitely many states of σ but taken at only finitely many positions in σ.

For a system S, we denote by $Comp(S)$ the set of all computations of S.

2.2   A Simple Programming Language

To present programs, we introduce a simple concurrent programming language (SPL) in which processes communicate by shared variables. The reader is referred to [MP91] for a description of the full language. Here, we will illustrate its syntax and semantics through an example.

Fig. 1 presents a simple program consisting of two processes communicating by the shared variable x, initially set to 0. Process P_1 keeps incrementing variable y as long as $x = 0$. Process P_2 has only one statement, which sets x to 1. Obviously, once x is set to 1, process P_2 terminates and some time later so does P_1, as soon as it observes that $x \neq 0$.

$$
\boxed{
\begin{array}{c}
x, \ y \text{: integer where } x = y = 0 \\[2mm]
P_1 :: \begin{bmatrix} \ell_0 : & \text{while } x = 0 \text{ do} \\ & [\ell_1 : \ y := y + 1] \\ \ell_2 : & \end{bmatrix}
\quad \| \quad
P_2 :: \begin{bmatrix} m_0 : & x := 1 \\ m_1 : & \end{bmatrix}
\end{array}
}
$$

Figure 1: Program PARA: A Simple Concurrent Program

We will show how to define a fair transition system S_P corresponding to program P.

- The *state variables* of system S_P are $V : \{\pi, x, y\}$. Variable π is a control variable ranging over subsets of the locations $\{\ell_0, \ell_1, \ell_2, m_0, m_1\}$. The value of π in a state denotes all the locations of the program in which control currently resides.

As states we take all possible interpretations that assign to the state variables values over their respective domains. For example, the initial state of program PARA is

$$\langle \pi : \{\ell_0, m_0\}, \ x : 0, \ y : 0 \rangle.$$

- The *transitions* of system S_P are $T : \{\tau_I, \ell_0, \ell_1, m_0\}$, where τ_I is the *idling transition*, and ℓ_0, ℓ_1, m_0 are transitions corresponding to the program statements.

Their transition relations are given by:

$$\rho_{\tau_I} \ : \ \pi' = \pi \ \wedge \ x' = x \ \wedge \ y' = y$$

$$\rho_{\ell_0} \ : \ \ell_0 \in \pi \ \wedge \ \left(\begin{array}{c} x = 0 \ \wedge \ \pi' = \pi - \{\ell_0\} \cup \{\ell_1\} \\ \vee \\ x \neq 0 \ \wedge \ \pi' = \pi - \{\ell_0\} \cup \{\ell_2\} \end{array} \right) \ \wedge \ x' = x \ \wedge \ y' = y$$

$$\rho_{\ell_1} \ : \ \ell_1 \in \pi \ \wedge \ \pi' = \pi - \{\ell_1\} \cup \{\ell_0\} \ \wedge \ x' = x \ \wedge \ y' = y + 1$$

$$\rho_{m_0} \ : \ m_0 \in \pi \ \wedge \ \pi' = \pi - \{m_0\} \cup \{m_1\} \ \wedge \ x' = 1 \ \wedge \ y' = y$$

- The *initial condition* of system S_P is Θ: $\quad \pi = \{\ell_0, m_0\} \ \wedge \ x = 0 \ \wedge \ y = 0$.
- The *justice set* of system S_P is $\mathcal{J} : \{\ell_0, \ell_1, m_0\}$.
- The *compassion set* of system S_P is $\mathcal{C} : \phi$, the empty set.

Requirement Specification Language: Temporal Logic

As a requirement specification language for reactive systems (under the qualitative model) we take *temporal logic* [MP91].

In this paper we use the temporal operators $\square$ and $\diamond$ and the entailment $p \Rightarrow q$ which is an abbreviation for the formula $\square(p \rightarrow q)$. In the underlying assertion language we use the location predicate at_ℓ_i, which is an abbreviation for the formula $\ell_i \in \pi$, stating that control is currently at location ℓ_i. We also use the expression $at\_\ell_{i,j}$ as an abbreviation for the disjunction $at\_\ell_i \vee at\_\ell_j$. We refer to a formula in the assertion language as a *state formula*, or simply as an *assertion*.

Specification of Properties

A temporal formula φ that is valid over a program P specifies a property of P, i.e., states a condition that is satisfied by all computations of P. As is explained in [MP91], the properties expressible by temporal logic can be arranged in a hierarchy that identifies different classes of properties according to the form of formulas expressing them.

Here we will consider only properties falling into the two most important classes.

- *Safety properties* are those that can be expressed by the formula $\square \psi$, for some past formula ψ. Here, we only consider *invariance formulas*, i.e., the case where ψ is an assertion. For example, the formula $\square(y \geq 0)$ states that y is nonnegative in all states appearing in computations of PARA.

- *Response properties* are those that can be expressed by the formula $p \Rightarrow \diamond q$, for past formulas p and q. Here, we only consider the case that p and q are assertions. For example, the response formula $\Theta \Rightarrow \diamond(at\_\ell_2 \wedge at\_m_1)$ is valid over program PARA. It claims that every state satisfying the initial condition of PARA is followed by a terminal state characterized by $at\_\ell_2 \wedge at\_m_1$. This implies that all computations of PARA eventually terminate.

2.3 Verifying Safety Properties

We present a proof rule for establishing the validity of a safety formula over a given transition system $P : \langle V, \Theta, \mathcal{T}, \mathcal{J}, \mathcal{C} \rangle$.

Verification Conditions

For a transition τ and state formulas p and q, we define the *verification condition* of τ, relative to p and q, denoted $\{p\}\tau\{q\}$, to be the implication:

$$(\rho_\tau \wedge p) \to q',$$

where ρ_τ is the transition relation corresponding to τ, and q', the *primed version* of the assertion q, is obtained from q by replacing each variable occurring in q by its primed version. Since ρ_τ holds for two states s and s' iff s' is a τ-successor of s, and q' states that q holds on s', it is not difficult to see that if the verification condition $\{p\}\tau\{q\}$ is valid, then every τ-successor of a p-state is a q-state. For a set of transitions $T \subseteq \mathcal{T}$, we denote by $\{p\}T\{q\}$ the conjunction of verification conditions, containing the conjunct $\{p\}\tau\{q\}$ for each $\tau \in T$.

In the context of program PARA, consider for example the verification condition of ℓ_1 with respect to assertions $y \geq 0$ and $y > 0$, i.e., $\{y \geq 0\}\, \ell_1\, \{y > 0\}$. Expanding the definition of the verification condition, this yields

$$\underbrace{\ell_1 \in \pi \wedge \pi' = \pi - \{\ell_1\} \cup \{\ell_0\} \wedge x' = x \wedge y' = y + 1}_{\rho_{\ell_1}} \wedge \underbrace{y \geq 0}_{p} \;\to\; \underbrace{y' > 0}_{q'}$$

which is valid. This shows that every ℓ_1-successor of a state satisfying $y \geq 0$ satisfies $y > 0$.

An Invariance Rule

The following rule can be used to establish the validity of the invariance formula $\Box p$.

$$
\text{INV} \quad
\begin{array}{ll}
\text{I1.} & \Theta \to \varphi \\
\text{I2.} & \{\varphi\}\mathcal{T}\{\varphi\} \\
\text{I3.} & \varphi \to p \\
\hline
& \Box p
\end{array}
$$

Premises I1 and I2 establish that the auxiliary assertion φ is initially true and is preserved by every transition of P. It follows that all states in the computations of P satisfy φ. By premise I3, they also satisfy p.

It often happens that assertion φ appearing in rule INV naturally splits into a disjunction $\varphi = \bigvee_{i \in M} \varphi_i$, where M is some finite index range such as $1, \ldots, m$. In this case, it may be easier to prove premises I1 and I2 of the rule in the form:

$$
\begin{array}{lll}
\text{I1.} & \Theta \to \varphi_i & \text{for some } i \in M \\
\text{I2.} & \{\varphi_i\}\, \mathcal{T}\, \{\varphi\} & \text{for every } i \in M
\end{array}
$$

Let us illustrate the application of rule INV for proving the property $\Box(y \geq 0)$ for program PARA. We take φ and p to be $y \geq 0$. Premise I1 for this case is

$$\underbrace{\cdots \wedge y = 0}_{\Theta} \quad \rightarrow \quad y \geq 0$$

which is obviously valid. For premise I2, we consider first the verification condition for transition ℓ_1

$$\underbrace{\cdots \wedge y' = y + 1}_{\rho_{\ell_1}} \wedge y \geq 0 \quad \rightarrow \quad y' \geq 0$$

which is also valid. All other transitions preserve the value of y and therefore trivially preserve $\varphi : y \geq 0$. Premise I3 holds since $\varphi = p$.

Proof Diagrams

As we become more experienced in conducting proofs according to rule INV, proofs need not be presented with full formal detail. However, identification of the structure of the verification conditions and how transitions may lead from a state satisfying some φ_i into a state satisfying some φ_j is helpful in increasing confidence in the correctness of the proof. Here we propose to represent this information by proof diagrams.

A *proof diagram* is a directed graph consisting of a finite set of nodes N and a set of directed edges E connecting the nodes. Each node n_i is labeled by an assertion φ_i, and each edge is labeled with a name of a transition. A subset of the nodes $I \subseteq N$ is identified as the set of *initial nodes*. An example of a proof diagram is presented in Fig. 2.

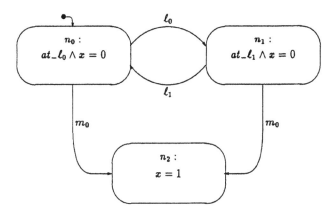

Figure 2: A Proof Diagram

If node n_i is connected to node n_j by an edge labeled by τ, we say that n_j is a τ-successor of n_i.

A proof diagram is defined to be *sound* if, for every nonterminal node $n \in M$ labeled by assertion φ and every transition $\tau \in \mathcal{T}$:

- If $n_1, \ldots n_k$ are the τ-successors of n for some $k > 0$, then the verification condition $\{\varphi\} \tau \{\bigvee_{i=1}^{k} \varphi_k\}$ is valid.

- If n has no τ-successor then the verification condition $\{\varphi\} \tau \{\varphi\}$ is valid.

It is obvious that a sound proof diagram identifies a set of verification conditions that can serve as premise I2 of rule INV. To account for premises I1 and I3, we define a diagram D to be *valid with respect to* assertion p if D is sound and the following implications are valid:

$$\Theta \rightarrow \varphi_I, \qquad \varphi_N \rightarrow p,$$

using the notation φ_K as an abbreviation for the disjunction $\bigvee_{i \in K} \varphi_i$, where K is either I or N^1.

Claim 1 *A diagram that is valid with respect to assertion p establishes the validity of the formula $\Box p$ over program P.*

Taking p to be $x = 0 \rightarrow at\_\ell_{0,1}$, it is not difficult to show that the proof diagram of Fig. 2 is valid with respect to p. This establishes the validity of the safety property $\Box(x = 0 \rightarrow at\_\ell_{0,1})$ over program PARA.

Statechart Conventions

There are several conventions inspired by the visual language of Statecharts [Har87] that improve the presentation and readability of proof diagrams. We extend the notion of a directed graph into a structured directed graph by allowing *compound nodes* that may encapsulate other nodes, and edges that may depart or arrive at compound nodes. A node that does not encapsulate other nodes is called a *basic node*.

We use the following conventions:

- Labels of compound nodes: a diagram containing a compound node n, labeled by an assertion φ and encapsulating nodes $n_1, \ldots, n_k$ with assertions $\varphi_1, \ldots, \varphi_k$, is equivalent to a diagram in which n is unlabeled and nodes $n_1, \ldots, n_k$ are labeled by $\varphi_1 \wedge \varphi, \ldots, \varphi_k \wedge \varphi$.

- Edges entering and exiting compound nodes: a diagram containing an edge e connecting node A to a compound node n encapsulating nodes $n_1, \ldots, n_k$ is equivalent to a diagram in which there is an edge connecting A to each n_i, $i = 1, \ldots, k$, with the same label as e. Similarly, an edge e connecting the compound node n to node B is the same as having a separate edge connecting each n_i, $i = 1, \ldots, k$, to B with the same label as e.

With these conventions we can redraw the proof diagram of Fig. 2 as shown in Fig. 3. Note that the common conjunct $x = 0$ has been factored out of nodes n_0 and n_1 and now appears as the label of the compound node encapsulating them.

---

[1]Note the abuse of notation by which we use I and N to denote sets of nodes as well as sets of the indices of these nodes. We hope that the ensuing ambiguity can always be resolved by the context.

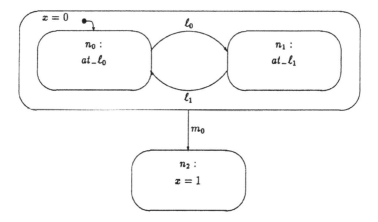

Figure 3: A Structured Proof Diagram

3   Real-Time Systems

The next model we consider introduces the metric aspect of time, and provides a measure for the time-distance between events as well as for the duration of activities in the system.

The specific model we present here was introduced and discussed in [HMP90],[HMP91], [HMP92]. A closely related model was presented in [AL92]. Many of the Process Algebra extensions to real-time, such as [NSY92], [MT90], and many others listed in [Sif91], are based on very similar assumptions.

3.1   Computational Model: Timed Transition System

As the time domain we take the nonnegative reals R^+. In some cases, we also need its extension $R^\infty = R^+ \cup \{\infty\}$.

A *timed transition system* (TTS) $S = \langle V, \Theta, \mathcal{T}, l, u \rangle$ consists of the components V, Θ, and $\mathcal{T}$, defined the same as for a fair transition system, and the two new components:

- A *minimal delay* $l_\tau \in R^+$ (also called *lower bound*) for every transition $\tau \in \mathcal{T}$.

- A *maximal delay* $u_\tau \in R^\infty$ (also called *upper bound*) for every transition $\tau \in \mathcal{T}$. It is required that $u_\tau \geq l_\tau$ for all $\tau \in \mathcal{T}$.

Note that the components $\mathcal{J}$ and $\mathcal{C}$ are eliminated.

We introduce a special variable T, sometimes called the *clock variable*. At any point in an execution of a system, T has a value over R^+ representing the current time. The set of variables $V_T = V \cup \{T\}$ is called the set of *situation variables*. A type consistent interpretation of V_T is called a *situation*, and the set of all situations is denoted by Σ_T.

Often, we represent a situation as a pair $\langle s, t \rangle$ where s is a state and $t \in \mathbb{R}^+$ is the interpretation of the clock T.

To simplify the formalism, we assume that all transitions are *self disabling*. This means that no transition $\tau \in \mathcal{T}$ can be applied twice in succession to any state, implying that τ is disabled on any τ-successor of any state, i.e., $\tau(\tau(s)) = \phi$ for any s.

Computations

A *computation* of a timed transition system is an infinite sequence of situations

$$\sigma : \langle s_0, t_0 \rangle, \langle s_1, t_1 \rangle, \langle s_2, t_2 \rangle, \ldots ,$$

satisfying:

- *Initiation:* $s_0 \models \Theta$ and $t_0 = 0$.

- *Consecution:* For each $j = 0, 1, \ldots,$

    - Either $t_j = t_{j+1}$ and $s_{j+1} \in \tau(s_j)$ for some transition $\tau \in \mathcal{T}$, or

    - $s_j = s_{j+1}$ and $t_j < t_{j+1}$. We refer to this step as a *tick step*, implying that time has progressed.

- *Lower bound:* For every transition $\tau \in \mathcal{T}$ and position $j \geq 0$, if τ is taken at j, there exists a position i, $i \leq j$, such that $t_i + l_\tau \leq t_j$ and τ is enabled on $s_i, s_{i+1}, \ldots, s_j$. This implies that τ must be continuously enabled for at least l_τ time units before it can be taken.

- *Upper bound:* For every transition $\tau \in \mathcal{T}$ and position $i \geq 0$, if τ is enabled at position i, there exists a position j, $i \leq j$, such that $t_i + u_\tau \geq t_j$ and

    either τ is not enabled at j,
    or τ is taken at j.

    In other words, τ cannot be continuously enabled for more than u_τ time units without being taken.

- *Time Divergence:* As i increases, t_i grows beyond any bound.

Unlike the untimed case, it is not necessary to require that every state has at least one transition enabled on it. This is because, even if all transitions are disabled, we can always take tick steps which ensures that all computations are infinite. Consequently, we no longer need the *idling transition* τ_I and omit it from the systems corresponding to programs.

The requirement of time divergence excludes *Zeno computations* in which there are infinitely many state-changes within a finite time interval [AL92].

Initially $x = b = y = 0$.

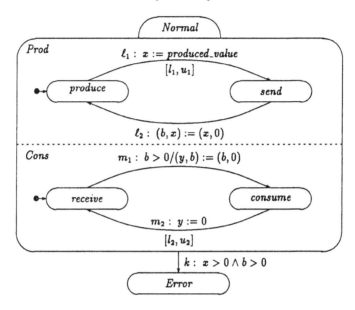

Figure 4: PROD-CONS a Producer Consumer system.

System Description by Timed Statecharts

A very convenient specification of timed systems can be obtained by extending the visual notation of Statecharts [Har87] by annotating each transition with a pair of numbers $[l, u]$, denoting the lower and upper time bounds of that transition. As an example, we present in Fig. 4 a timed specification of a producer-consumer system.

The diagram consists of two processes (automata): *Prod* and *Cons*, which operate concurrently. Process *Prod* represents a producer that produces a positive value in x and places it in the buffer variable b. Process *Cons* waits for b to become positive and then copies b to its working variable y while resetting b to 0.

A label of a transition in this Statechart specification has the form

$$name : c/assignment,$$

where *name* is an optional name of the transition (with no semantic meaning), c is a *triggering condition* which causes the transition to become enabled, and *assignment* is an optional assignment which is executed when the transition is taken. When the transition has the trivial triggering condition T, such as transition ℓ_1 in the diagram, we omit the separator '/' from the label. In this case, the transition is enabled whenever the state from which it departs (state *produce* in the diagram) is active.

In addition, each transition is optionally labeled by a pair of real numbers $[l, u]$, which specifies the minimal and maximal delays of the transition. Transitions that are not explicitly labeled are considered to be immediate, i.e., to have the time bounds $[0,0]$.

An interesting analysis question one would like to address in this situation is the conditions under which state *Error* is guaranteed to be unreachable. A simple calculation implies that $l_1 > u_2$ is a sufficient condition for the unreachability of *Error*. In the sequel we discuss an approach to the verification of such statements.

Timed Statecharts as a TTS

While we refer the reader to [KP92] for a full definition of the semantics of timed Statecharts, we show here how Statechart PROD-CONS of Fig. 4 can be viewed as a timed transition system.

As we see in the diagram, a Statechart contains *basic states* which do not contain other states and *compound states* which do. We refer to the direct descendants of a compound states as its *children*. Thus, the children of state *Prod* are *produce* and *send*, the children of *Cons* are *receive* and *consume*, and the children of *Normal* are *Prod* and *Cons*. States *Prod* and *Cons* are (exclusive) *or-states*. A basic state is considered active if the system is currently at this state. An or-state is active if precisely one of its children is active. State *Normal*, on the other hand, is an *and-state*. An and-state is active if all of its children are active. Or- and and-states correspond to sequential and parallel composition of their children, respectively.

The control variable π in the TTS representation of Statecharts ranges over sets of basic states. We adopt the notation by which a reference to a compound state names the set of basic states that are its descendants. For example, *Prod* refers to the set $\{produce, consume\}$.

Following is the identification of the constituents of the timed transition system corresponding to Statechart PROD-CONS.

- *State Variables*: $\{\pi, x, b, y\}$, where π ranges over subsets of
  $\{produce, send, receive, consume, Error\}$.

- *Initial Condition*: Given by
  $\Theta: \pi = \{produce, receive\} \wedge x = b = y = 0$.

- *Transitions, lower and upper bounds*: Listed in the following table. For simplicity, we omitted all conjuncts of the form $u' = u$ for any state variable u.

τ	ρ_τ	l_τ	u_τ
ℓ_1	$produce \in \pi \ \wedge \ \pi' = \pi - \{produce\} \cup \{send\} \ \wedge \ x' > 0$	l_1	u_1
ℓ_2	$send \in \pi \ \wedge \ \pi' = \pi - \{send\} \cup \{produce\} \ \wedge \ b' = x \ \wedge \ x' = 0$	0	0
m_1	$receive \in \pi \ \wedge \ \pi' = \pi - \{receive\} \cup \{consume\} \ \wedge \ b > 0 \ \wedge \ y' = b \ \wedge \ b' = 0$	0	0
m_2	$consume \in \pi \ \wedge \ \pi' = \pi - \{consume\} \cup \{receive\} \ \wedge \ y' = 0$	l_2	u_2
k	$\pi \cap Normal \neq \phi \ \wedge \ x > 0 \ \wedge \ b > 0 \ \wedge \ \pi' = \pi - Normal \cup \{Error\}$	0	0

Note that transition ℓ_1 takes any positive value as a "produced value." The reference to *Normal* in the relation for transition k, is equivalent to a reference to the set $\{produce, send, receive, consume\}$.

Timed Extension of the Textual Language

In the previous section (subsection 2.2), we introduced the simple programming language SPL for the qualitative model. What extensions, if any, are necessary to deal with real-time?

On the lowest level, very few extensions are necessary. At the minimum, it is only necessary to assign time bounds to the transitions associated with statements of the program. For example, we can assign uniform time bounds $l_\tau = L$ and $u_\tau = U$ to every transition.

It is obvious that with this time bounds assignment each SPL program can be viewed as a TTS.

With this timing assignment, we may reconsider a program such as PARA and claim for it some stronger properties. For example, the property of termination can now be quantified by saying that the program terminates within $3 \cdot U$ time units. In the following subsections we will show how such properties are specified and verified.

To distinguish between the interpretation of a program P as a fair transition system and its interpretation as a timed transition system (when provided time bounds for its transitions), we denote the latter as P_T.

3.2 Requirement Specification Languages

To specify properties of timed systems, we use the language of temporal logic with appropriate extensions. There have been several proposals for such extensions. Here we present only two of them.

One approach to the specification of timing properties presented in [HMP91] introduces a bounded version of most temporal operators, obtained by subscripting the operator by a timing constraint. For example, the formula $\Diamond_{\leq d}\, q$ holds at position i of a timed computation $\sigma : (s_0, t_0), (s_1, t_1), \ldots$ iff there exists a j, $i \leq j$, such that $t_j \leq t_i + d$ and q holds at j. With this notation, we can write the formula $p \Rightarrow \Diamond_{\leq d}\, q$, which expresses the *bounded response* property stating that every p should be followed by an occurrence of a q, after no more than d time units.

This language for the specification of timing properties, which we refer to as *metric temporal logic* (MTL), has been advocated in [KVdR83], [KdR85], and [Koy90], although an early proposal in [BH81] can be viewed as a precursor to this specification style.

Another approach to the specification of timed properties introduces a temporal function $\Gamma(\varphi)$, called the *age* of the formula φ. The age of the function measures the length of the largest interval, extending through the past to the present, in which φ has been continuously true. More precisely, the value of $\Gamma(\varphi)$ at position j in a computation σ is defined to be

> the largest t such that, for some $i \leq j$, $t = t_j - t_i$ and φ holds at all positions $i, \ldots, j$, or 0 if $(\sigma, j) \not\models \varphi$.

We denote by TL_Γ the logic obtained by extending temporal logic with the age function. Note that the value of $\Gamma(true)$ at situation $\langle s_i, t_i \rangle$ is always t_i, the current value of the clock variable T. Consequently, we allow formulas in TL_Γ to refer explicitly to the clock variable T. In this respect, TL_Γ can be viewed as an extension of the *Explicit Clock Temporal Logic* considered, for example, in [PH88], [HLP90], and [Ost90].

Referring to the clock T, we can specify the bounded response property by the formula
$p \wedge T = t_0 \Rightarrow \Diamond (q \wedge T \leq t_0 + d)$.

An assertion that may refer to the clock variable T or contain age expressions of the form $\Gamma(\psi)$, where ψ is an assertion, is called a *timed assertion*.

3.3 Verification of Age Formulas

For verifying properties specified by TL_Γ, we develop an extended version of rule INV.

Before presenting the rule itself, we present some axioms governing the behavior of age expressions:

AGE-RANGE :	$0 \leq \Gamma(\psi) \leq T$	for every formula ψ
AGE-FALSE :	$\neg \psi \rightarrow \Gamma(\psi) = 0$	for every formula ψ
UPPER-BOUND :	$\Gamma(En(\tau)) \leq u_\tau$	for every transition $\tau \in T$

We may use these axioms freely in any reasoning step. Note that a consequence of AGE-RANGE is that $T = 0$ implies $\Gamma(\psi) = 0$ for every ψ.

Verification Conditions

In preparation for rule INV, we introduced the verification condition $\{p\}\, \tau\, \{q\}$ whose validity ensures that every τ-successor of a p-state satisfies q. When considering computations of timed transition system, there are two ways to get from a situation to its successor: by taking a transition or by letting time progress (a tick step). Consequently, we introduce two verification conditions.

- The condition $\{p\}\, \tau\, \{q\}_\tau$ is given by $\rho_\tau^* \wedge p \rightarrow q'$, where ρ_τ^* stands for
$$\rho_\tau \wedge T' = T \wedge l_\tau \leq \Gamma(En(\tau)) \leq u_\tau.$$

- The condition $\{p\}\, tick\, \{q\}$ is given by $\rho_{tick} \wedge p \rightarrow q'$, where ρ_{tick} stands for
$$V' = V \wedge T' > T \wedge \bigwedge_{\tau \in T}(\Gamma'(En(\tau)) \leq u_\tau).$$

In any of these formulas we may need to evaluate the primed version of $\Gamma(r)$, denoted by $\Gamma'(r)$ for some assertion r. This is given by
$$\Gamma'(r) \;=\; \text{if } r' \text{ then } \Gamma(r) + T' - T \text{ else } 0.$$

A Rule for Timed Invariances

The following rule can be used to establish the validity of the formula $\Box p$ for a (possibly timed) assertion p over a timed transition system P_T.

T-INV	I1.	Θ_T	$\rightarrow$	φ
	I2.	$\{\varphi\}$	T	$\{\varphi\}_\tau$
	I3.	$\{\varphi\}$	$tick$	$\{\varphi\}$
	I3.	φ	$\rightarrow$	p
			$\Box p$	

Premise I1 refers to Θ_T, the timed version of the initial condition, which is defined as $\Theta \wedge T = 0$. Rule T-INV is complete for proving timed invariance formulas.

To present elaborate proofs, we again recommend proof diagrams. The only difference between the timed and untimed case is that, in the timed case, assertions may refer to the clock variable T and contain age expressions.

Moving to the timed case, we add to the definition of a sound (and valid) proof diagram the requirement

- For every $n_i \in N$ it is required that the tick verification condition $\{\varphi_i\}$ *tick* $\{\varphi_i\}$ is valid, implying that each of the assertions is preserved under the progress of time.

Let us consider the property stating that program PARA$_T$ terminates within 15 time units. In MTL, this can be specified by the formula $\Theta \Rightarrow \diamondsuit_{\leq 15}(at\_\ell_2 \wedge at\_m_1)$. In this form, this property appears to be a response property. However, this property is actually a *safety* property. We refer the reader to [Hen91] and [Pnu92] where it is pointed out that many liveness properties become safety properties when we consider their bounded version.

We will use rule T-INV via proof diagrams to establish the same property, expressed by the invariance

$$\Box(T \leq 15 \vee (at\_\ell_2 \wedge at\_m_1)).$$

This formula states that if more than 15 time units have elapsed, then the program must have terminated.

The proof diagram presented in Fig. 5 establishes the validity of this formula over program PARA$_T$.

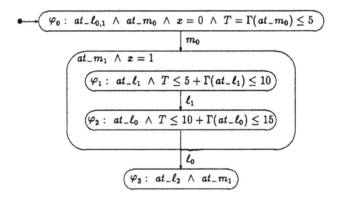

Figure 5: A Timed Proof Diagram

It is not difficult to show that the diagram is valid with respect to the assertion $T \leq 15 \vee (at\_\ell_2 \wedge at\_m_1)$.

Proving Untimed Properties of Timed Systems

The previous example concentrated on proving timed properties, i.e., properties in which time is explicitly mentioned. Another interesting class of properties consists of properties that do not refer to time directly but whose validity over a program P_T is a consequence of the timing constraints satisfied by the computations of P_T.

For example, the property $\Box(y \leq 3)$ is valid over all computations of program PARA$_T$ with uniform time bounds $[1,5]$. It is certainly not valid for the untimed computations of PARA$_T$.

In Fig. 6 we present a proof diagram that is valid with respect to the assertion $y \leq 3$.

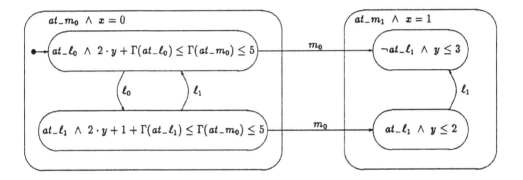

Figure 6: A Timed Invariance Proof Diagram

4 Hybrid Systems

The last model presented here is that of *hybrid systems*. This model allows some components of the system to modify their variables continuously, in addition to discrete components that modify their variables by transitions that change the values of variables in zero time.

4.1 Computational Model: Phase Transition System

A *phase transition system* (PTS) is given by $\Phi : \langle V, \Theta, \mathcal{T}, \mathcal{A}, l, u \rangle$. The components V, Θ, $\mathcal{T}$, l, and u are defined identically to their definition for a timed transition system. The set $V = V_d \cup V_c$ is partitioned into V_d the set of *discrete variables* and V_c the set of *continuous variables*. Continuous variables have always the type *real*. The new component is

- $\mathcal{A}$: A finite set of *activities*. Each activity $\alpha \in \mathcal{A}$ is a conditional differential equation of the form:

$$p \;\rightarrow\; \dot{x} = e,$$

where p is a predicate over V_d called the *activation condition* of α, $x \in V_c$ is a continuous state variable, and e is an expression over V. We say that the activity α *governs* variable x. Activity α is said to be *active* in state s if its activation condition p holds on s. Otherwise, α is said to be *passive*. Let G_x denote the set of activities that govern variable x.

It is required that the activation conditions of the activities that govern the same variable x be exhaustive and exclusive, i.e., at least one of them holds on any state but no two of them can hold simultaneously.

For simplicity, we require that transitions whose enabling condition depends on a continuous variable be immediate, i.e., have the time bounds $[0, 0]$.

Activity Successors

Consider a phase transition system Φ. An *activity selection* is a mapping $g : V \mapsto \mathcal{A}$, assigning to each continuous variable $x \in V_c$ an activity $g(x) \in G_x$ in its governing set.

Let $\langle s_1, t_1 \rangle$ and $\langle s_2, t_2 \rangle$ be two situations of Φ with $t_1 < t_2$. An *evolution* $\langle g, F \rangle$ from $\langle s_1, t_1 \rangle$ to $\langle s_2, t_2 \rangle$ consists of an activity selection g and a set of functions $F : \{ f_x(t) \mid x \in V \}$, one for each variable $x \in V$, that are differentiable in the interval $[t_1, t_2]$ and satisfy the following requirements for every $x \in V$:

- $f_x(t_1) = s_1[x]$ and $f_x(t_2) = s_2[x]$. Thus, the values of $f_x(t)$ at the boundaries of the interval $[t_1, t_2]$ agree with the interpretation of x by s_1 and s_2, respectively.

- If x is a continuous variable, and $p \to \dot{x} = e$ is the activity selected for x by g, then p holds at s_1 and f_x satisfies the differential equation

$$\tfrac{d}{dt} f_x(t) \;=\; e(F)$$

  holds in the interval $[t_1, t_2]$, where the expression $e(F)$ is obtained from e by replacing each occurrence of a variable y by the function $f_y(t)$.

- If $x \in V_d$ is a discrete variable, then $f_x(t) = s_1[x]$ for every $t \in [t_1, t_2]$.

- For every t, $t_1 \le t < t_2$, there is no immediate transition which is enabled on the state $s(t)$ defined as the interpretation assigning to each variable $y \in V$ the value $f_y(t)$.

In such a case we say that the situation $\langle s_2, t_2 \rangle$ is an *activity successor* of the situation $\langle s_1, t_1 \rangle$. Note that there exists at most one evolution from $\langle s_1, t_1 \rangle$ to $\langle s_2, t_2 \rangle$, for a given activity selection g. In fact, the functions F are uniquely determined by the selection g and the situation $\langle s_1, t_1 \rangle$.

Sampling Computations

A *sampling computation* of a phase transition system $\Phi : \langle V, \Theta, \mathcal{T}, \mathcal{A}, l, u \rangle$ is an infinite sequence of situations

$$\sigma \;:\; \langle s_0, t_0 \rangle, \; \langle s_1, t_1 \rangle, \; \langle s_2, t_2 \rangle, \; \ldots \;,$$

satisfying:

- *Initiation:* $s_0 \models \Theta$ and $t_0 = 0$.

- *Consecution:*   For each $j = 0, 1, ...,$

   - Either $t_j = t_{j+1}$ and $s_{j+1} \in \tau(s_j)$ for some transition $\tau \in \mathcal{T}$ — transition τ taken at j, or

   - $\langle s_{j+1}, t_{j+1} \rangle$ is an activity successor of $\langle s_j, t_j \rangle$ (implying $t_j < t_{j+1}$) — a continuous phase is executed at step j.

- *Bounds:*   Each transition $\tau \in \mathcal{T}$,

   - *can* be taken only after being continuously enabled for at least l_τ time units, and

   - *cannot* be continuously enabled for more than u_τ time units without being taken.

- *Time Divergence:*   As i increases, t_i grows beyond any bound.

System Description by Hybrid Statecharts

Hybrid systems can be conveniently described by an extension of timed Statecharts called *hybrid Statecharts*. The main extension is that states may be labeled by (unconditional) differential equations. The implication is that the activity associated with the differential equation is active precisely when the state it labels is active.

We illustrate this form of description by the example of *Cat and Mouse* taken from [MMP92]. At time $T = 0$, a mouse starts running from a certain position on the floor in a straight line towards a hole in the wall, which is at a distance X_0 from the initial position. The mouse runs at a constant velocity v_m. After a delay of Δ time units, a cat is released at the same initial position and chases the mouse at velocity v_c along the same path. Will the cat catch the mouse, or will the mouse find sanctuary while the cat crashes against the wall?

The Statechart in Fig. 7 describes the possible scenarios.

This diagram illustrates the typical interleaving between continuous activities and discrete state changes, which in this example only involves changes of control.

The specification (and underlying phase transition system) uses the continuous state variables x_m and x_c, measuring the distance of the mouse and the cat, respectively, from the wall. It refers to the constants $X_0, v_m, v_c,$ and Δ.

The idea of using Statecharts with continuous activities associated with certain states (usually basic ones) was already suggested in [Har84].

The Underlying Phase Transition System

Following the graphical representation, we will now identify the phase transition system underlying the picture of Fig. 7.

- *State Variables:* Given by $V_c = \{x_c, x_m\}$ and $V_d = \{\pi\}$. The variable π is a control variable whose value is a set of basic states of the Statechart.

Initially $x_c = x_m = X_0$.

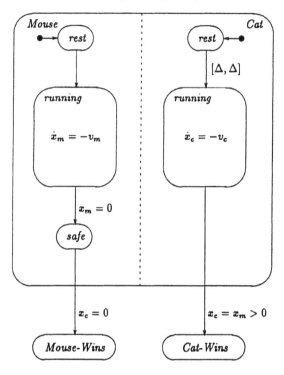

Figure 7: Specification of Cat and Mouse.

- *Initial Condition:* Given by

    Θ : $\pi = \{Mouse.rest, Cat.rest\} \wedge x_c = x_m = X_0$

- *Transitions:* Listed together with the transition relations associated with them. The transitions are named according to the states from which they depart.

Mouse.rest	:	*Mouse.rest* $\in \pi \wedge \pi' = \pi - \{Mouse.rest\} \cup \{Mouse.running\}$
Cat.rest	:	*Cat.rest* $\in \pi \wedge \pi' = \pi - \{Cat.rest\} \cup \{Cat.running\}$
Mouse.running	:	*Mouse.running* $\in \pi \wedge x_m = 0 \wedge$
		$\pi' = \pi - \{Mouse.running\} \cup \{Mouse.safe\}$
Mouse.safe	:	*Mouse.safe* $\in \pi \wedge x_c = 0 \wedge \pi' = Mouse\text{-}Wins$
Cat.running	:	*Cat.running* $\in \pi \wedge x_c = x_m > 0 \wedge \pi' = Cat\text{-}Wins$

- *Activities:* Four activities α_m and α_c represent the running activities of the two participants. Their equations sets are given by

$$
\begin{array}{lll}
\alpha_m^{on} & : & Mouse.running \in \pi \;\rightarrow\; \dot{x}_m = -v_m \\
\alpha_m^{off} & : & Mouse.running \notin \pi \;\rightarrow\; \dot{x}_m = 0 \\
\alpha_c^{on} & : & Cat.running \in \pi \;\rightarrow\; \dot{x}_c = -v_c \\
\alpha_c^{off} & : & Cat.running \notin \pi \;\rightarrow\; \dot{x}_c = 0
\end{array}
$$

- *Time Bounds:* For transition *Cat.rest* they are $[\Delta, \Delta]$. All other transitions are immediate.

System Description by Textual Programs

It is possible to extend the simple programming language SPLto represent timed and hybrid behaviors as well. The resulting language is a subset of the language *Statext* introduced in [KP92], which is shown there to have expressive power equal to that of hybrid Statecharts.

The main extensions are to allow a differential equation as an SPL statement, and the *preemption* statement $S_1 \cup S_2$. The intended meaning of the *preemption* statement is that S_1 is executed until a first step of S_2 is taken. When the first step of S_2 is taken, the remainder of statement S_1 is discarded.

We refer the reader to [KP92] for a sampling-computation semantics of this extension of SPL.

In Fig. 8, we present an extended SPL program that can be viewed as a hybrid version of program PARA.

$$
\boxed{
\begin{array}{c}
y\text{: integer where } y = 0 \\
x\text{: real \ where } x = 0 \\[1em]
\left[
\begin{array}{l}
\ell_0 : \ \textbf{while } x < 1 \textbf{ do} \\
\quad \left[\ell_1 : \ y := y + 1 \right] \\
\ell_2 :
\end{array}
\right]
\quad \| \quad
\left[
\begin{array}{l}
[m_0 : \ \dot{x} = 0.2] \ \cup \ [m_1 : \ \textbf{await } x \geq 1] \\
m_2 :
\end{array}
\right] \\[2em]
-\ P_1 \ - \qquad\qquad\qquad\qquad -\ P_2 \ -
\end{array}
}
$$

Figure 8: Program PARA$_H$: A Hybrid textual Program

In this program, process P_2 represents a continuous component that lets x grows linearly from 0 until it reaches a value $x \geq 1$. At that point, statement m_1 intervenes and shuts off the continuous process. Process P_1 is very similar to process P_1 in program PARA. It loops, incrementing y, as long as $x < 1$. Once process P_1 detects that $x \geq 1$, it terminates.

The following interprets program PARA$_H$ as a phase transition system.

$$
\begin{array}{lll}
V & = & V_c : \{x\} \ \cup \ V_d : \{\pi, y\} \\
\Theta & : & \pi = \{\ell_0, m_0, m_1\} \ \wedge \ x = y = 0
\end{array}
$$

$\mathcal{T}$: $\{\ell_0, \ell_1, m_1\}$ with transition relations:

$$\rho_{\ell_0} \;:\; \ell_0 \in \pi \;\wedge\; \begin{pmatrix} x = 0 \;\wedge\; \pi' = \pi - \{\ell_0\} \cup \{\ell_1\} \\ \vee \\ x \neq 0 \;\wedge\; \pi' = \pi - \{\ell_0\} \cup \{\ell_2\} \end{pmatrix} \;\wedge\; x' = x \;\wedge\; y' = y$$

$$\rho_{\ell_1} \;:\; \ell_1 \in \pi \;\wedge\; \pi' = \pi - \{\ell_1\} \cup \{\ell_0\} \;\wedge\; x' = x \;\wedge\; y' = y + 1$$

$$\rho_{m_1} \;:\; m_1 \in \pi \;\wedge\; x \geq 1 \;\wedge\; \pi' = \pi - \{m_0, m_1\} \cup \{m_2\} \;\wedge\; x' = 1 \;\wedge\; y' = y$$

$\mathcal{A}$: $\{\alpha_1, \alpha_2\}$ given by:

$$\alpha_1 \;:\; m_0 \in \pi \;\rightarrow\; \dot{x} = 0.2$$

$$\alpha_2 \;:\; m_0 \notin \pi \;\rightarrow\; \dot{x} = 0$$

$l = 1$ and $u = 5$ for ℓ_0 and ℓ_1; m_1 is immediate.

Requirement Specification Languages

At present, no special extensions to the requirement specification languages have been identified for hybrid systems. As in the case of the real-time model, we use either MTL or TL$_\Gamma$ for specifying properties of hybrid systems.

4.2 Verification of Age Formulas

Here we only consider verification of TL$_\Gamma$ formulas over hybrid systems. The major extension relative to the real-time model is in the verification conditions.

The verification condition $\{p\}\,\tau\,\{q\}_\tau$ remains with no change. However, instead of using the verification condition $\{p\}\,tick\,\{q\}$, we define a new condition $\{p\}\,cont\,\{q\}$ which is intended to ensure that every continuous phase leads from a p-situation to a q-situation.

The condition $\{p\}\,cont\,\{q\}$ is given by a conjunction of implications $\rho_{cont}^g \wedge p \rightarrow q'$, one for each activity selection g. The relation ρ_{cont}^g stands for

$$F^g(T) = V \;\wedge\; F^g(T') = V' \;\wedge\; T' > T \;\wedge\; \bigwedge_{\tau \in \mathcal{T}} (\Gamma'(En(\tau)) \leq u_\tau)$$
$$\wedge$$
$$\bigwedge_{x \in V_c} (p_x^g(V) \;\wedge\; \bigwedge_{\tau \in \mathcal{T}_0} \neg(\exists t : (T < t < T') : En(\tau)(F^g))$$

where $\mathcal{T}_0$ consists of the immediate transitions. We assume that, for a given g, we can solve the differential equations for the activities selected by g, and express the solutions as a formula involving t, V – the initial value of the variables at the beginning of the continuous step, and T – the initial value of t at the beginning of the continuous step.

For example, if the activity selected is $\dot{x} = 2$, then the solution for this selection is given by $f_x(t) = x + 2 \cdot (t - T)$. Let F^g denote the set of these solutions.

The expression $e(F^g)$ and the formula $En(\tau)(F^g)$ are obtained by replacing every occurrence of $x \in V$ by $f_x(t)$.

The first line in the formula states that the boundary values V and V' agree with the values of F^g at T and T', respectively. This line also states that $T' > T$ and that no transition becomes over-ripe as a result of the progress of time.

The second line states that the activation conditions selected by g all hold at V, and that no immediate transition becomes enabled in the middle of an evolution.

In both q' and ρ_{cont}, we need to evaluate $\Gamma'(r)$ for several assertions r. This is given by

$$\Gamma'(r) \;=\; \text{if } r \wedge r' \text{ then } \Gamma(r) + T' - T \text{ else } 0.$$

Note that, in the real-time case, it was sufficient to evaluate r at s'. This is because all state variables preserve their values in a tick step. In the hybrid case, the continuous state variables may change their values from s to s'. Consequently, $\Gamma(r)$ is incremented only if r holds at both s and s'.

In order to ensure that this definition actually measures the age of an assertion, we restrict our use of the expression $\Gamma(r)$ to assertions r that cannot change their truth value in the middle of a continuous step.

A Rule for Invariances

Having defined the two verification conditions, we can immediately formulate a rule for proving invariance formulas over hybrid systems.

H-INV		
	I1.	$\Theta_T \to \varphi$
	I2.	$\{\varphi\}\, T\, \{\varphi\}_T$
	I3.	$\{\varphi\}\, cont\, \{\varphi\}$
	I3.	$\varphi \to p$
		$\Box p$

We will illustrate the use of this rule on several examples.

For the first example, we prove that program $PARA_H$ also terminates within 15 time units. The proof diagram of Fig. 9 is valid with respect to the assertion $T \le 15 \vee (at\_\ell_2 \wedge at\_m_1)$.

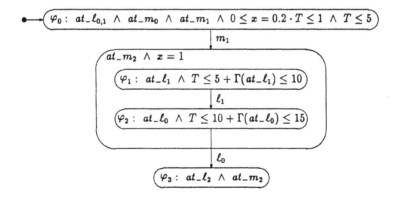

Figure 9: A Proof Diagram for Termination of PARA$_H$

The only new element in establishing this validity is checking that assertion φ_0 is preserved under a continuous step. The only relevant activity allocation function g is the one that picks α_1 for x, i.e., $g(x) = 1$. For this choice of g, the evolution of x is given by $f_x(t) = x + 0.2 \cdot (t - T)$. Consequently, the appropriate verification condition (after some simplifications) is

$$\underbrace{\pi' = \pi \ \wedge \ T' > T \ \wedge \ x' = x + 0.2 \cdot (T' - T) \ \wedge \ (\forall t : T < t < T' : x + 0.2 \cdot (t - T) < 1)}_{\rho^s_{cont}}$$

$$\wedge \ \underbrace{at\_\ell_{0,1} \ \wedge \ at\_m_0 \ \wedge \ at\_m_1 \ \wedge \ 0 \leq x = 0.2 \cdot T \leq 1 \ \wedge \ T \leq 5}_{p}$$

$$\rightarrow$$

$$\underbrace{at\_\ell'_{0,1} \ \wedge \ at\_m'_0 \ \wedge \ at\_m'_1 \ \wedge \ 0 \leq x' = 0.2 \cdot T' \leq 1 \ \wedge \ T' \leq 5}_{q'}$$

It is not difficult to see that this implication is valid.

This establishes that program PARA_H terminates within 15 time units.

Verifying a Property of the Cat and Mouse System

Consider the property that, under the assumption

$$\frac{X_0}{v_m} < \Delta + \frac{X_0}{v_c} \tag{1}$$

all computations of the Cat and Mouse system satisfy

$$\square(Cat.running \wedge (x_c = x_m) \rightarrow x_m = 0).$$

In Fig. 10, we present a proof diagram of this invariance property. In this diagram we use shorter names for the states of the Statechart. For example, $C.run$ stands for $Cat.running$. Transitions are identified by the names of the state from which they depart. For example, $M.rest$ refers to the transition connecting state $Mouse.rest$ to state $Mouse.running$ in the Statechart. We also use t_m for $\frac{X_0}{v_m}$, the time it takes the mouse to run the distance X_0.

It is not difficult to verify that the diagram is sound, including the preservation of all assertions under a continuous step. The only part that requires some more attention is showing that the φ_2 conjunct

$$X_0 - v_c \cdot (T - \Delta) > x_m = X_0 - v_m \cdot T$$

is maintained as long as x_m is nonnegative, which implies $T \leq t_m$. To show this, it is sufficient to show $v_c \cdot (T - \Delta) < v_m \cdot T$ which is equivalent to

$$\frac{v_m}{v_c} > 1 - \frac{\Delta}{T} \tag{2}$$

From inequality (1), we can obtain

$$\frac{v_m}{v_c} > 1 - \Delta \cdot \frac{v_m}{X_0}$$

which, using the definition of $t_m = \frac{X_0}{v_m}$, gives

$$\frac{v_m}{v_c} > 1 - \frac{\Delta}{t_m}. \tag{3}$$

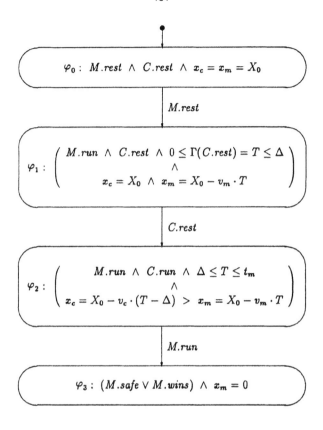

Figure 10: A Proof Diagram for the Safety of the Mouse

Since $T \le t_m$, the right hand side of (3) is not smaller than $1 - \dfrac{\Delta}{T}$ establishing (2).

It remains to show that

$$\underbrace{M.rest \,\wedge\, C.rest \,\wedge\, x_c = x_m = X_0}_{\Theta_T} \;\rightarrow\; \underbrace{M.rest \,\wedge\, C.rest \,\wedge\, x_c = x_m = X_0}_{\varphi_0} \quad (4)$$

$$\varphi_0 \,\vee\, \cdots \,\vee\, \varphi_3 \;\rightarrow\; \Big(C.run \,\wedge\, x_c = x_m \;\rightarrow\; x_m = 0\Big). \quad (5)$$

Note that, to simplify matters, we consider the initial state of all computations to be the one in which the two competitors are in $M.rest$ and $C.rest$, respectively, and that x_c and x_m are already set to X_0. Implication (4) is obviously valid. To check implication (5), we observe that both φ_0 and φ_1 imply $\neg C.run$, φ_2 implies $x_c > x_m$, and φ_3 implies $x_m = 0$.

This shows that under the assumption (1), property

$$\Box(Cat.running \,\wedge\, (x_c = x_m) \;\rightarrow\; x_m = 0)$$

is valid for the Cat and Mouse system.

References

[AL92]   M. Abadi and L. Lamport. An old-fashioned recipe for real time. In J.W. de Bakker, C. Huizing, W.P. de Roever, and G. Rozenberg, editors, *Proceedings of the REX Workshop "Real-Time: Theory in Practice"*, volume 600 of *Lect. Notes in Comp. Sci.* Springer-Verlag, 1992.

[BH81]   A. Bernstein and P. K. Harter. Proving real time properties of programs with temporal logic. In *Proceedings of the Eighth Symposium on Operating Systems Principles*, pages 1-11. ACM, 1981.

[Har84]   D. Harel. Statecharts: A visual approach to complex systems. Technical report, Dept. of Applied Mathematics, Weizmann Institute of Science CS84-05, 1984.

[Har87]   D. Harel. Statecharts: A visual formalism for complex systems. *Sci. Comp. Prog.*, 8:231-274, 1987.

[Hen91]   T.A. Henzinger. Sooner is safer than later. Technical report, Stanford University, 1991.

[HLP90]   E. Harel, O. Lichtenstein, and A. Pnueli. Explicit clock temporal logic. In *Proc. 5th IEEE Symp. Logic in Comp. Sci.*, pages 402–413, 1990.

[HMP90]   T. Henzinger, Z. Manna, and A. Pnueli. An interleaving model for real time. In *5th Jerusalem Conference on Information Technology*, pages 717–730, 1990.

[HMP91]   T. Henzinger, Z. Manna, and A. Pnueli. Temporal proof methodologies for real-time systems. In *Proc. 18th ACM Symp. Princ. of Prog. Lang.*, pages 353–366, 1991.

[HMP92]   T. Henzinger, Z. Manna, and A. Pnueli. Timed transition systems. In J.W. de Bakker, C. Huizing, W.P. de Roever, and G. Rozenberg, editors, *Proceedings of the REX Workshop "Real-Time: Theory in Practice"*, volume 600 of *Lect. Notes in Comp. Sci.* Springer-Verlag, 1992.

[KdR85]   R. Koymans and W.-P. de Roever. Examples of a real-time temporal logic specifications. In B.D. Denvir, W.T. Harwood, M.I. Jackson, and M.J. Wray, editors, *The Analysis of Concurrent Systems*, volume 207 of *Lect. Notes in Comp. Sci.*, pages 231-252. Springer-Verlag, 1985.

[Koy90]   R. Koymans. Specifying real-time properties with metric temporal logic. *Real-time Systems*, 2(4):255-299, 1990.

[KP92]   Y. Kesten and A. Pnueli. Timed and hybrid statecharts and their textual representation. In J. Vytopil, editor, *Formal Techniques in Real-Time and Fault-Tolerant Systems*, volume 571 of *Lect. Notes in Comp. Sci.*, pages 591–619. Springer-Verlag, 1992.

[KVdR83] R. Koymans, J. Vytopyl, and W.-P. de Roever. Real-time programming and asynchronous message passing. In *Proc. 2nd ACM Symp. Princ. of Dist. Comp.*, pages 187–197, 1983.

[MMP92] O. Maler, Z. Manna, and A. Pnueli. From timed to hybrid systems. In J.W. de Bakker, C. Huizing, W.P. de Roever, and G. Rozenberg, editors, *Proceedings of the REX Workshop "Real-Time: Theory in Practice"*, volume 600 of *Lect. Notes in Comp. Sci.* Springer-Verlag, 1992.

[MP91] Z. Manna and A. Pnueli. *The Temporal Logic of Reactive and Concurrent Systems: Specification.* Springer-Verlag, New York, 1991.

[MP92] Z. Manna and A. Pnueli. Models for reactive systems. Technical report, Dept. of Comp. Sci., Stanford University, 1992.

[MT90] F. Moller and C. Tofts. A temporal calculus of communicating systems. In J.C.M. Baeten and J.W. Klop, editors, *Proceedings of Concur'90*, volume 458 of *Lect. Notes in Comp. Sci.*, pages 401–415. Springer-Verlag, 1990.

[NSY92] X. Nicollin, J. Sifakis, and S. Yovine. From ATP to timed graphs and hybrid systems. In J.W. de Bakker, C. Huizing, W.P. de Roever, and G. Rozenberg, editors, *Proceedings of the REX Workshop "Real-Time: Theory in Practice"*, volume 600 of *Lect. Notes in Comp. Sci.* Springer-Verlag, 1992.

[Ost90] J.S. Ostroff. *Temporal Logic of Real-Time Systems.* Advanced Software Development Series. Research Studies Press (John Wiley & Sons), Taunton, England, 1990.

[PH88] A. Pnueli and E. Harel. Applications of temporal logic to the specification of real time systems. In M. Joseph, editor, *Formal Techniques in Real-Time and Fault-Tolerant Systems*, volume 331 of *Lect. Notes in Comp. Sci.*, pages 84–98. Springer-Verlag, 1988.

[Pnu92] A. Pnueli. How vital is liveness? In W.R. Cleaveland, editor, *Proceedings of Concur'92*, volume 630 of *Lecture Notes in Computer Science*, pages 162–175. Springer-Verlag, 1992.

[Sif91] J. Sifakis. An overview and synthesis on timed process algebra. In K.G. Larsen and A. Skou, editors, *3rd Computer Aided Verification Workshop*, volume 575 of *Lect. Notes in Comp. Sci.*, pages 376–398. Springer-Verlag, 1991.

Horizons of Parallel Computation

Gianfranco Bilardi* and Franco P. Preparata**

Abstract. This paper considers the ultimate impact of fundamental physical limitations—notably, speed of light and device size—on parallel computing machines. Although we fully expect an innovative and very gradual evolution to the limiting situation, we take here the provocative view of exploring the consequences of the accomplished attainment of the physical bounds. The main result is that scalability holds only for neighborly interconnections, such as the square mesh, of bounded-size synchronous modules, presumably of the area-universal type. We also discuss the ultimate infeasibility of latency-hiding, the violation of intuitive maximal speedups, and the emerging novel processor-time tradeoffs.

1 Introduction

Parallel computation has been for some time a hot topic for computer science research. The extraordinary technological advances—globally referred to as VLSI—which occurred over the last fifteen years exhibit the capability to enable what was previously the object of mainly academic speculation. Despite the enabling technology, there is wide consensus, eloquently and authoritatively expressed [S86, V90a, V90b], that parallel computation has not enjoyed to this day the development that was to be reasonably expected, notwithstanding some remarkable realizations (see, e.g., [Be92]). The main reason for this failed expectation has been convincingly identified [V90a] in the lack of an agreed-upon model of parallel computation, one that would unleash the independent development of hardware and software, the key feature of the extraordinary success of the von Neumann serial computer. While the central theme and outlook of this paper are of a different nature, the focus being on how physical limitations constrain the structure of large computers, the positive upshot of these considerations is that the resulting constraints can play an important role in identifying the appropriate model.

* Dipartimento di Elettronica ed Informatica, Università di Padova, Via Gradenigo 6/A, 35131 Padova, Italy. This author's work was supported in part by the Italian National Research Council and the Italian Ministry of University and Research.
** Department of Computer Science, Brown University, Providence, RI 02912-1910. This author's work was supported in part by NSF Grant CCR91-96152 and by ONR Contract N00014-91-J-4052, ARPA order 8225.

The unrelenting progress of computing technology over the past half-century is frequently expressed by sentences whose syntax is: parameter "so-and-so" has been improved by "so-large-a" factor every "so many" years. Such sentences naturally encourage the view of unbounded technological progress. The repercussion of this outlook upon the theory of computing machines is something we may dub the "topological view." In the topological view, a system is an interconnection of *sites*, (be they devices, modules, subsystems, etc.), so that communication between adjacent sites occurs with fixed delay (or, for that matter, instantaneously, if the fixed communication delay is interpreted as some kind of set-up time at the site). This view is commonly denoted "synchronous model," but we prefer the qualifier "topological" for the following reason. A *topology* (in our context, simply a directed graph) will always be implemented as a *geometry* (in our context, an assembly of wires and physical devices). The synchronous model corresponds to the assumption that timing of operations depends only upon the topology of the system and is independent of its realizing geometry (that is, it takes constant time to transmit through an edge regardless of its layout length); it is the basis of a number of significant results on size-time trade-offs, simulations between different topologies, achievable speed-ups, latency-hiding mechanisms, etc.. It must be understood that to some extent, through the clever deployment of a careful mix of technologies and architectural tricks, this view is supported by current computer engineering.

Nevertheless, any buildable machine will consist of physical components and thus will be subject to the laws (and limitations) of physics. Some of these limitations are of an absolute nature (finiteness of the speed of light), others are related to material science as we know it today. These constitute ultimate bounds to what is achievable, for what we know. We fully realize that the road towards these bounds will not end catastrophically, but will be more like a gradual evolution tempered by engineering insights. However, in this paper we take the provocative outlook of considering a technology for which these limitations are fully operative and with which arbitrarily large machines are to be built. Thus, we radically separate topological and geometric structures. The illustrated consequences are admittedly projected in the future, but involve principles that are lurking and must ultimately be reckoned with.

Several of the considerations and suggestions presented here do not entirely originate with this paper. They are an outgrowth of an intellectual climate to which an entire community of researchers has contributed over the years through both scholarly work and machine design. To them goes due credit.

2   Fundamental Limitations

Although it is very fruitful and appropriate to think of a computation as of an abstract process involving precisely defined mathematical objects—as, for example, the constituents of the Turing machine model—one should never lose sight of the fact that any concrete implementation of that process involves the utilization of physical phenomena. The physical reality will ultimately determine what can be accomplished by means of computing machines.

One may see that the present situation is vaguely reminiscent of the dichotomy between classical and modern views that characterized physics in the early part of this century: on one hand the inducement into indefinitely extrapolating current experience, on the other the awareness of limitations that alter the common-sense intuition of reality. When clock rates are of the order of $1MHz$, it is natural to view as instantaneous the signal propagation on a wire; when a transistor area is of the order of square millimeters, it is natural to view a size reduction by a factor of two as a desirable technological improvement not affecting the functionality of the device.

Both views have become shakier under the relentless technological progress that occurred in the past decade. The pillars of the revolution that ushered modern physics—relativity theory and quantum mechanics—become increasingly relevant to the structure of computing machines, by exhibiting some hard limitations to what is ultimately physically realizable. We shall now discuss these limitations.

1. Speed-of-light limitation. This is the crucial constraint. Speed of light is finite, and this fact is already quite relevant to computing systems. This relevance is striking when one considers that the duration of $1ns$ is already "long" for today's technology, and that in $1ns$ light travels a bare $30cm$. Although signal propagation on electric conductors is frequently governed by slower processes (such as charging or discharging a capacitive load) [MC80, BPP82, CM85], we shall assume that signal transmission time is proportional to the length of the connection.

2. Size limitation. It is reasonable to make reference to a *fixed* technology, characterized by a minimum attainable value of the "feature" [MC80] of an integrated circuit. This, of course, does not naively mean the preclusion of technological improvements (reductions of feature size) that are bound to occur in the near future; it simply means that forthcoming technological advances will ultimately lead to a situation where the same down-scaling mechanisms will no longer work. Quantum theory reveals the essential non-determinism of atom-size physical systems; this appears to indicate that there exists an absolute minimum size for a deterministic digital device (in other words, down-scaling is not endless).

3. Degree-boundedness. The topology of any digital network is a directed graph with bounded indegree and outdegree. This corresponds to assume the use of digital gates with bounded fan-in and fan-out, which is a well-known requirement if one wishes to use gates with basically homogeneous performance.

4. Planar layout. Although this is not a prescription dictated by any fundamental law, it is reasonable to assume that a digital computing system be physically realized by laying out its constituents on a plane. In a sense, this corresponds to the current common practice of printed-circuit-board assembly of integrated circuits. There are clear engineering reasons favoring this solution: ease of assembly, ease of maintenance, and ability to remove heat generated by switching devices. However, elimination of this assumption is inconsequential: In any case, system layout must occur in the three-dimensional space. Even overcoming serious engineering problems, a 3D-layout strategy will only result in a nonessential modification of the obtained conclusions: typically the replacement of square-root with cubic-root in some performance measures related to the physical diameter of the layout domain [Ros81].

These four limitations are the basis of the conclusions derived in the forthcoming sections.

3 Machine Modelling and Scalability

A pervasive objective of computer science is the development of increasingly large machines with the capabilities to solve increasing size instances of any given problem. This motivation has been a driving force in the brief history of the discipline.

A digital computer is a finite-state machine whose behavior is specified, in principle, by a transition function. Computer architecture is concerned with structural description of machines as assemblies of well-defined and relatively simple functional constituents. Typically, the description makes reference to a small collection of characteristic parameters, each representing the measure of some significant item or resource (for example, input size, memory size, etc.). Thus, a given architecture defines a "family" of machines.

In view of the size limitation discussed in Section 2, it is ideally desirable that machines of a given family be buildable with a homogeneous technology, i.e., by assembling increasing numbers of building blocks of fixed types. In common parlance, this property is called "scalability," and is one of the central objectives of computer architecture. In order to deal with this important notion under the limitations introduced above, we shall now attempt a simple formalization of scalability.

At the abstract level, a computation is a sequence of steps (state transitions) of the machine, and its cost is the number of steps. In a chosen physical implementation, however, each step has a duration (measured in seconds) and the cost of a computation is appropriately measured by execution time. For a class of machines, scalability means that the duration of one machine step is the same for all members of the family (i.e., in the appropriate units, the number of steps is a correct measure of running time). To deal with the more flexible notion of "degree of scalability," we propose the following definition.

Definition 1. Let $\mathcal{F} = \{M_k : k \in I\}$ be a family of machines, where I is a set of tuples of architectural parameters. With reference to a chosen physical implementation, we say that $\mathcal{F}$ has *slowdown* $\tau(k)$ if the maximum duration (measured in seconds) of any step of M_k is $\tau(k)$, for all values of k. We say that $\mathcal{F}$ is *strict-sense scalable* if $\tau(k) = O(1)$.

We now illustrate the previous definition with a few examples. Often the families arise by considering finite versions of structures theoretically defined as infinite machines.

Example 1. The most immediate example of a strict-sense scalable machine is a d-dimensional ($d = 1, 2, 3$) *cellular automaton*. We are referring here to the case where for, say, $d = 3$, $k = (k_1, k_2, k_3)$ and M_k consists of $k_1.k_2.k_3$ identical finite-state machines (with structure independent of k) placed at the points of integer coordinates of a parallelepiped of side-lengths k_1, k_2, and k_3, with near-neighbor connections. Observe that, if the structure of the finite-state machine were considered a free parameter, then the resulting family would no longer be strict-sense scalable. Indeed, a machine with a larger number of states requires a larger layout area, and hence a longer time to execute one state transition.

Example 2. One-tape Turing machines also form families of strict-sense scalable machines. Within a family, all members have identical finite-state control and M_k has k cells of tape. M_k is equivalent to a one-dimensional cellular automaton of k cells, each containing an instance of the Turing machine's finite-state control, with only one cell active at any time.

The fundamental reason why the above are families of scalable machines is that communication occurs only within bounded distance (essentially between spatially contiguous modules whose size is independent of k). These are the only examples of strict-sense scalable machines we know of. Consider now the following examples:

Example 3. In multihead Turing Machines, communication between heads introduces a delay proportional to tape length, which precludes strict-sense scalability.

Example 4. The von Neumann machine, or Random Access Machine(RAM) [CR73], M_m has a single memory of m addressable words, each of $\lceil \log_2 m \rceil$ bits (to store addresses), and a CPU tailored to $\lceil \log_2 m \rceil$-bit words. Under the speed-of-light limitation, the memory access time for M_m is $\Omega(\sqrt{m \log m})$ since, in the most favorable situation, the memory is laid out in a planar domain of diameter $\Omega(\sqrt{m \log m})$. These lower bounds are achievable so that $\tau(m) = \theta(\sqrt{m \log m})$, i.e., the von Neumann machine *is not* strict-sense scalable.

This conclusion may seem in contrast with the half century of indisputable success enjoyed by the von Neumann architecture. However, the "apparent scalability" of the RAM is due to the deployment of smaller and faster devices in the realization of increasing memory size. Indeed, by increasing m only by a fraction of the gain in device speed, $\tau(m)$ (essentially equal to the *clock cycle time*) has remarkably decreased with m. Moreover, commercial machines are augmentations of the abstract RAM with a memory hierarchy leading to different access times for different regions of memory. For programs exhibiting *locality* the result is a reduction of the average access time, hence of the observed $\tau(m)$.

Of central importance to parallel-computing are machine families based on the notion of network of processors.

Definition 2. A *network of processors* is a computing machine M characterized by three parameters: p, the number of processing elements (PE's), G, a directed graph of p vertices defining the processor interconnection, and m, the number of addressable memory cells of $\lceil \log_2 m \rceil$ bits each. Each PE is essentially a RAM with a memory of m/p cells, and is uniquely identified by an ID-tag (an integer between 0 and $p-1$). The PE's correspond to the vertices of G. The RAM repertoire of instructions is augmented with (one-step) communication primitives allowing a PE to exchange data with its (topological) *neighbors*.

We assume here that a network of processors is programmed in a Multiple Instruction Multiple Data (MIMD) mode [F66]. Specifically, all PE's execute the same program, but each PE has its own program counter. Although the communication primitives are restricted to adjacent PE's, addresses of instruction operands may range over the entire machine memory. Global memory accesses must be supported by specialized programs (and cannot be regarded as one-step operations). Network architectures are defined around a family of graphs of increasing sizes such as binary trees, meshes, hypercubes, etc.

Definition 3. Given a set of positive integers J, consider a family of directed graphs $\{G_p : p \in J, |G_p| = p\}$. We say that the machines $M_{p,G_p,m}$ form a *family of networks of processors*.

To assess the scalability of a network, let us focus first on the PE's. Clearly, a PE has a memory with $\theta((m/p)\log m)$ bits. Then, assuming that the CPU has a size comparable to or smaller than the size of the memory, the area of a PE is proportional to $(m/p)\log m$ and, due to the speed-of-light limitation on memory access time, $\tau(p,m) = \Omega(\sqrt{(m/p)\log m})$. The value of m/p will probably be dictated by a number of engineering tradeoffs. We assume here this value to be a constant (although most likely a big one) to maintain a fix ratio between memory area and CPU area as p grows. Then, we can regard $\tau(p,m)$ as essentially constant. (Indeed, for current machines $\log m$ is between 32 and 64, and 256 bits would allow to address each of the 10^{80} particles estimated to fill the universe.)

A more stringent constraint on $\tau(p,m)$ arises from network layout. Indeed, $\tau(p,m) = \Omega(L_p)$, where L_p is the length of the longest wire in the layout of G_p minimizing such length. It has been shown [L81] that $L_p = \Omega(\max(p, B_p)/D_p)$, where B_p is the bisection bandwidth and D_p is the topological diameter of G_p. We remark that, whereas networks with small diameter and high bandwidth appear desirable in the topological model, they are categorically penalized by the speed-of-light limitation, as the following table illustrates:

The table clearly singles out as highly desirable the mesh of processors described by the following definition:

Definition 4. For p a perfect square, the *p-processor mesh* is a network of PE's $\{P_{ij} : 1 \le i, j \le \sqrt{p}\}$, where the neighborhood of P_{ij} is $\{P_{i-1,j}, P_{i+1,j}, P_{i,j-1}, P_{i,j+1}\}$ (ignoring P's with indices out of range).

Table 1.

	B_p	D_p	L_p
BINARY TREE	$\theta(1)$	$\theta(\log p)$	$\Omega(\sqrt{p}/\log p)$
MESH	$\theta(\sqrt{p})$	$\theta(\sqrt{p})$	$\Omega(1)$
CCC	$\theta(p/\log p)$	$\theta(\log p)$	$\Omega(p/\log^2 p)$
CUBE	$\theta(p)$	$\theta(\log p)$	$\Omega(p/\log p)$

In a mesh, each processor can be laid out in area $O((m/p)\log m)$, and the entire network takes area $O(m\log m)$. Considering both memory accesses and near-neighbor communication, we conclude that $\tau(p,m) = \theta(\sqrt{(m/p)}\log m)$. Essentially, the slowdown is that due to the PEs, which we have seen to be almost insensitive to p (for constant m/p). Hence, we reach the central conclusion that the *mesh of processor is scalable*. By contrast, the binary tree, the hypercube [P77], and the CCC [PV81] are not scalable.

Although meshes and families of bidimensional cellular automata are all arrays of finite-state machines, there is a subtle but far reaching difference between the two families. Whereas nodes of a cellular automaton are indistinguishable from each other and independent of array size, nodes of a mesh are distinguished by their ID, which supports addressability and programmability, and their size increases, albeit slowly, with the array size.

4   The Mesh-Connected Structure

We have seen in the preceding section how, when considering very large machines, the speed-of-light limitation naturally leads to the mesh interconnection. Informally, the outstanding feature of the mesh interconnection is that its operation is essentially insensitive to the speed-of-light limitation. Clearly, other near-neighbor interconnections, such as the torus or the hexagonal mesh, would share the same feature. But these network are not substantially different from the square mesh, and we can restrict our considerations to the latter without significant loss of generality.

In this section we examine in some detail an important property of the mesh interconnection, namely, its ability to support a shared-memory programming style, a desirable feature from the user's viewpoint. Next, we consider the apparent infeasibility on the mesh under the speed-of-light limitation of the so-called "latency hiding," an accelerating mechanism that appears practicable in a more "classical" framework.

There is consensus on the fact that programming for a bounded-degree network in general, and for the mesh in particular, places on the programmer the burden of some tasks, such as *memory allocation*, i.e., assignment of each variable to a specific node of the network (private memory of some PE) where to store it, and *message routing*, i.e., the selection, for each message resulting from a memory reference, of a network path and a schedule between source and destination. It would definitely be convenient for the programmer if these tasks were handled somehow automatically by the compiler and by the runtime system. As is well known, the most serious drawback of this approach is represented by memory collisions, occurring among simultaneous memory references directed to the same network node. A number of solutions to this problem have been proposed, based both on randomized and on deterministic algorithms[MV84, UW87, AHMP87, Ran87, KU88, HB88].

These schemes are collectively referred to as P-RAM simulations, and each of them is categorized on the basis of its *slowdown*, i.e., the number of network steps needed to simulate a P-RAM step (a global memory reference). Fortunately, the mesh interconnection lends itself to a P-RAM simulation whose slowdown is of the same order as the intrinsic mesh-traversal time. Indeed, the randomized scheme proposed in [Ran87] for the butterfly network can be adapted in a relatively straightforward manner to simulate a p-processor P-RAM on a p-node mesh in time $O(\sqrt{p})$, with high probability [A.G. Ranade, private communication, 1992]. Since, on the average, for a set of p random references on a p-processor mesh, a substantial fraction of them are destined to nodes at distance $\Omega(\sqrt{p})$ from their respective sources, Ranade's result appears quite satisfactory and indicates the ability for the mesh to efficiently support a shared memory programming model of the P-RAM type, a feature which is highly desirable, and probably necessary, for a machine to be effectively usable. At the same time, however, it is by no means clear that it would be sufficient. We shall return to this issue in a later section.

Next, we turn our attention to the issue of "latency hiding" or "latency masking." *Latency l* (measured as a number of system's steps) is the time interval between the issue of a data request and the delivery of data to the requestor. Latency, an increasing function of the memory layout area, has been correctly targeted as a negative measure for a computing system. The following approach has been sometimes advocated to overcome latency.

In a network with n nodes, e edges, and latency l, each of $p \leq n$ processors is time-shared, suppose in a round-robin fashion, by a set of $s \leq l$ processes. The remaining $n - p$ nodes provide only routing and storage capabilities. A processor devotes to any given process one out of every l steps, so that the time interval between two consecutive steps of the same process is sufficient for a memory reference to be satisfied. The approach assumes that there are sp concurrent processes, for example, as the result of executing on a *physical* p-processor machine an algorithm written for a *virtual* machine with ps processors.

We now discuss how such an intriguing scheme can run into difficulties under the speed-of-light limitation on account both of bandwidth and of size constraints. We denote by "edge use" the utilization of a network edge to route a request/response between two adjacent processors. There-fore, each memory request accounts for l edge uses for its satisfaction. During an interval of duration l (latency cycle), ps memory references are issued and satisfied, so that psl edge uses are requested by the latency-hiding mechanism and only el uses are offered by the network. It follows that $psl \leq el$, that is,

$$ps \leq e. \tag{1}$$

For any bounded-degree network, $e = O(n)$, and inequality (1) yields $p = O(n/s)$. Thus, the average number of operations per step is $t = O(ps/l) = O(n)$, regardless of the value of p. Essentially, fewer processors can be active if any of them must be time-shared by more than one process. Under the speed-of-light limitation, and in particular for the mesh, $l = \theta(\sqrt{n})$. Therefore $t = O(\sqrt{n})$, whether we choose $p = n$ and $s = 1$ (all processors issuing a memory request $O(1/\sqrt{n})$ of the time), or $s = \theta(\sqrt{n})$ (only $p = \theta(\sqrt{n})$ processors issuing a memory request at each time unit).

By contrast, consider an n-node hypercube, for which $e = n \log n$ and $l = \theta(\log n)$. Choosing $p = n$ and $s = \log n$, which satisfies (1), yields a number of operations per step $t = O(n)$. Thus, under the synchronous assumption, the hypercube has the potential of fully masking latency. In-deed, this potential is exploited in some schemes to simulate a $(n \log n)$-processor P-RAM on a n-node hypercube, within $O(\log n)$ steps with high probability [V90b]. Unfortunately, under the speed-of-light limi-tation, the hypercube has a slowdown $\tau(n) = \Omega(n/\log n)$ (see Table 1), which translates into $O(\log n)$ operations per second. Moreover, the scheme also rests on a node-degree $\theta(\log n)$, which is technologically ques-tionable as n grows.

The preceding arguments appear to indicate that the difficulty encoun-tered is due to the bounded degree of the node (which limits the num-ber of edges in the network), or—if we allow arbitrary degree— to the width of the wires, which is ultimately responsible for long wires in high bandwidth networks. However, we shall argue that, asymptotically, the speed-of-light and the device-size limitations alone make it impossible to effectively mask latency, even if we paradoxically assume the deploy-ment of wires of zero width (thus allowing unlimited bandwidth as in a cross-bar network).

Indeed, a processor time-shared by s processes must use $\Omega(s)$ area to store their state information. For p processors, this requirement leads to overall network area $A = \Omega(ps)$, latency $l = \Omega(\sqrt{ps})$, and hence $O(ps/l) = O(\sqrt{ps})$ operations per second. In this situation, full latency masking occurs for $s = p$ (under the optimistic assumption that context switching between processes be doable in $O(1)$ time). For $s = p$, we have a machine (of course, a p-node mesh) of area $A = \theta(p^2)$ performing at most p^2 operations every p steps. But in the same area, we could have a p^2-processor mesh (not postulating unlimited bandwidth) that can emulate a p^2-processor P-RAM with the same overall performance (p^2 operations every p steps).

5 Synchronous Regions

Although the speed-of-light and device-size limitations ultimately appear to lead to machines whose structure on the large scale is of the (geometric) near-neighbor type (neighborly networks), the same limitations do not directly dictate the small and medium size structure of the machine. To obtain insight on some of the relevant factors, we analyze in more detail the fundamental features of communication as it occurs in digital systems.

Each communication action involves the transmission of a message from a source to a destination; the message consists of a number of bits (typically encoded as sequences of voltage transitions on suitable electric lines) which may be transmitted serially, in parallel, on in combination of these two basic modes. At the most elementary level, transmission occurs from driving gate to driven gate within a boolean network, from the instant the driving gate begins to switch, to the instant the driven gate begins an analogous transition. At a less elementary level, we have a memory read-out which runs from the instant a memory cell is selected to the instant the read-out information is usable at the output of some CPU register, etc...

In the above examples, as in any other, we recognize the following common features: an initial constant-duration set-up event (for example the switching of a driving transistor) is followed by a propagation event, which takes place in a selected support medium, and whose duration is an increasing function of the source to destination distance (for example, charging the capacity of the wire connected to the input gate of a driven transistor [BPP82].)

In all cases, it appears that the duration δ (delay) of a transmission event can be expressed as the sum of two terms: a constant set-up duration σ and a variable transmission time. Conveniently, the latter can be approximated as a linear function of the travelled distance, so that

$$\delta = \sigma + \alpha \ell. \tag{2}$$

This general form of the communication delay has some fundamental implications for parallel computation. Note first that, as long as the two terms of the right-hand side of (2) are comparable, the distance ℓ plays a negligible role in the transmission delay δ, to the point that for $\ell \leq \sigma/\alpha$ we may assume δ to be a constant. This indicates that within layout regions of geometric diameter σ/α distance becomes inconsequential: we may appropriately call such regions "synchronous", and they are correctly encompassed by the traditional synchronous model of VLSI. One should not naively infer, however, that purely technological parameters determine the size of synchronous regions. Architectural considerations may suggest a substantial enlargement of such domains by externally forcing the beginning and the end of communication events within the regions by means of a clock. Nevertheless, this approach typically introduces a slowdown with respect to the inherent speed of the deployed technology, which, beyond some limit, would offset any advantages accruing from architectural innovation. In consideration of such diverse factors, for the purposes of this paper we shall say that a *synchronous region is* implicitly defined as a layout domain where communication is allowed to take a single clock cycle.

Therefore, in the synchronous regions, the limitations that asymptotically dictate the geometric near-neighbor connection are not active constraints, and the interconnection topology is determined by other factors. Indeed, the opportunity arises to accelerate information transfer by adopting a low-diameter topology. However, if wire delay can be neglected, wire area remains an important factor and essentially constrains the available bandwidth across given sections of the machine. For example, the hypercube and its derivatives, whose bisection bandwidth is linear (or slightly sublinear) in the number of nodes, have quadratic (or nearly quadratic) area [Tho80]. Hence, within the fixed areas of the synchronous regions, only a number of nodes proportional to (or slightly larger than) the square root of that area can be connected according to those topologies. Therefore, the available area would be vastly underutilized by algorithms that can take more advantage of number of processors than they can do of bandwidth (e.g., consider systolic matrix multiplication).

Motivated by considerations of the type developed in the above paragraph, Leiserson [Lei85] proposed the concept of *area-universal* network. Informally, an area-universal network is one that can route any collection of messages almost as efficiently as any other network with similar layout area. This property is clearly desirable for a general-purpose computer, which at different times will have to execute algorithms with different communication requirements. However, a priori, the very existence of area-universal networks is not an obvious matter. Leiserson demonstrated the existence of some such networks in [Lei85] and called them *fat-trees*. A number of subsequent papers have been devoted to the subject [GL89, LM88, BB90]. Reporting the specific findings of these investigations goes beyond our present purposes. The crucial result is that there are networks that can solve any instance of the routing problem by losing at most some logarithmic factors (typically two) against any other network of similar area (even one designed specifically for that instance). Further improvements appear possible. These results are remarkable, and are the product of over a decade of investigations on the relation between bandwidth of networks and their layout area [Tho80, L81, V81, BL84, BP86].

In conclusion, we reach the view of an "asymptotically" large machine as a square mesh interconnection of small machines, each approximately of the size of the synchronous regions, exhibiting (in addition to the mesh structure) area-universal topologies. In the next section we shall elaborate on the possible impact of this mesh interconnection of area universal modules on the programming of parallel machines.

6   Considerations on Programming Models

It is of interest to speculate what programming model might be appropriate for the type of machine structure imposed by the physical constraints. This subject deserves a deep and systematic investigation well beyond the extent of this section, which offers only some preliminary considerations.

A convenient programming environment is provided by the *shared-memory* model. As we have seen in Section 4, the mesh supports an efficient implementation of shared memory, through the mechanism of P-RAM simulation. When this approach is adopted, a p-processor mesh will execute, on the average, $O(\sqrt{p})$ operations per unit time. We have also argued that this performance cannot be improved by latency-hiding techniques. It is well-known, however, that a number of algorithms of great practical interest exhibit considerable locality with respect to the mesh interconnection, that is, most of the memory references generated by any such algorithm are destined to nodes that are quite close to their respective source nodes, and hence do not incur the worst-case latency.

To illustrate this point, consider the problem of multiplying two $\sqrt{p} \times \sqrt{p}$ matrices and the two following solutions: (1) A uniprocessor system (von Neumann machine) with a memory of size $\theta(p)$, executing the standard serial algorithm, involving $\theta(p^{3/2})$ memory accesses and additions/multiplications. Since the memory is laid out in area $\theta(p)$, each memory access will take time $\theta(\sqrt{p})$ on the average, resulting in total execution time $\theta(p^{3/2} \cdot \sqrt{p}) = \theta(p^2)$. (2) A mesh-connected $\sqrt{p} \times \sqrt{p}$ network of processors, executing the well-known systolic algorithm for the problem [K82], which runs in time $\theta(\sqrt{p})$, performing $\theta(p)$ useful arithmetic operations per time step. This is essentially due to the fact that each arithmetic operation executed by a PE involves data stored in adjacent PE's. Thus, under the speed-of-light limitation, we have (without substantially altering the used area) a parallel solution using p processors that improves over the time of the best sequential solution by a factor of $p^{3/2}$, and therefore *greater* than p (at variance with the intuitive principle sometime called the Fundamental Law of Parallel Computation [S86], which arises in the synchronous model).

In general, up to an $O(\sqrt{p})$ factor in time could be gained in a mesh by minimizing the distance of references. Within the area-universal synchronous regions, the latency of individual references becomes less significant, as the distances are logarithmic. However, the $O(\sqrt{p})$ bisection bandwidth is still a bottleneck, and up to an $O(\sqrt{p})$ factor in time could be gained by an appropriate reduction of the bandwidth requirements on all sections of the network.

Unfortunately, the P-RAM style of programming does not allow control of data allocation and hence precludes the consideration of locality. Worse yet, all known methods to simulate P-RAMs on bounded-degree networks are based on memory allocations or maps (hashing in randomized approaches, and generalized expanders in deterministic ones) which randomize the correspondence between logical and physical address spaces, thereby destroying any locality implicit in the logical address space. These considerations motivate the remark that, beyond the support of shared memory, the adopted programming language should allow the programmer, when she desires to do so, to take a more direct control of the machine resource allocation. To what extent sophisticated compiler and runtime system techniques will be help in the objective of exploiting locality is an interesting question, which will no doubt receive much attention.

7   Processor-time Trade-off

Under the speed-of-light limitation, processing increasingly large input instances of a problem by a sequential algorithm will result not only in a larger number of steps, but also in a longer duration of each step, i.e., $\theta(\sqrt{A})$, for area A. This behavior naturally leads to parallelism, since—if the problem allows it—substantial speedups with respect to a uniprocessor systems are possible. If $O(A)$ processors can be used effectively, the machine will perform $O(\sqrt{A})$ useful operations per unit time. Further improvements are possible, as illustrated in Section 6, if the algorithm exhibits data locality.

It is then natural to wonder how amenable typical applications are to parallel solutions. The answer that seems to emerge from extensive research in the area know as "parallel algorithmics" [L91, KR90] is quite optimistic: to date, parallel algorithms have been developed for a large number of problems. In contrast, there is no known proof of inherent sequentiality for any "natural" problem. (P-completeness [C74, L75, KR90] arguments are often interpreted as proofs of inherent sequentiality. However, apart from the fact that such interpretation is based on the likely but yet unproven assumption that $NC \neq P$, it will be seen below that membership in NC is only loosely correlated with "physical" parallelizability.)

We now analyze more systematically the impact of the degree of parallelism, as measured by the number of processor in a P-RAM algorithm, on the efficiency of the computation, measured by the running time T under physical limitations.

A primary objective of "parallel algorithmics" is the reduction of S, the number of P-RAM steps executed to complete a given computation. An alternative criterion of performance is the product $W = pS$, known as "work." As W is the total number of operations that are executable if all processors are constantly kept busy, it seems more appropriate to use the term "potential work." Associated with this notion is the so-called "Brent's principle"[B74], stating that for a given problem the potential work $W = pS$ is a non-decreasing function of p, as we can always simulate a p-processor P-RAM with a p'-processor P-RAM ($p' < p$) of the same type with a p/p' slowdown. Brent's principle can be viewed as expressing a processor-time tradeoff.

We now wish to analyze this tradeoff under the speed-of-light limitation, which sharply separates the notions of time T and number of steps S. As the physical machine size is correctly measured by its area, rather than by its number of processors, potential work is appropriately expressed by the product AT. Here we naturally assume that the P-RAM be efficiently simulated on a mesh, with slowdown proportional to the machine diameter.

Let us consider a P-RAM algorithm whose execution on an input of size n, takes S parallel steps, p processors, and m memory cells. For concreteness, we assume that the entire input must be stored and that, for large p, m is proportional to p. Thus, $m = \theta(\max(n, p))$. The geometric diameter of a mesh with p processors and m memory cells is $\theta(\max(\sqrt{m}, \sqrt{p})) = \theta(\max(\sqrt{n}, \sqrt{p}))$. Therefore, given the assumed relation between m, n, and p, the simulated algorithm runs with the following performance:

$$T = S\max(O(\sqrt{n}), O(\sqrt{p})), \tag{3}$$

$$A = \max(O(n), O(p)). \tag{4}$$

For $p \leq n$, we have $T = O(S\sqrt{n})$ and $A = O(n)$. Any improvement in the P-RAM number of steps S translates into a corresponding improvement of the physical time T. In this situation, using fewer than $\Omega(n)$ processors leads to a clear waste of potential work. For $p > n$, instead, we have $T = O(S\sqrt{p})$ and $A = O(p)$, whence $AT^2 = O(S^2A^2) = O(W^2)$; this indicates that the product AT^2 is invariant, i.e., time is at a premium, or a doubling of the computation time allows a four-fold reduction of the area. In conclusion, the neat trade-off embodied by Brent's principle is not consistent with the speed-of-light limitation, which suggests a balancing of memory and processor resources.

To better illustrate the emerging trade-off, in the (p, S)-plane we can draw the isotemporal curves (isochrones) $\theta(S\sqrt{\max(n, p)}) = T_0$ (T_0 a constant). Any such curve delimits (together with the coordinate axes) a finite region of (p, S) values. Inside the region lie points corresponding to $T < T_0$ and outside lie points corresponding to $T > T_0$.

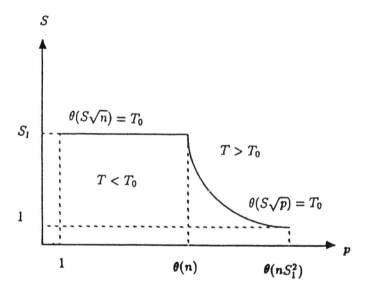

Fig. 1. An isochrone in the (S, p) plane

In the shown isochrone, we note that if a sequential algorithm exists with $p = 1$ and $S = S_1$, then no more than $\theta(nS_1^2)$ processors can ever be effectively used to speed up the solution of the problem. (This is due to the fact that nS_1^2 processors require area $\Omega(nS_1^2)$, whose traversal uses $\Omega(\sqrt{n}S_1)$ time, of the same order as the time of the sequential algorithm.) The preceding discussion could be adapted to account for locality, reaching qualitatively similar conclusions.

It is interesting observe that, in the context of P-RAM simulations, the balancing condition $p = n$ corresponds to the minimum value of the product AT. Indeed, T is a nonincreasing function of p, while, for $p \leq n, A$ is constant and, for $p > n, AT^2$ is constant. The product AT is conveniently interpreted as an expression of marginal utility for the user: in fact A is realistically proportional to the equipment cost, and, defining as T_{life} the commercially conventional lifetime of the equipment, T_{life}/T is the number of runs available to the user from one copy of the machine. Thus, for a given amount of resources, the policy achieving the largest number of runs is the one for which these resources are allocated to machines minimizing the AT-product.

In conclusion, it may be appropriate to make some observations on the widely investigated parallel complexity class NC [P79, C81], which contains exactly those problems that can be solved in polylogarithmic time by a PRAM with polynomially many processors. Membership in NC is often equated with parallel feasibility. Unfortunately, the correspondence is questionable in two ways. On the one hand, there are algorithms not of the NC type which are excellent parallel algorithms (e.g., many systolic algorithms); on the other hand, some NC algorithms require so many processors that, according to (3), they are practically slower than some known sequential algorithm for the same problem.

It must be strongly underscored, however, that while it is important to understand the impact of physical limitations on the performance of parallel algorithms, a deeper understanding of the structure of computational problems is often better obtained in abstract models of computation (for example, the class NC on the P-RAM) that are not encumbered by the physical limitations. Such models have played and will continue to play a vital role in the development of algorithms.

8 Conclusions

Technological progress in digital system engineering brings about a serious re-examination of the current models of parallel computing. In this paper, we have taken the extreme view of a technological situation where the ultimate physical limits represented by speed-of-light and device-size (under degree-boundedness) have been attained, and examined the consequences of such premises. These hypotheses appear to lead, naturally, to an asymptotically scalable parallel computing structure, consisting of a mesh-like neighborly interconnection of synchronous units, each of the latter being itself, for example, an area-universal network. While this conclusion appears to negatively constrain the feasible network choices, on the positive side it disposes in a sense of the topological chaos of potential computing structures, which represented a widely held view in past years. In addition, the convergence towards a "favorite" interconnection may provide the consensus model that would finally let hardware and software flourish autonomously.

We have also examined how the fundamental physical limitations challenge some principles and schemes that are quite natural within the currently prevailing synchronous model, such as latency masking and processor-time tradeoffs.

Of course, we do not naively suggest that the limit model discussed in this paper should govern near-term parallel computing. As history teaches us, the evolution towards the outlined situation is likely to be smooth and rich with engineering innovations. There is ample room for retention of the synchronous model for a long time, but we should be aware of what lies at the end of the road.

References

[AHMP87]   Alt, H., Hagerup, T., Mehlhorn, K., Preparata, F.P.: Simulation of idealized parallel computers on more realistic ones, SIAM Journal on Computing, 16, 5 (1987) 808-835

[BB90]   Bay, P., Bilardi, G.: Deterministic on-line routing on area-universal networks. Proceedings of the 31st Annual Symposium on Foundations of Computer Science, pages 297–306, October 1990

[Be92]   Bell, G.: A teraflop before its time, Comm. of the ACM, 35, 8 (1992), 26-47

[BL84]   Bhatt, S.N., Leighton, F.T.: A framework for solving VLSI graph layout problems, Journal of Computer and Systems Sciences, 28, 2 (1984), 300-342

[BP86]   Bilardi, G., Preparata, F. P.: Area-time lower-bound techniques with application to sorting, Algorithmica, 1, (1986), 65-91

[BPP82]   Bilardi, G., Pracchi, M., Preparata, F.P.: A critique of network speed in VLSI models of computation, IEEE Journal Solid-State Circuits, 17(1982), 696-702

[B74]   Brent, R.P.: The parallel evaluation of general arithmetic expressions, Journal of the ACM, **21**,2 (1974)201-206

[CM85]   Chazelle, B., Monier, L.: A model of computation for VLSI with related complexity results, Journal of the ACM, **32**, (1985) 573-588

[C74]   Cook, S.A.: An observation of time-storage tradeoff, JCSS, **9,3**, (1974)308-316

[C81]   Cook, S.A.: Towards a complexity theory of synchronous parallel computation, Enseign. Math. **27**,(1981) 99-124

[CR73]   Cook, S.A., Reckhow, R.A.: Time bounded random access machines, Journal of Comput. System Science, **7** (1973) 354-375

[F66]   Flynn, M.J.: Very high-speed computing systems, Proc. IEEE **54**, 12, (1966), 1901-1909

[GL89]   Greenberg, R. I., Leiserson, C.E.: Randomized routing on fat-trees. In Micali, S., editor, *Randomness and Computation*, 345–374. JAI Press, Inc., 1989.

[HB88]   Herley, K., Bilardi, G.: Deterministic simulations of PRAMs on bounded-degree networks, Proceedings of the 26th Annual Allerton Conference on Communication, Control, and Computing, Monticello, Illinois, (1988), 1084-1093

[KU88]   Karlin, A.,Upfal, E.: Parallel hashing - an efficient implementation of shared memory, Journal of the ACM, **35**, 4(1988) 876-892

[KR90]   Karp, R.M., Ramachandran, V.: Parallel algorithms for shared-memory machines, Handbook of Theoretical Computer Science: Algorithms and Complexity (J.v. Leeuwen, ed.) Elsevier-The MIT Press, 1990

[KRS90]   Kruskal, C.P., Rudolf, L., Snir, M.: A complexity theory of efficient parallel algorithms, Theoretical Computer Science, **71** (1990) 95-132

[K82]   Kung, H.T.: Why systolic architectures? Computer Magazine, **15**, 1, (1982), 37-46

[L75]   Ladner, R.E.: The Circuit Value problem is logspace complete for P, SIGACT News **7**, 1(1975), 18-20

[L91]   Leighton, F.T.: *Introduction to Parallel Algorithms and Architectures: Arrays-Trees-Hypercubes*, Morgan Kaufmann, 1991

[L81]   Leighton, F.T.: *Layouts for the Shuffle-Exchange Graph and Lower Bound Techniques for VLSI*, Ph.D. dissertation, Massachusetts Institute of Technology, Cambridge, Massachusetts, September 1981

[Lei85]   Leiserson, C.E.: Fat-trees: Universal networks for hardware-efficient supercomputing, IEEE Transactions on Computers, **C-34**,10 (1985) 892-900

[LM88]   Leiserson, C.E., Maggs, B.M.: Communication-efficient parallel algorithms for distributed random-access machines. Algorithmica, **3** (1988) 53-77

[MC80]   Mead, C., Conway, L.: *Introduction to VLSI Systems*, Addison-Wesley, 1980

[MV84]   Mehlhorn, K., Vishkin, U.: Randomized and deterministic simulations of PRAMs by parallel machines with restricted granularity of parallel memories, Acta Informatica, **21**, 4 (1984) 339-374

[P77]   Pease, M.C.: The indirect binary n-cube microprocessor array, IEEE Transactions on Computers, **C-26**, 5, (1977), 458-473

[P79]   Pippenger, N.: On simultaneous resource bounds, Proceedings of the 20th IEEE Symposium Foundation of Computer Sicence, (1979) 307-311

[PV81]   Preparata, F.P., Vuillemin, J.: The cube-connected cycles: A versatile network for parallel computation, Communications of the ACM, **24**, 5 (1981)300-309

[Ran87]   Ranade, A.G.: How to emulate shared memory, Proceedings of the 28th Annual Symposium on the Foundations of Computer Science,(1987), 185-192

[Ros81]   Rosenberg, A.L.: Three-dimensional integrated circuitry. In H.T. Kung, B. Sproull, and G. Steele, editors, Proceedings of the CMU Conference on VLSI Systems and Computations, Computer Science Press (1981), 69-80

[Smi81]   Smith, B. J.: Architecture and applications of the HEP multiprocessor system, Signal Processing IV, 298, (1981), 241-248

[S86]   Snyder, L.: Type architectures, shared memory, and the corollary of modest potential, Annual Review of Computer Science, **1** (1986) 289-317

[Tho80]   Thompson, C.D.: *A Complexity Theory for VLSI*. Ph.D. dissertation, Carnegie-Mellon University, August 1980

[UW87]   Upfal, E., Wigderson, A.: How to share memory in a distributed system, Journal of the ACM, **34**, 1(1987) 116-127

[V90a]   Valiant, L.G.: A bridging model for parallel computation, Communications of the ACM, 33,8 (1990), 103-111

[V90b]   Valiant, L.G.: General purpose parallel architectures, Handbook for Theor. Computer Science [J.v. Leeuwen, ed.], Elsevier-MIT Press, 1990

[V81]   Valiant, L.G.: Universality considerations in VLSI circuits, IEEE Transactions on Computers, **C-30**, 2, (1981) 135-140

Control Software for Virtual-Circuit Switches: Call Processing

Roy Campbell, Sean Dorward, Anand Iyengar, Chuck Kalmanek,
Gary Murakami, Ravi Sethi, Ce-Kuen Shieh, See-Mong Tan[1]

Abstract. The software architecture in this paper has evolved through a sequence of research projects at AT&T Bell Laboratories. We review the architecture and describe an experimental reimplementation.

Calls from each device attached to a virtual-circuit switch are managed by a software process, called a *line process*; the line process translates call requests from the device into a uniform device-independent internal protocol. Host computers and trunks can have numerous lines multiplexed over a single physical link. This process-per-line architecture leads to a profusion of specialized processes, most of them idle, with very simple contexts. Previous implementations used machine-dependent code to manage the processes.

The experimental implementation does basic call processing and was completed largely by three people in three months. It is portable. The architecture was reused, but the code was not. The relatively small effort supports the belief that the architecture is suited to call processing and dispels the myth that the complexity of control software prevents limited experiments.

1 Introduction

A *virtual circuit* is a pre-arranged route used for communication between devices such as host computers attached to a data network. The messages exchanged over this route are part of a *call* between the devices. *Call processing* consists of setting up and taking down calls; that is, selecting a route and making it possible for messages to flow along the route.

This paper describes experimental call-processing software developed for Xunet-2, a testbed for research on data communications [8]. The Xunet program began in 1986 as a collaboration between AT&T Bell Laboratories and the Universities of California at Berkeley, Illinois at Urbana-Champaign, and Wisconsin at Madison. Graduate student research is an integral part of Xunet; the experimental software began as a student project called *Archos*.[2]

Archos had just enough functionality to place calls between host computers, enough to demonstrate that switch-control software can be portable; that is, it can accommodate

---

[1] See Section 6 for how the authors worked together. Except as noted, the authors are at AT&T Bell Laboratories, Murray Hill, New Jersey 07974 USA. Roy Campbell is at the Department of Computer Science, University of Illinois, Urbana-Champaign, Illinois 61801 USA; Ce-Kuen Shieh is at National Cheng-Kung University, Tainan, Taiwan; See-Mong Tan is completing his military service in Singapore.

[2] The Archos switch-control software is unrelated to the real-time operating system ArchOS [11].

changes in hardware, including changes in the switch, the device interfaces, and the control computer that the call-processing software runs on. The initial implementation was largely completed by three students as a summer project—evidence of the flexibility of the software architecture that has evolved through a sequence of research projects at Bell Labs, especially TDK [12], [13]. Lessons from these projects are reviewed in Section 3. Archos itself is described in Section 4.

2 Xunet-2: A Nationwide High-Speed Testbed

Xunet stands for Experimental University Network. The goal of the Xunet testbed is to demonstrate high-speed wide-area communication between TCP/IP hosts over a virtual circuit backbone network. The network will also be used to explore techniques for handling communication between users that have other types of traffic, such as voice and video [8]. The Xunet backbone is based on Asynchronous Transfer Mode (ATM), which has been adopted for use in Broadband ISDN [2]. In ATM networks, data is sent in small, fixed size cells; error detection and correction are left to the endpoints. ATM networks will support asynchronous data traffic as well as *isochronous* traffic, such as voice and video, in which cells are transmitted at regular intervals.

Communication over Xunet-2

The initial Xunet-2 configuration connects routers at the four sites in Fig. 1 to a backbone with several switches and 45 Mb/sec trunks. The routers allow hosts on FDDI local-area networks to communicate over the backbone. For example, the host in Fig. 2 sends a packet over FDDI to the router, which picks it up and sends it over the backbone (not shown) to a router at the remote site. The packet is then forwarded by the remote router to the destination host.

In more detail, when a packet from a source host is received by the originating router, the router translates the packet's destination address into the identifier for a virtual circuit

Figure 1. Xunet-2 began with routers at four sites attached to a virtual-circuit backbone with 45 Mb/sec trunks.

177

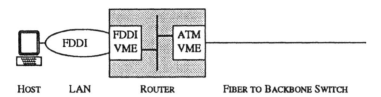

HOST   LAN   ROUTER   FIBER TO BACKBONE SWITCH

Figure 2. The Xunet-2 router serves as an interface between a local-area network and the virtual-circuit backbone.

connecting it to the destination router. If there is no such virtual circuit, the router initiates a call. The ATM-VME interface in the router fragments the packet and reformats it as ATM cells and transmits it over a fiber link to a switch on the backbone. In the present implementation, the fiber link operates at 200 Mb/sec. At the remote site, the cells are reassembled by the router, by its ATM-VME interface, which also does error detection, but not error recovery.

Research Program

"Although Xunet-2 only involves a few endpoints, the research program seeks to understand the problems of a large data network. We are interested in techniques that allow cost effective communication over a shared backbone for users with very modest requirements (e.g. 64 Kilobits/sec) while allowing other users to communicate at speeds up to 600 Megabits/sec. [8]"

The Archos software architecture (Section 4) was therefore chosen to accommodate a wide range of devices. The issues that arise when a device is attached to a network are similar to those that arise when networks are interconnected [3]; however, an overall design allows interface software to be distributed between the device and the network. For example, the software to interface the router in Fig. 2 to the backbone can run in the router, and control software for a host attached directly to an Xunet-2 switch can be split between the host and the switch-control computer.

3   Software Architecture

The Archos software architecture is largely borrowed from TDK [12], [13]; the main difference between the two is in the treatment of the signaling information that is exchanged to set up a virtual circuit.

The TDK software was built on the idea from [4], [10] of a separate process for each switchable stream, known as a *channel* or a *line*. McMahon [12] writes, "Focus for a moment on the asynchronous streams of input: requests for initiation or termination of service, . . . A single process for each stream, being independently scheduled, can block and wait for the next event from its line. By routing each independent input stream to a separate process, we can comb the multiple concurrent inputs into a manageable order . . . The main advantages of this organization are two. First, the unit of programming is single-thread. . . . Secondly, the idiosyncrasies of a single kind of line are concentrated in the process controlling that kind of line." The TDK architecture is referred to as a "process-per-line" or PPL architecture.

The illustration of the hardware and software architecture in Fig. 3 has a network with two switches, each labelled SW. The switch on the left is attached to two devices: an asynchronous terminal and a trunk. The second switch is attached to the other end of the trunk and to a host computer. An asynchronous terminal requires a single virtual circuit or channel, whereas hosts and inter-switch trunks have multiple channels that are multiplexed onto a single fiber. Each device is shown connected to the network by a hardware-software pair, the hardware part of the interface is represented by a thin unlabeled box, the software part by an ellipse. Vertical dotted lines go between the hardware and software parts of an interface. The software process for a terminal is called *termp*, the process for a trunk channel is *trunkp*, and the process for a host channel is called *hostp*.

Supervisory Events, Signaling Data

In Fig. 3, there are two paths over which information can flow, corresponding to the two routing map entries in a Datakit switch [7]. The user data path appears as a solid line, flowing from the terminal through both switches to the host.

The dashed lines represent a path for control information known as *supervision*, which flows between the device (or device interface) and the control software that runs in the control computer. Supervision uses a permanent virtual circuit, while the data channel is switched.

The data channel serves two purposes: it is connected to the control computer to exchange *signaling* information needed to establish a call, and it is connected to the endpoint during a call.

More formally, *supervisory events* are interrupt-like events used by the call-processing software to monitor and control the state of a call. Examples of supervisory events are OFFHK (read "off-hook"), which indicates readiness to communicate, and ONHK (read "on-hook"), which results in communication being terminated. *Signaling data* flows

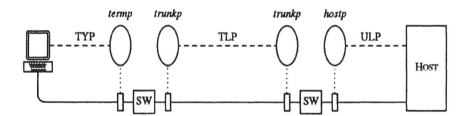

Figure 3. Each device is attached through a combination of hardware (thin unlabeled boxes) and software (ellipses).

from a device to the call-processing software in a node. An example of signaling data is the name of a destination to be called.[3]

Informally, the call-processing software must be ready at all times for a supervisory event to occur, whereas signaling data arrives only at certain times, presumably marked by supervisory events.

The use of control and data paths during call setup is illustrated in Fig. 4.

In (a), the user turns the terminal on, which causes the hardware line module to send a supervisory packet over a permanent virtual circuit through the switch to the controller. The controller then sets the routing map so that user data will flow to the controller.

In (b), user data flows to the control computer. The user types the name of the destination host which is packetized and sent as signaling data over the data path to the control computer. The software in the control computer routes the call and sets the routing map entries so that the data path is directed toward the destination host.

In (c), the solid (user) data path goes through the switch and on to the destination. Now if the terminal is turned off, the line module will send a supervisory packet over the supervision path to the controller, thus causing the connection to be torn down.

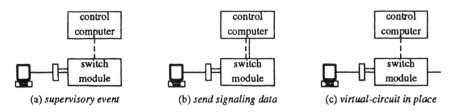

(a) *supervisory event* (b) *send signaling data* (c) *virtual-circuit in place*

Figure 4. An asynchronous terminal attached through a line module represented by a thin unlabeled box. Supervisory information flows through the switch along the dashed lines between the interface and the control computer. Data flows along the solid lines.

Multiplexed Interfaces

Host computers and inter-switch trunks support multiple virtual circuits. TDK uses a process-per-line for each virtual circuit and has a single virtual circuit over which the supervisory information for all virtual circuits is multiplexed.

When the *termp* process in Fig. 3 has translated the signaling information, it forwards the call request to the *trunkp* line process which manages the outgoing channel to the next switch. This message is sent via interprocess communication using the *Virtual Line*

[3] Call-processing terminology dates back to the earliest telephone networks. The supervisory events ONHK and OFFHK recall hooks for holding telephone receivers. When not in use, a receiver rested on a hook; it had to be taken off the hook before communication could occur. Hooks were invented in 1877. "Before 1878, there was no central-office switching and telephony was confined to private lines with a telephone at each end. The [supervisory] problem was simple . . . the caller simply shouted into the mouthpiece using words with long vowel sounds such as 'ahoy' and 'hello' " to get the attention of the called party [5].

Protocol or VLP, the internal protocol of TDK [13]. The *trunkp* process on the left must then communicate with a peer in the control computer of the switch on the right in order to forward the call.

A *trunkp* process establishes communication with a peer by sending a supervisory message over the single multiplexed channel. The route map in the switch is then set so that the peers can exchange signaling data over the data channel they control. The call is established by setting the route map again, this time to include the channel on the data path between endpoints.

Role of Device Interfaces

Each type of device has its own specialized interface, tailored to the needs of the device. The terminal interface module described above includes the physical level (electrical) conversion and start/stop character to packet conversion. In addition, there is an end-to-end protocol that allows the terminal interface to be controlled by a remote computer, including managing the RS-232 control leads, inserting delay between characters to match terminal timing constraints, and handling the BREAK line violation. The advantage of this approach is that multiple applications can be supported without changing the device interface.

In addition, the clear separation of supervision and signaling allowed "a modest implementation of the basic control problem of supervising many uncoordinated devices while allowing great flexibility in the implementation of vertical services that are achieved through signaling. ... we expect there to be a continuing evolution of new services and the language of signaling for these new services will continually evolve" [6].

4 Archos

Archos is a fresh C++ implementation of call processing, built on top of the Choices operating system [1]. Its internal protocol, Gulp, evolved from VLP. Gulp differs from the protocols used in TDK in that it sends both supervision and signaling data over a common signaling channel. Gulp also assumes an underlying reliable transport protocol, which simplifies the design of the signaling protocol.

Gulp: A Trunk Protocol

Gulp began as a protocol for establishing connections over trunks. As it evolved, Gulp was also used as the internal connection management protocol for Archos, and as the signaling protocol used with hosts. Thus, in Fig. 3, *termp*, *trunkp*, and *hostp* speak a uniform internal protocol with each other. The architecture nonetheless supports the use of different line protocols for different types of devices.

The messages of Gulp appear in Fig. 5. As in TDK, a *trunkp* process at one end of a trunk communicates with its peer across the trunk and with line processes within the same node. For clarity, messages from/to the peer begin with P, and messages from/to line processes within the same node begin with V. The number of message names can be reduced by overloading; for example, a single CALL message can play the role of both VCALL and PCALL.

MESSAGE FROM/TO		REMARK
Peer	Local Process	
PSTART		Synchronize with peer
PREADY		Acknowledge synchronization
PCALL	VCALL	Incoming call
PANS	VANS	Answer: call accepted
PNAK	VNAK	Negative answer: call not accepted
PHUP	VHUP	Hangup the call in progress
PHUPACK	VHUPACK	Hangup acknowledgement

Figure 5. Gulp messages.

A simplified automaton for Gulp appears in Fig. 6. Peer line processes at both ends of a trunk run the same protocol. Starting at the top of Fig. 6, a *trunkp* process synchronizes with its peer before processing any calls. One of the peers sends a START and waits for it to be acknowledged by READY; the automaton in Fig. 6 is for the peer that sends START. This synchronization occurs after every call setup-takedown cycle and after any error. For clarity, the additional transitions required for error recovery have been removed from Fig. 6.

Consider a call placed across a trunk. The line process at one end receives VCALL from some process at the same switch, and responds by sending PCALL to its peer and going into the *waitpeer* state. The call will be accepted when the peer returns a PANS.

At the other end of the trunk, the peer receives the PCALL, changes state to *translate*, and uses the dialstring to look up the outgoing line process. An available outgoing line process is sent a VCALL, which is propagated, perhaps onto the next switch, until an endpoint is reached. If the endpoint accepts the call, the acceptance propagates back along the path of the call request.

If at any point the translate function is unable find a line process, it sends a PNAK back across the trunk, along with an error code so that the various error cases—dialstring invalid, destination busy—can be distinguished.

Either end can hang up, resulting in the receipt of one of the signals VHUP and PHUP. A hang-up message propagates to the end of a virtual circuit and then an acknowledgement propagates back.

The assumption of reliable-delivery keeps Gulp simpler than it would be if lost messages had to be handled. Lost messages can lead to deadlocks with the protocol in Fig. 6. For example, consider a trunk process that makes the following transitions.

$$idle \xrightarrow{\text{PCALL}} translate \xrightarrow{\text{/VCALL}} waitline \xrightarrow{\text{VANS/PANS}} talk$$

From the point of view of this line process, the call is established and PANS has been sent.

But, suppose that the PANS notifying the peer across the trunk is lost, say due to a transmission error. The peer, by now in the *waitpeer* state, will deadlock awaiting a PANS or PNAK since the only signal that the sender of the lost message can send from its

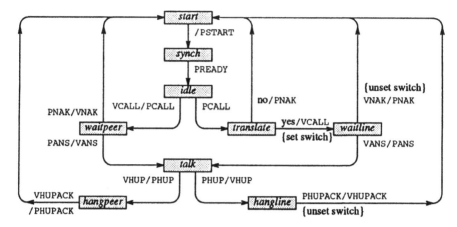

Figure 6. Simplified finite automaton for Gulp. State transitions are labeled with incoming and outgoing messages, separated by /. The label /START from state *start* represents a transition with an outgoing message, but no incoming message. The transition from state *idle* to *waitpeer*, labeled VCALL/PCALL, occurs when a VCALL arrives from a line process in the local switch/host, to which the response is an outgoing PCALL to the peer at the other end of the trunk.

talk state is a PHUP. In addition, the originator is not notified that the connection has been established

Automata for line processes can get quite complex. An approach to dealing with such complexity is explored in [14].

Common Signaling Channel

Instead of using the user data channel to exchange signaling data, Archos merges supervision and signaling for all channels on a trunk onto a single channel which we will refer to as a *common signaling channel*. Messages from a line process are multiplexed over the common signaling channel and demultiplexed at the other end of the trunk for delivery to its peer. In Fig. 7, a control message from a *trunkp* process goes to the common *trunkcp* process to be forwarded over the common signaling channel. The *trunkcp* process at the other end sends it to the peer *trunkp* process.

The Gulp messages VCALL and PCALL carry destination dialstrings, unlike the corresponding messages in TDK. This approach has the advantage of efficiency: in TDK, a virtual-circuit is set up to carry signaling data over a data channel; the time taken to write the routing map in the switch can be up to 75% of the time needed for call setup. The use of a common signaling channel is also more in keeping with standard signaling protocols, such as Q.931 (although Q.931 is substantially more complex than Gulp).

In the Archos implementation, the routing map is set in anticipation of the acknowledgment from the destination and in parallel with the propagation of call setup

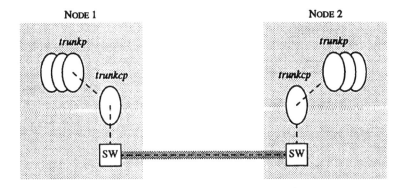

Figure 7. A *trunkp* line process communicates with its peer over a multiplexed common supervision channel, controlled by *trunkcp* processes in the nodes connected by the trunk.

information. That is, the switch's routing map is set in anticipation that the call will succeed. If the call is indeed successful, no further writes to switch memory are required when answer messages that accept the call are received.

Channel Contention

Channel contention occurs when both peers initiate calls at the same time by sending PCALL messages to each other, wishing to place calls on the same channel. The likelihood of channel contention is reduced by using a high-low scheme, where one peer allocates channels from high to low and the other allocates from low to high. This leaves only a small likelihood of collision when the last remaining channel over a trunk is allocated.

A priority scheme resolves contention for the last channel. The peer with low priority backs off and allows the high priority peer to continue its call. Priorities can be determined at system startup time; for example, by exchanging random numbers or unique switch identifiers.

5 Discussion

The design of Archos continues the "keep it simple" methodology of its predecessors. As a result, we were able to build a rudimentary control software quickly. In our implementation, there is little difference between hosts and trunks: both use Gulp. Although the response of a host or switch to an incoming call request are different, the protocol remains the same. The code for both is implemented using inheritance, so that the bulk of the Gulp code is shared.

Portability of Archos falls out of the portability of the Choices operating system. Archos relies on Choices to support lots of lightweight processes all executing in the same address space. New devices can be attached to a running switch by dynamically loading and linking appropriate software.

The process-per-line architecture leads to a profusion of specialized processes, most of them idle with very simple contexts. TDK managed these processes by using machine-dependent code. This machine dependence prompted portability as a goal for Archos. In Archos, the processes form a class hierarchy so they inherit common features and are implemented as persistent objects that, when idle, can be stored on disk.

Archos replaced the common supervision channel of TDK with a common channel carrying both signaling and supervision, which means that fewer packets need to be exchanged. The line state is still maintained in a process-per-line. We could take things even further: with devices that have a large number of homogeneous channels, like hosts and trunks, the line state can be kept in a single process corresponding to the process that communicates over the common signaling channel. The process-per-line approach would still be needed to attach other devices, such as terminals, which require customization on a per-line basis, as in TDK and Archos.

The process-per-line architecture remains a promising framework for attaching heterogeneous devices to a single network, although further work with more devices is needed to explore the architecture. Another approach to the problem of heterogeneity, which might lead to a different architecture than the process-per-line, would be to have the control computer support only one protocol for call establishment. The complexity of mapping from the device protocol to the network internal protocol would then shift to the device interface.

TDK has support for fault management of a single node. Further work is needed to add support in Archos for node-level or network-level fault management.

6 Acknowledgments

The Archos project was planned and led by Chuck Kalmanek and Ravi Sethi and implemented by Sean Dorward, Anand Iyengar, See-Mong Tan, and Gary Murakami, working closely together. After the summer project ended, Archos was completely rewritten by See-Mong Tan, under Roy Campbell's guidance at the University of Illinois. Ce-Kuen Shieh explored an alternative approach to portability.

See-Mong Tan began by completing the port of the Choices operating system to an AT&T 6386 computer. He wrote the disk and console drivers, ported the file system, made it possible to launch applications, and provided support for proxy objects. He also wrote a Datakit switch memory interface. Later, at Illinois, he redid Archos, adding an interface to the Xunet-2 switch.

Sean Dorward worked on the controller kernel; in particular, he was responsible for URP, the Universal Receiver Protocol [9], and the interface to the host. He also rewrote the TDK host line process.

Anand Iyengar designed and tested Gulp, unified the trunk and host line processes, and was largely responsible for the controller software running on Choices. He has since simplified Gulp, remaining true to the spirit of the description in Section 4.

Ce-Kuen Shieh ported TDK itself, rather than reimplementing the process-per-line architecture on top of a portable operating system. He isolating TDK's machine dependencies and made it run under a single process on the UNIX® operating system.

The Archos developers were at Bell Labs, but the development was split between Bell Labs and the University of Illinois. We got a lot of help from Milan Jukl and Bill Marshall of Bell Labs and from Dave Dykstra and Aamod Sane of the University of Illinois.

The experimental controller ran on `beren`, the machine in the top left corner in Fig. 8. The Choices source code remained in Illinois, so compilation was done on `babym`, the machine at the bottom of the figure. Access to `babym` was over a virtual-circuit network, Xunet-1, based on Datakit switches. The node "archos" in the center of the figure, served as both the test switch and as a node on Xunet-1; it was then controlled by the machine `control` on the left in the figure.

The experimental controller was debugged via a serial line between `beren` and another machine called `luthien`.

Experimental host software was tested using `west`, a machine running a local Research version of UNIX; we decided to work with a known version of the operating system. Note that each machine in Fig. 8 ran a different operating system.

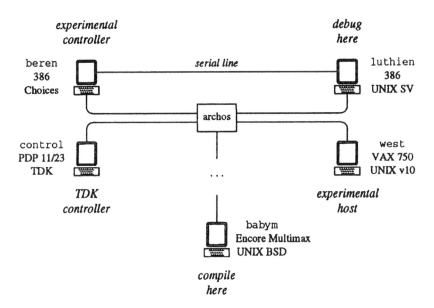

Figure 8. Experimental setup.

References

1. Campbell, R.H., Russo, V., and Johnston, G. Choices: the design of a multiprocessor operating system. In *Proc. USENIX C++ Workshop*, 1987, pp. 109-123.

2. CCITT Draft Recommendation I.361.

3. Cerf, V.G. and Kirstein, P.T. Issues in packet-network interconnection. *Proc. IEEE 66*, 11 (1978), 1386-1408.

4. Condon, J.H., Haley, C.B., McMahon, L.E., and Thompson, K. TPC: tiny phone company. 1978.

5. Fagen, M.D., Ed. *A History of Engineering and Science in the Bell System: The Early Years (1875-1925).* AT&T Bell Laboratories, Available from AT&T Technologies, Indianapolis (1-800-432-6600), 1975.

6. Fraser, A.G. Supervision of hosts and terminals. manuscript, 1982.

7. Fraser, A.G. Towards a universal data transport system. *IEEE J. Selected Areas in Communications SAC-1*, 5 (1983), 803-816.

8. Fraser, A.G., Kalmanek, C.R., Kaplan, A.E., Marshall, W.T., and Restrick, R.C. Xunet 2: a nationwide testbed in high-speed networking. In *INFOCOM*, Florence, Italy, 1992.

9. Fraser, A.G. and Marshall, W.T. Data Transport in a Byte Stream Network. *IEEE J. Selected Areas in Communications 7*, 7 (1989), 1020-1033.

10. Haley, C.B. A method for sharing process stacks in a telephone switch. September 15, 1978.

11. Jensen, E.D. ArchOS. In *ACM SIGOPS Workshop on Operating Systems in Computer Networks*, January 1985.

12. McMahon, L.E. An experimental software organization for a laboratory data switch. In *ICC '81, IEEE Intl. Conference on Communications*, Vol. 2, 1981, pp. 25.4.1-25.4.4.

13. McMahon, L.E. and Marshall, W.T. XUNET Programmer's Manual, Vol. I: Call Processing. April 1988.

14. Murakami, G.J. and Sethi, R. Parallelism as a structuring technique: call processing using the Esterel language. In *Proc. IFIP 92*, Elsevier, Madrid, 1992.

III. Artificial Intelligence, Cognitive Systems, and Man-Machine Communication

What Is Knowledge Representation, and Where Is It Going?

Ronald J. Brachman

AT&T Bell Laboratories
Murray Hill, NJ 07974, USA

Abstract. Since its very beginnings, Artificial Intelligence (AI) has rested on a foundation of formal representation of knowledge. To date, AI
systems have almost universally relied on knowledge bases of symbol-
ically encoded world knowledge and associated formal inference algorithms, which draw implicit conclusions from explicitly represented facts.
While Knowledge Representation – the research area that directly addresses languages for representation and the inferences that go along with
them – has always been important in AI, the 1980's saw a groundswell of
new work in the area, and as we engage the '90's, the field continues to
grow and evolve. In this brief overview, I introduce the area, outlining its
goals and some of its key concerns. I offer some brief historical remarks
and a short description of the evolution of the field over the last dozen
years, and conclude with some directions that will carry the field into
the mid-'90's.

1 Introduction

While Artificial Intelligence (AI) is a very broad area of research, one of the
constants in its 35-year quest for intelligent computational systems has been
its reliance on formal encodings of facts and rules that might allow a machine
to "know" something about its environment, its goals and plans, other agents,
and itself. From its very beginnings, AI research has proceeded (although often
implicitly) on the assumption that the knowledge needed to get along in the
world could be written down in some explicit, symbolic form, and then manipulated formally and used as needed. The incarnations of this hypothesis have
varied over the years, from McCarthy's "Advice Taker," to Newell and Simon's
"Physical Symbol System Hypothesis," to the "Knowledge is Power" slogan of
the expert system years, to Brian Smith's explicit statement of the "Knowledge
Representation Hypothesis" [26]. While potential alternatives such as artificial
neural nets and "reactive" systems (which do not use explicit representations)
have recently become popular, most of AI still rests securely on the foundation
of Knowledge Representation (KR).

While much early AI activity was directly concerned with representation
and reasoning, it was usually hidden within a larger effort aimed at natural
language understanding (NLU), medical diagnosis, robot planning, etc. But in
the last decade or so, KR has crystallized into its own subfield, with its own
special concerns and even its own international conference. These have been

extremely productive years, but as inevitably happens in any field as it matures, the questions and answers of KR have become less accessible to outsiders, and worries have been expressed that the subfield has perhaps lost touch with its original *raison d'être*.

Fortunately, recent activity seems to be addressing these concerns, and the field is now evolving in interesting and promising directions. My goal here is to introduce Knowledge Representation and its key issues, and give some indication of important directions for research in the '90's. While not attempting to define KR, I do want to attempt to give a feel for its central concerns. To that end, I will briefly mention some of the basic questions addressed by the field, and the various dimensions of research it comprises. In order to understand the future, it is important to get a sense of the past; thus I will next briefly outline progress in the field to date. Finally, I will discuss some of the current issues that preoccupy researchers in KR, and the directions they seem to imply for the field over the next few years. While this is by no means a comprehensive survey, I do hope to leave the reader with an impression of the broad scope of KR research and its continuing critical role in Artificial Intelligence.[1]

2 The Field

2.1 Basic Concerns

Interpretations of "knowledge representation" and its role in Artificial Intelligence vary widely, but at heart the idea is a simple and straightforward one: how do we impart knowledge of the world to a robot or other computational system so that, given an appropriate reasoning capacity, that knowledge can be used to allow the system to adapt to and exploit its environment?

The idea of "imparting knowledge" makes the goals of KR somewhat reminiscent of those of database and other information systems. But some key differences between AI's goals and more conventional computer science applications give rise to a very different set of emphases and central research issues. The main differences have to do with the need to deal with incomplete information, and with "commonsense" inferences. In conventional databases, records are completely specified, and if a fact is not explicitly recorded, it is assumed false. This is fine for payroll and airline reservation applications, where we expect all details to be known and all absent listings to be false. But consider how often humans need to act before they have a complete picture of their problem. We can easily begin preparations for a trip without knowing anything about specific flights from one city to another, the detailed physical layout of an airport, or the exact current exchange rate for a foreign currency. We can reason easily with disjunctive facts ("I'm going either to the supermarket or the pharmacy first, depending on traffic"), negative facts ("No one in this room is the culprit, so we had better keep looking for the guilty person"), quantified facts ("There will be at least 9

---

[1] This paper borrows substantially from an invited lecture and paper in the Eighth National Conference on Artificial Intelligence (AAAI-90) [4].

players available for the game next week, so we can safely schedule it"), and a host of other types of statements giving less than complete information.

When faced with the pervasive incompleteness of real-world information, we are usually able to make assumptions and predictions based on previous experience or just plain "common sense." We can infer that a city is accessible by air by any number of means (or just assume it if it is a major city), which would allow us to begin travel planning. We can predict based on past experience roughly how long it will take to get through customs at a major international airport. We can estimate exchange rates based on a quick glance at the newspaper, etc.

Every day, in virtually all of our activities, we make many even more basic assumptions, e.g., that (unless we've heard otherwise) our office has not been destroyed by earthquake, that someone named "George" is a male, that things persist in their places unless moved, etc. None of these things can be *proven*, yet they are absolutely fundamental to our success in adapting to and exploiting our environment. Commonsense inferences of this sort, and even logical inferences based on incomplete knowledge are far beyond the scope of current database technology. In fact, KR researchers have found that it is surprisingly difficult to design a reasoning system to make such inferences fast and reliably. Among the main stumbling blocks are finding an appropriate representation formalism and computing conclusions from it efficiently. Solving these problems is the crux of KR.

Thus, the central questions of KR research are these:

- in what form is knowledge to be expressed?
- how can a reasoning mechanism use a limited amount of knowledge to derive as much of the rest (i.e., implicit knowledge) as it needs?
- how can explicit and derived knowledge be used to influence appropriately the behavior of the system?
- what can the system do in the presence of incomplete or noisy information?
- how can the system make reasonable assumptions, and alter its beliefs appropriately when those assumptions fail?
- how can the system actually reason in the face of potentially overwhelming search and inference complexity (e.g., NP-hard or undecidable problems)?

Since most AI systems have explicit knowledge bases (KB) of one form or another, these key issues of representation and reasoning are pervasive. Indeed, almost anything that involves the above issues can be considered work in KR.

2.2 Aspects of the Field

KR has almost always been especially concerned with the design of *forms* for expressing information, ranging from informal memory models to complex formal languages. Among the key technologies that have been widely used, we find production systems, inheritance networks, direct uses of formal logics (first-order predicate logic or its Horn Clause fragment, for example), "procedural" representations, description logics (sometimes called "terminological" or "taxonomic" logics), associational formalisms, and hybrids of these, such as object-centered "frame" representations. Different approaches may be better suited to different problems, but much of KR has proceeded in pursuit of "general-purpose" languages and systems. In many cases, the interest has been in how to represent a fragment of knowledge in a formal structure, without regard for how it will be used.

However, it is now fairly widely held that it is virtually useless to consider a representation without considering the reasoning that is to be done with it. In much of KR the kind of reasoning that will be done is primary, and the structures used to represent the grist for the reasoning mill are secondary. "KR" now clearly stands for "Knowledge Representation and Reasoning." As a result, the study of KR is in general rooted in the study of logics,[2] where formal syntaxes of languages are accompanied by rules of inference and interpretations. This provides a standard for the correctness of an implemented "knowledge representation system"; without the logic, the only meaning of the representation language is the implementation itself. Many different types of reasoning are possible with the same syntax, and much of the concern in the field has been with "extra-logical" manipulations, such as belief revision (how to change what the system "believes" in light of new observations) and learning.

In addition to the above, the field has other sides to it, which provide it with a great richness, but also make it difficult to give a simple characterization. The variety of approaches also means that there are sometimes incomparable or conflicting goals in KR work. Much of it involves the form of knowledge, but increasingly, and appropriately, KR workers are dealing with *content* issues – that is, what is actually *in* the knowledge base rather than just what is its form. Among the other types of research endeavor in KR we see at least the following:

- *foundational mathematics* – KR has developed its own repertoire of complex logics, and has used various theoretical tools to analyze the connections between them as well as the complexity of computing various functions over the representation structures.
- *cognitive science* – one part of KR research is primarily interested in the structure of human thought and its parameters, either for its own sake or in order to design and understand variations on the theme.
- *representing knowledge* – part of KR involves actually producing domain theories. Recent work has been concerned with more general "ontologies" (high-level theories of the structure of the world), axiomatizations that stretch across domains, the production of large, reusable knowledge bases, and issues of knowledge engineering and acquisition.
- *reasoning* – beyond conventional deduction, many forms of domain-independent, commonsense reasoning (nonmonotonic reasoning, learning, etc.) are central to or overlap with KR.
- *technology* – KR researchers build systems to support a wide variety of AI applications. KR systems can include knowledge base management facilities, interface tools, query languages, acquisition tools, etc.

---

[2] This is not to say simply classical first-order predicate logic, but logics in general.

All in all, while the basic idea of "knowledge representation" is simple, the field as a whole is complex and variegated.

3 A Brief History of KR Research

In order to get a sense of KR as it now stands, let us take a brief look at how it has evolved. For a variety of reasons, a reasonable breaking point appears to be roughly around 1980, so I will first summarize the earliest days, and then the most important post-1980 developments.[3]

3.1 The Pioneering Days

In the early days of AI, KR was largely practiced as a subsidiary activity to more problem-specific tasks like NLU; prior to 1975 AI conferences did not even have separate sessions for KR. The roots of the field as we know it can be found in work on problem-solving and language understanding at MIT and CMU in the late 1960's, and emerging work on "semantic networks" at Bolt Beranek & Newman Inc. and elsewhere (graphical network formalisms that primarily facilitated associational processing by path-tracing and marker propagation).

In the 1970's, as AI grew, KR's horizons expanded rapidly. The major body of work seems to have begun in semantic networks, although there were occasional connections with formal logic, and numerous *ad hoc* formalisms. Many new representation languages were invented, although their intended scope and semantics were often unaddressed. At some point, it became generally assumed that KR systems were to be general-purpose support tools for virtually all of AI, and arguments about the superiority of one over another were often made with respect to anecdotal treatment of natural language examples. There were numerous arguments over what role – if any – mathematical logic should play in representing knowledge, and great discussion of whether "procedural" approaches were superior to "declarative" ones (see [16] for a summary of the arguments). These were exciting, pioneering days; there was plenty of territory to be staked out, and as many ways of representing knowledge as there were people interested in the topic. But, in general, KR work was very informal, and often, not terribly well-founded.

An important development in the mid-'70's was Minsky's frame paper [20]. Minsky was concerned with more realistic commonsense reasoning, and his proposals for using prototypes and defaults, complex object descriptions, "differential diagnoses" of situations, etc., invigorated the KR community and led to the development of numerous frame representation systems (although most of them did not really address Minsky's key insights).

Also in the mid-'70's, the lack of semantic accounts of representational formalisms and misunderstandings of the role of logic were also growing concerns

---

[3] See [11] for an extensive but non-homogenized catalogue of the field as of the late '70's; see also [13] and [19]. For a more technical and comprehensive review of the field in the mid-'80's, see [18].

(e.g., see [28] and [16]). Fortunately, towards the end of the decade, things began to sort themselves out, and the calls for treatment of semantics were increasingly heeded. In some cases, frame and semantic net systems were defined in terms of standard logics. In others, predicate logic was used directly as a representation medium. Generally speaking, a more formal approach slowly began to take root.

By 1980, four representational paradigms were ascendant: semantic networks, frames, predicate logic, and production systems (popularized in Expert Systems). A few people were experimenting with approaches that combined pairs of these. Most proposals were still "general purpose," although there were several subareas of KR where reasoning of a specialized sort (e.g., qualitative physics – see below) was primary and representation was tailored to the task. There were even some *de facto* standards emerging in the various frame and network representations, such as composite objects with slots, generalization hierarchies, inheritance of properties, and procedural attachment. Resource-limited processing and meta-description were popular topics. Qualitative physics and other reasoning areas had their own growing communities. And a strange new world of "nonmonotonic reasoning" was beginning to be explored [1; 24].

Despite the beginnings of more widespread formalization and some basic standard apparatus for frame systems, the picture painted by a community-wide survey in 1980 [11] was still one of *ad hoc* methodology and heterogeneity. Most KR groups were building their own systems, which were used only by themselves, and there was still significant disagreement on many fundamental issues.

3.2 The 1980's

Since 1980 many things have changed. The last dozen years have been impressively productive, there is widespread agreement on many issues, and the methodology in the field is now much more uniform. Among the general trends that have characterized KR research over the last twelve years that are almost unanimously perceived as significant (although not uniformly as positive), we have at least the following:

– KR work has become increasingly *technical*. This seems to represent a decline in the kind of loose meta-discussion popular in the 1970's and an increase in interest in getting some real work done. On the other hand, the increase in technical detail has made KR work much harder to comprehend for those not already involved, and has helped draw KR away from the other areas of AI with which it had traditionally been allied (e.g., NLU).
– KR work has also increasingly focused on *theory*; more theorems and proofs than ever before have appeared in recent KR papers and the body of mathematics in support of KR has grown dramatically. A formal semantics is now an obligatory accompaniment of the description of a novel KR system. This upsurge in KR theory has seemingly come at the expense of experimentation and system-building. While the injection of theory and rigor allows us to be able to determine if programs really work and has given us KR systems with precise formal semantics (a clear improvement over work typical

of the pre-1980 era), the pendulum may have swung too far, inadvertently causing a rift between the formalists and those concerned with applications, and causing less and less of the KR literature to have any impact on the rest of AI or on practice.

- The community has moved away from "procedural representations" to a radically *declarative* worldview. KR work has increasingly focused on what our representations say (e.g., about the world) and less on how to control procedures that process them. The field as a whole seems to have warmly embraced classical logic with standard model-theoretic semantics.

- Almost paradoxically, there has been increased focus in the KR community on general types of *reasoning*, shifting from the older concentration on language design to the arena of different types of inference (e.g., temporal, "abductive," "case-based"). This is a good sign, in that the older formalisms could rarely be evaluated because it was never clear what they meant or what inferences they sanctioned.

- Another trend of note is a *concentration* of work in a small set of areas, most notably nonmonotonic reasoning and qualitative reasoning (see below). A look at recent conference proceedings reveals how large a number of people have flocked to a very small set of issues.

Within the context of these more global trends, there have been numerous notable technical developments in KR over the last decade that have given the field its current directions. Here I briefly gloss over some of the more obvious happenings to give a flavor of what caught the fancy of the KR community.

Easily the most noticeable KR area at recent conferences has been that of *"nonmonotonic reasoning"* (NMR), wherein formal approaches are proposed to handle the fact that a great deal of reasoning is based not so much on known facts, but rather on reasonable assumptions.[4] Since information learned at some future time may falsify a default assumption, many commonsense reasoning situations are inherently nonmonotonic. Classical logics are monotonic, in that new facts do not invalidate old conclusions (if T and N are sets of sentences and s is a sentence, $T \models s$ implies $T \cup N \models s$). Thus, new approaches are needed to handle defaults, exceptions, and other nonmonotonic phenomena.

The last dozen years has seen the introduction of numerous formalisms for NMR, including circumscription, Default Logic, autoepistemic logics, conditional logics, and many variants of inheritance systems. Some of these are semantic, or consistency-based systems (e.g., they depend on a certain default being consistent with an entire KB) and some are syntactic (e.g., they depend on paths through a graph). An important insight has been the use of "minimal models" as the semantic basis of many nonmonotonic systems.

Work in NMR has typically been extremely technical, and the field has spent much of its time concentrating on a few specialized problems of limited scale. In addition, most proposed mechanisms have significant computational problems. All told, this has caused many to worry that the contribution of NMR to mainstream AI in the 1980's was relatively minimal.

---

[4] For a more comprehensive introduction to this area, see [12], [15], and [24].

In the '80's there was also tremendous growth in interest in *qualitative reasoning*, usually about continuous physical systems (thus it is usually called "qualitative physics" (QP)) [2; 27]. The work has its roots in work on engineering problem-solving at MIT in the 1970's, Hayes' work on Naive Physics, and in early work on how devices work by Rieger and Grinberg. As with other fields, QP does not have a single coherent view, and people differ on the key goals. But generally, QP is about how physical devices work, including (1) what are appropriate representational primitives for the salient features of devices and their behavior? (2) given a physical artifact and an initial situation, how do we construct a description of how that artifact works? and (3) how do we use this description to perform interesting tasks like diagnosis and design? Most agree that explanations of how things work have qualitative, temporal, and causal components.

While NMR and QP shared the KR limelight in the '80's, they were by no means the only technical activities. A number of other topics with keen interest emerged:

- In the early days of KR, it was relatively uncommon to consider including *probabilistic information* in general formalisms. While Bayesian/decision-theoretic approaches were attractive, since they allowed one to maximize expected value even in cases that were not statistically significant, they were problematic because they either required you to assume that everything was conditionally independent or that everything was dependent. In the '80's work on Bayes networks [23] yielded representations that could express partial dependence and partial independence. This allowed one to tackle large-scale decision problems from a formal probabilistic perspective, and it should have some important practical implications.
- By the mid-'80's, combining multiple types of representation into *hybrid systems* became popular. In a division of representational labor, specialized subsystems stitched together might provide the power to handle realistic domains without forcing a single uniform, too-powerful logic.[5] Hybrids of various sorts were developed, including several marrying logic and frames; sorted logics grew in popularity, and commercial expert system shells generally offered several loosely integrated types of representation.
- One important criterion for separation of hybrid components distinguished between terminology (knowledge about the meanings of terms, independent of the existence of any objects exemplifying those terms) and assertion (knowledge of contingent facts) [7]. A large family of *"description logic"* systems has developed based on this split, first explored in technical detail in KRYPTON [6] (these systems ultimately attribute their roots to work done on KL-ONE [10] in the late '70's and early '80's). Description logics have been studied and implemented in a number of countries; an extensive body of mathematical results has been built up, and some systems have been used in commercial applications.

---

[5] The problem with logics being "too powerful" is that it may be impossible to actually compute anything with them. See below.

- An influential piece of work that grew out of this work on hybrid representation and description logics involved proofs of the *computational complexity* of the term subsumption inference [8]. The results were surprising: small syntactic changes in a representation language can lead to dramatic changes in inference complexity (a seemingly insignificant addition to a simple language caused the basic inference problem to go from polynomial to exponential complexity [assuming $P \neq NP$]). There soon followed a large number of analyses of the complexity of reasoning with various related term-subsumption languages, as well as complexity results for abductive reasoning, default inheritance, etc.

- Another important thread in the '80's was the attempt to reason based on catalogues of past experience, appropriately indexed. By drawing analogies to the current situation, a *case-based reasoning* system may be able to reuse or revise a previously stored solution. This work has looked at memory structures for case-based reasoning in general and in legal argumentation, medical diagnosis, etc.

- In the '80's we began to see the rise of projects developing *very large knowledge bases*, for example, the CYC project [17], which is attempting to encode millions of fragments of "consensus reality" in an encyclopedic knowledge base. Such projects have begun to raise a host of issues previously unaddressed, simply because of their magnitude. More generally, with the contemplation of significant investment of time and energy into single KB's, concern has begun to develop about the reusability of KB's, knowledge base management issues, general issues of "ontology," and even standards for representation languages. One community-wide effort is exploring the possibility of developing an "interlingua" that could be used to share KB's from one project to another, even if the projects used different KR languages [14].

- There were a number of other topics pursued rather vigorously by the KR community, among them truth-maintenance systems, temporal reasoning, "model-based" reasoning, abductive reasoning (reasoning to best explanation), "vivid" reasoning (which involves compressing knowledge to simple, database-like forms from which inference can be reduced to fast retrieval), reasoning about mental systems (including intensionality, goals and commitments, explicit and implicit belief, and combining evidence), and continued and expanding work on a few network representation systems.

- A final intriguing development of the 1980's was the beginning of exploration of *connections to other fields*, including decision theory, database theory, control theory, and economics.

Beyond its own technical progress, KR benefited from the commercialization of AI in the 1980's. It began to have an impact on the "real world" via Expert System shells sold to the public and used in commercial applications. While the KR technology that supported most commercial Expert Systems work was somewhat simple and had been developed long before, some of the larger shells included multiple representational components (typically rules, frames, and some logical representation). With rule-based programming becoming an acceptable alternative – not to mention the widespread use of logic programming (which bears some relationship to KR) – KR made its way into the mainstream of technology.[6]

4 A 1990 Assessment

Despite the somewhat oversimplified nature of the above comments, it should be clear that KR has evolved extensively since the early days of the field. As of two years ago, at least, work was substantially more formal and rigorous than it was prior to 1980, fewer implemented systems were being discussed, and a small number of issues had absorbed great attention. In the 1980's, the field moved to center stage in AI, owing to a number of factors, such as conference "best papers," journal special issues, eye-catching problems and projects, widespread use of Expert System shells, and a dedicated international conference.

But at the end of the '80's, shadowing the accomplishments and vigor of the field, was a sense of concern. In 1990, in my AAAI-90 talk on "The Future of Knowledge Representation," I pointed out some fairly widespread worries about KR and the potential degradation of its contribution to the rest of AI. For example, many people had begun to feel that the emphasis on formal logic had gone too far, and that important experimental work was being squeezed out by increasingly ethereal theoretical concerns. Much of the work being done exhibited little regard for realistic problems: more theorems were being proved, but it seemed to many that they were less and less interesting or relevant to the real world. In general, as KR focused more on self-generated technical problems, it seemed to move farther from the rest of AI that it was originally intended to support. In 1990, the question of the relevance and future of KR research was an oft-discussed one amongst both KR researchers and concerned outsiders.

5 Where Are We Going?

While the research area of Knowledge Representation has not changed radically since 1990, there are strong signs that the field is awakening to those challenges voiced two years ago. There are some noticeable shifts in interest in the field that bode well for the next few years, such as a re-awakening concern for system-building and serious experimentation, and growing attention to ways to reason given real-world computational constraints. The 1992 version of the international KR conference [22] has emphasized the real-world impact of KR

---

[6] Another development of importance for KR was the resurrection of interest in "connectionist" architectures, some forms of which directly contradict explicit symbolic representation in their basic assumptions. We do not have time to explore the complexities of the issues raised by neural nets and other non-symbolic architectures, but in general, the jury is still out. It also appears that something important might be gained from synergy between connectionist approaches and more traditional symbolic approaches.

ideas and importance of experimentation as a complement to theoretical work. And a recent IFIP workshop brought together researchers from core KR and from qualitative reasoning with the express purpose of bridging the gap between producers of KR technology and one set of consumers.

With these promising general directions in mind, let us take a quick look at some of the trends and interests that are likely to continue to carry us through the next few years. Please bear in mind that anything resembling a prediction is of necessity speculative.

Logic, rigor, and theory. The emphasis on rigor in KR will probably continue, and all told, this is a positive trend. Despite disgruntlement in some circles it is also likely that the declarative, "logicist" program will continue to dominate, although we might see a procedural backlash of some sort, and serious discussion of the role that intended use plays in the form of knowledge. However, there does seem to be a growing appreciation of the fact that the well-trodden areas (e.g., in NMR) are at a point of diminishing theoretical returns. An exciting change seems to be increased interest in testing ideas against the real world and more serious experimentation (e.g., see [21]).

Task-specific representations. It seems that KR specialists are reacquainting themselves with the broader tasks of AI (e.g., planning, NLU, model-based diagnosis), and this will lead to more task- and problem-oriented KR ideas, rather than the increasingly detached, totally general approaches of the past. For example, an extensive DARPA-sponsored initiative on planning is bringing together planning and KR people to develop a state-of-the-art KR language specifically geared to planning applications. In another direction, we should begin to see the viability of extensible KR systems that can be tailored to specific tasks or domains (e.g., see [3]).

Computational tractability. In the 1980's there was growing interest in at least formal measures of computational complexity in KR systems. This more academic approach now appears to be blossoming into attempts to take very seriously real-world constraints on the tractability of inference. People are beginning to realize that if something doesn't work *fast*, it doesn't really work at all. The concern with realistic reasoning manifests itself in numerous ways, including attempts to find approximate reasoning methods that work quickly, judicious use of incomplete algorithms, transformation of knowledge bases from general to specialized forms for which fast procedures exist, attempts to do very quick reasoning on "obvious" subproblems, and niche uses of limited languages. A recent AAAI workshop on tractable reasoning indicated that this is an up-and-coming topic in KR.

More practical efforts. The concern with realistic performance is just one side of an encouraging general trend hinted at above. Numerous KR people really want to see their systems used, and are pushing their efforts to be more responsive to potential consumers. Case-based reasoning has become a realistic approach to some commercial problems. Some description logic systems (e.g., CLASSIC, see [5]) are now being used in commercial products. One corollary to this activity is that there will be more pressure on KR-based approaches to be truly competitive with conventional approaches (e.g., combinatorial optimization algorithms). No longer will it be helpful just to advertise that a system embodies an "AI technique" – the techniques will have to stand on their own convincing performance. The AI/KR community will probably wake up to the fact that practitioners in other fields will not really listen unless they can be shown definitively that your system can perform robustly and well on key problems.

Nonmonotonic reasoning. Intuitions about the meaning of nonmonotonicity and its different incarnations have become better identified in recent years. Since so much work in NMR has become incremental progress on relatively technical problems, the excitement has died down a bit, and the NMR community is becoming more realistic. Computational reality is now more of a concern, with energy now being directed at ways to make NMR more practical and more mainstream.

Large KB's. Very large knowledge-based systems will soon be commonly upon us. With this, issues that have occupied the database world will come to concern KR developers, although perhaps complicated in interesting ways by the logical interpretation of KR languages. Among such concerns, we might see sharing of KB's (see below), persistent object stores, dealing with outdated or suspect information, "drift" of terminology, and infrastructure issues such as ownership and commercial value of represented information. Incremental revision will be of paramount importance, since KB's will exist over longer periods of time. Indeed, the entire area of "knowledge base management" is already becoming increasingly important, highlighting issues of version control, global integrity of KB's, principles of KB organization, and belief revision. Knowledge acquisition will of necessity move closer to mainstream KR – with very large knowledge bases, automatic and semi-automatic acquisition will become the *sine qua non* of KB's. Issues of "ontology" will be among the most important and most discussed about in the next few years. How to build an appropriate "upper model" – the topmost levels of a large hierarchy of commonsense knowledge, how to integrate parts created by different people, and how to control revisions will be important considerations. Finally, much will be learned from trying to build CYC, although serious obstacles (e.g., difficulty of timely inference in a large enough KB, reconciliation of pieces built by different authors, and general skepticism of the utility of a KB built without a particular use in mind) may prevent it from being anything other than an exciting first experiment.

Knowledge base sharing. Serious work is now underway on understanding how to share knowledge amongst projects and even between systems implementing very different representation languages. As the investment in large knowledge bases increases over the next few years, the incentive to reuse knowledge rather than re-represent it anew will also grow. At this point a fairly comprehensive "interlingua" language has been specified [14], with the hope being that specific representations could be translated into such an interlingua and then translated out into a completely different representation language.

KR standards. A related issue is that of standards. As attempts are made to share or reuse knowledge bases, standardization of at least interfaces to KB's will grow in importance. There are also some incipient efforts trying to invent standard knowledge representation languages. These may have some success when limited to specific subfields or problem areas, and when enough experience has already been gained to allow wise choices based on proven utility. But I also suspect that, because of the diversity of approaches in the field and current lack of incentives for standardizing, the results of any general standards work will be less than ideal for the foreseeable future.

KR to the people. It is probable that by the millennium "knowledge systems" will be a common commercial concept. This has important implications for the future of KR. Among other things, KR components will increasingly find themselves in the hands of non-experts, raising a new set of issues, such as how to make KR systems more usable, how to explain reasoning in terms comprehensible to normal human beings, how to allow visualization of knowledge in a large KB, and how to facilitate KB maintenance by non-experts. Indeed, maintenance is absolutely critical if KR tools are to be of any use in commercially significant software projects.

Probability and statistics. Two years ago, I predicted that work on statistical and probability-based reasoning would become more closely associated with mainstream KR. Now, I am not so sure. While challenges to deductive reasoning such as the need to handle noisy data, frequency information (e.g., in learning), and "fuzzy" concepts are still important, much work on reasoning with uncertainty seems caught up with itself in the way that nonmonotonic reasoning had become in the latter half of the 1980's. The issues are still very important, but little impact on mainstream AI has been felt in the last two years. However, in the long run, I do think we will see some profound and impressive results from the more statistics-oriented view of KR.[7]

Knowledge representation and machine learning. Research on machine learning in AI has been flourishing for a number of years, but only recently have the representations used for problems and hypotheses begun to approximate the complexity of those used in KR research. I think we can expect to see more serious collaborations between the two fields in the near future, seriously extending the range of problems that learning techniques can handle.

6   Conclusion

Knowledge Representation has occupied a central place in Artificial Intelligence since its very beginnings. Although it originally played a relatively hidden, supporting role, in the last dozen years it has taken center stage, evoking strong independent interest in important and difficult technical problems, and developing its own specialist community. The sharpening of interests in KR has been something of a double-edged sword. Work has become more rigorous, deeper, and built more on previous results than ever before. But it has also in part

---

[7] One intriguing possibility is that the statistical nature of many real-world phenomena may lead to fast inference procedures with a stochastic element [25].

meandered away from the mainstream of AI that it was originally intended to support.

Fortunately, we now see signs that KR researchers are paying more attention to issues of practicality, impact, and support for specific tasks that will help the area make a key contribution to AI in the future. Given that KR has developed a substantial body of knowledge and machinery, and has recently begun to make an impact on the "real world," the next few years promise exciting developments, both for students of representation and reasoning and Artificial Intelligence in general.

References

1. D. G. Bobrow, editor. Special Issue on Non-Monotonic Logic. *Artificial Intelligence*, 13(1–2), April 1980.
2. D. G. Bobrow, editor. Special Volume on Qualitative Reasoning about Physical Systems. *Artificial Intelligence*, 24(1–3), December 1984.
3. A. Borgida and R. Brachman. Customizable classification inference in the ProtoDL description management system. In *Proc. First International Conference on Information and Knowledge Management (CIKM-92)*, Baltimore, MD, November 1992.
4. R. J. Brachman. The future of knowledge representation. In *Proc. AAAI-90*, pages 1082–1092, Boston, MA, July 1990.
5. R. J. Brachman. 'Reducing' CLASSIC to practice: Knowledge representation theory meets reality. In Nebel et al. [22].
6. R. J. Brachman, R. E. Fikes, and H. J. Levesque. KRYPTON: A functional approach to knowledge representation. *IEEE Computer*, 16(10):67–73, October 1983.
7. R. J. Brachman and H. J. Levesque. Competence in knowledge representation. In *Proc. AAAI-82*, pages 189–192, Pittsburgh, PA, August 1982.
8. R. J. Brachman and H. J. Levesque. The tractability of subsumption in frame-based description languages. In *Proc. AAAI-84*, pages 34–37, Austin, TX, August 1984.
9. R. J. Brachman and H. J. Levesque, editors. *Readings in Knowledge Representation*. Morgan Kaufmann, San Mateo, CA, 1985.
10. R. J. Brachman and J. G. Schmolze. An overview of the KL-ONE knowledge representation system. *Cognitive Science*, 9(2):171–216, April–June 1985.
11. R. J. Brachman and B. C. Smith. Special Issue on Knowledge Representation. *SIGART Newsletter*, 70, February 1980.
12. D. W. Etherington. *Reasoning with Incomplete Information*. Pitman, London, 1988.
13. N. V. Findler, editor. *Associative Networks: Representation and Use of Knowledge by Computers*. Academic Press, New York, 1979.
14. M. R. Genesereth, R. E. Fikes, and et al. Knowledge interchange format, version 3.0 reference manual. Technical Report Logic-92-1, Computer Science Department, Stanford University, 1992.
15. M. L. Ginsberg, editor. *Readings in Nonmonotonic Reasoning*. Morgan Kaufmann, San Mateo, CA, 1987.
16. P. J. Hayes. In defence of logic. In *Proc. IJCAI-77*, pages 559–565, Cambridge, MA, August 1977.

17. D. B. Lenat and R. V. Guha. *Building Large Knowledge-Based Systems*. Addison-Wesley, Reading, MA, 1990.
18. H. J. Levesque. Knowledge representation and reasoning. In *Annual Review of Computer Science, Volume 1*, pages 255–287. Annual Reviews Inc., Palo Alto, CA, 1986.
19. D. V. McDermott. The last survey of representation of knowledge. In *Proceedings AISB/GI 1978*, pages 206–221, 1978.
20. M. Minsky. A framework for representing knowledge. In P. H. Winston, editor, *The Psychology of Computer Vision*, pages 211–277. McGraw-Hill, New York, 1975. Also in [9].
21. D. Mitchell, B. Selman, and H. Levesque. Hard and easy distributions of SAT problems. In *Proc. AAAI-92*, pages 459–465, San Jose, CA, July 1992.
22. B. Nebel, C. Rich, and W. Swartout, editors. *Principles of Knowledge Representation and Reasoning: Proceedings of the Third International Conference (KR92)*, Cambridge, MA, October 1992. Morgan Kaufmann.
23. J. Pearl. *Probabilistic Reasoning in Intelligent Systems: Networks of Plausible Inference*. Morgan Kaufmann, San Mateo, CA, 1988.
24. R. Reiter. Nonmonotonic reasoning. In *Annual Review of Computer Science, Volume 2*, pages 147–186. Annual Reviews Inc., Palo Alto, CA, 1987.
25. B. Selman, H. Levesque, and D. Mitchell. A new method for solving hard satisfiability problems. In *Proc. AAAI-92*, pages 440–446, San Jose, CA, July 1992.
26. B. C. Smith. Reflection and semantics in a procedural language. Technical Report MIT/LCS/TR-272, Laboratory for Computer Science, Massachusetts Institute of Technology, January 1982.
27. D. S. Weld and J. de Kleer, editors. *Readings in Qualitative Reasoning about Physical Systems*. Morgan Kaufmann, San Mateo, CA, 1990.
28. W. A. Woods. What's in a link: Foundations for semantic networks. In D. G. Bobrow and A. M. Collins, editors, *Representation and Understanding: Studies in Cognitive Science*, pages 35–82. Academic Press, New York, 1975. Also in [9].

Creating a Design Science of Human-Computer Interaction

John M. Carroll

Computer Science Department
IBM Thomas J. Watson Research Center
Box 704, Yorktown Heights, NY 10598 U.S.A.

Abstract. An increasingly prominent task of computer science is to support the analysis and design of computers as things to learn from, as tools to use in one's work, as media for interacting with other people. Human-Computer Interaction (HCI) is the speciality area that addresses this task. Through the past two decades, HCI has pursued a broad and ambitious scientific agenda, progressively integrating its research concerns with the contexts of system development and use. This has created an unprecedented opportunity to manage the emergence of new technology so as to support socially responsive objectives.

1 Introduction

HCI (Human-Computer Interaction) has emerged relatively recently as a focal area of computer science research and development. Some of the reasons for this are straightforwardly technical: HCI has evoked many difficult problems and elegant solutions (for example, in work on direct manipulation, user interface management systems, task oriented help and instruction). Other reasons for this are broadly cultural: the province of HCI is the view people have of computing technology and the impact that technology has on their lives, in that sense it is the visible part of computer science. The most recent reasons are commercial: as the underlying technologies of computing become commodities, inscribed on generic chips, the non-commodity value of computer products resides in applications and user interfaces, that is, in HCI.

The area has evolved rapidly in the past two decades as it has struggled to define for itself intellectual substance and practical technique, that is to say, both a basis in science and a utility in system and software development. In this essay I sketch the history of HCI as four approaches to creating a design science of HCI. Though this "history" must of course largely be a construction of the historian, I think the exercise is justified as a means of fathoming not merely what the field was or has been, but what is it now and what it may become.

2 Precursor: Software Psychology

It is unavoidably unfair to look back in judgment at earlier work; what is obvious today is obvious *because* prior work advanced and clarified things. Yet we must look back if we wish to understand and evaluate where a field has been and where it might be going. The work that constitutes the historical foundation for current HCI, was called "software psychology" in the 1970s; it is well summarized in Ben Shneiderman's 1980 book of that title [31].

This work had two distinctive methodological axioms: First, it assumed the validity of a received view of what system and software development is like, namely, the so-called waterfall model of top-down decomposition and discretely sequenced stages with well-specified interfaces [28]. Second, it assumed that there were two central roles for psychology to play within this context: (a) to produce general descriptions of humans interacting with systems and software, descriptions which could be compiled into "guidelines" to be used by developers and (b) to directly verify the usability of systems and software as (or more typically, after) they were developed.

These axioms proved to be problematic. The waterfall idealization of design turned out to be an unnatural and unwanted imposition on designers (e.g., [2]). It is only ever observed in severely regimented work environments and probably only makes sense as a crude management tool for very large-scale projects. As computer research and development diversified in the 1970s and 1980s, small and distributed personal work organizations became increasingly commonplace.

The roles assumed for software psychologists were also problematic. The two envisioned roles became a division of labor: research people (mainly in universities) worked on getting general descriptions of users and on framing their implications as guidelines; human factors specialists tried to apply these guidelines. This division did not work particularly well. From the standpoint of its practical goals, the research of this period tended to overgeneralize from seriously unrepresentative situations (undergraduates standing in for programmers, 50-line programs standing in for business systems, and teletypes standing in for display tubes). In order to obtain statistically reliable results, researchers often ended up studying outrageous contrasts (organized versus disorganized menus, structured versus scrambled code). The researchers understood little about the use and non-use of guidelines and often produced nearly vacuous advice.

Psychologists and others playing the human factors specialist role were frustrated trying to use and encourage use of these guidelines. They were frustrated in their other role of verifying the usability of finished systems, both because the methodological tools they had (chiefly the direct-contrast experiment that focuses on showing that a difference exists among alternatives) were too weak and too uninformative to allow them to serve as anything more than gatekeepers. Human factors people were often seen merely as a sort of bureaucratic assurance hurdle standing in the way of heroic developers. And they often were.

The origins of HCI in software psychology posed two problems that became touchstones for the field during the 1980s. One of these was the problem of determining what design and development work is really like and understanding how it might be supported. If what's going on is not an orderly waterfall from requirements to assurance, what is it and can it be improved? The other problem was that of determining what content the field of psychology, and perhaps social science more broadly, might have to offer HCI and how that content could best be cultivated and applied in the development context.

3 Iterative development

Starting in the 1970s, empirical studies of the design process began to paint a picture that to some extent explained *why* the waterfall model was difficult to practice. Designers, as observed in these studies, appear to be very locally driven; they may work on a single requirement at a time, embody it in a scenario of user interaction to understand it, reason about, address it, and test the partial solution — all perhaps quite incompletely — then finally move on to consider other requirements. Through the course of this piecemeal process, they sometimes radically reformulate goals and constraints. But this is not a chaos; it is a highly involuted, highly structured process of decomposing problems of unbounded complexity into smaller subproblems that can be concretely, albeit partially, resolved in a set of subsolutions that iteratively constrain design work of broader scope (e.g., [11, 22]).

With such a description of design work in hand one can consider approaches to supporting design, alternatives to the waterfall approach of imposing a rational structure on the activity. One can try to support the observed patterns of activity. One inspiration for this came from the work of the great industrial designer Henry Dreyfuss who had pioneered an empirical approach in the 1940s [12]. Dreyfuss' approach institutionalizes an accommodation to designers' propensity for concrete, incremental reasoning and testing. It incorporates four central ideas: (1) early prototyping with (2) the involvement of real users, (3) introduction of new functions through familiar "survival forms," and (4) many cycles of design iteration.

A typical example is Dreyfuss' design work on airplane interiors for Lockheed (pp. 70-71, 129-135). Dreyfuss sent two associates back and forth across the U.S. on commercial flights to inventory passenger experiences. They found that passengers were often baffled by design details like water taps that were unnecessarily novel (p. 71); they were impressed that people wanted to think of airplane seats as armchairs not as "devices" (though increasingly they are and will be devices, pp. 131-132). Initial designs were prototyped in a Manhattan warehouse and a full flight of "passengers" were hired to occupy the mock-up for 10 hours: to store carry-on luggage, to eat meals, to use lavatories. This concretized requirements for seating, storage space, lavatory-door latches, and so forth — and permitted low-cost, iterative reworking of the original designs.

Through the decade of the 1980s, the inevitability of an empirical orientation toward system and software design rapidly evolved from a somewhat revolutionary perspective [16] to an establishment view. It provided early and critical motivation and direction for research on user interface management systems [34], and it transformed "rapid prototyping" into a necessary requirement for system development methodologies [35, 36].

Empirical design requires new management techniques to identify stopping criteria. One technique for providing such criteria is to measure aspects of user performance throughout the development process and to stop design iterations when improvement becomes asymptotic [15]. Another technique is to incorporate users into design discussion throughout prototype development, and to publicly negotiate design goals and criteria on-goingly [18]. A third is to codify measurable usability specifications as part of specifying the design [7]. All of these can be used together [37].

Recent work on empirical design has adapted Michael Scriven's [29] classic analysis of curriculum evaluation, and his concept of "mediated evaluation," integrating analytic evaluation of a design's structure (what Scriven called "intrinsic evaluation") with empirical evaluation of its efficacy (what he called "pay-off evaluation"). Building an intrinsic evaluation, a rich analysis of a prototype's implicit design goals and its positions on inherent tradeoffs among goals, facilitates systematic attributions from pay-off evaluation of user experience and/or performance to specific design features [e.g., 9, 20].

In a word, the last two decades have significantly clarified what actual design practice is like, and have identified a range of techniques for managing this practice to produce more useful and usable systems.

4 Analytic models

The second problem-area bequeathed to modern HCI by earlier work in software psychology was that of identifying robust social scientific content that could guide system development. The first significant work was efficiency modeling, systematically analyzing critical human performance parameters like keystrokes [3]. This work was broadly grounded both in the then-current "information processing" approach to cognitive science and in traditional human factors interests in metrics. Initially, it was argued that these models provided a comprehensive paradigm for scientifically-grounded HCI design ([24] but cf. [6]). Their actual impact has been more narrow, though they have been usefully applied in domains where relatively low-level user performance efficiency matters (e.g., modeling telephone operator scripts [17]).

Beginning in the 1980s, efficiency models were supplemented by analytic models addressed to the mapping from commands (and other user interface symbology) to application functions (and other referents). These mapping models sought to characterize the factors that make command languages easier to learn and use (e.g., [4, 27, 32]). Much of this discussion focussed on the notion of consistency, on the fact that the suitability of a command named "pull" depended on the existence of a complementary command named "push" (versus, say, one named "grab"). Consistency turned out to be highly intentional [4], significantly idiosyncratic [14], and even questionable as a general objective in design [19]. Nevertheless, promoting consistency in user interface and application design has become a prominent practical issue [25], and these models are the foundation for our current understanding of it.

Mapping models addressed a broader range of psychological phenomena than efficiency models: they considered performance beyond keystroke-level parameters and they considered learning — at least to the extent of learning times and characteristic learning difficulties. Since the mid-1980s, analytic modeling has taken an increasingly comprehensive view of use and usability. For example, naturalistic studies of new users' learning problems highlighted the need to study and to design support for *whole* systems and *whole* user tasks [5]; studies of performance highlighted the need to consider the entire planning-execution-evaluation cycle of user activity [26]; the emergence of open architectures for analytic models highlighted the need to incorporate a variety of social and behavioral factors [1].

Efficiency and mapping considerations are now folded into a matrix of psychological and social factors including attitudes, experiences and feelings of users about computer tools they are to use, work-group coordination of learning and skill, and specific impacts of technologies on the structure and interactions of jobs. The emergence of "contextualist" research [5, 13, 18, 26, 37, 38] helped to legitimize in-depth, qualitative analysis of user activity over significant spans of time, serving goals more significant than solitary selections or command interactions — it better integrated research concerns with contexts of real use. To a considerable extent these trends helped to reform the zeitgeist of cognitive science itself, away from simple "information processing" models and towards a more intellectually ambitious social constructivism grounded in real human activities (e.g., [21, 30, 33, 39]).

The development of work on analytic models in HCI has not been simply a technical shift toward "higher" levels of description. First, what has happened is more accurately seen as a broadening in which more levels of analysis are taken into consideration (though there is urgent need for more systematic integration). But second, this broadening of analytical interests both reflects and has helped to create a far more integral role for HCI in computer science and the computer industry. Through the 1980s, there was growing recognition that the cornerstone of new technology is its suitability for human use. The reasons for this are moral (we are in a position to realize the worst fears of the 19th-century Luddites); they are technical (software and hardware white elephants still abound today); and they are commercial (everything except usefulness to people can, after a few years, be inscribed on a chip). By raising the scope of its analyses and the breadth of its ambitions, HCI has become a premier focus for the future of computer science and technology.

5 Design rationale

The two lines of development in HCI, iterative development and analytic models, are converging, I think, in a new framework for HCI that fully integrates research and development activity. This framework is design rationale; its essence is the broad reification of the design process and its products. Systematizing design rationale supports explicit discussion and debate about what was intended, considered, planned, decided, and accomplished in a project, helping to force out hidden assumptions and dependencies earlier and continuingly. Moreover, codifying a design discourse creates an audit trail from which to draw and save lessons to guide future work. In this sense, design rationale is simultaneously a paradigm for deliberative practice and for action science [8].

An enormously varied range of design rationale work is underway in HCI today (e.g., [23]). Two current projects in the Watson Research Center illustrate the twin facets of reifying process and reifying product. In one of these, we are building a multimedia design history database. We had observed in prior work that members of design teams sometimes spontaneously construct an oral history of stories and episodes encapsulating and preserving key elements of the vision and development of their work. The oral mode is fundamentally social, and thus can support teambuilding even while it promotes diversity and personal viewpoint; it fosters historical development, that is, the reconstruction of the past to make better sense of the present. We are now collecting such stories in video and building a browsing tool to explore the implications of making the oral history of a design project more easily and systematically available [10].

In another project, we are developing use-oriented vocabularies for representing the products of design, that is, a framework for representing software and systems in terms of the user tasks they restructure. The restructuring of human tasks is the most important impact of computing, and we need better means to talk about these impacts and better control over them. Our approach is to represent a computer as a set of scenarios of use that are supported, enabled or obstructed, and further, to analyze each scenario into a set of causal schemas specifying how features of the system facilitate or impede the scenario. Such representations allow more articulate design discussion and planning for specific interventions. Discussion and analysis can go forward at the relatively coarse grain of scenarios (e.g., a programmer investigating the behavior of a particular user interface component) or at the finer resolution of causal relations constituting the scenarios (e.g., the tradeoffs of example-based documentation in such situations; see [8]).

The emergence of design rationale as a focal area of HCI may be the culmination of prior work on iterative design and analytic models. Iterative design is consistent with the reality of design work, but that alone does not make it a practical paradigm for designing useful and usable systems. Its fundamental problem has always been that without explicit goal and process management, it is indistinguishable from trial-and-error thrashing. Reifying a design history as it occurs creates an object to focus criticism and planning.

Analogously, work on analytic models has provided a rich and diverse conceptual foundation for HCI, but this alone does not give the models real and practical value in guiding design reasoning. In fact, modeling is still largely a form of commentary and description in HCI, not a proactive part of the design process. Reifying the use of an artifact as it is designed creates the kind of abstract understanding that HCI as a science needs to cumulate and develop. And at the same time, it allows social science to directly underwrite design decisions, via the circumstances, tasks, and motives of use.

Nevertheless, many questions remain to be answered about how comprehensive a paradigm design rationale can be for HCI. A key to this is the now-open question of whether building an explicit rationale can actually provide a unifying representation across the broad range of research and development activities: design, evaluation, redesign, training, documentation, maintenance, and science-building. This will be an area of great importance to HCI in the next decade.

6 What have we learned?

I have tried to stress two major themes in this essay: first, that significant progress has been made on the two touchstone issues bequeathed to modern HCI by pioneering efforts in software psychology during the 1970s; and second, that new possibilities for consolidating and integrating this progress are crystallizing now under the banner of design rationale.

We now have an accurate understanding of the nature of system and software design work as practiced. This is not to say we are able to effectively support design work, but rather that — in my opinion — we are ready to pose and address the right questions in order to achieve that. We have a range of robust and appropriate methodological abstractions. Again, this is not to say that the science base we need is there now, but I believe we have developed a sufficiently broad understanding of what is involved to make steady and real progress on building a science of HCI. My suggestion is that progress in understanding the nature of design and development work and in determining what cognitive and social science abstractions can best be pursued and applied in such work can be leveraged in both its rate and its relevance by better integration.

It is exciting to see that the emerging role of social and cognitive science in computer science and the computer industry is *far more* diverse, pervasive and critical than imagined in the 1970s. As it has turned out, that role was not to support a received view of design, but to help overturn it, and to help clarify the real nature of design. Neither was that role merely to apply academic psychology as human factors assurance; it was indeed to play a part in driving the evolution of social and cognitive science, and the recognition that computers can be deliberately designed to facilitate human activity and experience only when social and cognitive requirements drive the design process throughout.

There is unprecedented potential for interdisciplinary synergy here: social science has always borne the vision of what human society might become, but it has chronically lacked the means to do anything substantially constructive; computer science — quite the converse — cannot avoid causing substantial social restructuring. An integrated and effective HCI can be a turning point in both disciplines, and, perhaps, in human history.

Acknowledgements

I am grateful to Jürgen Koenenmann-Belliveau, Dan Diaper, Bob Mack, Dianne Murray, Mary Beth Rosson and Kevin Singley for comments on drafts of this essay.

References

1. P.J. Barnard: Applying cognitive theory: Human-computer interaction as a case study. Hillsdale, NJ: Erlbaum, in preparation

2. F.P. Brooks: The mythical man-month. Reading, MA: Addison-Wesley, 1975

3. S.K. Card, T.P. Moran, A. Newell: The psychology of human-computer interaction. Hillsdale, NJ: Erlbaum, 1983

4. J.M. Carroll: What's in a name? An essay in the psychology of reference. New York: W.H. Freeman, 1985

5. J. M. Carroll: The Nurnberg Funnel: Designing minimalist instruction for practical computer skill. Cambridge, MA: M.I.T. Press, 1990

6. J.M. Carroll, R.L. Campbell: Softening up hard science: Reply to Newell and Card. Human-Computer Interaction, 2, 227-249, 1986

7. J.M. Carroll, M.B. Rosson: Usability specifications as a tool in iterative development. In H.R. Hartson (Ed.) Advances in Human-Computer Interaction. Norwood, NJ: Ablex, 1985, pp. 1-28

8. J.M. Carroll, M.B. Rosson: Getting around the task-artifact cycle: How to make claims and design by scenario. ACM Transactions on Information Systems, 10/2, 181-212, 1992

9. J.M. Carroll, M.K. Singley, M.B. Rosson: Integrating theory development with design evaluation. Behaviour and Information Technology, 11, 1992 in press

10. J.M. Carroll, M. Van Deusen, J. Karat, S. Alpert, M.B. Rosson: Raison d'Etre: Embodying design history and rationale in hypermedia folklore. IBM Research Report, 1992

11. B. Curtis, H. Krasner, N. Iscoe: A field study of the software design process for large systems. Communications of the ACM, 31, 1268-1287, 1988

12. H. Dreyfuss: Designing for people. New York: Simon and Schuster, 1955

13. P. Ehn: Work-oriented design of computer artifacts. Hillsdale, NJ: Erlbaum, 1989

14. G. Furnas, T.K. Landauer, L. Gomez, S. Dumais: Statistical semantics: Analysis of the potential performance of keyword information systems. Bell System Technical Journal, 62, 1753-1806, 1983

15. M. Good, T.M. Spine, J. Whiteside, P. George: User-derived impact analysis as a tool for usability engineering. CHI'86, Conference on Human Factors in Computing Systems. (Boston, April 13-17). New York: ACM, pp. 241-246, 1986

16. J.D. Gould, S.J. Boies: Human factors challenges in creating a principal support office system — The speech filing approach. ACM Transactions on Office Information Systems, 1, 273-298, 1983

17. W.D. Gray, B.E. John, M.E. Atwood: The precis of project Ernestine, or, An overview of a validation of GOMS. CHI'92 Conference on Human Factors in Computing Systems. Monterrey, California, May 3-7, 1992, pp. 307-312

18. J. Greenbaum, M. Kyng: Design at work: Cooperative design of computer systems. Hillsdale, NJ: Erlbaum, 1991

19. J. Grudin: The case against user interface consistency. Communications of the ACM, 32, 1164-1173, 1989

20. T.K. Landauer: Let's get real: A position paper on the role of cognitive psychology in the design of humanly useful and usable systems. In J.M. Carroll (Ed.), Designing interaction: Psychology at the human-computer interface. New York: Cambridge University Press, 1991, pp. 60-73

21. J. Lave: Cognition in practice: Mind, mathematics, and culture. New York: Cambridge University Press, 1988

22. A. Malhotra, J.C. Thomas, J.M. Carroll, L.A. Miller: Cognitive processes in design. International Journal of Man-Machine Interaction, 12, 119-140, 1980

23. T.P. Moran, J.M. Carroll (Eds.): Design rationale. Hillsdale, NJ: Erlbaum, in press

24. A. Newell, S.K. Card: The prospects for psychological science in human-computer interaction. Human-Computer Interaction, 1, 209-242, 1985

25. J. Nielsen (Ed.): Coordinating user interfaces for consistency. New York: Academic Press, 1989

26. D.A. Norman, S.W. Draper: User centered system design. Hillsdale, NJ: Erlbaum, 1986

27. S.J. Payne, T.R.G. Green: Task-Action Grammars: The model and its developments. In D. Diaper (Ed.), Task analysis for human-computer interaction. Chichester: Ellis Horwood, 1989, pp. 75-107

28. W.W. Royce: Managing the development of large software systems. Concepts and techniques. Proceedings of WESTCON, August 1970

29. M. Scriven: The methodology of evaluation. In R. Tyler, R. Gagne, & M. Scriven (Eds.), Perspectives of curriculum evaluation. Chicago: Rand McNally, 1967, pp. 39-83

30. D.A. Schön: The reflective practitioner: How professionals think in action. New York: Basic Books, 1983

31. B. Shneiderman: Software psychology: Human factors in computer and information systems. Cambridge, MA: Winthrop, 1980

32. B. Shneiderman: Direct manipulation: A step beyond programming languages. IEEE Computer, August 1983, 57-62

33. L.A. Suchman: Plans and situated actions: The problem of human-machine communication. New York: Cambridge University Press, 1987

34. P.P. Tanner, W.A.S. Buxton: Some issues in future user interface management system (UIMS) development. In G.E. Pfaff (Ed.), User interface management systems: Proceedings of the workshop on user interface management systems held in Seeheim, FRG, November 1-3, 1983. New York: Springer Verlag, 1985, pp. 67-79

35. A.I. Wasserman, D.T. Shewmake: Rapid prototyping of interactive information systems. ACM Software Engineering Notes, 7, 171-180, 1982

36. A.I. Wasserman, P.A. Pircher, D.T. Shewmake, M.L. Kersten: Developing interactive information systems with the user software engineering methodology. IEEE Transactions on Software Engineering, SE-12(2), 326-345, 1986

37. J. Whiteside, J. Bennett, K. Holtzblatt: Usability engineering: Our experience and evolution. In M. Helander (Ed.), Handbook of Human-Computer Interaction, Amsterdam: North-Holland, 1988, pp. 791-817

38. J. Whiteside and D. Wixon: Improving human-computer interaction — a quest for cognitive science. In J.M. Carroll (Ed.), Interfacing thought: Cognitive aspects of human-computer interaction. Cambridge, MA: Bradford/MIT Press, 1987, pp. 337-352

39. T. Winograd, F. Flores: Understanding computers and cognition: A new foundation for design. Norwood, NJ: Ablex, 1986

IV. Robotics, Image and Vision

Sensing Robots

Michael Brady,
Robotics Research Group
Department of Engineering Science
University of Oxford

1   Introduction

Robots have become a key component of computer-integrated manufacturing systems, for a number of reasons: (i) they are increasingly *cost effective*: the tumbling cost of electronics has meant that robot arms are fifty times more powerful now than they were thirty years ago, yet they have risen in cost at only one quarter the rate at which labour has; (ii) they can work effectively in *hostile environments* including forges, spray paint shops, and in nuclear installations; but, most importantly, (iii) they produce *consistent, high quality products*, particularly cars and consumer electronics. In the past, the major applications have been in automating existing processes, such as forging, die casting, spot welding, and spray painting. Currently, the major growth is in assembly robots, particularly in electronics, though the greatest potential is the development of entirely new products, particularly mechatronic devices. Industrial robots vary in shape, size, and strength and have evolved for specific applications. However, they overwhelmingly share one characteristic: they do not sense the world in which they operate. This implies that they cannot tolerate uncertainty such as a mismatch between the real world and their internal model of it. In particular, they cannot deal with unexpected events, such as dropping a part. In practise, insensate robots demand expensive fixturing, reducing their cost effectiveness. Worse, it limits the applications to which they have to date been put.

Robotics research, such as the examples given in this paper, aims primarily to provide robot structures with sensors to enable them to solve reliably new classes of problems. The resulting systems continuously operate according to sense-process-act cycles, though practical systems comprise multiple control loops operating at different rates. Many sensors have been investigated, including sonar, infrared, radar, vision, proximity, touch, and force. They are chosen for a particular application according to their cost, signal-to-noise, and bandwidth. Inevitably, the information provided by any single sensor is uncertain, necessitating control regimes that tame uncertainty, such as Kalman filtering or stochastic optimal control. As well, considerable attention has been paid to schemes for integrating the information provided by different sensors. The real-time demands of practical applications and the bandwidths of sensor processing, particularly vision, necessitate novel computer architectures.

The sensor-based robot systems we describe are:

- a free-ranging robot vehicle (section 3) that uses sonar sensors to detect obstacles encountered along its nominal trajectory, and which can make appropriate detours to avoid them, even if this entails re-planning the entire trajectory;

- a real-time implementation (section 4) of algorithms that can compute the three-dimensional layout of the scene a free ranging vehicle is driving through, and can determine which parts are driveable. The systems work by tracking a set of point features of the image surface ("corners") that need to be extracted from the image sequence accurately and reliably;

- a four-camera system (section 2) developed by Durrant-Whyte and his colleagues (11) to track several targets, typically people, as they move about in a room. The section introduces the Kalman filter that is used in other systems described in the paper. The novelty of the Oxford work is that the equations of the Kalman filter have been completely partitioned, and implemented on a fully decentralised (Transputer based) architecture. The system degrades gracefully in the sense that if one or more of the cameras is unplugged, it continues to track successfully, albeit with increased uncertainty in the positional estimates of the targets;

- a four degree-of-freedom stereo head/eye platform (section 5) that is compact, reliable, relatively cheap, yet fast and accurate. It is intended to be mounted on the AGV described above for visual navigation through narrow gaps amongst moving obstacles.

- a parallel implementation (section 6) of an algorithm that recognises instances of parameterised geometric objects in cluttered scenes and simultaneously determines the position, pose, and parameters of the instance.

2 Decentralised Kalman filtering

This section introduces the Kalman filter and describes an application of it to surveillance. The Kalman filter maintains an estimate of the state of a system and a covariance estimate of its uncertainty. Bar-Shalom and Fortman (1) provide a lucid introduction to the theory of Kalman filtering The application of the Kalman filter to sensor-guided control is used to reduce the discrepancy between the planned and actual states of a vehicle increase, as does the state uncertainty, when no sensor measurements are made, see (8) for more detail and illustrations. Suppose the vehicle senses a planar surface. The uncertainty orthogonal to the wall decreases sharply; but continues to increase in the direction tangential to the wall. If a second wall is sensed, the state uncertainty is sharply reduced.

The Kalman filter has the property that, under certain reasonable assumptions, it is an optimal state estimator. Not that it is without problems in practice. Among the more severe of these are (i) the difficulty of computing a good *initial* state estimate ; (ii) the difficulty of determining appropriate gain matrices; and (iii) the difficulty of identifying and approximation real plants in the simple form shown.

The Oxford Robotics Group has not contributed to the theory of the Kalman filter so much as to the way in which it may be computed. In a typical fielded system, a set of sensors make independent measurements of components of the state and report them, at each step, to a central processor that runs the Kalman filter. If one of the sensors ceases to operate, the system continues to run, albeit with increased state uncertainty. If, however, the central processor ceases to operate, the whole system fails. An obvious alternative design is to distribute the Kalman filter amongst the sensors (in the current parlance this makes them "smart" sensors) and enable them to communicate their state estimates amongst themselves. Rao et. al. (11) have shown that the equations of the Kalman filter can be partitioned so that such a fully decentralised system converges to the same global optimum as the centralised system. The system degrades gracefully as "smart" sensors cease to operate, and upgrades gracefully as new "smart" sensors are introduced into the system.

Durrant-Whyte and his colleagues have developed a distributed implementation of the Kalman filter based on an architectural component that they call *LISA*: the *L*ocally *I*ntelligent *S*ensor *A*gent. The *LISA* is a small card that comprises a Transputer module with 500KB of memory, two serial-to-parallel interfaces (CO11), and two serial line connections to other *LISA*s. Recent work has developed a second generation *LISA*, and used groups of them to control a process plant and to control the sensing and actuation of a robot vehicle called *OXNAV*.

The first application of these ideas (11) was in collaboration with British Aerospace's (BAe) Sowerby Research Centre, as part of an Esprit collaboration *SKIDS*. Four cameras are placed in the corners of a room that is 10 metres by 6 metres. They are multiplexed through a single image processing system (on grounds of cost, ideally there would be four such), and then through an interface card, to four Transputers that are fully interconnected. One Transputer is dedicated to each camera, and receives from the image processing system, at each time step (currently 1/7th second), a difference image that gives a (poor) representation of image motion as seen from that camera. At each iteration, a Transputer (i) performs a connected component analysis to find moving blobs in its difference image; (ii) finds the point at the centre of the bottom of the blob (hopefully this corresponds to the feet on the floor); (iii) knowing the camera transformation from the world frame, de-projects the ray through this point to intersect it with the ground plane; (iv) transmits this estimate to the other three cameras and receives theirs; and (v) computes the updated Kalman estimate of the positions of the moving objects. (10) shows how the system can be extended to track several moving targets. The graceful degradation refered to above is confirmed in practice as the system continues to track targets as one, then two, cameras are unplugged and then plugged back in.

3   Autonomous Guided Vehicle

The second application concerns an Autonomous Guided Vehicle (AGV). Our research aimed to equip autonomous guided vehicles, in particular a state-of-the-art British product developed by GEC (in collaboration with the Caterpillar company) designed for transporting material around factories, with sensory capabilities, and with planning capabilities that rely upon sensed data. The AGV is controlled using an industrial controller that integrates Information from an infrared ranging system that reads reflecting bar-coded targets, and from odometry. The fielded industrial system uses a *landbase* software system that models the pathways and places in a factory and is used for route planning. For safety, the vehicle is equipped with a plastic bumper that stops the vehicle on contact with an unexpected obstacle. The vehicle follows cubic spline trajectories planned between set points established in the landbase. Implicitly, it assumes that the real factory environment in which the AGV operates matches exactly the software model that is enshrined in the landbase. The sensing system of the industrial system is very accurate: the vehicle always knows where it is. Unfortunately, it doesn't know where anything else is: as we noted in the Introduction, the AGV's environment must conform to its internal model if it is to operate effectively and safely.

We have equipped the vehicle with a number of sonar sensors. These are multiplexed into a Transputer system that interfaces to the vehicle's industrial controller. The vehicle sets out to follow a planned trajectory, but may encounter obstacles located by the sonar sensors. An algorithm determines if the obstacle can be sidestepped by a simple detour around it, in which case a cubic spline patch is inserted into the planned trajectory. If it is considered that the object cannot be by-passed in this manner, a search algorithm that contains a model of the environment (without unexpected obstacles) is called to formulate a new trajectory to the goal.

As noted in the Introduction, sensor data is always uncertain. Recent work on the sonar guided vehicle aims to integrate decision theory with the Kalman filter and a probabilistic model of possibly moving obstacles to determine dynamically the optimal policy (trajectory). Suppose that the AGV detects the presence of an unexpected obstacle partially blocking its path. The gap between the obstacle and the environment may be navigable, in which case the by-pass strategy will work; but the sensor uncertainty may mean that the AGV has to get closer to the obstacle to be sure. By the time it is sure, it may transpire that the gap is not after all navigable, in which case an unnecessary price (motion plus sensing) has been paid. Perhaps, the robot should have earlier chosen to cut its losses, instead planning an entirely different route? To achieve this kind of decision making, we assume that prior information about the environment is available, but unexpected obstacles may appear at random positions. To handle the uncertainty, we adopt a Bayesian approach to build the statistical models for encountering unexpected obstacles, which are based on assumed prior distributions and updated dynamically by sensor data. These statistical models provide quantified uncertainty costs to be used to assign merits to each portion of a path. When the robot searches for an optimal path, it takes the uncertainty cost into account in making a decision. Based on prior information and sensor data, we have shown that the proposed method allows our robot to cope with unexpected obstacles, plan an optimal path and learn global knowledge from its traversals in real time.

Suppose that the AGV plans a path, say the straight line between the current position and the goal shown in figure 1. The path is sent to the

AGV's GEM80 controller and the AGV will move along this path until the sonar sensors detect unexpected obstacles. If a stationary obstacle such as O_1 shown in Figure 1 partially blocks the path, the local planner (obstacle avoidance) adjusts the speed and heading of the robot to avoid it in real time. If the planned path is completely blocked by an obstacle such as O_2, the local planner reduces the robot speed until it stops and requests an alternative path from the global planner. The global planner increases the cost of the current portion of the path to infinity and replans an alternative path using equation (2) for the robot to reach the goal. If more obstacles are found, path search will continue in the same way until all paths have been attempted. If none is successful the AGV returns to the start node and reports failure.

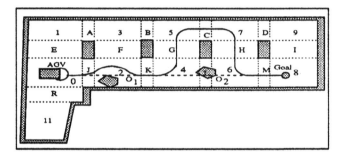

Figure 1: The AGV tries to reach a goal

Based on the statistical models we have proposed, the mobile robot is able to learn global knowledge from path execution. Therefore, if the mobile robot frequently encounters obstacles which block the way completely in a portion of the path, the cost of this partial path will quickly increase so that this partial path is removed from planning for some time. As its cost function decays exponentially, this portion of the path will be a candidate path later and the robot will try it again. Figure 2 shows that the robot chooses an arc path rather than the straight one because obstacles have appeared frequently during past traversals. But the robot will try the straight line path from time to time, depending upon the exponential decay rate.

The layered perception system developed for the AGV is used for active sensor control and distributed sensor fusion to support a layered control strategy. All sensing layers operate independently, but are loosely coupled. Communication between them is used to realize sensor data fusion. The high bandwidth controller we have designed is shown in Figure 3. It has three control layers which in turn consist of a network of

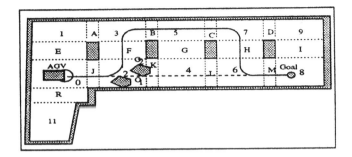

Figure 2: *Turtle* chooses an arc path

sensing and control nodes, namely local intelligent control agents(LICA).

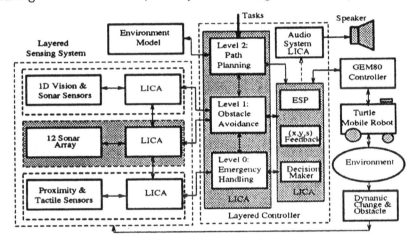

Figure 3: The Block Diagram of Distributed Transputer Architecture

4   Visual guidance of the AGV

Our work on visual guidance of the AGV is an exploration of the concept of "active vision", which aims at purposive control of the viewpoint of a system that has a continuing existence. This raises a number of important problems: (i) how to control viewpoint? (ii) what is the control state, observables, and control law of the system? (iii) how is uncertainty represented and tamed? (iv) where should the system look next, and to what end or purpose? (v) how should speed/time requirements be met? and (vi) how should the environment be represented? The goals of active vision systems include navigation, sensor-guided assembly, "model-based" image coding, surveillance (see section 2), search for an object, determination of grasp points on an object, and response to threat.

In an Esprit project *VOILA*, we have been collaborating with the Roke Manor Research Laboratory on a real-time implementation of a structure from motion algorithm *DROID* originally developed in (7). *DROID* determines the three-dimensional structure of a scene by tracking image features over a sequence of frames. It works as follows:

1. The state of the system at time t consists of a set of feature points in space, each of which has an associated vector

$$[x_i(t) \; y_i(t) \; z_i(t) \; \epsilon_x^i(t) \; \epsilon_y^i(t) \; \epsilon_z^i(t) \; \lambda_i]^\top.$$

   The first three components are the estimated three-dimensional position of the feature. The second three components are the semi-axes of an ellipsoidal representation of the uncertainty of the points position. Initially, the uncertainty is low in the image coordinates, but large in depth. As the vehicle circumnavigates a feature, the uncertainty in depth is reduce by the simple technique of intersecting ellipsoids. The final component λ is a flag that says whether the feature is temporarily invisible (eg because it is occluded).

2. Given an estimate of the motion between the imaging position at time t and time $t + 1$, the state prediction at time $t + 1$ can be made, and, after perspective projection using a pinhole model, the positions of the feature points in the $t + 1$st image can be predicted.

3. Features can be extracted from the $t + 1$st image. Originally, features defined by image autocorrelation were used. Recently, we have developed a novel corner finder, and this has significantly improved the accuracy of the system. This is by far the most computationally intensive step of the computation.

4. The *correspondence* is computed between the predicted locations of points in step 2 and the feature points found in step 3. Ambiguous matches are decided by matching descriptions of the predicted and found points that involve the intensity value and gradients.

5. The state estimate is updated.

6. The image locations of the feature points are triangulated, using the Delaunay triangulation that minimises long thin triangles. The

triangles are deprojected into the scene (recall that the z component of each feature point has been estimated. The surface normal of each deprojected triangular facet is computed. Driveable regions are computed as the transitive closure of the facets lying close to the horizontal plane, starting just in front of the vehicle.

Wang and Brady (13) report a number of careful experiments with the *DROID* algorithm using cameras mounted on the robot vehicle described in the previous section and which can compute its position using the on-board infrared sensor. There is no integral action in the controller, but subject to this limitation, velocity and position estimates are reasonably accurate. However, precise camera calibration is required, and, in view of the inevitable vibrations of the mobile robot, this is the most sensitive part of the system. Recently, we have developed a stereo matching system based on the same set of "corner" points, and integrated it with the structure from motion system.

5   Real-time gaze control for a robot head

The remarkable performance of the animate visual system, particularly its speed and reliability, derive in part from the active control of attention. This has lead to the construction recently of a number of multiple degree-of-freedom robot "heads" (9). For a vision system in a dynamic world to respond to visual stimuli or to achieve some perceptual purpose, either the visual direction of the robot head, or the focus of attention of the vision system, or both, must be controlled to speed up or simplify image processing. To achieve these purposes, both a precisely engineered camera/eye platform (robot head) and a robust gaze control algorithm and architecture are essential.

Despite the considerable developments in machine vision made over the past ten years, most machine vision systems are still only able to survive in simplified, relatively static and controlled environments. One of the major difficulties in engineering real-time machine vision systems that contend with a dynamically changing world is that they need extremely high bandwidth. More powerful high speed processing hardware/architecture/software is needed. However, it has been realised that relying only on the performance improvement of the processing hardware/architecture is by itself insufficient. An active, responsive, and dynamic vision system is required for operation in uncontrolled changing environments.

To this end, we have constructed a four degree-of-freedom stereo head/eye platform that is compact, reliable, relatively cheap, yet fast and accurate. It is intended to be mounted on the AGV described in section 3 for visual navigation through narrow gaps amongst moving obstacles. More fundamentally, the head enables us to investigate the interactions between image processing and the active control of attention and visual direction. We seek to understand if the behaviour of the cameras and resources can be actively controlled by perception, and to what extent (and how) perception can be improved.

We have constructed a common-elevation platform based on DC motors coupled to harmonic drive gearboxes that substantially reduce the mechanical backlash which typically limits the performance of geared systems. The camera vergence can attain a rate of $530°s^{-1}$ and accelerations of $7000°s^{-2}$. The joint motion control architecture comprises a processor and pulse-width modulation amplifier for each motor, the four processors being coordinated by a supervisory processor that additionally interfaces to a network of Transputers, on which the gaze control algorithms are implemented ((4) provides more detail). The gaze control algorithm is a two-layered motion process: the inner loop achieves open-loop saccadic motions to intercept a target, while the outer loop provides smooth pursuit and achieves what physiologists call the opto-kinetic reflex, vestibular-ocular reflex, and tracking. The controller is designed as a closed-loop inverse kinematic structure. The motion model and intrinsic parameters of the system are learned automatically by· making deliberate motions. At time of writing, the controller is fully operational with simple visual stimuli.

6 Parallel object recognition using SUP/INF networks

Current approaches to model-based object recognition (6) require the computer to maintain a separate model for each object to be recognised. But consider the example of an industrial pallet that confronts the AGV described above. Pallets come with a wide variety of numbers of slats and different aspect ratios. The typical model-based approach maintains one model for each type of pallet. To overcome this, Reid has developed a recognition system for parametrically varying classes of models (12). A model is described parametrically. In the case of the pallet, the parameters might include length, width, height, number of slats and slat separation.

Reid's object recognition system maintains a series of estimates of the upper and lower bounds of each parameter. If two or more parameters are inter-related, a change in the bounds of one affects the bounds of the others. Upper and lower bounds can be processed by the SUP/INF method of automatic theorem proving for arithmetic, introduced by Bledsoe (2), and applied to object recognition by Fisher and Orr (5) Models are represented as region-edge-vertex networks whose nodes are the SUP/INF bounds and whose links define not only the model geometry but also the constraints between parameters (eg length/height ≈ 3). Simple rules propagate changes in bounds from one parameter to its dependents.

The operation of Reid's algorithm and the often tight parameter bounds it computes simultaneously with the determination of the position and pose of objects in real range data are described in (12). Though the program works surprisingly quickly (typically recognising objects in a few seconds), it is too slow for real time industrial applications. This motivated the search for a parallel implementation of the algorithm. A key problem is to allocate object models to a distributed set of processors. We have developed a method to do this, and we have implemented Reid's algorithm on a network of transputers.

There are two main reasons for implementing the algorithm on a MIMD architecture. First, the localised activity (due to a change in parameter bounds) which then spreads throughout the network does not fit the SIMD model well. Second, whenever the bounds of a parameter are changed, the changes are propagated along the arcs emanating from its SUP/INF block to its dependents. This invites communication between separate processes, each corresponding to a SUP/INF block, suggesting communicating sequential processes. We have implemented the algorithm on a network of Transputers, giving particular attention to the automatic allocation of processes to the typically small number of processors. We have explored the use of neural networks for this task (3).

Acknowledgements

The distributed Kalman filter and its application to surveillance is due to my colleague Hugh Durrant-Whyte and his students Bobby Rao and John Leonard. Chris Harris of Plessey and his colleagues invented the DROID algorithm whose parallel implementation is reported in this paper. The work described here was in collaboration with Ian Reid, Fenglei Du, Huosheng Hu, and Han Wang. David Murray, Phil McLauchlan, Ian Reid, and Paul Sharkey have shared their experiences of building a similar head for surveillance applications. Work on this paper was supported by the Science and Engineering Research Council ACME Directorate, by the EC on the VOILA and SKIDS contracts. Nikki Clack and Sara Morris defend the author from intrusions.

References

[1]Y Bar-Shalom and T E Fortman. *Tracking and Data Association.* Academic, 1988.

[2]W.W̃. Bledsoe. The sup-inf method in presburger arithmetic. Technical report, Technical Report Memo ATP 18, Dept of Math and Computer Science, Univ of Texas, 1974.

[3]Michael Brady, Huosheng Hu, Han Wang, and Steve Udall. Parallel algorithms in vision and robotics. In B. Ford, editor, *Parallel Computation.* Oxford University Press, 1992.

[4]Fenglei Du and Michael Brady. Real-time gaze control for a robot head. In *Proc. 2nd Int. Conf. Advanced Robotics and Computer Vision*, Singapore, Sept. 1992.

[5]R. B. Fisher and M. J. L. Orr. Geometric reasoning in a parallel network. *International Journal of Robotics Research*, 10(2):103–122, 1991.

[6]W. E. L. Grimson and T. Lozano-Pérez. Model based recognition and localization from sparse range or tactile data. In *Proceedings of the 1st International Conference on Computer Vision, 93–101*, London, 1987.

[7]C G Harris and J M Pike. 3D positional integration from image sequences. In *Proc. 3rd Alvey Vision Conference*, Cambridge, Sept. 1987.

[8]John J. Leonard and Hugh F. Durrant-Whyte. *Directed sonar sensing for mobile robot navigation.* Kluwer Academic Publishers, 1992.

[9]D. W. Murray, F. Du, P. F. McLauchlan, I. D. Reid, P. M. Sharkey, and Michael Brady. *Design of stereo heads*, pages 155–175. MIT Press, 1992.

[10]B. S. Y. Rao. *Data Fusion Methods in Decentralized Sensing Systems.* PhD thesis, Dept. Engineering Science, Oxford University, 1991.

[11] B.S.Y. Rao, Durrant-Whyte H.F., and Sheen J.A. A fully decentralized multi-sensor system for tracking and surveillance. *Int. J. Robotics Research*, 12, 1992.

[12] Ian Reid. *Recognizing Parameterized Objects from Range Data*. PhD thesis, Dept. Engineering Science, Oxford University, Michaelmas Term 1991.

[13] Han Wang, C Bowman, Michael Brady, and C Harris. A parallel implementation of a structure-from-motion algorithm. In G. Sandini, editor, *Proc. ECCV'92, Second European Conference on Computer Vision*, Genova, Italy, May 1992. Springer Verlag.

Fundamentals of Bicentric Perspective

Buys Ballot Laboratory, Utrecht University
Princetonplein 5, 3584 CC Utrecht, The Netherlands

Abstract. Bicentric perspective is the study of the projection of 3D space from a *pair* of fiducial points instead of a single one ("centric", or "natural" perspective). In contradistinction with centric perspective, in bicentric perspective some 3D structure is preserved in the projection. This structure is of two different kinds: it is either purely *optical* or of a mixed opto–mechanical nature. The optically specified structure is conveyed by the pair of centric projections alone, whereas the opto–mechanical information depends also on a knowledge of the kinematical state of the two sensors.

1 Introduction

I will use anthropomorphic terminology throughout: The two projection centers are the "eyes", the line defined by them the "interocular axis", their mutual separation the "interocular distance". I label the centers "right eye" and "left eye".

I take the interocular axis as the X axis of a Cartesian capitocentric coordinate system. The Z-axis is the vertical, and the Y axis the posterior to anterior ("straight ahead") direction. I disregard the posterior halfspace ($y < 0$). It is geometrically evident that the geometries in all planes (so called "epipolar planes") through the interocular axis are identical. (Figure 1, the eyes are at ($\pm 1, 0, 0$).)

I single out the horizontal plane ($z = 0$) in order to study this geometry in a simplified 2D setting. The (minimum) angle ε between any such halfplane and the horizontal halfplane is the "elevation", reckoned positive for positive z coordinates.

In the epipolar planes I will consider various parametrizations, the Cartesian (ξ, η) being one example. For the horizontal plane ($\varepsilon = 0$) the parameters (ξ, η) coincide with (x, y). The Cartesian coordinates are subject to the constraint $y > 0$ or $\eta > 0$ (forward halfspace, or upper halfplane).

Another useful parametrization is by the angles (φ_L, φ_R), that I will refer to as the "surveyor's parametrization". These coordinates represent the raw observations for the case of a land surveyor who performs sightings of landmarks with the help of two graduated circles, placed at disparate positions. For a fiducial point $\mathcal{P}$ these angles are given by

$$(1) \qquad \varphi_L = \arctan \frac{\xi + a}{\eta}, \varphi_R = \arctan \frac{\xi - a}{\eta},$$

in terms of the Cartesian parametrization. Here a denotes half the interocular separation. The surveyor's angles are both in the range $\|\varphi_L\|, \|\varphi_R\| < \pi/2$.

In most cases it is advantageous not to use surveyor's coordinates as such, but to switch to "symmetric angle coordinates" instead. The reason is that the two sightings will be very close if the surveyor's base line is short with respect to the distances from landmarks of interest. Then symmetric and antisymmetric combinations of the

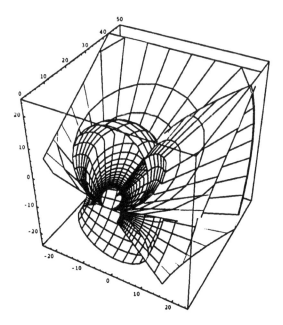

Figure 1: Surfaces of constant version, vergence and elevation.

surveyor's angles behave in essentially different ways. From an operational point of
view it may well be preferable to measure these combinations in some direct manner,
instead of indirectly via the surveyor's system.

I define the binocular version λ and the "binocular vergence" γ in terms of the
surveyor's parameters as

$$(2) \qquad \lambda = \frac{1}{2}(\varphi_L + \varphi_R), \gamma = \frac{1}{2}(\varphi_L - \varphi_R).$$

Notice that the symmetrical angle coordinates are subject to the constraint $\gamma + \|\lambda\| \le$
$\pi/2$.

In the geometrical picture the version (λ) is not reckoned from the origin (mid-
point of the interocular axis), but from an "egocenter" that lies on the negative
η-axis on the circle through the eyes and the fiducial point. (Figure 2.) The egocenter shifts as you move the fiducial point about, although for all practical purposes it
almost coincides with the origin, thus the version is *almost* the same as the azimuth
(reckoned from the Y-axis, positive towards the X axis) in conventional polar coordinates. The vergence (γ) is half the angle under which the fiducial point "sees" the
left and right center. Note that this angle is also subtended by half the interocular
distance as "seen" from the vertex (point most distant from the orgin on the Y-axis)
of the "Vieth-Müller circle", that is the circle through the eyes and the fiducial point.
This indicates that the vergence is very close to the reciprocal of the diameter of
this circle, an thus a good measure for the *bicentric nearness* of this locus.

This construction goes as far back as Euclid[2], that is *ca.* 350 B.C.

The choice of parametrization is of course completely arbitrary and indeed is

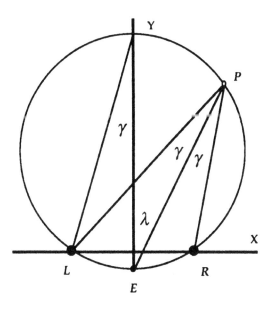

Figure 2: Symmetric angle coordinates.

essentially irrelevant from the formal standpoint. However, from an *operational* viewpoint one system may be far more convenient than another. One reason is that some parameters are subject to immediate operational methods of measurement, whereas others have to be derived via indirect procedures. As an external geometer you would probably use measuring tape to fix the position of $\mathcal{P}$ in terms of the Cartesian system. As a surveyor with limited access to the region to be surveyed you may set up facilities for angular measurement at the projection centers and reckon in the surveyor system. A more important reason to prefer one system of parametrization over an other is the sensitivity of the parametrization to the inevitable experimental tolerances. For instance, the bicentric nearness is very vulnerable with respect to small errors in the surveyor's system.

As a binocular human being version and vergence seem to be the natural choice: it can be shown that humans are highly insensitive to the actual value of the vergence, whereas the version (visual direction) is sensed quite well[1]. This is not to say that the human observer is effectively monocular: Various *derivatives* of the vergence are apparently sensed with considerable acuteness.

In any opto–motor system you will typically measure directly in the surveyor's coordinates. These coordinates are most simply converted into motor commands. This implies an a priori calibration of the apparatus. (*E.g.*, the angles have to be referred to a common reference frame.)

In any purely optical system you have only the left and right *images*. To simplify the analysis I will assume that the correspondence is given and that both sensors are calibrated to measure angles in radians. (Here various—all interesting—alternative systems could have been defined and studied. I pick a fairly obvious and important case here.) In practical cases the head will turn towards and the eyes will fixate the target, which is typically many interocular distances away. Then the vergence will be unknown because of the lack of a common reference frame for the left and right sensors, although various derivatives of the vergence with respect to version and elevation can possibly be measured rather precisely. These are the "disparity", "disparity gradient", and so forth. The version will also be small (because of the head movements) and will be known quite well, except for some unkown (and possibly appreciable) systematic deviation.

In the optomotor case the 3D structure that can be recovered depends on the tolerances in the surveyor's angular measurements and the quality of the head–eye calibration. In the optical case the recoverable structure must be a function of the derivatives of the version that are robust against unknown version shifts. The importance of this distinction can be illustrated vividly by noticing that in degenerate cases there need not be any optical information *at all*. A single point of light in the dark is an example. (No spatial derivatives can be defined or observed!) Although this is the surveyor's dream, human observers can't localize it very well. This is the so called "autokinetic effect": one perceives a more or less randomly wandering light point on a dark field[5]. Clearly the human observer doesn't function much like a surveyor. In this paper I consider mainly the optical case.

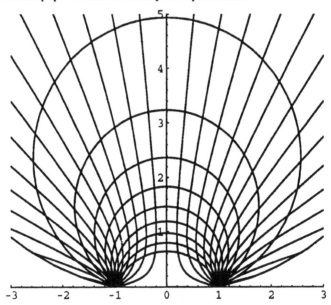

Figure 3: Superimposed congruences of Vieth–Müller circles and Hillebrand hyperbolæ.

To conclude the introduction I mention the already obvious fact that the loci of constant vergence are circles passing through both eyes:

$$(3) \qquad \xi^2 + (\eta - a \cot 2\gamma)^2 = \left(\frac{a}{\sin 2\gamma}\right)^2,$$

commonly known as the "Vieth–Müller–circles". The loci of constant version are rectangular hyperbolæ with the origin as center, that pass through the eyes:

$$(4) \qquad (\xi \cos \lambda - \eta \sin \lambda)(\xi \sin \lambda + \eta \cos \lambda) = \frac{a^2}{2} \sin 2\lambda.$$

These are known as the "Hillebrand-hyperbolæ".

Introspective reports suggest that human observers (with fixed head) judge their Hillebrand hyperbolæ to be the "straight rays" through the egocenter, and the Vieth-Müller circles as the equidistance loci. (Figure 3.)

The nexus defined by the congruences of Vieth–Müller circles and Hillebrand hyperbolæ is thus a very special one, and its importance for human vision makes that it is illustrated and discussed in handbooks on human binocular vision. It is less well known in computer vision and robotics. The reason is that—unlike the human observer case—one usually relies heavily on precise prior calibration of the stereo rig. Even so, inevitable tolerances will induce uncertainties that will be structured on the pattern of these "natural" directions.

2 Orthothomics of the Hillebrand Hyperbolæ and Vieth-Müller Circles

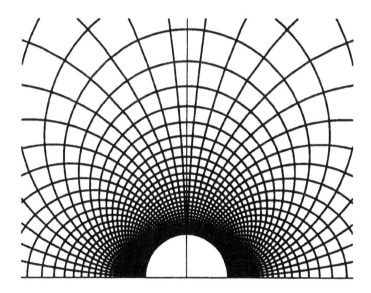

Figure 4: Congruence of Vieth–Müller circles and the orthotomic congruence.

Any curve congruence induces another curve congruence of "orthotomics" that cuts it everywhere at right angles. In the case of the Vieth-Müller circles (equation 3) and Hillebrand hyperbolæ (equation 4) these orthotomics are the field lines of the gradients of the vergence and version respectively. (Figure 4.)

The Vieth-Müller circles and their orthotomics obviously form systems of orthogonal circle pencils, very much like the field lines and equipotential curves of the electric dipole.

We have two dual elliptic and hyperbolic pencils of circles. Notice that the orthotomics of the Vieth–Müller circles don't just radiate out from the origin as one would like them to. (After all the circles appear like equidistance circles, thus their orthotomics had better act like rays though the origin.) They sprout forth from the interocular interval and indeed start their course on a reasonable path. However, eventually they curve back and move *towards* the epipolar axis again, which is certainly an awkward feature.

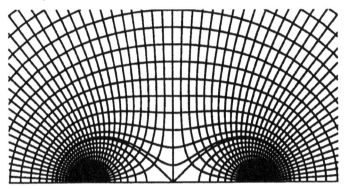

Figure 5: Congruence of Hillebrand hyperbolæ with the orthotomic congruence. Notice that the orthotomics are either simply connected, or come in two disjunct branches. The separatrix is a lemniscate.

The orthotomics of the Hillebrand hyperbolæ are more complicated. (Figure 5.) It turns out that the orthotomics are a family of "Ovals of Cassini" with the eyes as foci. (I don't think these have appeared in the literature before, but I did not perform an extensive historical search.) The product of the distances d_L, d_R to left and right eyes is constant on any such oval. The ovals of Cassini are fourth order curves:

$$(5) \qquad ((\xi + a)^2 + \eta^2)((\xi - a)^2 + \eta^2) = d_L^2 d_R^2.$$

These curves come in three varieties: convex ovals that encircle both eyes, nonconvex ovals that encircle both eyes, and *a pair* of (convex) ovals, each encircling *one* eye. There is also a singular member, a lemniscate with a double point at the origin.

Thus the "near field" behavior is qualitatively different from the "far field" behavior. This is already evident from the Hillebrand hyperbolæ themselves. Since they appear as "straight rays" through the egocenter, it is natural to associate to each fiducial point a "bicentric direction" that is obtained by projecting it to the vault of heaven (infinite distance from the egocenter) by way of a Hillebrand hyperbola. You then obtain a pattern in which each eye has its own system of directions in the near field whereas these merge to a single bicentric direction system in the far field.

In the near field the congruence of orthotomics looks like a mess. Since the hyperbolæ appear as rays through the origin one would like the orthotomics to be roughly convex ovals with the origin as center. Even the single connected ovals have concave indentations in the near field. Such concavities mess up the regular field of visual directions. This is illustrated by the fact that you can see the frontal face and *both* the left and right side of a small cube (smaller than the interocular distance) in the near field (as one may easily verify with the help of a match box), something that is absolutely impossible for the case of (mono–)centric perspective.

The interpretation of the Hillebrand–hyperbolæ as subjective rays and Vieth–Müller circles as subjective equidistance loci is only reasonable in the far field and for not too large versions: the orthotomics of the hyperbolæ should be convex ovals, and of the circles they should move away from the origin. This limits the reasonable region to versions less than $\pm\pi/4$ and distances in excess of a. In practice this is always realized. This limitation is also useful for another reason.

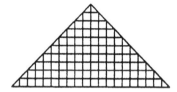

Figure 6: Superimposed congruences of Vieth–Müller circles and Hillebrand hyperbolæ in λ–γ-space. (These are the *same* congruences as depicted in figure 3!)

The halfplane $y > 0$ corresponds to the parameter *triangle* $\gamma + \|\lambda\| \leq \pi/2$. The sides of this triangle correspond to infinity ($y \mapsto \infty$), and the left and right eye. The interocular stretch and the two semi–infinite stretches of the interocular axis starting at the eyes map to the vertices of the triangle. Thus the map is highly degenerated. The restriction indicated above limits the map to a rectangle with the eyes at two endpoints of one side whereas infinity maps to the opposite side. (Such a parameter rectangle would be a very useful representation of the surveyor's space, because the tolerance regions for landmarks map to equal sized circles, no matter their position.)

In the parameter triangle the system of Vieth-Müller circles and Hillebrand hyperbolæ map to a nice Cartesian lattice. (Figure 6.) Luneburg[4] may have been the first to study this map in some detail.

3   Metric of the Halfplane $y > 0$

The derivatives of a fiducial point with respect to the parameters yield the "moving frame" (e_λ, e_γ)(Figures 7 and 8.)

(6)
$$e_\lambda = \tfrac{2a}{\sin 2\gamma}(\cos 2\lambda\, e_\xi - \sin 2\lambda\, e_\eta),$$

$$e_\gamma = -\tfrac{2a}{\sin^2 2\gamma}(\sin 2\lambda \cos 2\gamma\, e_\xi + (1 + \cos 2\lambda\, \cos 2\gamma)\, e_\eta).$$

Of course these frame vectors are neither normalized, nor orthogonal. They make a good basis though, except at large versions.

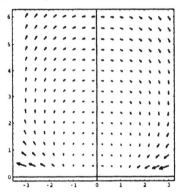

Figure 7: The e_λ vector field.

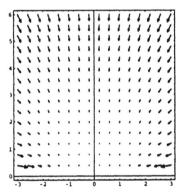

Figure 8: The e_γ vector field.

The scalar producs of the frame vectors immediately yield the metric of the half plane $y > 0$ expressed in terms of the symmetric angle coordinates. If one plots fixed stretches in the principal directions of the metric one obtains a nice picture of Tissot's indicatrices[7], thus making the warping of the map visible. (Figures 9 and 10, the eyes are at $x = \pm 1, y = 0$.)

The metric itself permits one to express distances and angles in the halfplane in terms of the symmetric angle parameters. Since these are invariant against Euclidean movements one thus obtains important sets of invariant expressions. Since the metric tensor depends on the vergence, not just on its angular derivatives, such invariants are useful to the surveyor (in the optomotor system), but useless to the human observer.

Of course this metric is nothing but the Pythagorean formula $ds^2 = d\xi^2 + d\eta^2$ of the Euclidean plane in other guise! The representation in the λ–γ–parameter plane is interesting though. Only at a point right in front of the eyes at half an interocular

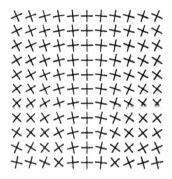

Figure 9: The Euclidean metric in the λ–γ–space.

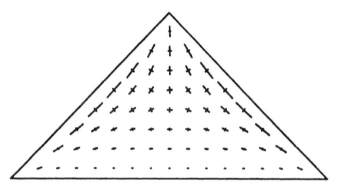

Figure 10: The Euclidean metric in the upper half plane. By comparison with the previous figure you can assess the Tissot principal directions and magnifications of the correspondence.

distance from the origin do you observe isotropy, at any other location the metric looks highly *anisotropic*.

The metric also appears as very *inhomogeneous*: Near the horizon very tiny angular deviations suffice to define an Euclidean unit of length. This indicates that the surveyor will run into trouble in the far field.

Other interesting metrics are obtained by an explicit analysis of tolerances. An example is the surveyor's method. Assuming fixed tolerances in the angular measurements one obtains an Euclidean metric in the (ξ, η) parameter triangle. Mapped back into the halfplane one obtains an inhomogeneous and anisotropic metric that degenerates towards infinity ($y \mapsto \infty$). (Figure 11.) It appears that the surveyor is in business at nearby distances and in the more or less forward direction. Otherwise the uncertainties in the localization in the upper halfplane become prohibitive. Notice that the uncertainties in the azimuthal direction grow proportionally with distance, whether in the radial direction they grow with the square of the distance. Thus objects will tend to "grow flat" when you move them away from the surveyor, an effect that is also evident in introspective reports from human observers.

The case of human vision is in most respects quite unlike that of the surveyor. The human doesn't use the equivalence of a pair of graduated circles. Instead, the version is measured much like the surveyor's angles. (More or less constant tolerance.) The vergence is not obtained as the difference of two versions though. Human observers don't measure vergence at all, but can find vergence gradients with great precision. An intermediate case would be a surveyor with one graduated circle for the version, and some kind of optical ranging device for the vergence. For many feasible instruments the tolerance in the vergence will be a *constant relative tolerance*, instead of a *constant absolute* one. The reason is that the vergence is a small angle, and smaller angles will usually be processed with increased magnification.

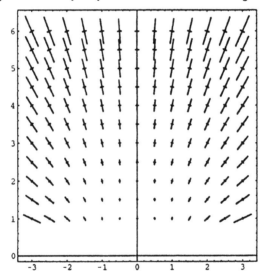

Figure 11: The surveyor's metric in the upper half plane.

For such an observer we obtain a metric that is much more isotropic. (Figure 12.) For more or less forward directions the uncertainties in the upper halfplane are close to circular, their size growing proportional with the distance. Combined with a head movement fixation capability, this would certainly make an excellent general purpose binocular system.

4   Iseikonic Transformations

Consider the "translations" in the parameter triangle $(\lambda, \gamma) \mapsto (\lambda + \lambda_0, \gamma + \gamma_0)$. Such translations are produced by *eye movements*. Because the eyes merely *rotate* in their orbits, the natural perspective for the individual eye is not at all affected and the *optical* information is not affected either. In these translations in the symmetric angle parameter space we have a prime example of a transformation that can be detected by the surveyor, but not by the human observer. Such transformations are

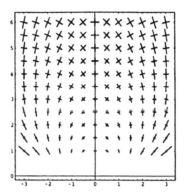

Figure 12: Metric in the upper halfplane of constant tolerance in the version, but constant *relative* tolerance in the vergence. Eyes at $(\pm 1, 0)$.

known as *iseikonic transformations*. (Figure 13.)

Two (different) physical configurations that are related by such an iseikonic transformation yield *exactly* the same optical stimulation of the brain, and only differ in the state of strain of the eye muscles. To distinguish such configurations is thus a pure *motor feat*. It turns out that the human observer is unable to perform such a feat, that is, with the head fixed (only eye movements) all configurations related by iseikonic transformations are—at least to a very good approximation—perceptually equivalent.

In machine vision any uncertainty in the kinematic calibration has to show up as an unknown iseikonic transformation. Thus these transformations are also of interest in the optomotor case if one cares about tolerances.

It is very simple to construct "iseikonic invariants": derivatives $d^n\gamma/d\lambda^n$ of any order $n \geq 1$ are obviously invariant against iseikonic transformations. After transforming these invariants to the Cartesian (ξ, η) system, we obtain slanted curvature elements at various positions that are perceptually equivalent. Here I am especially interested in the lowest two orders, basically slant and curvature.

The first order yields:

$$(7) \qquad \frac{d\gamma}{d\lambda} = a \frac{(\xi^2 - \eta^2 - a^2)\frac{d\eta}{d\xi} - 2\xi\eta}{\eta(\xi^2 + \eta^2 + a^2) - \xi(\xi^2 + \eta^2 - a^2)\frac{d\eta}{d\xi}},$$

or, asymptotically for the far field near the straight ahead direction ($\xi \mapsto 0, \eta \mapsto \infty$), $\frac{d\eta}{d\xi} = -\frac{1}{\gamma}\frac{d\gamma}{d\lambda}$. Thus it is immediately obvious that the optical observer must confuse distance and slant. If you know the distance (γ) by any other independent means (motor system, visual "cue"), you can find the slant. (Figure 14. The eyes are at $\xi = \pm 1$.)

For the second order a surprise is in store. The exact expression for the second order invariant is very complicated (although easy to construct with a symbolic algebra package!) and not very enlightening. This time I give the invariant "in reverse", that is the Euclidean curvature κ expressed in terms of the first and second order iseikonic invariants times half the interocular distance a (thus $a\kappa$) is given by

Figure 13: Two different physical configurations that are isokonically equivalent. Such configurations are indistinguishable to the human observer.

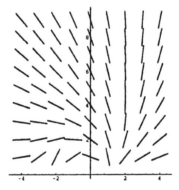

Figure 14: A field of slope contact elements.

the somewhat cumbersome expression:

$$(8) \quad \frac{(-1 + (\frac{\partial \gamma}{\partial \lambda})^2 - \frac{1}{2}\frac{\partial^2 \gamma}{\partial \lambda^2}\cot 2\gamma - \frac{1}{\sin 2\gamma}(\frac{1}{2}\frac{\partial^2 \gamma}{\partial \lambda^2}\cos 2\lambda + \frac{\partial \gamma}{\partial \lambda}\sin 2\lambda - (\frac{\partial \gamma}{\partial \lambda})^3 \sin 2\lambda))}{(1 - (\frac{\partial \gamma}{\partial \lambda})^2 + 2(\frac{\partial \gamma}{\partial \lambda})^2 \frac{1 + \cos 2\lambda \cos 2\gamma}{\sin^2 2\gamma} + 2\frac{\partial \gamma}{\partial \lambda}\frac{\sin 2\lambda}{\sin 2\gamma})^{3/2}},$$

However, the asymptotic expression for the far field and the (more or less) straight ahead direction, *frontal* view (vanishing slant) and high curvature is simply

$$(9) \quad \frac{d^2 \gamma}{d\lambda^2} = -\frac{1}{a}\frac{d^2 \eta}{d\xi^2}.$$

In this case the Euclidean curvature is optically specified by the second order iseikonic invariant! This is the content of Rogers'[6] "disparity gradient". Of course this is only *approximately* true. The influence of finite distance, version and curvature can be gleaned from the somewhat better approximation (κ denotes the curvature):

$$(10) \qquad a\kappa = -2\gamma - \frac{d^2\gamma}{d\lambda^2} + 4\lambda\frac{d\gamma}{d\lambda} + 3\frac{\lambda}{\gamma}\frac{d\gamma}{d\lambda}\frac{d^2\gamma}{d\lambda^2} \cdots$$

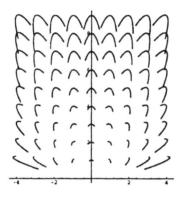

Figure 15: A field of curvature contact elements.

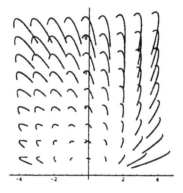

Figure 16: A field of slope–curvature contact elements.

The approximate conservation of curvature under iseikonic transformations is apparent for the fields of sloped curvature contact elements illustrated in figures 15 and 16 (again: the eyes are at $\xi = \pm1$, $\eta = 0$). For each element the disparity fields agree to the second order.

A more quantitative analysis corroborates these informal observations. Here are a few examples:

Take an interocular distance of 65 mm and look at some highy curved object, say a sphere with radius of 1 cm. I will vary the distance from the *punctum proximum* (about 18 cm) to amply out of reach (2 m). First I compute the second order invariant for frontoparallel attitude and frontal view at arm's length (50 cm). The

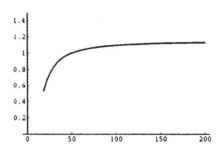

Figure 17: The effect of distance misjudgement on curvature estimation.

value is $\frac{\partial^2 \gamma}{\partial \lambda^2} = 7.48358$. Now I estimate the Euclidean curvature for this value of the invariant, but various distance estimates (18 cm to 200 cm). I plot the ratio of the curvature needed to yield the same value of the iseikonic invariant to the true curvature. This is of course unity if the distance estimate is 50 cm. The result is clearcut (see figure 17): It hardly matters if you misjudge distance, except in the very near field. You don't have to know the vergence in order to judge the curvature.

This result differs sharply from the case of slant judgements. Since the first order iseikonic invariant is approximately the slant *times* the vergence, any distance misjudgement influences the slant estimate seriously.

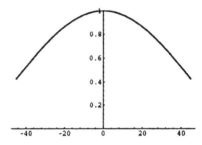

Figure 18: The effect of version misjudgement on curvature estimation.

The effects of version and slant on the curvature estimates can be studied in a similar manner. I stay with the same numerical example.

I compute the curvature needed to keep the second order iseikonic invariant constant as a function of the version angle. Viewing distance is arm's length. I plot the ratio of this curvature to the true curvature as a function of the version. This ratio is of course unity at frontal viewing. It is clear from figure 18 that the effect of any finite version not taken into account by the observer is slight (less than 10 % say) in a *range* of versions subtending 30 to 40 degrees, most certainly a range that will accommodate uncertainties in head fixation.

The effects of a non-frontoparallel attitude are interesting because the observer is in no position to measure the slant if the distance is not known by independent means. I use the same general technique as before. Viewing distance is arm's length, viewing direction forward (no version). I compute the curvature needed to keep the second order iseikonic invariant at a constant value under variation of the slant angle.

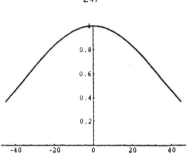

Figure 19: The effect of slant misjudgement on curvature estimation.

I use slant angle up to 45 degrees in both directions. Again, the effect is slight. (See figure 19.) For slant angles of about forty degrees you are wrong by about a factor of two, in a slant *range* of thirty to forty degrees the effect is below 10 %. This latter range is amply sufficient in the case of viewing the object under manipulative control (turning a small object in your hand). If the observer is not in control, large slant values may well be present of course. Although you can control for version by head rotations, this is not possible for the slant: You would need head translations, and some independent knowledge to correct for the effect of slant.

5 The 3D Case

In 3D space the geometry is the same in all planes through the interocular axis ("epipolar planes", see figure 20). Thus a good parametrization will be based on this cylindrical symmetry. Symmetric angle coordinates in the epipolar planes augmented by the elevation are indeed convenient parameters.

The surfaces of constant *elevation* are simply planes through the interocular axes. Each of these planes can be fitted out with one and the same system of Vieth–Müller circles and Hillebrand hyperbolæ. Indeed, the geometry in all epipolar planes is identical to the two dimensional case discussed above.

The surfaces of constant vergence (see figure 21) are torical surfaces that self intersect on the interocular axis. For large distances (smal vergences) this self intersection is very minor, and tends towards a tangency. One obtains what the german geometers call a "Dorntorus" (a "spine" torus). If the observer looks at a plane in its environment, the loci of constant vergence on that plane are the intersections of the plane with these torical surfaces. The loci can have very complicated shapes. (One may have (among more) concentric ovals, or the various ovals of Cassini. There is no relation at all with the ovals of Cassini that appear as the orthotomics of the Hillebrand hyperbolæ though.) For the related case of optic flow such loci have been studies because of their practical importance in aviation. ("Blur zones[8]".)

The surfaces of constant version are the Hillebrand hyperbolæ, rotated about the interocular axis. (Figure 22.) In general these surfaces also self intersect. Asymptotically they appear as right circular cones with the epipolar axis as axis of symmetry.

It is an easy matter to derive the moving frame, the metric and the affine connection (the Christoffel symbols) in terms of this parametrization. Iseikonic transformations are translations in the triangular $(\lambda, \gamma, \varepsilon)$ prism if we assume for the moment

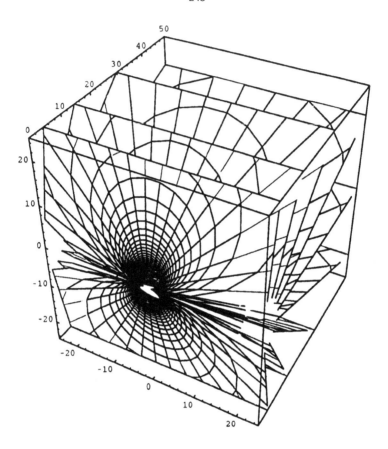

Figure 20: Surfaces of constant elevation. Eyes at $(\pm 1, 0, 0)$.

that the eyes make synchronized excursions in the elevation and avoid differential cyclotorsion. (Note that an ε-translation is just a rotation about the interocular axis.) In reality cyclotorsion certainly comes into play. The present treatment is only a preliminary one. It may be too early to spend an effort to treat any specific system of binocular eye movements in depth, because little certainty exists as to their relevance. The monocular observer with stationary head tends to perform eye movements according to Listing's law. Head movements lead to movements of the eyes more like the gimballed movements typical of the artificial heads.

A surface in space can be parametrized in the form $\gamma(\lambda, \varepsilon)$. The optical observer can measure the various mixed derivatives of the vergence with respect to both version and elevation. It is of some interest to try to derive Euclidean invariants of the surface, say its mean and Gaussian curvature, in terms of these observables. It is a straightforward exercise to do the differential geometry in terms of this parametrization—in principle. In practice the expressions are very cumbersome indeed, and even with the assistance of a symbolic algebra package the exact expressions are not particularly enlightening. The initial terms of a Taylor expan-

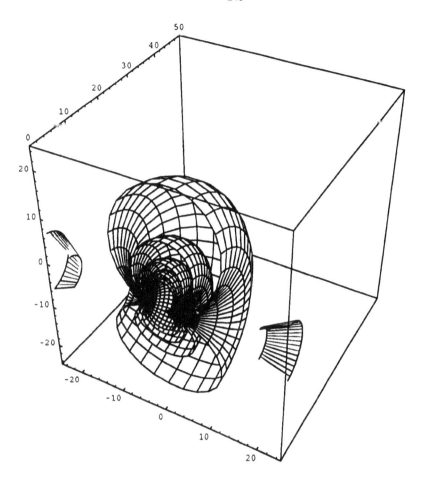

Figure 21: Surfaces of constant vergence. Eyes at $(\pm 1, 0, 0)$.

sion near the straight ahead direction, frontal attitude and large distance reveals the essential structure though.

For these approximate conditions one has: ($\lambda = 0$; $(\frac{\partial \gamma}{\partial \lambda})^2 + (\frac{\partial \gamma}{\partial \epsilon})^2$ vanishes; a denotes half the interocular distance):

$$(11) \qquad Ka^2 = (\frac{\partial^2 \gamma}{\partial \lambda^2} \frac{\partial^2 \gamma}{\partial \epsilon^2} - (\frac{\partial^2 \gamma}{\partial \lambda \partial \epsilon})^2) + (\frac{\partial^2 \gamma}{\partial \lambda^2} + 2\frac{\partial^2 \gamma}{\partial \epsilon^2})\gamma + 2\gamma^2 + O[\gamma]^3,$$

and

$$(12) \qquad Ha = \frac{1}{2}(\frac{\partial^2 \gamma}{\partial \lambda^2} + \frac{\partial^2 \gamma}{\partial \epsilon^2}) + \frac{3}{2}\gamma + O[\gamma]^3,$$

where K denotes the Gaussian, and H the mean curvature, much as one would have guessed offhand. (Think of $d\lambda/\gamma$ and $d\epsilon/\gamma$ as approximate Cartesian coordinates in a Monge parametrization!) The distance terms reflect the approximate central projection (the surface of equal distance is not planar, but has approximate curvature

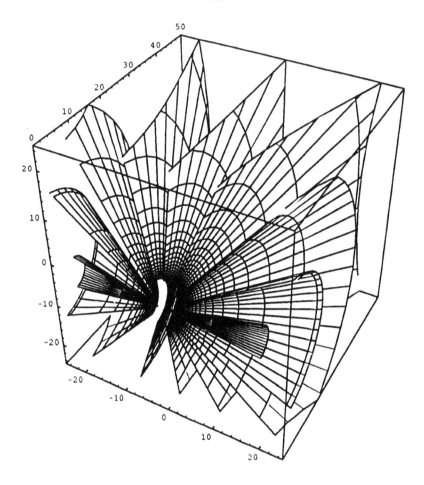

Figure 22: Surfaces of constant version. Eyes at $(\pm 1, 0, 0)$.

a/γ) and the at first sight surprising different factors for the version and elevation are due to the difference between the Vieth–Müller torus and a sphere.

The effect of a slant is also quite simple: Merely scale the expressions given above by the factor

$$(13) \qquad (1 + (\frac{1}{\gamma}\frac{\partial\gamma}{\partial\lambda})^2 + (\frac{1}{\gamma}\frac{\partial\gamma}{\partial\epsilon})^2)^{-1},$$

for the mean curvature, and by the square of this factor for the Gaussian curvature. For small slants the effect is again a minor one.

The effect of version is also relatively minor. The conclusion is that the simple frontoparallel, forward approximations are typically quite good in cases of practical interest. This conclusion can also be reached by more elementary (affine) methods[3]. It turns out that the datum available from the optical methods is equivalent to a knowledge of the projection of Dupin's indicatrix.

References

[1] C.J.Erkelens and H.Collewijn: Eye movements and stereopsis during dichoptic viewing of moving random-dot stereograms. Vision Research **25**, pp. 1689-1700, 1985

[2] H.E.Burton: The optics of Euclid. J.Opt.Soc.Am. **45**, pp. 357-372, 1945

[3] J.J.Koenderink and A.J.van Doorn: Second-order optic flow. J.Opt.Soc.Am. **A**, **9**, pp. 530-538, 1992

[4] R.K.Luneburg: Mathematical analysis of binocular vision. Princeton University Press, Princeton NJ, 1947

[5] C.O.Roelofs and H.G.van der Waals: Autokinetische Bewegungsempfindung. Z.f.Psychologie **147**, pp. 358-400, 1940

[6] B.Rogers and R.Cagenello: Disparity curvature and the perception of three-dimensional surfaces. Nature **339**, pp. 135-137, 1989

[7] A.Tissot: Mémoire sur la représentation des surfaces et les projections des cartes géographiques. Paris, 1881

[8] T.C.D.Whiteside and G.D.Samuel: Blur zone. Nature **225**, pp. 94-95, 1970

Acknowledgement Jan Koenderink is supported by the Dutch ministry of economic affairs (SPIN project "3D Computer Vision") and the ESPRIT "InSight" Basic Reaearch Action of the EC.

Digital HDTV: A Technical Challenge

by

Arun N. Netravali
AT&T Bell Laboratories
Murray Hill, New Jersey 07974
USA

Abstract. All digital HDTV systems over different media such as terrestrial broadcast, satellite, and coaxial or fiber cable are being proposed, implemented and tested in several countries. This paper presents technical challenges faced by such systems. First, in order to conserve the scarce terrestrial spectrum, bandwidth compression is required. Even after compression, picture quality has to be perceptibly better than today's TV and the cost of decompression in the HDTV set has to be kept small. Secondly, digital HDTV has to be receivable by all the people receiving the broadcast of current TV and has to fit within the spaces left in the present spectrum allocation. Finally, digital HDTV has to support all the functionality that we have gotten used to with today's TV (e.g., videotape recorders). This paper reviews these technical challenges and proposes one solution that addresses these challenges.

I. Introduction

No single technological innovation over the past 100 years has touched human lives as much as television (TV). Today, there are many countries (including developed countries such as the U.S.A.) where television is more often found in a household than a telephone. Television technology initially created for sports, entertainment and news, has rapidly proliferated to other domains: for example, medical and education. Standards for today's television were created in the 50's and 60's. Since then the camera, display, signal processing and semiconductor technology have made rapid advances. Time has come to exploit these advances and give consumers crisper pictures and high quality sound so that they can experience "theatre at home," and this is the goal of HDTV.

A number of challenges need to be faced in creating the new HDTV system. First, in order to exploit the growing synergies between entertainment, telecommunications and computing, and to allow distribution of HDTV over a variety of media (e.g., terrestrial broadcast, cable, satellite, VCR), the HDTV must be all digital. Technical challenges in creating an all-digital HDTV are reviewed in this paper. It should be pointed out that there are numerous other challenges that also need to be overcome before a global standard allowing free and easy exchange of HDTV programs can take place.

The technical challenges facing all digital HDTV fall into three classes. First, the digitized HDTV signal occupies too large a bandwidth and therefore needs to be compressed so that it can fit after modulation in the spaces (called taboo channels) left in the terrestrial spectrum. The picture quality after compression has to be perceptibly superior so that consumers will be enticed to make the investment in the HDTV set. Also, the cost of the decompression has to be small so that it can become part of the consumer television set. The modulation scheme used for terrestrial broadcast has to be robust to fit in the taboo channels and should not interfere with the current television which will be simulcast for a number of years. In addition, the HDTV broadcast should be able to cover all the people receiving the current television broadcast. Finally, the digital HDTV signal should be able to provide all (and perhaps more) functionalities that we currently have in television. An example of this is the analog VCR. We have gotten used to storing and retrieving video signals in an analog VCR in different modes (fast forward, reverse, etc.). How does one provide such functionality with compressed digital signal?

The remaining part of this paper is organized in four sections. The next two sections deal with requirements on compression, followed by requirements on transmission. Next, we propose a solution that meets these requirements. Our conclusions are summarized in the last section.

II. Compression Requirements

The basic digital video compressor and decompressor are shown in Figure 1. As mentioned earlier, the function of the compressor is to reduce the bit rate as much as possible without sacrificing the picture quality required for the service[1]. In addition, a number of other requirements have to be satisfied, particularly in the cable, satellite and broadcast environment. In this section we outline these requirements so that they will serve as a guide in evaluating the proposal we present in Section IV.

The first requirement, of course, is to achieve transparent coding for the class of pictures that are typically used in the particular service. In entertainment and sports applications, the picture material may contain high detail, complex (not necessarily predictable) motion and a large number of frequent scene cuts or changes. The picture material may be created by an HDTV camera or synthesized by a computer or an arbitrary mixture of the two. In a number of situations, the source material may contain noise (e.g., old film or electronic news gathering cameras). The ability to compress such diverse material is indeed very challenging and different from either video teleconferencing or the multimedia applications. Moreover, the picture quality standard accepted and practiced in the cable and the broadcast industry is significantly more demanding than what is practical in videoconferencing or multimedia applications.

The second requirement is that the compressed HDTV bit stream must not be very fragile. Of course, compressed bit streams are always more fragile than raw compressed digital HDTV. However, their robustness to transmission impairments can be significantly improved by error correction and ghost cancellation techniques. In addition, the compression algorithm must be such that a large fraction of the errors that escape the error correction mechanism can be concealed and their effects localized both in terms of space (i.e., horizontal and vertical dimensions of a picture) and time (i.e., the number of frames).

In a cable or broadcast environment, a viewer may change from channel to channel with no opportunity for the transmitter to adapt itself to such channel changes. It is important that the buildup of resolution following the channel change takes place quite rapidly so that the viewer can make a decision to either stay on the channel or change further depending upon the content that he wishes to watch.

A cable, satellite or broadcast environment has only a few transmitters which do compression but a large number of receivers which have to do decompression. Therefore, the economics is dictated to a large extent by the cost of decompression. The choice of the compression algorithm ought to make the decompression extremely simple by transferring much of the cost to the transmitter, thereby creating an asymmetrical algorithm. The existing video standards such as px64 kbit/sec for videoconference and MPEG for multimedia do not explicitly incorporate this requirement. In a number of situations, cost of the encoder is also important (e.g., camcorder). Therefore, a modularly designed encoder which is able to trade off performance with complexity but which creates the data decodable by a simple decompressor may be the appropriate solution. Obviously, this tradeoff will change as a function of the integrated circuits technology.

In a number of instances, the original source material may have to be compressed and decompressed several times. In studios it may be necessary to store the compressed data and then decompress it for editing. Such multiple encodings of the signal is bound to increase the visibility of the coding artifacts; however, a choice of the coding algorithm should minimize the loss of quality associated with multiple encodings.

It is commonly believed that much of the material for the services based on digital compressed HDTV will be from films. The conversion from film to HDTV using 3:2 pull down creates a unique type of correlation in the signal. It is desirable for the compression algorithm to automatically detect such correlation and adapt itself to achieve a high degree of efficiency without increasing the complexity of the receiver.

The technology for storage of digital signals on a variety of media has made significant strides over the last few years. If the compressed digital signal is stored on a digital tape recorder, then some of the functions that we have become accustomed to should be easy to provide from the compressed digital signal. These include fast forward and backward searches, still frames, etc. This was an important consideration in the development of the MPEG algorithm.

As we move toward digital HDTV, we see a large number of possible picture resolutions (e.g., NTSC, CCIR-601, HDTV). It is desirable for the compression scheme to be compatible over these different resolutions. This will allow, for example, an HDTV decompressor to encode the compressed NTSC, PAL, as well as CCIR-601 signals without much duplication of the hardware. Also, a compatibility between the transmission formats chosen for the NTSC, PAL, CCIR-601 and HDTV signals would be desirable. Moreover, such a common transmission format should allow easy interconnection or transmission over different media and telecommunications networks.

In a number of situations, particularly in the cable head end, one may wish to add an insert into a compressed digital bit stream. It is desirable to add the insert without having to fully decode the signal. If only a small part of the coded bit stream can be affected and these effects can be localized on the picture signal, then the adding of inserts can become less damaging to the original signal.

It is clear by looking at these requirements that the broadcasting, cable, and satellite applications have requirements that are different from teleconferencing and multimedia applications. Therefore, it is not surprising that a different class of algorithms would suit these applications.

III. Transmission Requirements

Highly compressed digital TV signals need protection from transmission impairments. The nature of transmission impairments is different for different physical media. Terrestrial broadcast, cable (coaxial or fiber), satellite and digital videotape recorders are among media over which future digital HDTV may be distributed. Of these, terrestrial broadcast is the most imperfect medium and therefore is given most of the consideration in this section. The only spectrum spaces (taboo channels) left are the 6 Mhz bands sandwiched between bands that carry current analog TV. Moreover, a taboo channel in one region is usually an active analog TV channel for geographical regions surrounding it. Thus, digital HDTV has to be robust in spite of the interference from adjacent channels as well as cochannels (i.e., in the same band of frequencies) carrying analog TV. This can always be done by increasing the power of the transmitted HDTV signals. However, it is extremely important that a digital HDTV signal transmitted in the taboo spaces does not create visible degradation of the current TV both in the adjacent and cochannels carrying analog TV. This requires that the power levels be maintained low and the visible pattern of interference from digital HDTV look more like high frequency random noise that is perceptibly less visible. Thus, terrestrial broadcasting is constrained severely by interference considerations.

Another aspect of digital HDTV that is extremely important to broadcasters is the coverage area. Broadly speaking, terrestrial broadcast of digital HDTV should be receivable by all the people who currently watch "over the air analog TV," with no change in the transmitter locations even though HDTV will be transmitted with substantially low power due to interference considerations. One of the difficulties is that unlike the analog TV which gracefully degrades as the distance between the receiver and the transmitting tower is increased, digital TV could abruptly cease to be received. This so called "cliff effect" can be minimized by clever choice of modulation and compression techniques. Among the choices that can be made to prevent the cliff effect, a choice that keeps the receiver complexity low is clearly the preferred one. Such a solution can create high-quality pictures for receivers that are close to the transmitter and pictures that are at least as good as current TV for regions which are in the far fringes from the transmitter. In the next section we present a proposal for a digital HDTV system that meets almost all of these requirements.

IV. A Digital HDTV System

As an example we describe the system proposed by Zenith and AT&T (called DSC-HDTV) to the Federal Communications Commission in the United States[2]. The DSC-HDTV compression system uses a color television source signal of 994 Mbit/second bit rate which is compressed to a variable bit rate of between 8.6 and 17.1 Mbit/second without sacrificing image quality.

Video compression exploits three basic types of redundancy[3]. Motion Compensation removes temporal redundancy, spatial frequency transformation removes spatial redundancy, and perceptual weighting removes amplitude redundancy by putting quantization noise in less visible areas. Temporal processing occurs in two stages. The motion of blocks and pixels from frame to frame is estimated using hierarchical block matching. Using the motion vectors, a displaced frame difference (DFD) is computed. The DFD generally contains a small fraction of the information in the original frame. The DFD is transformed using a two-dimensional discrete cosine transform (DCT) prior to removal of the spatial redundancy. Each new frame of DFD is analyzed prior to coding to determine its rate versus perceptual distortion characteristics and the dynamic range of each coefficient. Quantization of the DCT coefficients is performed based on the perceptual importance of each coefficient, the precomputed dynamic range of the coefficients, and the rate versus distortion characteristics. The perceptual criterion uses a model of the human visual system to determine a human observer's sensitivity to color, brightness, spatial frequency and spatial-temporal masking. This information is used to minimize the perception of coding artifacts throughout the picture. Parameters of the Encoder are optimized to handle the scene changes that occur frequently in entertainment and sport events, and in channel changes made by the viewer.

IV.1 Video Encoder

The Video Encoder is shown in Figure 2. Its main parts are Motion Estimator, Forward Analyzer, Encoder Loop and Buffer. The Motion Estimator produces motion vectors which are compressed and sent to the Buffer for transmission. The Forward Analyzer analyses each frame before it is processed in the Encoder Loop. The motion vectors and control parameters resulting from forward analysis are input to the Encoder Loop which outputs the compressed prediction error to the Buffer. The Encoder Loop parameters are weighted by the buffer state which is fed back from the Buffer.

The coding parameters are controlled in part by forward analysis. The Encoder output data consists of some global parameters of the video frame computed by the Forward Analyzer and of DCT coefficients that have been selected and quantized according to a perceptual criterion. The chrominance bit rate is generally a small fraction of the total bit-rate without perceptible chrominance distortion.

IV.2 Motion Estimation

Motion is estimated in stages on a block-by-block basis using the luminance frames only. A block consists of 8x8 pixels. At each state the best block match is defined to be that which has the least absolute difference between blocks. The results from one stage are used as a starting point for the next stage to minimize the number of block matches per image. The Motion Estimator is capable of handling large frame-to-frame displacements typical of entertainment and sport scenes. Finally, the block size of motion estimation is adapted spatially to those places in the picture which could have the most benefit within the limit of the compressed motion vector bit rate.

The Motion Estimator compares a block of pels in the current frame with a block in the previous frame by forming the sum of the absolute differences between the pels, known as the prediction error. Each block in the current image is compared to displaced blocks at different locations in the previous image and the displacement vector that gives the minimum prediction error is chosen as being the best representation of the motion of that block. This is the motion vector for that block. The end result of motion estimation is to associate a motion vector with every block of pels in the image.

The Motion Estimator is shown in Figure 3. To reduce the complexity of the search, hierarchical motion estimation is used in which a first stage of coarse estimation is refined by a second, finer estimation. The first stage matching is performed on the images after they have been decimated by a factor of two both vertically and horizontally. This reduces both the block size and the search area and greatly reduces the size of the Motion Estimator. A coarse block size of 16Hx8V pixels in the decimated image is used with 1 pixel accuracy. The motion vectors that are generated are passed to the second stage which performs a search centered around this coarse estimate. The motion vectors generated from the first stage are used by the Fine Motion Estimator that can estimate the motion of 8x8 pixel blocks to within sub-pixel accuracy. The total search area is 96Hx80V pixels.

The second motion estimator stage generates the prediction errors of the 8x8 pixel blocks for each location within the search area. The prediction errors of the coarse blocks are derived from the sums of the appropriate small block prediction errors. The final stage of the Motion Estimator uses the prediction errors to generate the motion vectors by finding the minimum prediction error for all blocks in every location. The resulting motion vectors are then passed to the Motion Vector Selector.

Given the motion vectors from the coarse and fine motion estimator stages, the Motion Vector Selector must select the set of motion vectors that will give the best prediction of the next frame while limiting the bit rate of the compressed motion vector data to be in a range.

This is achieved by sending two resolutions of motion vectors. The first set represents the motion vectors of the coarse blocks which are unconditionally transmitted, and the second set represents the motion vectors for 8x8 pixel blocks. However, all of the 8x8 pixel block motion vectors may not be transmitted, only those which can be sent within the bit budget remaining after the coarse motion vectors have been sent.

IV.3 Transform Coding

The Encoder Loop in Figure 2 generates a transformed and quantized displaced frame difference (DFD) using the motion vectors, perceptual thresholds and loop control parameters. The motion vectors are applied to the predicted frame which is stored in a separate buffer. The displaced frame (DF) is scaled by a DF-factor and subtracted from the input frame. This yields the DFD which contains only a fraction of the original image. The DFD is spatially transformed using the DCT and the coefficients are then adaptively quantized. The coarseness of quantization of individual coefficients is adjusted in local regions of the image. This represents adaptation to the limitations of human vision while minimizing the amount of transmitted information. Fast recovery from channel errors and channel changes is facilitated by DF scaling.

IV.4 Vector Quantization

Rather than quantizing the 64 coefficients of a block according to a fixed scheme, a set of non-uniform quantizers is used. A Quantizer Selection Vector (QSV) is a 64 element vector in which each element represents one out of three quantizers or a drop command. Less than 2,000 QSV's are used and are sufficient to quantize all luminance coefficients; they constitute the Luminance QSV Code Book. Similarly there are two 500 QSV Chrominance Code Books.

The QSV's of the luminance code book are successively applied to a luminance super block consisting of four 8x8 blocks. One quantizer (or drop command) of the set of 64 of one QSV is applied to the four coefficients of the super-block that are in corresponding locations in each of the four 8x8 blocks. Chrominance QSV's are similarly applied to chrominance superblocks of six 8x8 blocks (16Hx24V). Quantization errors are computed and are compared to a perceptual error threshold; the result is summed to produce the selection error for the vector. The optimal vector is selected by considering both selection error and bit rate.

IV.5 Perceptual Criterion

This refers to matching the coding algorithm to the characteristics of the human visual system (HVS). The following properties are used: Frequency sensitivity, Contrast sensitivity, Spatial masking and Temporal masking. Frequency sensitivity refers to the property of the HVS that tolerates more quantization error at high frequencies than at low frequencies. Contrast sensitivity refers to flat field stimuli. This sensitivity varies with the brightness of the flat field and perceptual thresholds are adjusted accordingly. Coding includes a model of spatial masking which adjusts the perceptual threshold based on the amount of local texture present at each location in the input. Texture refers to the amount by which the input deviates from a flat field. Temporal masking refers to the increase of the perceptual threshold for high frequencies when there is motion in the scene. The perceptual criterion is implemented by the calculation of perceptual thresholds to be used in the quantizers. Separate luminance and chrominance perceptual thresholds are generated. They are not transmitted but are used to optimize the transmitted information and minimize perceptible artifacts.

IV.6 Channel Buffer and Formatter

The Buffer (Figure 2) regulates the variable input bit rate into an output bit rate for transmission of between 8.6 and 17.1 MBit/sec. Errors in variable-length coded data cause errors long after the error is past. To avoid error propagation, the data are packed into slices with header information. A slice corresponds to a fixed region in the original image. Motion vectors, quantizer selection vectors and quantized coefficients are variable length encoded. The Formatter arranges these data intermixed with various coding parameters of fixed length. The state of the Buffer is calculated periodically and relayed back to the Forward Analyzer. Here the perceptual thresholds are altered to prevent overflow or underflow of the buffer.

IV.7 Transmission System

The transmitter block diagram is shown in Figure ?. The variable video bit rate supplied by the Video Encoder is converted to a constant symbol rate. The addition of audio and ancillary data, forward error control data and sync data results in a symbol rate of 10.76 Msymbol/second. The transmission bytes are arranged in a "Data Frame," timed identical to an NTSC Frame. One Data Frame contains two "Data Fields" and one Data Frame is divided into 525 "Data Segments" all in correspondence with NTSC "frame," "field" and horizontal line, respectively.

All data are transmitted in accordance with a bi-rate scheme. Sync signals, one pair of stereo audio signals, and a fixed portion of the ancillary signals are always transmitted at 1 bit/symbol. The other audio pair and the remaining ancillary signals are always transmitted at 2 bits/symbol. Video data are transmitted at 1 or 2 bits/symbol as determined by the Video Encoder. DC and low frequency coefficients, quantizer scale factors, DF-factor and buffer fullness constitute the most important data and are always transmitted at 1 bit/symbol. The remaining video data are transmitted at 1 bit/symbol up to the attainment of a global target distortion (related to buffer fullness) corresponding to a desired picture quality. The rest of the video data is transmitted at 2 bits/symbol. Side information for receiver interpretation of the data is provided by the Video Encoder and is encoded in the Transmission Bit Map, transmitted twice at 1 bit/symbol during the first four data segments of each field.

IV.8 Interference Rejection

The decreased cochannel spacing between NTSC and DSC-HDTV transmitters requires special measures in the DSC-HDTV receiver as mentioned. The system uses a receiver Comb-Filter that has nulls at or very near the interfering NTSC cochannel's visual, aural and chroma carriers and thus rejects most of the interference. The correlation between Comb-Filter output symbols can be removed by digital pre- and post-coding. Both precoder and Comb-Filter are placed at the transmitter. Due to the digital operation on an essentially random sequence the transmitted spectrum remains flat and noise-like so that the property of minimum interference into an NTSC cochannel is retained.

These advantages are offset by a loss of 3 dB in signal-to-noise ratio. This can, however, be prevented when no significant NTSC cochannel interference is present. In that case, the Comb-Filter is switched out and a digital post-coder is used instead. The latter device does not have the 3 dB S/N ratio loss. A measured error rate in both modes using the pseudo-random field sync signal is used to decide which of the two circuits shall be active. This arrangement allows receiver simplification when simulcasting comes to an end.

IV.9 Modulation

The DSC-HDTV receiver has to operate reliably under severe cochannel interference conditions, as described. The Interference Rejection System only works after the receiver is properly tuned to the desired DSC-HDTV station. Tuning is greatly facilitated by a pilot signal. CW signals are potential sources of interference into NTSC receivers. There is, however, a region in the 6 MHz NTSC television channel where this potential is significantly reduced. This is at the low end of the channel where the NTSC receiver has considerable IF attenuation. Therefore, the data signal modulation chosen is Vestigial Side Band (VSB) with the carrier (suppressed) low in the band at the same frequency as the pilot. The modulated signal is designated "4-VSB" when the modulating signal consists of 4-level symbols and "2-VSB" when modulated by 2-level symbols.

There is some risk involved in adding a slight amount of pilot. The very long-time average of the data signal is zero but over shorter time spans the average may be negative which can decrease or even cancel the pilot. This can be avoided by subjecting groups of data to a modulo-4 bit addition until the average is positive. The addition is encoded in the 12 symbols following data segment sync.

The low-level modulator is followed by a SAW filter that includes dispersion in the form of constant-slope varying group delay. The only transmitted data that occur so regularly that they would cause a noticeable, non-random interference pattern on an NTSC receiver, are the data segment syncs. To reduce this effect, even though minor, the data dispersion operation is introduced. As a result, the random level of the data adjacent to the sync spreads into the sync data. This reduces the visibility of the described interference.

The transmitter is operated with a maximum Effective Radiated Power (ERP) which is a minimum of 12 dB less than current NTSC transmitters. At UHF, a portion of this power reduction may be used to reduce antenna gain in order to reduce beam-steering effects which can cause excessive level tilts over the 6 Mhz channel in some locations.

V. Conclusions

We have presented in this paper the technical challenges that must be overcome so consumers can experience high definition television. While challenges are considerable, there are a number of solutions and indeed the technology required to create the HDTV infra-structure (i.e., HDTV cameras, displays, VCR's) is already available. We presented a solution that adequately meets all the requirements. It is clear that all the pieces of technology are in hand and since people want to see clear pictures at home, HDTV will become widespread before the end of this decade.

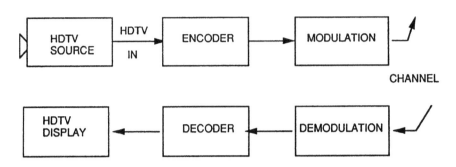

FIGURE 1: HDTV Compression and Decompression

261

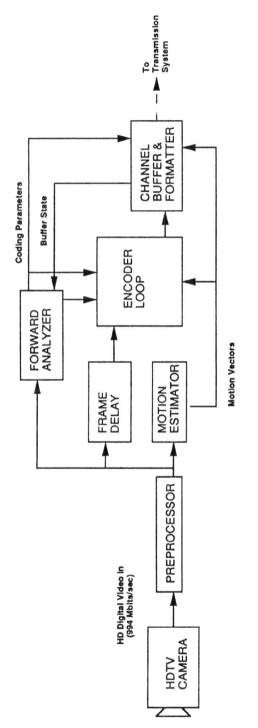

FIGURE 2: Video Encoder

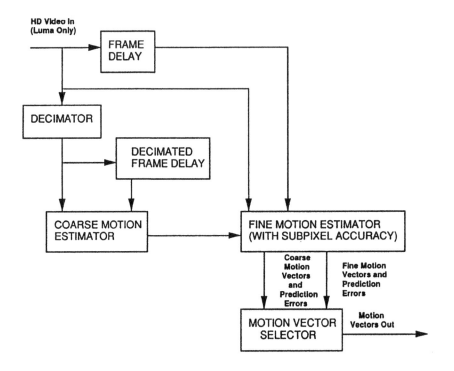

FIGURE 3: MOTION ESTIMATOR

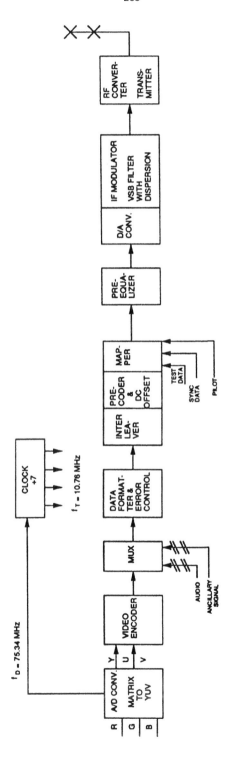

FIGURE 4: DSC-HDTV Transmitter Block Diagram

REFERENCES

1. "A High Performance HDTV Codec" by A. Netravali, E. Petajan, S. Knauer, K. Matthews, R. Safranek, P. Westerink. Paper delivered at the National Association of Broadcasters (NAB) Technical Conference, Las Vegas, Nevada, (USA), April 18, 1991.

2. Digital Spectrum-Compatible HDTV: "Technical Details." Monograph published by Zenith Electronics Corporation and AT&T Bell Laboratories, September 23, 1991.

3. "Digital Pictures, Representation and Compression" by A. Netravali, B. Haskell, Plenum Press 1988, New York.

V. Signal Processing, Control, and Manufacturing Automation

Autonomous Control

K. J. Åström

Department of Automatic Control
Lund Institute of Technology
Box 118, S-221 00 Lund, Sweden

Abstract. Several years of industrial use of adaptive control has led to an improved understanding of the issues involved in designing such controllers. Combined with recent research in system identification, control system design, robust control, adaptive control it is now possible to design adaptive controllers with significantly enhanced capabilities.

1. Introduction

The conventional approach to adaptive control is to recursively estimate parameters of a model and to design a controller with given specifications based on the estimated model. A problem with this approach is that the user must determine suitable specifications. This is a nontrivial task. What can be achieved depends on many factors, process dynamics, disturbances and controller complexity. Failure to find suitable specifications results in a controller with poor performance. The conventional adaptive control formulation thus automates some aspects of the control problem but not all. It is interesting to note that estimation of achievable performance is an important aspect of classical methods for tuning controllers. See Ziegler and Nichols (1942), where an estimate of the achievable bandwidth was obtained by determining the frequency where the plant has a phase lag of 180°. It seems natural to use ideas from classical controller tuning to obtain reasonable specifications for an adaptive controller. In this way we can obtain controllers that can find suitable performance criteria from experiments on the process. Such systems are called autonomous.

2. Performance Assessment

To design a controller it is necessary to have information about the desired closed loop behavior and the characteristics of the process and its environment. Specifications on desired behavior must naturally match the properties of the process and its environment. Typical specifications include requirements on load disturbance attenuation, sensitivity to measurement noise and modeling errors, and set point following. The information required for performance assessment includes process dynamics, constraints and disturbances. It is important to have some assessment of achievable performance before attempting to do a control system design. Such questions were at the center of interest in classical control theory. See, e.g., Truxal (1955) and Horowitz (1963). The questions have, however, largely been forgotten during the intensive development of modern control theory as was pointed out in the IEEE Bode Lecture given by G. Stein in 1989.

In this section we will present some performance limits that are simple and useful for obtaining realistic specifications for a control problem. The results are based on the gain crossover frequency ω_{gc}, which is defined as the lowest frequency where the magnitude of the loop transfer function L has unit magnitude. For frequencies below ω_{gc} the loop gain is higher than one and it is normally less than one for higher frequencies. Parameter ω_{gc} is a reasonable measure of the frequency where feedback is effective.

It is convenient to write the transfer function of the process as $L_{mp}L_{nmp}$ where L_{mp} is the minimum phase part that has all poles and zeros in the left half plane and L_{nmp} is the non-minimum phase part. This can be normalized by requiring that the L_{nmp} has unit magnitude. The loop transfer function L is the product of the transfer functions of the plant and the controller. A well designed controller is normally minimum phase. The non-minimum phase part of the loop transfer function is thus equal to the non-minimum phase part of the plant transfer function.

In the estimates given below Bode's relations for minimum phase systems will be approximated with

$$\arg L_{mp}(i\omega_{gc}) \approx n \frac{\pi}{2} \tag{1}$$

See Bode (1945). Assume that it is desired to have a phase margin larger than ϕ_m and let the gain crossover frequency be ω_{gc}. It then follows that

$$\arg L(i\omega_{gc}) > \phi_m - \pi \tag{2}$$

The following is a brief summary of results in Åström (1993).

2.1 Stable Minimum Phase Systems

Systems that are stable and minimum phase are relatively easy to control because plant dynamics poses no limitations on performance. Any crossover frequency can be obtained by a compensator with sufficient phase lead. A phase lead is, however, accompanied by a high gain. The following is a conservative estimate of the gain N required for a given phase lead ϕ

$$N_\infty = e^{2\phi} \tag{3}$$

Notice that the gain increases very rapidly with increasing phase lead. If the controller has high gain, measurement noise will be amplified and cause inadmissible control signals. For minimum phase systems the achievable performance is thus limited by measurement noise. Plant uncertainty also introduces limitations on the achievable bandwidth.

2.2 Stable Non-minimum phase Systems

For stable non-minimum phase systems the crossover frequency is limited by the nonminimum phase parts of the system. Consider a system with the loop transfer function L. Let ϕ_m be the desired phase margin and let n_{gc} be the slope at ω_{gc}. It then follows from (2) that

$$\arg L_{nmp}(i\omega_{gc}) > \phi_m - \pi - n_{gc} \frac{\pi}{2} \tag{4}$$

The function on the left hand side typically decreases monotonically. The inequality thus gives an upper bound for the crossover frequency. An upper bound for $n_{gc} = 0$ is thus obtained, since the slope n_{gc} must be negative at ω_{gc}. Notice that there is a tradeoff since ω_{gc} increases with increasing n_{gc}. To have a robust system it is desirable that n_{gc} should be small. The bounds given by (4) are illustrated with an example.

EXAMPLE 1—Systems with dead-time
For a plant with a dead time we have $L_{nmp}(s) = e^{-sL}$. Assuming $\phi_m = \pi/2$, $n_{gc} = -0.5$ it follows from Equation (4) $\omega_{gc} < \pi/2L$. Notice that the L_{nmp} has a phase lag of 90° at this frequency. □

2.3 Unstable Systems

Consider systems with right half plane poles. Equation (4) still holds but the function on the left hand side is now an increasing function of ω_{gc}. The inequality thus gives a lower bound on the crossover frequency. We illustrate this with an example.

EXAMPLE 2—Systems with an unstable pole
Consider a system with a right half plane pole at $s = a$. The nonminimum phase part of the transfer function then becomes $L_{nmp}(s) = (s+a)/(s-a)$ and the inequality (4) becomes

$$\omega_{gc} > a \arctan\left(\frac{\phi_m}{2} - n_{gc} \frac{\phi}{4}\right)$$

With $n_{gc} = -1$ and $\phi_m = \pi/4$ we get $\omega_{gc} > 2.4a$. □

For unstable systems there is a lower limit on the crossover frequency, which is determined by the unstable pole. Notice that for real poles the severity of the constraints increases as the pole moves further from the origin.

2.4 Summary

There are many ways to make an assessment of the achievable performance of a system. Here we have given some inequalities for the gain crossover frequency. It is suggested that estimation of such features should be part of an adaptive controller. To use the inequalities it is necessary to estimate time delays, and poles and zeros in the right half plane. If these quantities are determined it is possible to analyze if suggested specifications are reasonable and to determine specifications automatically. In addition to the properties discussed here it is useful to also estimate noise characteristics and model uncertainty. See Åström (1991).

3. Relay Feedback

Relay feedback is a powerful method of exciting a dynamical system and to estimate useful system characteristics. The key idea is that many systems will exhibit stable limit cycles when subject to relay feedback. The frequency and the amplitude of the limit cycle are determined by system features and give useful insight into system properties. The idea of using the excitation provided by relay feedback to tune simple controllers was proposed by Åström and Hägglund (1984b). The method has been applied very successfully in several industrial products. There are also several interesting variations of the method, see Schei (1991). There are several interesting questions related to existence and stability of the limit cycles obtained. In this paper we will not discuss these problems. For simplicity the discussion will be based on describing function analysis, see Atherton (1975). There are, however, also exact methods, see Tsypkin (1984) and Åström and Hägglund (1984a).

3.1 Phase Crossover Characteristics

The behavior of the plant transfer function at the phase crossover frequency, i.e. the frequency ω_{180}, where the phase lag is 180°, is of particular interest for design of PID controllers. It gives an estimate of the achievable closed loop bandwidth and it is also the basis for the Ziegler-Nichols tuning procedure. The frequency ω_{180} can be determined automatically from an experiment with

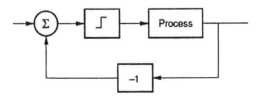

Figure 1. Determine the phase crossover frequency ω_{180} from an experiment with relay feedback.

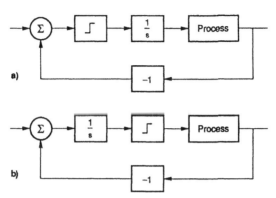

Figure 2. Two ways to determine the frequency ω_{90} by using relay feedback.

relay feedback as is shown in Figure 1. By making the observation that the describing function of a relay is the negative real axis it follows that the system oscillates with a frequency that is close to ω_{180}. See Atherton (1975). The frequency can be determined from zero crossings of the limit cycle. The magnitude of the transfer function can be determined by a simple harmonic analysis. In practice it is useful to introduce hysteresis in the relay. The describing function is then a line parallel to the negative real axis. Such a measurement will give the value of the transfer function at a frequency close to ω_{180}.

A slight modification of the experiment shown in Figure 1 gives other frequencies of interest. Figure 2 shows an experiment that gives the frequency ω_{90}, i.e. the frequency where the plant has a phase lag of 90°. The frequency ω_{270} can be obtained in a similar way by introducing a lead network instead of an integrator. Notice that there are two different versions of the experiment depending on the order of the integrator and the relay.

3.2 Closed Loop Experiments

Relay feedback can also be applied to closed-loop systems. Figure 3 shows an experiment that can be used to determine the amplitude margin on-line. Let L be the loop transfer function, i.e. the combined transfer function of the

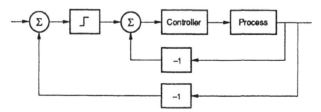

Figure 3. Using relay feedback to determine the amplitude margin of the closed loop system.

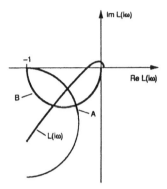

Figure 4. Frequencies obtained by different experiments with relay feedback.

controller and the plant. The closed-loop transfer function is then

$$G_{cl}(s) = \frac{L(s)}{1 + L(s)} \tag{5}$$

The experiment with relay feedback then gives an oscillation with the frequency such that the phase lag of $G_{cl}(i\omega)$ is 180°. It then follows from (5) that this is also the frequency where $L(i\omega)$ has a phase lag of 180°, i.e. the phase crossover frequency. If the relay has hysteresis, then a conformal mapping argument shows that the experiment gives the frequency, where the loop transfer function intersects part of the circle

$$\left| L(i\omega) - 1 + i\frac{1}{2a} \right| = \frac{1}{2a}$$

which is shown as curve A in in Figure 4. By introducing an integrator in series with the relay, the frequency where $G_{cl}(i\omega)$ has a phase lag of 90° is obtained. This occurs where the Nyquist curve of the loop transfer functions intersects the circle

$$\left| L(i\omega) + \frac{1}{2} \right| = \frac{1}{2} \tag{6}$$

which is shown as curve B in Figure 4.

3.3 Summary

In this section we have given several methods to estimate the frequencies ω_{90}, ω_{180} and ω_{270}. These frequencies are useful in order to determine the performance limitations imposed by process dynamics. In Lundh and Åström (1992) it is shown how this idea is used to design an adaptive controller. In Smith and Doyle (1992a) it is suggested to use relay experiments to estimate uncertainty bounds.

4. Interaction of Identification and Control

The desire to have compatible criteria for control and identification was one of the motivations for introducing the maximum likelihood method or the prediction error method. See Åström (1967) and Åström (1970). The idea is that the error under minimum variance control is equal to the error in predicting the output over the control horizon. The maximum-likelihood method for system identification minimizes the same prediction error. The fact that control and identification criteria are compatible is also one of the reasons why the simple self-tuner based on minimum variance control and least squares estimation, see Åström and Wittenmark (1973), has many nice properties.

In the very vigorous development of system identification that has taken place during the last 20 years it has sometimes been forgotten that design of a feedback controller is a main reason for doing identification. This viewpoint has however recently been reemphasized in a number of papers. The paper Schrama (1992) presents an iterative method for obtaining compatible control and identification criteria. Related problems are discussed in Lee *et al.* (1992), Zang *et al.* (1992), Hakvoort *et al.* (1992), Smith and Doyle (1992b), Rivera *et al.* (1992), and Gevers (1991).

We will investigate the interplay between identification and control for the particular case of pole placement control and least squares estimation. It turns out that the problem has a very simple solution in this case.

4.1 Pole Placement Control

The pole placement design method is simple and well-known, see e.g. Åström and Wittenmark (1973). Consider a process described by the model

$$Ay = Bu + v \qquad (7)$$

where u is the control signal y the measured variable and v a disturbance signal. All signals are assumed to be discrete time signals where the sampling interval is the time unit. Furthermore A and B are polynomials in the forward shift operator. Let the controller be

$$Ru = Ty_{sp} - Sy \qquad (8)$$

where y_{sp} is the set point and R, S and T are polynomials. The polynomials R and S satisfy the diophantine equation

$$AR + BS = A_cA_o \qquad (9)$$

where the desired closed loop polynomial is A_oA_c. This equation has many solutions, it is customary to choose the simplest one that gives a causal controller but it is also possible to introduce auxiliary conditions. Integral action is obtained by finding a solution such that $R(1) = 1$. High frequency roll-off is obtained by requiring that $S(1) = 1$. See Åström and Wittenmark (1990). In Lundh and Åström (1992) it is shown how to choose the sampling period and the polynomials $A_m(q)$ and $A_o(q)$ from experiments with relay feedback.

The polynomial T is given by $T = \alpha A_o$, where $\alpha = A_c(1)/B(1)$. If $R(1) = 0$ it also follows that $T(1) = S(1)$. Combining (7) and (8) we get

$$
\begin{aligned}
y &= \alpha \, \frac{B}{A_c} \, y_{sp} + \frac{R}{A_c A_o} \, v \\
u &= \alpha \, \frac{A}{A_c} \, y_{sp} - \frac{S}{A_c A_o} \, v
\end{aligned}
\tag{10}
$$

This equation shows that constant disturbances v will not give steady state errors if $R(1) = 0$.

The sensitivity function is $AR/A_o A_c$. Polynomials A_o and A_c are typically chosen to give good rejection of disturbances and insensitivity to modeling errors and measurement noise.

4.2 Least Squares Estimation

In adaptive control and automatic tuning it is attempted to perform modeling and control design automatically. One approach is to used standard system identification methods (Ljung (1987), Söderström and Stoica (1989)) to obtain a model. The control law is then generated by applying some control design method. As always when problems are solved automatically it is essential to have a good understanding of the problem in order to do this.

To perform system identification it is necessary to have information about the purpose of the modeling. Since discrete time methods are used it is also necessary to choose a reasonable sampling period. Both choices require prior information about the system. In automatic tuning this information must be acquired automatically. There are many ways to do this. One way, proposed in Åström and Hägglund (1984b), is to use relay feedback to acquire the information. This idea is evaluated in Lundh and Åström (1992), where it is shown that the approach gives good results for pole placement control.

There is another important issue in system identification that also must be considered. The result obtained when fitting a low order model to data generated by a complex process critically depends on the input signal used and on the criterion for identification. It is interesting to note that these matters are very nicely handled by the simple self-tuner based on minimum variance control and least squares estimation given in Åström and Wittenmark (1973). First the criteria used to fit the model is the one-step prediction error. Under minimum variance control the criterion is the same because the control error is also the one-step prediction error. See Åström (1970). When identification is done in closed loop the input signal is also the one used by feedback control. These are two reasons why the simple self-tuner has such good properties.

Least squares is a common way to perform parameter estimation. The model (7) is then fitted to data in such a way that the mean square value of the error

$$e_i = F(Ay - Bu) \tag{11}$$

is minimized. In this expression F denotes the transfer function of the data filter. One reason for choosing the criterion given by (11) is that the calculations are simple because the error is linear in the parameters of the polynomial.

The parameters obtained depend critically on the properties of the input signal and the filter transfer function F. When parameter estimation is done in connection with adaptive control the natural signals in the feedback loop are used. The signals are thus given by the problem. The user can however choose the filter F. This has largely been done heuristically. In the next section it will be shown that there is a rational way of choosing the filter.

4.3 Main Result

It is desirable to formulate the adaptive control problem in such a way that the goals for control and identification are compatible. If this is done it means that a model is fitted in such a way that it matches the ultimate use of of the model.

Consider the situation when the goal is to control a plant with transfer function P_0. A controller is designed using pole placement based on the approximate model whose transfer function is $P = B/A$. To compute the control law the parameters of the polynomials A and B are estimated using least squares as discused in Section 2, and the controller is then determined by the pole placement method as was discussed in Section 3. Let u_0 and y_0 denote the inputs and outputs obtained when controlling the actual plant and let u and y denote the corresponding signals when the controller controls the design model. The control performance error can then be defined as

$$e_{cp} = y_0 - y \tag{12}$$

We have the following result

THEOREM 1
The identification error e_i and the control performance error e_{cp} are identical if identification is performed in closed loop and if the transfer function of the data filter is chosen as

$$F = \frac{R}{A_o A_m} \tag{13}$$

Proof: The proof is a straightforward calculation. We have

$$y_0 = \frac{P_0 T}{R + P_0 S} y_{sp} \tag{14}$$

and the control signal for the true plant is

$$u_0 = \frac{T}{R + P_0 S} y_{sp} \tag{15}$$

The corresponding signals for the nominal plant are obtained simply by omitting the index 0 on y_0, u_0 and P_0. The control performance error then becomes

$$
\begin{aligned}
e_{cp} &= \left(\frac{P_0 T}{R + P_0 S} - \frac{PT}{R + PS} \right) y_{sp} = \frac{RT(P_0 - P)}{(R + P_0 S)(R + PS)} y_{sp} \\
&= \frac{R(P_0 - P)}{R + PS} u_0 = \frac{AR(P_0 - P)}{A_o A_m} u_0
\end{aligned} \tag{16}
$$

where the first equality follows from (12) and (14). The second equality is obtained by a simple algebraic manipulation. The third follows from (15) and the last equality follows from (9). Equations (11) and (13) now imply

$$e_i = e_{cpe}$$

which completes the proof. □

Remark. Notice that the denominator of the filter (13) is given by $A_o A_m$, which are given by the specifications.

Remark. Notice that for a controller with integral action the filter (13) is a bandpass filter.

The results can be used in several different ways. One possibility for offline design is to use an iterative scheme of the type suggested in Schrama (1992). Another application is in adaptive controllers based on least squares estimation and pole placement design. In this case it is simply a matter of using the ordinary adaptive algorithm with the data filter given by (13). Notice that it is only the numerator of the filter that has to be adapted.

5. Conclusions

In adaptive control it is customarily assumed that specifications are given a priori and the interest is focused on methods for modeling and control design. In traditional approaches to tuning the focus has instead been to determine reasonable specifications. The modeling and design methods used have however been fairly primitive. Therefore it seems reasonable to try to combine the approaches. In this paper this has been done by introducing methods for performance assessment. It is shown how relay experiments can be used for controller tuning and that criteria for identification and control criteria can be made compatible by a proper choice of the data filter.

Acknowledgements

The results presented in this paper have been supported by the Swedish National Board for Industrial and Technical Development under contract 92-04014P.

References

Åström, K. J. (1967): "Computer control of a paper machine—An application of linear stochastic control theory." *IBM Journal of Research and Development*, 11:4, pp. 389–405.

Åström, K. J. (1970): *Introduction to Stochastic Control Theory*. Academic Press, New York. Translated to Russian, Japanese and Chinese.

Åström, K. J. (1991): "Assessment of achievable performance of simple feedback loops." *International Journal of Adaptive Control and Signal Processing*, 5, pp. 3–19.

Åström, K. J. (1993): "Intelligent tuning." In *Proceedings of IFAC 4th International Symposium on Adaptive Systems in Control and Signal Processing, Grenoble 1992*. Pergamon Press. Invited Plenary Paper. To appear.

Åström, K. J. and T. Hägglund (1984a): "Automatic tuning of simple regulators." In *Preprints 9th IFAC World Congress*, pp. 267–272, Budapest, Hungary.

Åström, K. J. and T. Hägglund (1984b): "Automatic tuning of simple regulators with specifications on phase and amplitude margins." *Automatica*, 20, pp. 645–651.

Åström, K. J. and B. Wittenmark (1973): "On self-tuning regulators." *Automatica*, 9, pp. 185–199.

Åström, K. J. and B. Wittenmark (1990): *Computer Controlled Systems— Theory and Design*. Prentice-Hall, Englewood Cliffs, New Jersey, second edition.

Atherton, D. P. (1975): *Nonlinear Control Engineering—Describing Function Analysis and Design*. Van Nostrand Reinhold Co., London, UK.

Bode, H. W. (1945): *Network Analysis and Feedback Amplifier Design*. Van Nostrand, New York.

Gevers, M. (1991): "Connecting identification and robust control: A new challenge." Technical Report 91.48, CESAME, Universé Catholique de Louvain, Louvain-la-Neuve, Belgium.

Hakvoort, R. G., R. J. P. Schrama, and P. M. J. Van den Hof (1992): "Approximate identification in view of LQG feedback design." In *1992 American Control Conference*, volume 4, Chicago, Illinois.

Horowitz, I. M. (1963): *Synthesis of Feedback Systems*. Academic Press, New York.

Lee, W. S., B. D. O. Anderson, R. L. Kosut, and I. M. Y. Mareels (1992): "On adaptive robust control and control-relevant system identification." In *1992 American Control Conference*, volume 4, Chicago, Illinois.

Ljung, L. (1987): *System Identification—Theory for the User*. Prentice Hall, Englewood Cliffs, New Jersey.

Lundh, M. and K. J. Åström (1992): "Automatic initialization of robust adaptive controllers." In *Preprints 4th IFAC Symposium on Adaptive Systems in Control and Signal Processing*, pp. 439–444, Grenoble.

Rivera, D. E., J. F. Pollard, and C. E. García (1992): "Control-relevant prefiltering: A systematic design approach and case study." *IEEE Transactions on Automatic Control*, 37:7, pp. 964–974.

Schei, T. S. (1991): "A new method for automatic tuning of PID control." In Commault *et al.*, Eds., *Proceedings of the First European Control Conference, ECC 91*, Grenoble, France, volume 2, pp. 1523–1527, Paris. Hermes.

Schrama, R. J. P. (1992): "Accurate models for control design: The necessity of an iterative scheme." *IEEE Transactions on Automatic Control*. To appear.

Smith, R. S. and J. C. Doyle (1992a): "Closed loop relay estimation of uncertainty bounds for robust control models." Private communication.

Smith, R. S. and J. C. Doyle (1992b): "Model validation: A connection between robust control and identification." *IEEE Transactions on Automatic Control*, 37:7, pp. 942–952.

Söderström, T. and P. Stoica (1989): *System Identification*. Prentice Hall.

Truxal, J. (1955): *Automatic Feedback Control System Synthesis*. McGraw-Hill, New York.

Tsypkin, Y. Z. (1984): *Relay Control Systems*. Cambridge University Press, Cambridge, UK.

Zang, Z., R. R. Bitmead, and M. Gevers (1992): "Disturbance rejection: On-line refinement of controllers by closed loop modelling." In *1992 American Control Conference*, volume 4, Chicago, Illinois.

Ziegler, J. G. and N. B. Nichols (1942): "Optimum settings for automatic controllers." *Trans. ASME*, 64, pp. 759–768.

Analog and Digital Computing

Roger W. Brockett

Division of Applied Sciences, Harvard University
Cambridge, MA 02138

Abstract

It is clear that digital signal processing is growing in importance, fulfilling functions that were once carried out exclusively by analog means. At the same time the analog point of view, as represented by neural networks and adaptive control is also developing in new directions. Prompted by these considerations, this paper attempts to put into perspective recent work on analog computing. Some basic definitions are proposed and used to classify some examples from the literature.

1 Introduction

Stonehenge has not been used for the purpose for which it was built for many years and slide rules have, for the most part, been replaced by digital calculators and digital computers. Yet, the idea of analog computing refuses to go away. There seem to be two main reasons for this. In the first place, animals perform acts that require data processing that is far beyond anything now possible with the fastest digital computers and one can not entirely dispel the notion that this is because biological systems compute in ways that are intrinsically different from, and superior to, the standard digital computer. Secondly, there does not exist any comprehensive theory that postulates the existence of a set of circuit elements, tolerances, noise mechanisms, etc. and establishes fundamental limitations on the performance of an analog computer made from the given parts. Thus there can be no general theory attesting to the superiority of digital or analog computing because we do not have a sufficiently powerful theory of analog computation.

*This work was supported in part by the National Science Foundation under Engineering Research Center Program, NSF D CDR-8803012 and by the US Army Research Office under grant DAAL03-86-K-0171, and DARPA grant AFOSR-89-0506

Over the years there have been many attempts to develop methods for treating these issues. Throughout his work on computing von Neumann maintained a strong interest in analog methods. It would appear from [1] and [2] that he wrote less about analog computing and more about logical automata not because he felt that digital computing was more interesting but because it proved to be a more tractable subject. He mentions the idea that the "primary language" of the brain (perhaps meaning the "machine language" of the brain) is something far different from the instruction set of a digital computer and offered the opinion that new mathematics would be required to understand it. In the early 1940's McCulloch and Pitts [3] had put forth a mathematical model for a neuron and somewhat later Norbert Wiener with his work on estimation theory [4] and Claude Shannon with his work on information theory [5] provided a whole range of new mathematical ideas associated with communication. The practical use of these ideas has grown slowly, having been held back for many years by the expense of the equipment necessary for their implementation. Today their effect is widely felt and the importance of these ideas for computing is still growing.

In spite of the efforts extended, progress toward a theory of analog computing has been slow. The purpose of this essay is to offer a brief appraisal of past results and to propose some new points of view that allow one to more directly compare analog and digital systems. This work is prompted, in part, by the current interest in artificial neural networks but also by the biological relevance of analog computing and Hebb's model of learning [6]. It seems that we can safely predict the emergence of technologies which will identify appropriate structures for using a combination of parallel processing (analog or digital) and sequential processing to solve various perceptual problems involving data fusion, low level motion control, motion planning, etc. and ideas of the type being discussed here will have a role in these activities.

2 Continuous vs. Episodic Computing

To begin with we wish to distinguish between "computers" that continuously process a data stream acting as a transducers or filters as opposed to "computers" that are episodic or ballistic in the sense that the computation has a very definite beginning point and ending point. (The term episodic is inspired by its current use in learning theory.) Providing a transformed version of a sound wave in which all frequency components outside the range between 200Hz and 300Hz are suppressed exemplifies filtering whereas using Newton's method to solve for the roots of an equation exemplifies episodic computing. In the first instance a computation has no definite starting or ending point; the computational process begins to produce results immediately. In the second case there is a definite beginning and end to the computation and the results are not useful until the end of the computation is reached.

Making a satisfactory distinction between analog and digital computing requires some care because, from a certain point of view, all computing is analog computing.

Digital computers use voltages, currents, charges, magnetic states, etc. to represent the data that is being manipulated and the program that is manipulating it. Thus to be faithful to the standard way of thinking we need to look deeper. Some computing proceeds by following a segmented path with the duration of the segments being determined by a clock and the end point of segment being determined by an equilibrium state. In the simplest case, the trajectory for each segment is generated by a set of **triangular differential equations**, triangular in the sense that the equations can be ordered so that the right-hand side of the first equation depends only on the first variable, the right-hand side of the second equation depends on the first and the second variable, etc. as suggested by

$$\dot{x}_1 = f_1(x_1)$$
$$\dot{x}_2 = f_2(x_1, x_2)$$
$$\dots\dots\dots\dots\dots\dots$$
$$\dot{x}_n = f_n(x_1, x_2, \dots, x_n)$$

The number of equations permitted here is limited by the length of the time interval between clock pulses and the maximum propagation delay. Systems that can be described by such a triangular family of differential equations may be said to be **digital systems** if there is a fixed and finite set of possible equilibrium states such that every trajectory flows from one of them to another one during each segment. Digital systems can be used to do either filtering or episodic computing. **The flows associated with digital computing are punctuated, triangular, and flow from one equilibrium state to another** in that any given segment of the flow involves the relatively rapid transition from one equilibrium state to another following a path along which only one variable is changes at a time. By **parallel digital computing** it is meant that the flow is permitted to involve simultaneous transitions as long as they are decoupled.

By contrast, **analog computing** does not require a fixed and finite set of equilibrium states but rather the implementation may possess a manifold of equilibrium states. The resting point of a given trajectory is determined by the initial conditions. Analog computing can be used to operate on a steady stream of input data. If $u(\cdot)$ is the input then systems taking the form $dx/dt = f(x, u)$ act as filters. During normal operation the differential equation is not re-initialized but is simply driven by u. We may identify explicitly an output $y = h(x, u)$. Ordinary analog filters as found in radio and television receivers are common examples. On the other hand, it is also possible to do episodic computing with an analog system. In this case the data of the problem is coded as initial conditions for a system of differential equations that have time as the independent variable. The variables governed by the differential equations are then allowed to flow to their steady state value. This steady state value then codes the "answer". The differential equation must be re-initialized and allowed to flow to steady state each time a new computation is to be done. In this case the computer generates a whole trajectory but only the end point is of interest. The end point may be anywhere on a manifold of dimension one or greater. When doing this type of analog computing we launch a trajectory and see where it comes to rest.

Input-output systems such as quantizers have a very great sensitivity, or gain, at certain points and low gain at others. Equilibrium points which are such that the trajectories passing near them are strongly contracted in one subspace and strongly expanded in a complementary space are said to be hyperbolic. Thus regions of high gain, yielding sharp dividing lines in the phase portrait, are characteristic of digital systems and also of dynamical systems with hyperbolic equilibrium points. A key idea is that in a digital system the flows only encounter two dimensional hyperbolic points. At a dividing point there are only two possible directions to go. This means that one can use very high gain with little danger than an inaccuracy will drive the trajectory to an incorrect final state. This allows us to more precisely characterize digital flows **as flows that consist of a sequence of high gain, two dimensional, hyperbolic encounters.**

In contrast, analog quantities have a certain range of values associated with them, often fixed by the nature of the physical principles that govern the variables involved in their operation. Potential differences generated by electrochemical effects will not exceed a certain voltage, the concentration of calcium, potassium or sodium ions will not exceed a certain molarity, etc. The smallest differences between analog quantities that can be reliably used are limited by the precision of the analog implementation and, ultimately by thermal noise. Thus the set of trajectories that are useful for doing analog computing are constrained in that they must avoid saturation and be sufficiently distinct so as to avoid ambiguity. **Hyperbolicity is the scourge of analog computing** because it can only be faithfully simulated by a system with a large dynamic range. Its effects are felt strongly in the case of episodic computing with free end point whereas the quasi-fixed end point situation is better protected against its ravages.

The final point that we want to make in this section concerns the independent variable, time. **Time is a special analog quantity** in that, by comparison with voltages, currents, molarities, etc. it is not as severely constrained by the dynamic range problem. Analog implementations that use divisions of the time axis delineated by pulses, for example, can possess a larger dynamic range than can systems that use electrical or chemical coding. With the exception of time, it seems that in practical situations analog variables are capable of no more than about eight bits of precision or about one part in 256. This limitation applies not only to the input and output data but it also applies to the data generated as the computation proceeds. Thus we might expect to be able to build an analog device that adds two seven bit numbers but we can not expect to multiply two seven bit numbers unless we code the answer in some way that lets us represent it as two different quantities such as a least significant part and the most significant part.

3 Towards a more Formal Treatment

Why use a dynamical system to evaluate a function? Why not use a resistive network or some other "static" relationship? The answer to these questions lies in the consideration of energy. If we compute with passive elements then the energy level associated with the output signal is less than that of the input and in a cascade of such operations the signal level will eventually become unacceptably small. Amplifiers are needed to save the day. But amplifiers transfer energy and this means that the dynamics of energy flow must be considered.

Analog computations, regardless of whether they are done electrically, mechanically, or chemically, are more robust if they involve smooth characteristics. However some useful functions are discontinuous or at least non-differentiable functions of the data. For example, analytic functions of a set of variables and their absolute values, i.e. functions which take the form $y = y(u_1, u_2, \ldots, u_m, |u_1|, u_2|, \ldots |u_m|)$ appear in the study of sorting. It is important to realize that because the asymptotic (for large time) value of the solution of a differential equation is not necessarily a continuous function of the initial data or parameters, even for systems described by analytic vector fields, it makes sense to study the problem of realizing such functions with smooth systems.

In a recent paper [13] it was shown that the equation

$$dH/dt = \left[H, [H, N]\right] \quad ; \quad [A, B] \stackrel{\text{def}}{=} AB - BA$$

can be used to compute a great variety of useful functions. For example it can be used as a sorter of real numbers. The connectivity of the circuit needed to implement this equation is not especially dense but there is an extremely sparsely connected circuit obtained by restricting this equation to the tridiagonal symmetric matrices, that will sort numbers operating in episodic mode. It seems intuitive that it requires a higher level of interconnection to compute functions in filter mode than it does to compute in the ballistic sense, although we are unaware of any precise result along these lines.

The difference between digital episodic and analog episodic computing may be illustrated by this same equation. When we initialize this equation with $H(0)$ having eigenvalues $1, 2, \ldots, n$ we know that the equilibrium state will be characterized by a permutation matrix. (See [13].) When we use it as an eigenvalue solver, we are on an isospectral manifold and will flow to a diagonal matrix characterized by the eigenvalues of $H(0)$ but we must think of the equilibrium point as being an analog quantity. This is a pure analog situation. Thus we can distinguish between finite state episodic computing and unconstrained episodic computing. the former generalizes ordinary digital computing and includes it as a special case.

The Problem of Finding a Smooth Realization. Let P be a compact subset of $\mathbf{R}^{2m}$ and let y be an analytic map P into $\mathbf{R}$. Find a compact analytic manifold X, analytic vector fields $f, g_1, g_2, \ldots, g_m$, on X, and an analytic function h mapping M

into **R** such that the system

$$dx/dt = f(x) + g_1 u_1 + g_2 u_2, \ldots, g_m u_m$$
$$y(t) = h(x(t))$$

has among its equilibrium points, exactly one which is asymptotically stable and this equilibrium point, which we denote as $x(u)$, is such that

$$h(x(u)) = y(u_1, u_2, \ldots, u_m, |u_1|, |u_2|, \ldots, |u_m|)$$

Example: This problem formulation suggests specific questions such as that of generating $y(t) = |u(t)|$ using an analytical differential equation in the way discussed. This can be done, for example, with $dx/dt = uz^2; dz/dt = -uxz; y = x^2$. Note that here there are three equilibrium points for u positive and just one for u negative. For u positive the stable ones occur where x equals the square roots of u. For u negative there are no stable roots.

An elementary, but useful, function of two variables is their maximum value. How can we compute the maximum of u and v, in continuous time, with an arbitrarily small delay and with nothing but smooth functions? One possible way is two use the three differential equations which show up in out paper [13].

Median filters are widely used in signal processing to suppress outliers in time sequences. If $\{u(k)\}$ is a sequence, the p-median filtered version of $\{u(k)\}$ is a sequence $\{v(k)\}$ with $v(k)$ being the median of the p elements which surround $u(k)$. Of course the median is not a differential function of the u's but nonetheless we can compute it as the steady state value of a system which involves only multiplication.

4 Subspace Filters

In addition to episodic analog computing there are many interesting examples of the analog implementation of nonlinear filtering. Neural networks that adjust their weights are good examples. Such systems are often said to incorporate learning. The idea here is very well known. It shows up in a variety of places but perhaps most prominently in the literature on adaptive arrays. See, for example [11]. One views a time function as defining a trajectory in an inner product space **H**. The time function is an additive combination of a part that is "interesting" and a part that is "uninteresting". It is assumed that the interesting and uninteresting parts lie in complementary subspaces of **H** and that one knows, *aprori*, something about relative sizes of the interesting and uninteresting parts. In such cases it is often recommended that one do a principle component analysis and reject the unwanted part of the signal by nulling out the subspace in which it lies.

With this in mind, consider the following system of equations from reference [12].

$$\dot{Q}(t) = u(\sigma)u^T(t) - u^T(t)Qu(t)Q(t) : Q(0) = I/\sqrt{m}$$
$$\dot{\Theta}(t) = \Theta(t)Q(t)\Theta^T(t)N - N\Theta(t)Q(t)$$
$$y(t) = \Theta^T(t)\Lambda\Theta(t)u(t)$$

with N being the diagonal matrix $\text{diag}(1, 2, \ldots, n)$.

This set of equations describes a system that works in the following way. The equation for Q generates a symmetric matrix which can be thought of as the sample covariance of the input u. (We assume that u has zero mean.) The equation

$$\dot{\Theta}(t) = \Theta(t)Q\Theta^T(t)N - N\Theta(t)Q$$

is related to the equation

$$\dot{H} = [H, [H, N]]$$

by the change of variables $\Theta Q \Theta^T = H$. If Q is constant Θ flows to a steady state value that makes $\Theta Q \Theta^T$ diagonal with the largest eigenvalue of H in the first diagonal spot, the next largest eigenvalue of H in the second diagonal, etc. If Q is changing slowly relative to the time constant of the equation for Θ then Θ will track the eigenvectors of the sample covariance. Finally, by appropriate choice of Λ, a diagonal matrix, we can add the components of u back together to get the output y. If we let some diagonal elements of Λ be zero we will suppress those components exactly.

5 Coding

One way to get a high precision result from a analog device is to **read the output in digital form from qualitative features of the trajectory.** Strange attractors provide a way to build a high gain amplifier that does not saturate but it is not yet clear that one can do general computing this way. Apparently the so-called sigma-delta analog to digital converters work on the basis of a principle of this type. It appears that their operation can be thought of as one in which the input drives a chaotic system and the output is generated by reading digits of the digital representation of the input from a property of the orbit. The major problem to be solved before one can extend this mode of computation to a more general setting is that of finding a natural way for the input to influence the strange attractor and to better understand which methods of converting the trajectory into an output are effective. Should the input influence the system at just at one moment or should it be allowed to influence constantly but on a time scale that is slow compared with the period of the attractor. Perhaps one does not want a strange attractor but rather a tightly nested set of periodic solutions that are stable but with Floquet multipliers near one in magnitude.

We have proceeded above as if the only way to do analog computing is to code the numerical values being manipulated as voltages or concentrations etc. However, in principle, the representation of data in terms of physical variables can be done in many ways. Examples include the standard mechanisms used in communication such as amplitude modulations of a sinusoid of a fixed frequency, frequency modulations about a fixed frequency. Phase modulation at a fixed frequency etc. Biological systems appear to make extensive use of pulse frequency modulation and pulse phase modulation. Throughout VLSI design and implicit in the models appearing above, only the most naive coding consisting of modeling instantaneous value of the data as the instantaneous value of a physical variable, has been used. A consideration of noise and parametric uncertainties suggest that more sophisticated modulation schemes may be useful.

With this in mind we remark that if we start with the system used above

$$\dot{H} = [H, [H, N]]$$

and change variables according to $Z(t) = e^{-iNt}H(t)e^{iNt}$ then z satisfies the equation

$$\dot{Z} = [Z, iN] + [Z, [Z, N]]$$

This equation can be split into real and imaginary parts according to

$$Z = (\cos Nt)H(\cos Nt) - (\sin Nt)H(\sin Nt) + i(\cos Nt)H \sin Nt) - (\sin Nt)H(\cos Nt)$$

and replaced by a system of real equations. In the notation

$$iZ(t) = A(t) + iB(t)$$

we have

$$\frac{d}{dt}\begin{bmatrix} A & B \\ -B & A \end{bmatrix} =$$

$$\left[\begin{bmatrix} 0 & N \\ -N & 0 \end{bmatrix}, \begin{bmatrix} A & B \\ -B & A \end{bmatrix}\right] + \left[\begin{bmatrix} A & B \\ -B & A \end{bmatrix}, \left[\begin{bmatrix} A & B \\ -B & A \end{bmatrix}, \begin{bmatrix} 0 & N \\ -N & 0 \end{bmatrix}\right]\right]$$

If N is diagonal with distinct entries and if H has unrepeated eigenvalues then of course Z approaches a constant as t goes to infinity. The interconnection terms in the expression for $\dot{z}_{ij}$ are all amplitude modulated sinusoidal signals with zero average value. Thus this equation represents an alternative form of $\dot{H} = [H, [H, N]]$ which the communication is done via the amplitudes of sine waves, even though the equation itself is time invariant.

6 Other Structures

Because the solutions of simultaneous differential equations for which time is the independent variable provide a natural realization of "parallel" computing, and because spatially discretized partial differential equations of the evolution type are, by their very nature, local in space, there is a certain amount of insight about digitally realized parallel computing with limited processor communication which is to be gleaned from the classical mathematics of ordinary and partial differential equations. Until recently the principal use of this type of thinking has been to guide numerical analysts in their efforts to find better ways to map partial differential equations onto fine-grain parallel computers. Indeed, prior to the appearance of work on neural network theory showing that some combinatorial optimization algorithms can be solved by systems of differential equations, it was widely thought that differential equations and discrete optimization were about as far apart as two mathematical subjects can be. Far from considering combinatorial problems, over the years the main bulk of the effort on analog computation emphasized simulation. Tantalizing as these ideas are, the classical results on the theory of ordinary and partial differential equations are essentially limited to guiding work on the realization of linear filters, one and two dimensional Gaussian smoothing, and other Green's function problems.

There is considerably less known about the structures which might be effective in solving some of the harder problems involving data driven behavior. examples of importance include (adaptive) vector quantization, clustering, nonlinear regression, learning theory, etc. There are a number of "standard" filters, such as the median filter, whose usefulness is well established and which do, in some limited sense, involve combinatorics and differential equations. The implementation of a median filtering analog form would involve at least a partial sorting of numbers. However the problem of finding a system of differential equations of the evolution type whose connectivity is modest and which will solve matching problems, evaluate selected integrals, identify clusters etc. remains largely unsolved. In nature, extremely complex cognitive tasks, such as those involved in processing visual information, seem to be accomplished through the combined effort of an identifiable number of processing modules with relatively high connectivity, which communicate the results of their work using a more sparsely connected network. Does there exist a theory which speaks to the efficiency of such structures?

7 Acknowledgement

The ideas in this paper have been sharpened and clarified by conversations with my colleagues James Clark and Woodward Yang.

8 References

1. John von Neumann, **The Computer and the Brain**, Yale University Press, New Haven, 1958.

2. John von Neumann, **Theory of Self-Reproducing Automata**, University of Illinois Press, Urbana, IL, 1966.

3. W. S. McCulloch and W. Pitts, "A logical calculus of the ideas immanent in nervous activity", Bulletin of Math. Biophysics, Vol. 5, (1943) pp. 115–133.

4. Norbert Wiener, **Extrapolation, Interpolation and Smoothing of Stationary Time Series**, MIT Press, Cambridge, MA and John Wiley, New York, 1949.

5. C. E. Shannon, "A Mathematical Theory of Communication", **Bell Systems Technical Journal**, Vol. 27, (1948), pp. 379–423 (part I) and pp. 623–656, (part II).

6. D. O. Hebb, **The Organization of Behavior**, John Wiley, New York, 1949.

7. R. M. Gray and A. Gresho, **Adaptive Quantization**, John Wiley, New York, 1991.

8. R. W. Brockett, "Smooth Dynamical Systems Which Realize Arithmetical and Logical Operations," in *Lecture Notes in Control and Information Sciences. Three Decades of Mathematical Systems Theory.* (H. Nijmeijer and J. M. Schumacher, eds.) Springer-Verlag, Berlin, 1989, pp. 19-30.

9. G. B. Clayton, **Data Converters**, John Wiley, New York, 1992.

10. E. A. Guillemin, **Passive Network Synthesis**, John Wiley, New York, 1965.

11. B. Widrow and Stearns, **Adaptive Signal Processing**, Prentice-Hall, Englewood Cliffs, New Jersey, 1985.

12. R. W. Brockett, "Dynamical Systems That Learn Subspaces," **Mathematical System Theory: The Influence of R. E. Kalman**, (A.C. Antoulas, Ed.) Springer Verlag, Berlin, 1991, pp. 579–592.

13. R. W. Brockett, "Dynamical Systems That Sort Lists, Diagonalize Matrices and Solve Linear Programming Problems," **Linear Algebra and its Applications**, Vol 146, pp. 79-91, 1991, (also *Proceedings of the 1988 IEEE Conference on Decision and Control*, (1988) pp. 799-803.)

14. R. W. Brockett, "Least Squares Matching Problems," **Linear Algebra and Its Applications**, Vols. 122/123/124, pp. 761-777, 1989.

15. R. W. Brockett, "Sorting With the Dispersionless Limit of the Toda Lattice," in **Hamiltonian Systems, Transformation Groups and Spectral Transform Methods**, CRM, (J. Harnad and J.E. Marsden, Eds.) Université de Montréal, Montréal, Canada. pp. 103-112 (with A. M. Bloch)

16. R. W. Brockett, "An Estimation Theoretic Basis for the Design of Sorting and Classification Networks", in **Neural Networks**, (R. Mammone and Y. Zeevi, Eds) Academic Press, 1991, pp. 23-41.

17. R. W. Brockett, "A Gradient Flow for the Assignment Problem", Progress in System and Control Theory (G. Conte and B. Wyman, Eds.) Birkhauser, 1991 (with Wing Wong) pp. 170-177.

18. R. W. Brockett, "Differential Geometry and the Design of Gradient Algorithms", in **Differential Geometry** (Robert Green and S.T. Yau, Eds.) **AMS**, 1992. (to appear)

19. Misha Mahowald and Rodney Douglas, "A Silicon Neuron", **Nature**, Vol. 354, pp. 515–518, Dec. 1991.

20. Carver Mead, Analog VLSI and Neural Systems, Addison Wesley, Reading, MA, 1989.

21. A.L. Hodgkin and A.F. Huxley, Propagation of Pulses, **J. of Physiology, (London)**, Vol. 117, pp. 500–544, 1952.

22. R. W. Brockett, "Pulse Driven Dynamical Systems", in **Dynamics, Control and Feedback**, (Alberto Isidori and T. J. Tarn, Eds.), Birkhäuser, Boston, 1992.

Stochastic Control and Large Deviations

Wendell H. Fleming*
Division of Applied Mathematics, Brown University
Providence, RI 02912

Abstract

Large deviations theory is concerned with asymptotic estimates of probabilities of rare events associated with stochastic processes. A stochastic control approach to large deviations is outlined. Both problems of small random perturbations and large deviations from ergodicity are considered. For large deviations of Markov diffusion processes, PDE - viscosity solution methods are mentioned. Another stochastic control formulation, applicable to a broad range of large deviations problems is due to Dupuis and Ellis. This approach reduces many aspects of large deviations to the theory of weak convergence of probability measures.

1   Introduction

Large deviations theory is concerned with asymptotic estimates of probabilities of rare events associated with stochastic processes. Let A^ε be an event associated with some stochastic process x_t^ε, with exponentially small probability in the sense that

$$(1.1) \qquad -\lim_{\varepsilon \to 0} \varepsilon \log P(A^\varepsilon) = V^0.$$

When $P(A^\varepsilon)$ satisfies (1.1), then A^ε is said to have a large deviations property and V^0 is the large deviations rate. Similarly, one may seek a large deviations property for expectations $E\Phi^\varepsilon(x_\cdot^\varepsilon)$ of the form

$$(1.2) \qquad -\lim_{\varepsilon \to 0} \varepsilon \log E\Phi^\varepsilon(x_\cdot^\varepsilon) = V^0.$$

There is a well developed literature on large deviations. The reader may consult, for instance [A] [FW] [St] [V].

---

*Partially supported by NSF under grant DMS-900038, by AFOSR under grant F49620-92-J-0081DEF and by ARO under grant DAAL03-86-K-0171

Large deviations problems arise in a wide variety of applications in science and technology. These include: rare overloads in queueing systems [PW], signal tracking in communication systems [K], nonequilibrium thermodynamics (chemical reaction rates) [Sch], statistical mechanics [E] and quantum physics (tunnelling) [Si].

Large deviations results are closely connected with changes of probability measure, under which the event A^ε which is rare under probability measure P is no longer rare under a new probability measure P^ε. Typically, the Radon-Nikodym derivative dP/dP^ε has an exponential form. One needs to determine the dominant contribution to the exponent, when ε is small. Changes of probability measure are often useful in simulating rare events. If $P(A^\varepsilon)$ is extremely small, then sampling according to probability measure P is unlikely to produce the event A^ε. The method of quick simulation samples according to a changed probability measure under which A^ε is much more probable. This technique is also called "importance sampling", see [DK] [PW]. If x_t^ε is a continuous time Markov process, then the desired change of probability measure from P to P^ε typically arises through a change of generator. Changes of generator can be viewed as the result of controlling the process x_t^ε. The desired P^ε results from choosing a control which is optimal, according to a suitably chosen criterion. In this brief survey we illustrate through some "model problems" an approach based on a certain logarithmic transformation and PDE – viscosity solution techniques [FSn, Chap. 6]. Recently Dupuis – Ellis [DE] introduced a different technique, also formulated in stochastic control terms, which is applicable to a wide variety of large deviations problems (Section 5).

In Section 2 we consider large deviations for processes x_t^ε which are small random perturbations of deterministic dynamical systems. Such large deviations problems are often said to be of Freidlin–Wentzell type. The change of probability measure then arises from a Girsanov transformation, corresponding to a change of drift in the stochastic differential equation which x_t^ε satisfies. The optimal change of drift can be found by solving a first order partial differential equation (PDE). This PDE is the Hamilton–Jacobi equation associated with a calculus of variations problem of minimizing an associated action functional.

In Section 3 a different class of large deviations problems, called of Donsker–Varadhan type, is considered. The corresponding stochastic control problem involves minimization of an infinite time horizon, average cost per unit time expected cost criterion. The minimum expected cost is interpreted as a dominant eigenvalue. In Section 4, we mention some recent work on risk sensitive optimal control, which makes use of both Freidlin–Wentzell and Donsker–Varadhan types. Risk sensitive control theory provides a link between stochastic and deterministic robust approaches to the disturbance rejection problem in control theory.

2 Small random perturbations

Let us outline a stochastic control approach to Freidlin–Wentzell type large deviations by considering the following model problem. Let $I\!\!R^n$ denote n-dimensional euclidean space, and let $O \subset I\!\!R^n$ be open, bounded with smooth boundary ∂O. Consider x_t^ε satisfying

$$(2.1) \qquad dx_t^\varepsilon = f(x_t^\varepsilon)dt + \sqrt{\varepsilon}db_t, \ t \geq 0,$$

$$(2.2) \qquad x_0^\varepsilon = x$$

with b_t an n-dimensional brownian motion under some probability measure P. Assume that f is Lipschitz continuous. Let τ^ε be the exit time of x_t^ε from O. In (1.2) we take

$$(2.3) \qquad \Phi^\varepsilon(x_\cdot^\varepsilon) = \exp[\varepsilon^{-1} \int_0^{\tau^\varepsilon} q(x_t^\varepsilon)dt],$$

where q is continuous and $q \leq 0$. Then it turns out that the large deviations rate is

$$(2.4) \qquad V^0 = \min_{\eta_\cdot, \theta} \int_0^\theta F(\eta_t, \dot\eta_t)dt$$

$$(2.5) \qquad F(x, v) = \frac{1}{2}|v - f(x)|^2 - q(x),$$

and $\eta_\cdot$ belongs to the class of smooth, $I\!\!R^n$ - valued functions such that $\eta_0 = x$ and $\eta_\theta \in \partial O$ for some $\theta < \infty$. If $f \equiv 0$, then (2.5) is the classical action integrand.

The stochastic control approach to this model problem is as follows. Let us replace the drift $f(x_t^\varepsilon)$ in (2.1) by another drift $\underline{u}(x_t^\varepsilon)$, which is to be chosen suitably. The stochastic differential equation (2.1) is replaced by

$$(2.6) \qquad dx_t^\varepsilon = \underline{u}(x_t^\varepsilon)dt + \sqrt{\varepsilon}db_t^\varepsilon, \ t \geq 0,$$

with $x_0^\varepsilon = x$ where b_t^ε is a brownian motion with respect to a probability measure P^ε related to P via Girsanov's Theorem. We call $\underline{u}$ a feedback control (or Markov control policy.) The goal is to choose $\underline{u}$ to minimize

$$J^\varepsilon(x; \underline{u}) = E_x^\varepsilon \int_0^{\tau^\varepsilon} f(x_t^\varepsilon, \underline{u}(x_t^\varepsilon))dt,$$

where the subscript x indicates the initial state in (2.2). An optimal feedback control $\underline{u}^\varepsilon$ is found by dynamic programming, as follows. Consider the value function

$$(2.7) \qquad V^\varepsilon(x) = \inf_{\underline{u}} J^\varepsilon(x; \underline{u}).$$

Then V^ε satisfies the nonlinear elliptic PDE

$$(2.8^\varepsilon) \qquad 0 = \frac{\varepsilon}{2}\Delta V^\varepsilon(x) + \min_{v \in I\!R^n}[v \cdot \nabla V^\varepsilon(x) + F(x,v)], \; x \in O,$$

$$(2.9) \qquad\qquad V^\varepsilon(x) = 0, \; x \in \partial O.$$

The optimal feedback $\underline{u}^\varepsilon$ is found by taking arg min over v in (2.8^ε):

$$(2.10) \qquad\qquad \underline{u}^\varepsilon(x) = f(x) - \nabla V^\varepsilon(x).$$

See [FSn, Sec. 4.5].

By using PDE - viscosity solution methods, it is not difficult to show that $V^\varepsilon \to \bar{V}^0$ uniformly on O, where $\bar{V}^0$ is the unique viscosity solution to the first order equation (2.8^0) with (2.9). See [FSg] and for related results [FSn, Chap. 7]. Equation (2.8^0) is the Hamilton–Jacobi equation for the calculus of variations problem (2.4), and $\bar{V}^0 = V^0$ where $V^0(x)$ is the left hand side of (2.4) for initial data $\eta_0 = x$.

To see that $V^0(x)$ is indeed the large deviations rate, by using (2.5) one finds that $\phi^\varepsilon = \exp[-\varepsilon^{-1}V^\varepsilon]$ satisfies the linear elliptic PDE

$$(2.11) \qquad 0 = \frac{\varepsilon}{2}\Delta\phi^\varepsilon(x) + f(x) \cdot \nabla\phi^\varepsilon(x) + \frac{q(x)}{\varepsilon}\phi^\varepsilon(x), \; x \in O,$$

$$(2.12) \qquad\qquad \phi^\varepsilon(x) = 1, \; x \in \partial O.$$

Since $-\varepsilon \log \phi^\varepsilon \to V^0$ as $\varepsilon \to 0$, the large deviations formula (1.2) follows from the Feynman – Kac formula.

There is a more refined version of this large deviations result, which expresses $\phi^\varepsilon(x)$ in the form of a WKB - type asymptotic series in powers of the small parameter ε. However, this asymptotic series expansion holds only in an open set $O_1 \subset O$ where V^0 is smooth. The complement $O\backslash O_1$ is a closed set of Hausdorff dimension $\le n - 1$. See [FSg] and for related results [FJ], [FSn, Chap. 6].

For such applications as the problem of rare overloads in queueing systems, the nearly deterministic process x_t^ε is a Markov chain rather than a nearly deterministic Markov diffusion governed by a stochastic differential equation. In that case logarithmic transformations lead to stochastic control problems of a form described in [Sh], [FSn, Sec. 6.8].

3   Large deviations from ergodicity

Let us now consider a different class of large deviations problems, which belong to the type introduced by Donsker and Varadhan [DV]. Let x_t be a stochastic process, considered for $0 \leq t \leq T$ where T is finite but large. The role of the small parameter ε is now taken by T^{-1}. In place of (1.2) one seeks a result of the form

$$(3.1) \qquad \lim_{T \to \infty} \frac{1}{T} \log E\Phi^T(x_.) = \lambda,$$

where λ is a constant not depending on the initial state of x_t. See [DV] [St] [V].

To indicate a stochastic control approach to such large deviations problems, let us suppose that x_t is an ergodic Markov process with generator G, and that

$$(3.2) \qquad \Phi^T(x_.) = \exp \int_0^T \ell(x_t)dt.$$

Let

$$\phi(T, x) = E_x \exp \int_0^T \ell(x_t)dt,$$

$$V(T, x) = \log \phi(T, x).$$

Then (3.1) states that

$$(3.3) \qquad \lim_{T \to \infty} \frac{V(T, x)}{T} = \lambda.$$

If we use the heuristic that as $T \to \infty$

$$(3.4) \qquad \phi(T, x) \sim \psi(x) \exp(\lambda T), \quad \psi(x) > 0,$$

then one expects (under suitable assumptions) that

$$(3.5) \qquad \lambda\psi = G\psi + \ell(x)\psi.$$

Let $W = \log \psi$. Then λ and W should satisfy

$$\lambda = \mathcal{H}(W) + \ell(x),$$
$$(3.6)$$
$$\mathcal{H}(W) = e^{-W} G(e^W).$$

In the stochastic control interpretation, (3.5) is identified as the dynamic programming equation for an infinite time horizon stochastic control problem. The constant λ is the minimum average cost per unit time, and $W(x)$ is the cost potential. Again heuristically, one may think of λ as a dominant eigenvalue for the operator $G + \ell(x)$ and ψ as a corresponding positive eigenfunction This interpretation is not essential in order that a Donsker–Varadhan large deviations formula (3.3) hold. However, one needs the function $W = \log \psi$ for the stochastic control interpretation of λ.

Let us describe the stochastic control problem only in the following illustrative special case. Let x_t be a Markov diffusion in $I\!\!R^n$ satisfying the stochastic differential equation

$$(3.7) \qquad dx_t = f(x_t)dt + db_t,$$

with $x_0 = x$ and b_t a brownian motion with respect to some probability measure P. We assume:

(A) $f, \ell \in C^1(I\!\!R^n)$ with f_x, ℓ_x bounded. Moreover, all eigenvalues of $f_x(x)$ have real parts bounded above by $- a$ for some $a > 0$.

The generator of the Markov diffusion x_t is

$$G\psi = \frac{1}{2}\Delta\psi + f(x) \cdot D\psi.$$

Equation (3.6) becomes this case

$$(3.8) \qquad \lambda = \frac{1}{2}\Delta W + f(x) \cdot \nabla W + \frac{1}{2}|\nabla W|^2 + \ell(x).$$

This is equivalent to equation (3.5) for $\psi = \exp W$. By writing

$$\frac{1}{2}|\nabla W|^2 = \max_{w \in I\!\!R^n}[w \cdot \nabla W - \frac{1}{2}|w|^2]$$

equation (3.8) becomes the dynamic programming PDE for the following infinite horizon average cost per unit time control problem. The state ξ_t of the process being controlled satisfies

$$(3.9) \qquad d\xi_t = [f(\xi_t) + \underline{w}(\xi_t)]dt + d\tilde{b}_t,$$

where $\underline{w}(\xi_t)$ is a control applied at time t and $\tilde{b}_t$ is a brownian motion with respect to some probability measure $\tilde{P}$. The criterion to be *maximized* is

$$(3.10) \qquad J(x; \underline{w}) = \liminf_{T \to \infty} \frac{1}{T}\tilde{E}_x \int_0^T [\ell(\xi_t) - \frac{1}{2}|\underline{w}(\xi_t)|^2]dt.$$

It can be shown that (3.8) has a solution for λ, W, such that $W \in C^2(I\!\!R^n)$ and ∇W is bounded. See [FM2]. The maximum over $\underline{w}$ of $J(x; \underline{w})$ is λ (which does not depend on the initial state x.) Moreover,

$$\lambda = J(x; \underline{w}^*), \quad \underline{w}^*(x) = \nabla W(x).$$

4 Risk sensitive optimal control

There are various approaches to treating disturbances in control systems. In stochastic control, disturbances are modelled as stochastic processes (random noise.) On the other hand, in robust control theory disturbances are modelled deterministically. The theory of risk sensitive optimal control provides a link between stochastic and deterministic approaches.

For linear systems with quadratic cost criteria, H - infinity optimization provides a method for robust control design. The disturbance attenuation problem is one of those considered in robust H - infinity control theory. If a state space formulation is used, an associated "soft constrained" differential game arises naturally. See Basar–Bernhard [BB]. The stochastic control counterpart is a linear exponential quadratic regulator (LEQR) problem, introduced by Jacobson [Jac]. His analysis of the LEQR problem leads to the same differential game. Glover and Doyle [GD] gave a further connection between the LEQR problem and H - infinity control via a minimum entropy principle.

An interesting question is to find for nonlinear systems, or nonquadratic cost criteria, similar connections between stochastic and robust control approaches to disturbance attenuation problems. Whittle [W1] [W2] introduced an interesting approach to this question, using large deviations ideas. Whittle considered problems on a finite time horizon $0 \leq t \leq T$, and used Freidlin – Wentzell type "small noise" asymptotics of the kind mentioned in Section 2. In [FM1] [Jam] Whittle's formula for the optimal large deviations rate was obtained using PDE - viscosity solution methods, in a special case when the process being controlled is governed by a stochastic differential equation.

For infinite horizon risk sensitive control problems, Donsker - Varadhan type large deviations principles similar to those outlined in Section 3 are needed. One obtains a nonlinear version of the eigenvalue problem (3.5). Equation (3.6) is replaced by the Isaacs equation for a stochastic differential game, with an expected average cost per unit time as payoff [R] [FM2]. Finally, by considering double limits $T \to \infty, \varepsilon \to 0$ the infinite horizon game becomes a deterministic differential game, which has a natural role in robust nonlinear control theory.

Let us indicate this connection with robust control theory, again considering a model problem. Consider a disturbance attenuation problem, modelled deterministically as

$$(4.1) \qquad \frac{d\xi_t}{dt} = g(\xi_t, u_t) + w_t, \ t \geq 0$$

with $\xi_0 = x$ where u_t is a control chosen with the intent of "attenuating" the disturbance w_t. To avoid explaining differential game ideas here, suppose that $u_t = \underline{u}(\xi_t)$ where the feedback $\underline{u}$ has already been chosen. Consider the problem of choosing $w.$ to maximize

$$(4.2) \qquad J(x; w.) = \liminf_{T \to \infty} \frac{1}{T} \int_0^T [\ell(\xi_t) - \frac{1}{2}|w_t|^2]dt.$$

The dynamic programming equation is the deterministic analogue of (3.8):

$$(4.3) \qquad \lambda = f(x) \cdot \nabla W + \frac{1}{2}|\nabla W|^2 + \ell(x),$$

$$f(x) = g(x, \underline{u}(x)).$$

To obtain this as the limit of a risk sensitive stochastic control problem, we introduce a small parameter ε and let x_t^ε be the solution to (2.1) – (2.2). Let

$$(4.4) \qquad \phi^\varepsilon(T, x) = E_x \exp \frac{1}{\varepsilon} \int_0^T \ell(x_t^\varepsilon) dt$$

We again assume that f, ℓ satisfy assumptions (A), Section 3. For fixed $\varepsilon > 0$, we use the heuristic

$$\phi^\varepsilon(T, x) \sim \psi^\varepsilon(x) \exp(\varepsilon^{-1}\lambda^\varepsilon T),$$

and let $W^\varepsilon = \varepsilon \log \psi^\varepsilon$. As in (3.8) we obtain for λ^ε and $W^\varepsilon(x)$ the equation

$$(4.5) \qquad \lambda^\varepsilon = \frac{\varepsilon}{2}\Delta W^\varepsilon + f(x) \cdot \nabla W^\varepsilon + \frac{1}{2}|\nabla W^\varepsilon|^2 + \ell(x).$$

There is a solution with $W^\varepsilon \in C^2(\mathbb{R}^n)$ and $|\lambda^\varepsilon| \leq M$, $|\nabla W^\varepsilon(x)| \leq M$ for suitable M. An easy limiting argument as $\varepsilon \to 0$ gives λ and Lipschitz continuous W such that (4.3) holds in the viscosity sense. Moreover, for every disturbance w and every $T < \infty$

$$(4.6) \qquad W(\xi_T) + \int_0^T [\ell(\xi_t) - \frac{1}{2}|w_t|^2]dt \leq W(x) + \lambda T.$$

If $\ell \geq 0$, then $\lambda \geq 0$. For robust control theory, one would like to decide whether $\lambda > 0$ or $\lambda = 0$. Suppose that $f(0) = \ell(0) = 0$ and $\ell(x) > 0$ for $x \neq 0$. Also suppose that $W(x)$ has a minimum at some point x^*, with $W(x^*) = 0$ and that W is differentiable at x^*. Then (4.3) holds at x^*, and hence $x^* = 0$ if $\lambda = 0$. If in addition $\xi_0 = 0$, then (4.6) implies for all disturbances w and each T

$$(4.7) \qquad \int_0^T 2\ell(\xi_t)dt \leq \int_0^T w_t^2 dt.$$

If $\ell(x)$ is quadratic, then (4.7) is a familiar condition in robust control theory [I]. Of course, a quadratic ℓ does not satisfy the condition ℓ_x bounded in assumption (A), and hence a different result must be expected. For instance, if $n = 1$, $f(x) = -ax$ with $a > 0$ and $\ell(x) = Mx^2$, then (4.3) has a quadratic solution $w(x) = Kx^2$ with $\lambda = 0$ provided $a^2 \geq 2M$. If $a^2 < 2M$, the solution of the finite time maximization problem explodes at some $T^* < \infty$, and there is no infinite horizon, average cost per unit time control problem.

5 Another stochastic control approach

The recent paper of Dupuis and Ellis [DE] gives a stochastic control formulation and obtains results applicable to a wide variety of large deviations problems, in continuous or discrete time. Included are small random perturbations, with possibly discontinuous statistics as well as large deviations from ergodicity. In the discrete time formulation, relative entropy functions are used in defining cost functions for the stochastic control problems. In case of large deviations from ergodicity, empirical measures have the role of state variables.

References

[A]   R. Azencott: Grandes deviations et applications, Springer LNM No. 774, 1980.

[BB]   T. Basar and P. Bernhard: H^∞ - Control and Related Minimax Design, Birkhauser, Boston, 1991.

[DV]   M. D. Donsker and S. R. S. Varadhan: Asymptotic evaluation of certain Markov process expectations for large time, I, I, III, Comm. Pure Appl Math $\underline{28}$ (1975) 1–45, 279–301; $\underline{29}$ (1976) 389–461.

[DE]   P. Dupuis and R. S. Ellis: A stochastic control approach to the theory of large deviations, preprint.

[DK]   P. Dupuis and H. J. Kushner: Stochastic systems with small noise, analysis and simulation: a phase locked loop example, SIAM J. Appl Math. $\underline{47}$ (1987) 643–661.

[E]   R. S. Ellis: Entropy, Large Deviations and Statistical Mechanics, Springer Verlag, 1985.

[FJ]   W. H. Fleming and M. R. James: Asymptotic series and exit time probabilities, Annals of Probability (to appear).

[FM1]   W. H. Fleming and W. M. McEneaney: Risk sensitive control and differential games, Brown Univ. LCDS Report No. 92-1.

[FM2]   W. H. Fleming and W. M. McEneaney: Risk sensitive control with ergodic cost criteria, Proc. 31st IEEE CDC, 1992.

[FSn]   W. H. Fleming and H. M. Soner: Controlled Markov Processes and Viscosity Solutions, Springer Verlag, 1992.

[FSg]   W. H. Fleming and P. E. Souganidis: Asymptotic series and the method of vanishing viscosity, Indiana U. Math J. $\underline{38}$ (1989) 293–314.

[FW]   M. I. Freidlin and A. D. Wentzell; Random Perturbations of Dynamical Systems, Springer Verlag, 1984.

[GD]   K. Glover and J. C. Doyle: State-space formulae for all stabilizing controllers that satisfy an H_∞ - norm bound and relations to risk sensitivity, Systems Control Lett. 11 (1988) 167–172.

[I]   A. Isidori: Robust regulation of nonlinear systems, MTNS Abstracts, Kobe, Japan (1991).

[Jac]   D. H. Jacobson: Optimal stochastic linear systems with exponential criteria and their relation to deterministic differential games, IEEE Trans Automat. Control AC-18 (1973) 124–131.

[Jam]   M. R. James: Asymptotic analysis of nonlinear stochastic risk-sensitive control and differential games, Math of Control, Signals and Syst. (to appear).

[K]   H. J. Kushner: Approximation and Weak Convergence Methods for Random Processes, MIT Press, 1984.

[PW]   S. Parekh and J. Walrand: Quick simulation of excessive backlogs in networks of queues, IMA vols. in Math and Appl. No. 10, 439–470, Springer-Verlag, 1986.

[R]   T. Runolfsson: Stationary risk-sensitive LQG control and its relation to LQG and H - infinity control, Proc 29th IEEE CDC, 1990, 1018–1023.

[Sch]   Z. Schuss: Theory and Applications of Stochastic Differential Equations, Wiley, 1980.

[Sh]   S-J Sheu: Stochastic control and exit probabilities of jump processes, SIAM J. Control Optimiz. 23 (1985) 306–328.

[Si]   B. Simon: Instantons, double wells and large deviations, Bulletin Amer Math Soc 8 (1983) 323–326.

[St]   D. W. Stroock: An Introduction to Large Deviations, Springer-Verlag, 1984.

[V]   S. R. S. Varadhan: Large Deviations and Applications, SIAM, 1984.

[W1]   P. Whittle: A risk sensitive maximum principle, Syst. Contr. Lett. 15 (1990) 183–192.

[W2]   P. Whittle: A risk sensitive maximum principle: The case of imperfect state observation, IEEE Trans Auto, Control (to appear).

Differential-Geometric Methods: a Powerful Set of New Tools for Optimal Control

Department of Mathematics, Rutgers University
New Brunswick, NJ 08903

Abstract. Differential-geometric methods can and have been successfully used in control theory, not only to pose and solve new problems, but also to get new insights and prove new results about classical problems of optimal control. In particular, they yield new results on local controllability, continuity properties of value functions, the structure of reachable sets, and the properties of optimal trajectories. For large classes of systems given by controlled differential equations with real-analytic right-hand sides, these methods make it possible —in conjunction with the theory of subanalytic sets— to prove piecewise analyticity of the value function and the existence of a piecewise smooth optimal feedback.

1 Introduction

Since its early days in the 1950's, the development of finite-dimensional, deterministic control theory has proceeded along essentially two main parallel tracks. The first one is the study of *linear systems*, and of a host of related problems such as static and dynamic stabilization, linear-quadratic control, linear time-optimal control, various "geometric" problems —e.g. tracking, disturbance decoupling, disturbance attenuation, noninteracting control— and linear identification and adaptive control. The second one is the study of *general* nonlinear systems $\dot{x} = f(x, u)$, possibly linear in the control u, posssibly required to satisfy some technical conditions such as differentiability of f, but not subject to any special "algebraic" requirements. Not surprisingly, the first line of inquiry has led, thanks to the algebraic structure, to a very rich body of theory for a very narrow class of systems, while the second one has produced some theorems of great generality, whose ability to yield useful results for specific nonlinear problems often turns out to be disappointingly limited.

However, since the early 1960's a new line of research began to emerge, starting with the pioneering work of R. Hermann [3] in 1963, followed later by that of C. Lobry [6] in 1970, and then by that of Brockett [2], Krener [5], Sussmann-Jurdjevic, and others in the early 1970's, and by a veritable explosion in the late 70's and the 80's, some of whose achievements are described, e.g., in the books [4,8,10]. This research makes systematic use of *differential-geometric methods* (henceforth abbreviated as DGM's). Our purpose here is to provide a brief outline of some of the applications of DGM's, using simple examples and stressing the comparison with classical approaches.

Differential geometry studies *differentiable manifolds endowed with "geometric" structures such as connections, Riemannian metrics, symplectic forms, foliations, group structures (Lie groups), group actions, bundle structures, etc.* For this

---

[1] This work was supported in part by NSF Grant DMS-8902994.

purpose, it has developed a general language and a distinctive philosophy, referred to here as the "differential geometric point of view," and outlined in Section 2 below.[2]

The distinctive feature of the work using DGM's in control theory is the adoption of this point of view, rather than the use of the specific structures of traditional differential geometry. DGM's are applied in control theory in three major ways:

1. To get new insights into *classical* problems of optimal control theory, such as local and global controllability, and the structure and properties of optimal trajectories, reachable sets, value functions, and optimal synthesis.

2. To study nonlinear control problems that are intrinsically differential-geometric, because (i) their natural state space is a differentiable manifold —such as $\mathbb{R}^3 \times SO(3)$ for the kinematics of a rigid body, $\mathbb{R}^3 \times SO(3) \times \cdots \times SO(3)$ for the kinematics of a system of several rigid bodies linked by spherical joints, or the tangent bundles of the above spaces for more realistic control problems where the controls are accelerations and torques— and/or (ii) the dynamics and controls are naturally related related to the geometry.

3. To develop general theories of "geometric" nonlinear problems such as feedback linearization, feedback equivalence, smooth feedback stabilization, tracking, path finding, observer design, disturbance decoupling, noninteracting control, disturbance attenuation —including nonlinear analogues of H^∞ theory— and other nonlinear versions of various well-known problems of linear control theory, for which the language and tools of differential geometry are essential even at the level of problem formulation (cf. the books [4,8]).

In this note we concentrate mainly on the first of the three types of applications. Our goal is to show that *DGM's are already useful and necessary even to study classical optimal control questions that do not appear to be "differential-geometric,"* and to argue our case we will present several simple examples of classical problems and show how DGM's provide new insights.

2 The Differential-Geometric Point of View

Suppose we want to prove that, if A is an $m \times n$ real matrix, then there are nonsingular square matrices P, Q of the appropriate sizes such that PAQ has, for some k, the 2×2 block form $\begin{pmatrix} I_k & 0 \\ 0 & 0 \end{pmatrix}$, where I_k is the identity matrix. An *algebraist* would do it by showing that A can by transformed into the desired form by elementary row and column operations, and that every such operation corresponds to left or right multiplication by a nonsingular matrix. A *geometer* would regard A as the matrix of a linear map $L : \mathbb{R}^n \ni x \to L(x) = Ax \in \mathbb{R}^m,$[3] and then would forget that $\mathbb{R}^n$ is $\mathbb{R}^b$ and $\mathbb{R}^m$ is $\mathbb{R}^m$, and regard both $\mathbb{R}^n$ and $\mathbb{R}^m$ as abstract linear spaces V, W. He would then let $W_1 = L(V)$, write $V = V_1 \oplus V_2$, where V_2 is the kernel of L, pick a basis $f_1, \ldots, f_k$ of V_1, and a basis $f_{k+1}, \ldots, f_n$ of V_2, combine them to get a basis $\mathbf{f} = (f_1, \ldots, f_n)$ of V, define $g_i = L(f_i)$ for $i = 1, \ldots, k$, show that $(g_1, \ldots, g_k)$ is a basis of W_1, extend this to a basis $\mathbf{g} = (g_1, \ldots, g_m)$ of W, and then observe that the matrix of L with respect to $\mathbf{f}$ and $\mathbf{g}$ has the desired block form.

---

[2]   Defining differential geometry as the study of certain geometric objects is, of course, circular, but the circularity is unavoidable, since —for this as for any other area of mathematics— the list of structures commonly regarded by practitioners as part of a subject is determined by its history rather than by a general definition.

[3]   Here, and throughout the paper, vectors in $\mathbb{R}^n$ are written as columns.

This elementary example captures the essence of the geometric point of view. Rather than work with spaces of tuples of numbers, geometers like to think about points in abstract spaces and about "geometric objects" such as lines, subspaces, linear maps (if the space has a linear structure that makes these things meaningful), or curves and surfaces and fields of directions in more general settings. Points are not tuples of numbers, even though they can be represented as such in various ways, by choosing coordinates. Geometers intensely dislike coordinates, and use them sparingly. No coordinate system is regarded as "natural" or preferred. This has a cost, namely, that one cannot define geometric objects by referring to a particular coordinate system. A geometric definition should preferably be formulated in coordinate-free language. If this cannot be done, and coordinate systems have to be used, then they should *all* be used and treated equally. A geometric object $\mathcal{O}$ should have a well defined *coordinate representation* $\mathcal{O}^\kappa$ with respect to every coordinate system κ. Naturally, one does not not require that $\mathcal{O}^\kappa$ be the same for all κ, but that the various representations be related in appropriate ways. For example, on an n-dimensional *linear space* V over $\mathbb{R}$, the coordinate systems are linear 1-1 onto maps $\kappa : V \to \mathbb{R}^n$. Then any two such systems $x = \kappa(v) \overset{\text{def}}{=} v^\kappa$, $y = \tilde{\kappa}(v) \overset{\text{def}}{=} v^{\tilde{\kappa}}$, are linearly related, i.e. the coordinate change map $L : v^{\tilde{\kappa}} \to L(v^\kappa) = \tilde{\kappa} \circ \kappa^{-1}$ is linear. For this reason one can do *linear algebra*, and define linear objects such as lines, planes and segments, and linear concepts such as linear independence. (For example, linear independence of k vectors $v_1, \ldots, v_k$ can either be defined using coordinates —e.g. by the condition that the matrix $(v_1^\kappa, \ldots, v_k^\kappa)$ have rank k, which would then have to be proved to be independent of the choice of κ— or in coordinate-free language, by requiring that $c_1 = \ldots = c_k = 0$ whenever $\sum_{i=1}^k c_i v_i = 0$. Either definition is acceptable, but geometers always prefer coordinate-free formulations.)

Differential geometry operates on abstract spaces M of points that are not thought of as tuples of numbers, but can be represented in various ways by means of tuples of numbers. These *coordinate representations* are called *charts*. (Formally, an n-dimensional chart on a set X is a one-to-one map κ from a subset $D(\kappa)$ of X —the *domain* of κ— onto an open subset $Im(\kappa)$ of $\mathbb{R}^n$.) Contrary to what happens in the linear case, a chart κ need not assign coordinates to all possible points, but one requires that every point be in the domain of some chart. (A set $\mathcal{A}$ of charts with this property is called an *atlas*.) Most importantly, one does not require that the (partially defined) transformations $\tilde{\kappa} \circ \kappa^{-1}$ relating two charts be linear, and so linear concepts such as lines and planes are not well defined. On the other hand, many other classes of objects are well defined. Exactly which objects can be defined depends, of course, on the atlas $\mathcal{A}$ used to endow M with a structure. The smaller $\mathcal{A}$ is, the easier it is for a definition to be invariant under coordinate changes. So reducing an atlas $\mathcal{A}$ —i.e. replacing $\mathcal{A}$ by a smaller atlas $\tilde{\mathcal{A}}$— corresponds to *enriching* a structure, and enlarging the class of geometric objects.

Differential geometry is specifically interested in *differentiable structures*. A n-dimensional *structure of class C^k* on M is an atlas $\mathcal{A}$ on M such that the domain $\kappa(D(\kappa) \cap D(\tilde{\kappa}))$ of every associated coordinate change $L = \tilde{\kappa} \circ \kappa^{-1}$ is open in $\mathbb{R}^n$, and L is of class C^k there. (As usual, we allow $k = +\infty$ and $k = \omega$, and "C^ω" means "real-analytic.") A set M endowed with a C^k structure of class is a C^k *manifold*. If $k \geq 1$ then M is a *differentiable manifold*.

A simple example of a differentiable manifold is the two-dimensional sphere S^2, defined to be the set of points (x_1, x_2, x_3) such that $x_1^2 + x_2^2 + x_3^2 = 1$. One can define a chart κ whose domain is the open upper hemisphere $H^+ = \{x : x_3 > 0\}$ by observing that, on H^+, $x_3 = +\sqrt{x_1^2 + x_2^2}$, so each point $p = (x_1, x_2, x_3) \in H^+$ is determined by $\kappa(p) = (x_1, x_2)$. This, of course, is only one chart, and its domain does not cover the whole sphere. To get a true atlas, notice that H^+ is a neighborhood of the "north pole" $(0,0,1)$. However (thinking geometrically!) every $p \in S^2$ is the "north pole" for some Cartesian coordinate system in $\mathbb{R}^3$. So what we have done for $(0,0,1)$ works for any $p \in S^2$, and we can get a chart covering a neighborhood of p. So we have produced enough charts to cover all points, i.e. we have constructed an atlas $\mathcal{A}$. If $\kappa, \tilde{\kappa} \in \mathcal{A}$ arise from Cartesian coordinates y and z in $\mathbb{R}^3$, then $z_i = \sum_{j=1}^{3} a_{ij} y_j$, and so if $\kappa(p) = (y_1, y_2)$, $\tilde{\kappa}(p) = (z_1, z_2)$, then $z_i = a_{i1} y_1 + a_{i2} y_2 + a_{i3} \sqrt{y_1^2 + y_2^2}$ if $p \in D(\kappa) \cap D(\tilde{\kappa})$. So all the coordinate changes are C^ω, and S^2 is a C^ω manifold.

The sphere S^2 has a well defined *tangent space* $T_p S^2$ at each point p, consisting of all those vectors in $\mathbb{R}^3$ that are starting directions of C^1 curves from p that stay in S^2. In other words, $v \in T_p S^2$ iff $v = \dot{\gamma}(0)$, where $\gamma : [0, \varepsilon) \to \mathbb{R}^3$ is C^1, $\gamma(0) = p$, and $\gamma(t) \in S^2$ for all t. Since $\|\gamma(t)\| = 1$, it is easy to see that $\gamma(0) \perp p$. Conversely, for any $v \in \mathbb{R}^3$ such that $v \perp p$ we can construct a curve γ, e.g. by letting $\gamma(t) = \nu(p + tv)$ (where $\nu(w) = w/\|w\|$). Then $\gamma(t) = (p + tv)/(\sqrt{1 + t^2})$ —using $v \perp p$— so that $\gamma(t) = p + tv + o(t)$ and $\dot{\gamma}(0) = v$. So $T_p S^2$ is exactly the set of $v \in \mathbb{R}^3$ that are orthogonal to p. Notice that $T_p S^2$ varies as p changes. In particular, on a sphere it does not make sense to compute, for instance, the sum of two velocity vectors v_1, v_2 at different points p_1, p_2, since v_1 and v_2 live in different linear spaces.

The definition of tangent vectors for S^2 can be extended to arbitrary differentiable manifolds M. A "tangent vector" at $p \in M$ is defined intrinsically by first defining what it means for a curve $\gamma : I \to M$ to be C^1, and for two C^1 curves $\gamma, \delta : [0, \varepsilon) \to M$ such that $\gamma(0) = \delta(0) = p$ to be *tangent* at time 0. (This is done by referring to a chart κ with $p \in D(\kappa)$, and showing that the definition does not depend on the choice of κ.) Tangency is then an equivalence relation among C^1 curves starting at p, and the *tangent vectors at p* are the equivalence classes. If $\gamma : [0, \varepsilon) \to M$ is a C^1 curve from p whose class is v, then we write $v = \dot{\gamma}(0)$.

The set of tangent vectors at p is the *tangent space* at p, denoted by $T_p M$. Then every $v \in T_p M$ has a well defined representation v^κ with respect to every chart κ with $p \in D(\kappa)$ (obtained by picking any C^1 curve $\gamma : [0, \varepsilon) \to M$ with $\dot{\gamma}(0) = v$ and letting $v^\kappa = \dot{\gamma}^\kappa(0)$, where $\gamma^\kappa = \kappa \circ \gamma$). Of course, v^κ depends on κ. But,

$$\text{if } \kappa_1, \kappa_2 \text{ are charts and } p \in D(\kappa_1) \cap D(\kappa_2), \text{ then } v^{\kappa_2} = J(\kappa_2, \kappa_1)(p^{\kappa_1}) v^{\kappa_1}, \quad (1)$$

where $J(\kappa_2, \kappa_1)$ is the Jacobian matrix of the map $\kappa_2 \circ \kappa_1^{-1}$. Conversely, if we specify a collection $\{v^\kappa\}$ of vectors in $\mathbb{R}^n$, for all charts κ such that $p \in D(\kappa)$, and these vectors transform according to (1), then the v^κ are the representations of a unique $v \in T_p M$, so we could equally well have defined a tangent vector to be such a collection $\{v^\kappa\}$. As explained before, both definitions are acceptable in differential geometry, but geometers prefer the first one because it is more "cordinate-free".

The dual space $T_p^* M$ of $T_p M$ is the *cotangent space* of M at p, and its elements are called *covectors* at p. A covector $\lambda \in T_p^* M$ has coordinate representations λ^κ, that are taken to be *row vectors*. The λ^κ obey the following transformation law:

$$\text{if } \kappa_1, \kappa_2 \text{ are charts and } p \in D(\kappa_1) \cap D(\kappa_2), \text{ then } \lambda^{\kappa_2} = \lambda^{\kappa_1} J(\kappa_1, \kappa_2)(p^{\kappa_2}). \quad (2)$$

Notice that *vectors and covectors are intrinsically different objects*, because their transformation laws (1) and (2) are different. If φ is a real-valued C^1 function on some neighborhood of p —the concepts of "neighborhhod" and "C^1 function" are well defined, using charts— then we can define its *gradient* $\nabla \varphi(p)$ at p to be the functional $\lambda \in T_p^* M$ given by $\langle \lambda, v \rangle = \frac{d}{dt}\big|_{t=0} \varphi(\gamma(t))$, where γ is any C^1 curve from p such that $\dot{\gamma}(0) = v$. Then *the gradient of a function is a covector, not a vector*.

Having defined tangent vectors, it is obvious how to define vector fields and integral curves. A *vector field* is a function f that to every $p \in M$ assigns a tangent vector $f(p) \in T_pM$. If $I \subseteq \mathbb{R}$ is an interval, we call a C^1 curve $\gamma : I \to M$ an *integral curve* of f if $\dot{\gamma}(t) = f(\gamma(t))$ for all $t \in I$, where $\dot{\gamma}(t)$ is defined to be $\dot{\delta}_t(0)$, and $\delta_t(s) = \gamma(t+s)$. The concept of a C^k vector field is well defined on any C^{k+1} manifold. In particular, on a C^1 manifold we can talk about C^0 vector fields, and the usual local existence theorem for solutions of initial value problems $\dot{x} = f(x)$, $x(t_0) - x_0$ holds. If uniqueness also holds (for example, if f is C^1) then we say that f is a $C^{0,u}$ vector field, and use exponential notation for the flow of f, i.e. we write xe^{tf} for $\gamma_{x,f}(t)$, where $\gamma_{x,f}$ is the maximal integral curve of f which goes through x at time 0.

In control theory we study differential equations $\dot{x} = f(x, u)$ involving a parameter u, and for there to be true control u must take at least two values. So we have to work with *systems*, involving *at least two vector fields*. Clearly, then, one should look for operations that combine vector fields to get new ones. Besides the linear operations, there is an important binary operation that, to any two C^1 vector fields f, g, associates their *Lie bracket* $[f, g]$, defined in coordinates by $[f, g]^\kappa = \frac{\partial g^\kappa}{\partial x} \cdot f^\kappa - \frac{\partial f^\kappa}{\partial x} \cdot g^\kappa$ (writing both f^κ and g^κ as columns of functions, so that $\frac{\partial f^\kappa}{\partial x}$ and $\frac{\partial g^\kappa}{\partial x}$ are square matrices of functions). An easy computation shows that the above representations transform like a vector field, so there is a well defined vector field $[f, g]$. According to the basic differential-geometric philosophy, the Lie bracket ought to have an important control-theoretic meaning for non-linear systems, and should be definable in an intrinsic way. Remarkably, both facts are true, and the intrinsic definition actually explains why the Lie bracket matters in control theory. In fact:

$$[f, g](p) = \lim_{t \to 0} t^{-2}(pe^{tf}e^{tg}e^{-tf}e^{-tg} - p) . \qquad (3)$$

The control-theoretic importance of this will be discussed below in Section 3.1.

If M is a C^∞ manifold, we use $\Gamma^\infty(TM)$ to denote the set of all C^∞ vector fields on M. Then $[f, g] \in \Gamma^\infty(TM)$ whenever f, g are in $\Gamma^\infty(TM)$. A *Lie subalgebra* of $\Gamma^\infty(TM)$ is a linear subspace L of $\Gamma^\infty(TM)$ such that $f, g \in L \Rightarrow [f, g] \in L$. If $S \subseteq \Gamma^\infty(TM)$, then there is a smallest Lie subalgebra $\mathrm{Lie}(S)$ of $\Gamma^\infty(TM)$ containing S, called the *Lie algebra generated by* S.

3 Some Examples

We now present some simple examples, to illustrate how DGM's work, and to show the difference between their power and that of classical control theory methods such as the Pontryagin Maximum Principle (PMP). Since lack of space prevents us from dicussing the general theory, we will work with a fairly limited class of problems, namely, with *minimum time problems* for C^∞ control-linear systems of the form

$$\Sigma : \quad \dot{x} = f_0(x) + u_1 f_1(x) + \ldots + u_m f_m(x) , \quad x \in M , \quad u = (u_1, \ldots, u_m) \in U , \quad (4)$$

where the state space M is a C^∞ manifold, and $f_0, \ldots, f_m$ are C^∞ vector fields on M. The *control space* U is assumed to be a compact, convex subset of $\mathbb{R}^m$ with a nonempty interior. If $f_0 \equiv 0$ and $0 \in \mathrm{Int}\, U$, then we say that Σ is *driftless*. (If M and the f_i are C^ω, then we call Σ a C^ω *system*.) For $a \leq b$, we let $\mathcal{U}(a, b)$ denote the set of all measurable functions $\eta : [a, b] \to U$, and write $\mathcal{U}$ for the set $\cup\{\mathcal{U}(a, b) : -\infty < a \leq b < \infty\}$. A *control* for Σ is a member of $\mathcal{U}$. We write $f(x, u)$ for $f_0(x) + u_1 f_1(x) + \ldots + u_m f_m(x)$. If $\eta \in \mathcal{U}(a, b)$, an η-*trajectory* of Σ is an absolutely continuous curve $\gamma : [a, b] \to M$ such that $\dot{\gamma}(t) = f(\gamma(t), \eta(t))$ for almost all $t \in [a, b]$. We use $\mathrm{Tr}(\Sigma, \eta)$ to denote the set of all η-trajectories of Σ, and define $\mathrm{Tr}(\Sigma)(a, b) = \cup\{\mathrm{Tr}(\Sigma, \eta) : \eta \in \mathcal{U}(a, b)\}$, $\mathrm{Tr}(\Sigma) = \cup\{\mathrm{Tr}(\Sigma, \eta) : \eta \in \mathcal{U}\}$. If

$\gamma \in \text{Tr}(\Sigma, \eta)$, $\eta \in \mathcal{U}(a,b)$, then (i) a, b, $b-a$, $\gamma(a)$ and $\gamma(b)$ are, respectively, the *initial time*, the *terminal time*, the *duration*, the *initial point* and the *terminal point* of γ, and are denoted by $\tau_-(\gamma)$, $\tau_+(\gamma)$, $T(\gamma)$, $x_-(\gamma)$, $x_+(\gamma)$; (ii) (γ, η) is called an *admissible pair*; (iii) if $p = x_-(\gamma)$, $q = x_+(\gamma)$, $T = T(\gamma)$, then γ *goes from p to q in time T*, and η *steers p to q in time $T(\gamma)$*, and write $\gamma : p \xrightarrow{T} q$ and $\eta : p \xrightarrow{T} q$. We use $\text{Adm}(\Sigma)$ to denote the set of all admissible pairs of Σ. We write $\gamma : p \rightsquigarrow q$ if $(\exists T \geq 0)(\gamma : p \xrightarrow{T} q)$, and similarly for $\eta : p \rightsquigarrow q$. If there is an $\eta \in \mathcal{U}$ such that $\eta : p \rightsquigarrow q$ (resp. $\eta : p \xrightarrow{T} q$), then we say that q is Σ-*reachable* (resp. Σ-*reachable in time T*) from p, and that p is Σ-*controllable* (resp. Σ-*controllable in time T*) to q.

If $S \subseteq M$, we use $\mathcal{R}^\Sigma(S)$ (resp. $\mathcal{R}^\Sigma(\leq T; S)$, $\mathcal{R}^\Sigma(T; S)$, $\mathcal{C}^\Sigma(S)$, $\mathcal{C}^\Sigma(\leq T; S)$, $\mathcal{C}^\Sigma(T; S)$) to denote the set of all points q such that q is Σ-reachable from p (resp. Σ-reachable from p in time $\leq T$, Σ-reachable from p in time T, Σ-controllable to p, Σ-controllable to p in time $\leq T$, Σ-controllable to p in time T) for some $p \in S$. (If $S = \{p\}$, $p \in M$, then we write $\mathcal{R}^\Sigma(p)$, etc. instead of $\mathcal{R}^\Sigma(\{p\})$, etc.) We call Σ *controllable* if $\mathcal{R}^\Sigma(p) = M$ for all $p \in M$ (i.e. if $\mathcal{C}^\Sigma(p) = M$ for all $p \in M$).

Our hypotheses clearly imply the uniqueness and local existence of trajectories. We call Σ *complete* if it has no explosions, i.e. if for every a, b, $\eta \in \mathcal{U}(a,b)$, $\bar{t} \in [a, b]$, $\bar{p} \in M$ there is a $\gamma \in \text{Tr}(\Sigma, \eta)$ such that $\gamma(\bar{t}) = \bar{p}$. (This will happen, e.g., if M is compact, or if $M = \mathbb{R}^n$ and the f_i satisfy a linear growth bound $\|f_i(x)\| \leq C(1 + \|x\|)$.) If Σ is complete and S is compact, then *all the sets* $\mathcal{R}^\Sigma(\leq T; S)$, $\mathcal{R}^\Sigma(T; S)$, $\mathcal{C}^\Sigma(\leq T; S)$, $\mathcal{C}^\Sigma(T; S)$, *are compact*.

Reachable sets are related to controllable sets as follows. Define the *reversed* system Σ^- to be the system $\dot{x} = -f(x, u)$, $x \in \Omega$, $u \in U$. Then the controllable sets for Σ are the reachable sets for Σ^-, and viceversa.

A system Σ is *small-time locally controllable (STLC) to* (resp. *from*) a set S if for every $T > 0$ the set S is contained in the interior of $\mathcal{C}^\Sigma(\leq T; S)$ (resp. $\mathcal{R}^\Sigma(\leq T; S)$). Clearly, Σ is STLC to S if and only if Σ^- is STLC from S.

A *boundary trajectory* is a $\gamma \in \text{Tr}(\Sigma)$ such that $x_+(\gamma) \in \partial \mathcal{R}^\Sigma(\leq T, x_-(\gamma))$ for some $T > T(\gamma)$. (Here $\partial X \overset{\text{def}}{=} \text{Clos}\, X - \text{Int}\, X$.) The *value function* $V^\Sigma : M \times M \to \mathbb{R} \cup \{+\infty\}$ is defined by letting $V^\Sigma(p, q) = \inf\{T(\gamma) : \gamma \in \text{Tr}(\Sigma), \gamma : p \rightsquigarrow q\}$. (In particular, $V^\Sigma(p, q) = +\infty$ if $q \notin \mathcal{R}^\Sigma(p)$.) If we specify a *target set* S — i.e. a nonempty closed subset S of M— we then define the *value function* V_S^Σ by $V_S^\Sigma(p) = \inf\{V^\Sigma(p, q) : q \in S\}$. A trajectory γ such that $T(\gamma) = V^\Sigma(x_-(\gamma), x_+(\gamma))$ (resp. $x_+(\gamma) \in S$ and $T(\gamma) = V_S^\Sigma(x_-(\gamma))$) is called a *time-minimizer* (resp. an *S-time-minimizer*) for Σ. We let $\mathcal{M}(\Sigma)$ (resp. $\mathcal{M}_S(\Sigma)$, $\mathcal{B}(\Sigma)$) denote the set of all time-minimizers (resp. S-time-minimizers, boundary trajectories) for Σ. (If $S = \{p\}$, $p \in M$, we write V_p^Σ, $\mathcal{M}_p(\Sigma)$.) Clearly, $\mathcal{M}_S(\Sigma) \subseteq \mathcal{M}(\Sigma)$. Our assumptions then imply that, if Σ is complete, then (i) V^Σ *is lower semicontinuous* (LSC); (ii) *for every $p, q \in M$ such that $V^\Sigma(p, q) < +\infty$ there is a $\gamma \in \mathcal{M}(\Sigma)$ such that $\gamma : p \rightsquigarrow q$*; (iii) V_S^Σ is LSC and $(\forall p \in M)((V_S^\Sigma(p) < +\infty) \Rightarrow (\exists \gamma \in \mathcal{M}_S(\Sigma))(x_-(\gamma) = p)$ for every closed S. Moreover, $V_S^\Sigma(p) \geq 0$ for all $p \in M$, and $V_S^\Sigma(p) = 0$ if and only if $p \in S$. Finally, V_S^Σ is continuous if and only if Σ is STLC to S.

The *Pontryagin Maximum Principle* (PMP) gives necessary conditions for a trajectory γ to be in $\mathcal{M}(\Sigma)$ and for γ to be in $\mathcal{B}(\Sigma)$. To state the PMP, we first define the *Hamiltonian lift* Σ^* of Σ. Assume first that M is open in $\mathbb{R}^n$. The *Hamiltonian* H^Σ of Σ is the function $H^\Sigma : M \times \mathbb{R}^n \times U \to \mathbb{R}$ given by $H^\Sigma(x, z, u) = \langle z, f(x, u) \rangle$. Then Σ^* is the control system $\dot{x} = \frac{\partial H^\Sigma}{\partial z}(x, z, u)$, $\dot{z} = -\frac{\partial H^\Sigma}{\partial x}(x, z, u)$, with state space $M \times (\mathbb{R}^n - \{0\})$ and control space U. (The first equation just says that $\dot{x} = f(x, u)$, so every $\xi \in \text{Tr}(\Sigma^*)$ is of the form $t \to \xi(t) = (\gamma(t), \zeta(t))$, where $\gamma \in \text{Tr}(\Sigma)$ and $\zeta(t) \neq 0$.) Now, if M is a general manifold, then Σ^* makes parfect sense, provided that $\zeta(t)$ is interpreted as a *covector* at $\gamma(t)$. The state space of Σ^* is now $T^{\#}M$, where $T^{\#}M = \{(x,z) : x \in M, z \in T_x^*M, z \neq 0\}$ (so $T^{\#}M$ is the "cotangent bundle T^*M with the 0 section removed"). An admissible pair (ξ, η) for Σ^* is *H-minimizing* if there is a constant $\zeta_0 \geq 0$ such that $H^{\Sigma}(\xi(t), \eta(t)) = \min\{H^{\Sigma}(\xi(t), u) : u \in U\} = -\zeta_0$ for almost all $t \in [\tau_-(\gamma), \tau_+(\gamma)]$. If $\zeta_0 = 0$, then (ξ, η) is *zero-H-minimizing*. A *Pontryagin extremal* (resp. an *abnormal Pontryagin extremal*) is an admissible pair (γ, η) for which there is a ζ such that $(\gamma, \zeta) \in \text{Tr}(\Sigma^*, \eta)$ and (γ, ζ, η) is H-minimizing (resp. zero-H-minimizing). The PMP says that *if $\gamma \in \text{Tr}(\Sigma, \eta)$, then: (i) if $\gamma \in \mathcal{M}(\Sigma)$, then (γ, η) is a Pontryagin extremal, and (ii) if $\gamma \in \mathcal{B}(\Sigma)$, then (γ, η) is an abnormal Pontryagin extremal.*

3.1 Local controllability of the "Reeds-Shepp car" and Lie brackets

Consider the three-dimensional system Σ_{RS} given by $\dot{x}_1 = u\cos\theta$, $\dot{x}_2 = u\sin\theta$, $\dot{\theta} = v$, with state variables x_1, x_2, θ, and controls u, v, subject to $|u| \leq 1$, $|v| \leq 1$. Think of Σ_{RS} as describing the motion in a plane of a vehicle $\mathbf{V}$ that has, at each time, a position (x_1, x_2) and an orientation θ. Then $\mathbf{V}$ can move forwards and backwards but not sideways, and its orientation can be controlled as well. The state space M is not really $\mathbb{R}^3$, but $\mathbb{R}^2 \times S^1$, since θ is an angle. (This will be important later.) Our objective is to understand how to drive $\mathbf{V}$ from any given initial configuration (x_1^-, x_2^-, θ^-) to any other terminal configuration (x_1^+, x_2^+, θ^+) in minimum time. (This problem was studied by Reeds and Shepp in [9] using *ad hoc* techniques, and by Sussmann and Tang in [11] with control theory methods.)

A first natural question is to investigate the *controllability* and *local controllability* of Σ_{RS}. It is easy to verify directly, using combinations of small forwards and backwards motions and small rotations, that Σ_{RS} is STLC to and from any point. Let us see whether we can recover this using classical optimal control techniques, e.g. the PMP. Clearly, a driftless system Σ is not STLC from p if and only if, for arbitrary $T > 0$, the *constant trajectory* $t \to \gamma(t) = p$, $0 \leq t \leq T$ is in $\mathcal{B}(\Sigma)$. Now, the PMP gives a necessary condition for $\gamma \in \mathcal{B}(\Sigma)$, and this yields a sufficient condition for STLC from p. In our case, this simply amounts to the condition that the linearization of our equations around $\bar{p}$ be controllable, and it is easy to see that this condition fails. So *the sufficient condition arising from the PMP does not cover this case.*

Now contrast this with the differential geometric approach. Notice first that by using constant controls $(u, v) = (\pm 1, 0)$, $(u, v) = (0, \pm 1)$ we can move freely along the directions of the vector fields f, g with components $(\cos\theta, \sin\theta, 0)$ and $(0, 0, 1)$. So we have two "directly controllable" directions. To have STLC we must be able to move our vehicle forwards and backwards in three independent directions, so we are missing just one direction. At this point, a differential geometer would remind us that there is a binary operation on vector fields called the *Lie bracket*, which does precisely what we need, namely, associate to any two vector fields f and g a new vector field $h = [f, g]$ such that, even if one cannot directly steer the system along trajectories of h, one can approximately achieve the same effect by combining f- and g-motions. Identity (3) tells us how to produce a curve $t \to \delta(t)$ whose direction to second order is $[f, g](p)$ (i.e. $\delta(t) = t^2[f, g](p) + o(t^2)$), all whose points can be reached from p by combining forwards and backwards f- and g-motions, even though δ itself need not be a permissible motion. So, if $[f, g](p)$, $f(p)$, $g(p)$ are linearly independent, then it is as though we really had three linearly independent directions of motion, and STLC from p should follow, if we are in three dimensions. (For a rigorous proof, apply the Inverse Function Theorem to the map $(t, s, \tau) \to$

$\sigma(t)e^{sf}e^{\tau g}$, where σ is the C^1 curve given by $\sigma(t) = pe^{\sqrt{t}f}e^{\sqrt{t}g}e^{-\sqrt{t}f}e^{-\sqrt{t}g}$ for $t \geq 0$ and $\sigma(t) = pe^{\sqrt{-t}g}e^{\sqrt{-t}f}e^{-\sqrt{-t}g}e^{-\sqrt{-t}f}$ for $t \leq 0$.)

For Σ_{RS}, h is easily seen to have components $(\sin\theta, -\cos\theta, 0)$. So h is precisely the "missing" third direction of sideways motion. Then $f(p)$, $g(p)$, $h(p)$ are linearly independent for each p. So STLC holds. So *by using Lie brackets we have been able to derive a result that was beyond the power of the Maximum Principle.*

3.2 Lie Algebras and Chow's Theorem

The local controllability proof given above can in fact be carried out under much more general situations. The key idea is to iterate the procedure and compute all possible higher-order brackets such as $[f_i, [f_j, f_k]]$ or $[[f_i, f_j], [f_k, [f_l, f_m]]]$. Then STLC from and to p should follow, provided that the directions at p of all these brackets linearly span the space of all possible directions. This turns out to be a true, rigorous theorem, known as "Chow's Theorem," which in additon is remarkably easy to prove. (Cf. Krener [5]. The systematic use of Chow's Theorem in control theory was first advocated by R. Hermann in [3]). We associate to a system Σ its *accessibility Lie algebra* L^Σ, defined by $L^\Sigma = \mathrm{Lie}(\{f_0, f_1, \ldots, f_m\})$. We say that Σ has the *Lie algebra rank property* (LARP) a $p \in M$ if $L^\Sigma(p) = T_pM$, where $L^\Sigma(p) = \{X(p) : X \in L^\Sigma\}$. Chow's Theorem then says that, *if Σ has the LARP at p and is driftless, then it is STLC to and from p.*

3.3 Lie Brackets, Normal Forms and the Lobry Picture

The fact that the Lie bracket is intrinsic is often used as follows: suppose we know that certain numbers E_j, defined in terms of brackets, are nonzero at a point p. Using this, it may be possible to find a chart κ with respect to which our problem is in a simpler "canonical form," and the E_j will still be $\neq 0$ in the κ-representation. We illustrate this method by outlining the rigorous theory of the "Lobry picture," which appeared in C. Lobry's path-breaking 1970 paper [6].[4]

We study the *local structure of the reachable set* from a point p, for a three-dimensional control system of the form $\dot{x} = f(x) + ug(x)$, $-1 \leq u \leq 1$, where f, g are C^2 vector fields on a open subset Ω of $\mathbb{R}^3$. Let $X = f - g$, $Y = f + g$. Let $S_{XY}(p)$, $S_{YX}(p)$ be, respectively, the XY- and YX-surfaces from p, i.e. $S_{XY}(p) = \{pe^{tX}e^{sY} : t \geq 0, s \geq 0\}$, $S_{YX}(p) = \{pe^{sY}e^{tX} : t \geq 0, s \geq 0\}$, so that each surface looks like a —smoothly deformed— two-dimensional closed quarter-plane, and the two surfaces are glued at their boundary, which is the union of the two half-curves $L_X(p) = \{pe^{tX} : t \geq 0\}$, $L_Y(p) = \{pe^{tY} : t \geq 0\}$. Our goal is to outline a rigorous formulation and proof of the assertion that, *if $f(p)$, $g(p)$, $[f, g](p)$ are linearly independent. then, locally, the reachable set from p is the set that lies between $S_{XY}(p)$ and $S_{YX}(p)$.* It turns out that, using DGM's, we can provide both a correct mathematical formulation and a rigorous proof.

Theorem 1. *Assume that Ω is an open subset of $\mathbb{R}^3$, $k \geq 2$, f and g are C^k vector fields on Ω, Σ is the system $\dot{x} = f(x) + ug(x)$, $x \in \Omega$, $|u| \leq 1$, and $p \in \Omega$ is such that $f(p)$, $g(p)$, $[f, g](p)$ are linearly independent. Let $X = f - g$, $Y = f + g$. Then there exist a $T > 0$, a $\rho > 0$, a cubic C^k chart κ of radius ρ centered at p, and a C^k function $\varphi : (-\rho, \rho)^2 \to (-\rho, \rho)$, such that $\varphi(x_1, x_2) = x_1 x_2(1 + \psi(x_1, x_2))$ —where $\psi \in C^{k-2}$, $\psi(0, 0) = 0$, and $|\psi(x_1, x_2)| < 1$ for $|x_1| < \rho$, $|x_2| < \rho$— with the property that, if $\mathcal{R} = \mathcal{R}^\Sigma(\leq T; p)$, then*

---

[4]   I am indebted to H. Schättler for suggesting the approach presented here.

$$\kappa(\mathcal{R} \cap D(\kappa)) = \{(x_1, x_2, x_3) : x_1 \geq 0,\, x_2 \geq 0,\, 0 \leq x_3 \leq \varphi(x_1, x_2)\}\,. \tag{5}$$

Moreover, the sets $S^- = \kappa^{-1}(\{(x_1, x_2, x_3) : x_1 \geq 0,\, x_2 \geq 0,\, x_3 = 0\})$, $S^+ = \kappa^{-1}(\{(x_1, x_2, x_3) : x_1 \geq 0,\, x_2 \geq 0,\, x_3 = \varphi(x_1, x_2)\})$ *are precisely the intersections with* $D(\kappa)$ *of the sets* $S_{XY}^T(p)$, $S_{YX}^T(p)$, *defined by* $S_{XY}^T(p) = \{pe^{tX}e^{sY} : 0 \leq t \leq T,\, 0 \leq s \leq T\}$, $S_{YX}(p) = \{pe^{sY}e^{tX} : 0 \leq t \leq T,\, 0 \leq s \leq T\}$.

Remark. A *cubic chart of radius* ρ *centered at* p is a chart κ such that $\kappa(p) = 0$ and $Im(\kappa)$ is the cube $(-\rho, \rho)^3$.

OUTLINE OF THE PROOF. We let $Z = [X, Y]$ (so Z is a C^{k-1} vector field) and define an Ω-valued map F by $F(x_1, x_2, x_3) = pe^{x_3 Z}e^{x_2 Y}e^{x_1 X}$. Then F is well defined and of class C^k near $(0, 0, 0)$ (because the curve $t \to pe^{tZ}$ is C^k, since Z is C^{k-1}) and its Jacobian at $(0, 0, 0)$ is nonsingular. Therefore, there is a $\bar{\rho} > 0$ such that, if $0 < \rho \leq \bar{\rho}$, then F is 1-1 on the cube $C(\rho) = (-\rho, \rho)^3$, the image $N(\rho) = F(C(\rho))$ is open, and the restriction $F\lceil C(\rho)$ of F to $C(\rho)$ has a C^k inverse $\kappa_\rho : N(\rho) \to C(\rho)$. Then κ_ρ is a cubic C^k chart centered at p, $D(\kappa_\rho) = N(\rho)$, $X^{\kappa_\rho} \equiv (1, 0, 0)$, and $Y^{\kappa_\rho} \equiv (\alpha_1, 1 + \alpha_2, \alpha_3)$, where the α_i are C^{k-1} functions on $C(\rho)$ that vanish when $x_1 = 0$. Then $\alpha_i = x_1 \tilde{\alpha}_i$, where the $\tilde{\alpha}_i$ are C^{k-2}. Also, $Z^{\kappa_\rho} \equiv (\beta_1, \beta_2, \beta_3)$, where the β_i are of class C^{k-1}, and $\beta_1 \equiv \beta_2 \equiv \beta_3 - 1 \equiv 0$ wherever $x_1 = x_2 = 0$, so that $\beta_i = x_1 \hat{\beta}_i + x_2 \check{\beta}_i$ for $i = 1, 2$, and $\beta_3 = 1 + x_1 \hat{\beta}_3 + x_2 \check{\beta}_3$, where the $\hat{\beta}_i$, $\check{\beta}_i$ are C^{k-2} functions. Then $Z = [X, Y]$ implies $\beta_i = \frac{\partial \alpha_i}{\partial x_1}$. So $\frac{\partial \alpha_i}{\partial x_1} \in C^{k-1}$, so the $\tilde{\alpha}_i$ are C^{k-1}, since $\tilde{\alpha}_i(x_1, x_2, x_3) = \int_0^1 \frac{\partial \alpha_i}{\partial x_1}(sx_1, x_2, x_3)ds$. But then $\tilde{\alpha}_i = \beta_i - x_1 \frac{\partial \tilde{\alpha}_i}{\partial x_1}$, and therefore $\tilde{\alpha}_i = x_1 \hat{\alpha}_i + x_2 \check{\alpha}_i$ for $i = 1, 2$, $\tilde{\alpha}_3 = 1 + x_1 \hat{\alpha}_3 + x_2 \check{\alpha}_3$, where $\hat{\alpha}_i = \hat{\beta}_i - \frac{\partial \tilde{\alpha}_i}{\partial x_1}$, $\check{\alpha}_i = \check{\beta}_i$, so that the $\hat{\alpha}_i$ and $\check{\alpha}_i$ are C^{k-2}. This shows that $Y^{\kappa_\rho} = Y_0 + x_1^2 \hat{Y} + x_1 x_2 \check{Y}$, where $Y_0 \equiv (0, 1, x_1)$, $\hat{Y} \equiv (\hat{\alpha}_1, \hat{\alpha}_2, \hat{\alpha}_3)$, $\check{Y} \equiv (\check{\alpha}_1, \check{\alpha}_2, \check{\alpha}_3)$. So, by changing coordinates via κ_ρ, we have put (X, Y) in the "normal form" $X = (1, 0, 0)$, $Y = (0, 1, x_1) + o(||x||^2)$. From now on, we identify $N(\bar{\rho})$ with $C(\bar{\rho})$ via κ_ρ.

Now, the YX-surface is easy to compute, since the Y-trajectory from p is just the positive part of the x_2 axis, and the X-trajectories are just lines $\dot{x}_1 = 1$, $\dot{x}_2 = \dot{x}_3 = 0$. To compute the XY-surface, we let $\Phi(t, s) = pe^{tX}e^{sY}$, and observe that Φ is well defined and C^k for (t, s) near $(0, 0)$. Moreover, the derivatives $\frac{\partial \Phi}{\partial t}(0, 0)$ and $\frac{\partial \Phi}{\partial s}(0, 0)$ are equal, respectively, to $X(p)$ and $Y(p)$, so they are linearly independent. This means, by the Implicit Function Theorem, that there is an open square $U = (-T, T)^2$ in $\mathbb{R}^2$ such that Φ is defined on U, $\Phi(U)$ is a two-dimensional surface of class C^k, $\Phi(U) \subseteq N(\bar{\rho})$, the restriction $\Phi\lceil U$ of Φ to U is one-to one, and its inverse $(\Phi\lceil U)^{-1} : \Phi(U) \to U$ is C^k. From now on, we restrict the domain of Φ to U, so Φ is a mapping into $N(\bar{\rho})$, i.e. into $C(\bar{\rho})$. Moreover, if we let $\pi(x_1, x_2, x_3) = (x_1, x_2)$, then $\Psi = \pi \circ \Phi$ maps $(0, 0)$ to $(0, 0)$ and its Jacobian matrix at $(0, 0)$ is the identity matrix. Therefore, given any sufficiently small $\rho > 0$, there is an open neighborhood $V_\rho \subseteq U$ of $(0, 0)$ in $\mathbb{R}^2$ which is mapped by Ψ in a one-to-one and onto fashion, and with a C^k inverse, onto the square $(-\rho, \rho)^2$. Then $\Phi(V_\rho)$ is precisely the graph of a C^k function $\varphi_\rho : (-\rho, \rho)^2 \to \mathbb{R}$. The function φ_ρ vanishes when $x_1 = 0$ or $x_2 = 0$ (since $\Phi(t, 0) = (t, 0, 0)$ and $\Phi(0, s) = (0, s, 0)$). So $\varphi_\rho(x_1, x_2) = x_1 x_2 \tilde{\varphi}_\rho(x_1, x_2)$, where $\tilde{\varphi}_\rho \in C^{k-2}$. In particular, by picking ρ sufficiently small, we can guarantee that φ_ρ takes values in $(-\rho, \rho)$, so $\Phi(V_\rho) \subseteq C(\rho)$. Since $\alpha_i = x_1(1 + x_1 \hat{\alpha}_i + x_2 \check{\alpha}_i)$ for $i = 1, 2$, and $\alpha_3 = x_1(1 + x_1 \hat{\alpha}_3 + x_2 \check{\alpha}_3)$, we can make sure, by making ρ even smaller if needed, that $\alpha_3 > 0$ on C_ρ whenever $x_1 > 0$, and also that $\alpha_2 > 1/2$ and $|\alpha_1| < 1/2$ on C_ρ. Then, with such a choice of ρ, we have $S_{XY}^T(p) \cap N(\rho) = S^+(\rho)$, and $S_{YX}^T(p) \cap n(\rho) = S^-(\rho)$, where $S^+(\rho)$, $S^-(\rho)$ are, respectively, the intersections of $\Phi(V_\rho)$ and the square $(-\rho,\rho)^2 \times \{0\}$ with the set $\{(x_1,x_2,x_3) : x_1 \geq 0,\ x_2 \geq 0\}$.

From now on we just write $\kappa = \kappa_\rho$, $\varphi = \varphi_\rho$, $\tilde{\varphi} = \tilde{\varphi}_\rho$, $S^+ = S^+(\rho)$, $S^- = S^-(\rho)$.

Let us now show that, possibly after shrinking ρ, we can assume that $\frac{\partial \varphi}{\partial x_1} > 0$ when $0 < x_1 < \rho$, $0 < x_2 < \rho$. Along a Y-trajectory $t \to x(t)$ we have $\dot{x}_1 = \alpha_1 = x_1^2 \hat{\alpha}_1 + x_1 x_2 \check{\alpha}_1$, $\dot{x}_2 = 1 + \alpha_2 = 1 + x_1^2 \hat{\alpha}_2 + x_1 x_2 \check{\alpha}_2$, and $\dot{x}_3 = \alpha_3 = x_1(1 + x_1 \hat{\alpha}_3 + x_2 \check{\alpha}_3)$. On the other hand, $x_3 = \varphi(x_1,x_2)$, so $\dot{x}_3 = \frac{\partial \varphi}{\partial x_1} \dot{x}_1 + \frac{\partial \varphi}{\partial x_2} \dot{x}_2$. Plugging in the values of the $\dot{x}_i$, we see that $\frac{\partial \varphi}{\partial x_2} = x_1(1 + o(1))$. Hence $\frac{\partial^2 \varphi}{\partial x_1 x_2}(0,0) = 1$. Therefore $\tilde{\varphi}(0,0) = 1$. Now, $\frac{\partial \varphi}{\partial x_1} = x_2(\tilde{\varphi} + x_1 \frac{\partial \tilde{\varphi}}{\partial x_1})$. By shrinking ρ, we can assume that $\tilde{\varphi} + x_1 \frac{\partial \tilde{\varphi}}{\partial x_1} > 0$ on $(-\rho,\rho)^2$, and then $\frac{\partial \varphi}{\partial x_1} > 0$ when $x_2 \geq 0$, proving our claim. Also, if we define $\psi = \tilde{\varphi} - 1$, then we have shown that $\psi(0,0) = 0$, and then we can assume that $|\psi| < 1/2$ throughout $(-\rho,\rho)^2$ by shrinking ρ.

If we now define $\mathbf{R}$ to be the right-hand side of (5), then all we need is to show that $\mathcal{R}^* = \mathbf{R}$, where $\mathcal{R}^* = \mathcal{R} \cap N(\rho)$.

The set $\mathbf{R}$ is clearly closed in $C(\rho)$, and has the property that, if $q \in \mathbf{R}$, then qe^{tX} and qe^{tY} are in $\mathbf{R}$ for $t \leq 0$, t sufficiently small. (The conclusion about qe^{tX} is trivial unless $q \in S^+$. But in that case the function $\zeta = \varphi - x_3$ vanishes at q and is increasing along the X-trajectory from q, and then $\zeta(qe^{tX}) \geq 0$ for $t > 0$, t small. But this means that qe^{tX} lies below the graph of φ, as desired. The conclusion for qe^{tY} is trivial unless $q \in S^-$. But in that case it follows from the fact that α_3 is ≥ 0 for $x_1 \geq 0$, so $Y(q)$ points up if $q \in S^-$.) From this it follows easily that every trajectory γ that starts at p, stays in $N(\rho)$, and corresponds to a bang-bang control (i.e. a piecewise constant control with values ± 1), is entirely contained in $\mathbf{R}$. Then the same conclusion is true for an arbitrary measurable control $u(\cdot)$ with values between -1 and 1, since every trajectory is a limit of trajectories for bang-bang controls. On the other hand, there is a time $\tilde{T} > 0$ such that every trajectory that starts at p and is defined on an interval of length $\leq \tilde{T}$ stays in $N(\rho)$. Now replace T by $\min(T,\tilde{T})$, and shrink ρ further so that $5\rho < T$. Then $\mathcal{R} \subseteq \mathbf{R}$. Moreover, if $x = (x_1,x_2,x_3) \in \mathbf{R}$ then $x_1 \geq 0$, $x_2 \geq 0$, and $\varphi(x_1,x_2) - x_3 \geq 0$, whereas $\varphi(0,x_2) - x_3 \leq 0$, since $\varphi(0,x_2) = 0$ and $x_3 \geq 0$. Therefore there is a t such that $0 \leq t \leq x_1 < \rho$ for which $\varphi(x_1 - t, x_2) = x_3$. This means that $\tilde{x} = (x_1 - t, x_2, x_3)$ is in S^+. Therefore $\tilde{x} = p^\kappa e^{\tau X^\kappa} e^{\sigma Y^\kappa}$, for some $(\tau,\sigma) \in V_\rho$. The bounds $|\alpha_1| < 1/2$, $\alpha_2 > 1/2$ imply that $\sigma < 2\rho$ and $\tau < 2\rho$. So x is reachable from p in time $< 5\rho$. Since $5\rho < T$, we see that $x \in \mathcal{R}$. Hence $\mathbf{R} \subseteq \mathcal{R}$, and our proof is complete. ∎

3.4 Geometric Selections and Optimal Control of the "Reeds-Shepp Car"

Let us return to the minimum-time control problem for the system Σ_{RS} of 3.1. We know that Σ_{RS} is STLC from every point, and this easily implies that, given any pair (p,q) of points, there is a $\gamma \in \mathcal{M}(\Sigma_{RS})$ that goes from p to q. We would now like to understand the structure of the time-minimizers.

We would also like to find nice "sufficient classes" S. Call a class S of trajectories *sufficient for time-optimal control* (STOC) for a system Σ if for every pair p, q such that $q \in \mathcal{R}^\Sigma(p)$ there is a $\gamma \in S \cap \mathcal{M}(\Sigma)$ such that $\gamma : p \rightsquigarrow q$. (Notice that we do not demand that $S \subseteq \mathcal{M}(\Sigma)$ or that $\mathcal{M}(\Sigma) \subseteq S$.) The reason for studying such families is that, if S is STOC, then the problem of finding a time-minimizer from p to q can be reduced to the problem of finding a $\bar{\gamma} \in S$ that minimizes time among all $\gamma \in S$ that go from p to q. If S is very small, then this is likely to be a much more tractable problem. For a general complete Σ, two obvious examples of sufficient families are: (i) $\mathrm{Tr}(\Sigma)$ and (ii) the class $\mathcal{P}(\Sigma)$ of all γ such that (γ,η) is a

Pontryagin extremal for some η. Then $\mathcal{M}(\Sigma) \subseteq \mathcal{P}(\Sigma)$, but in general $\mathcal{M}(\Sigma) \neq \mathcal{P}(\Sigma)$, since the PMP is necessary but not sufficient for optimality. This suggests that to find nice sufficient classes one might start by applying the PMP, which enables us to replace $\mathrm{Tr}(\Sigma)$ by $\mathcal{P}(\Sigma)$, and then try to eliminate those elements of $\mathcal{P}(\Sigma)$ that are not optimal, perhaps using more sophisticated necessary conditions for optimality. There is, however, an intrinsic limitation to this strategy, namely, *the possibility that optimality by itself might not suffice as a criterion for selecting a small class*. It may happen that $\mathcal{M}(\Sigma)$ is too large, and to get a truly interesting sufficient class S one has to make a further selection, and not insist on the inclusion $\mathcal{M}(\Sigma) \subseteq S$.

The Reeds-Shepp example provides a striking illustration of this phenomenon. Consider the "left turn" system Σ_{LT} given by $\dot{x}_1 = u\cos\theta$, $\dot{x}_2 = u\sin\theta$, $\dot{\theta} = 1$, $|u| \leq 1$. Clearly, $\mathrm{Tr}(\Sigma_{LT}) \subseteq \mathrm{Tr}(\Sigma_{RS})$. Moreover, if $\gamma \in \mathrm{Tr}(\Sigma_{LT})$ and $T(\gamma) \leq \pi$, then $\gamma \in \mathcal{M}(\Sigma_{RS})$. So we see that $\mathcal{M}(\Sigma_{RS})$ is too large, because it contains —if $T \leq \pi$— all the η-trajectories for all $\eta \in \mathcal{U}(0,T)$ that are of the form $\eta(t) = (u(t), 1)$, *for an arbitrary measurable function* $u(\cdot) : [0,T] \to [-1,1]$. However, since the state space of Σ_{RS} is 3-dimensional, it would be nice to find a family $\mathcal{U}_0$ of controls depending on 3 continuous parameters, such that the class $S = \cup\{\mathrm{Tr}(\Sigma_{RS},\eta) : \eta \in \mathcal{U}_0\}$ is STOC. This requires that we make a selection within $\mathcal{M}(\Sigma_{RS})$.

The following *geometric selection method* turns out to work. Call a system Σ *degenerate* if whenever $\gamma_1, \gamma_2 \in \mathrm{Tr}(\Sigma)$ are such that $x_-(\gamma_1) = x_-(\gamma_2)$ and $x_+(\gamma_1) = x_+(\gamma_2)$ then $T(\gamma_1) = T(\gamma_2)$. Then, if Σ is degenerate and complete, one can easily show that all the sets $\mathcal{R}^\Sigma(p)$ are closed. Now fix some value $\hat{u} \in U$ of u. Assume that $\eta \in \mathcal{U}(0,T)$, $\gamma \in \mathrm{Tr}(\Sigma, \eta)$, $\gamma : p \rightsquigarrow q$, and find $\hat{\gamma} \in \mathrm{Tr}(\Sigma, \hat{\eta})$ such that $\hat{\gamma}(T) = q$, where $\hat{\eta} : [0,T] \to U$, $\hat{\eta}(t) \equiv \hat{u}$. Let $\tau = \inf\{t \in [0,T] : \hat{\gamma}(t) \in \mathcal{R}^\Sigma(p)\}$. Then $\hat{\gamma}(\tau) \in \mathcal{R}^\Sigma(p)$, because $\mathcal{R}^\Sigma(p)$ is closed. So there exist $\tilde{\tau} \geq 0$, $\tilde{\eta} \in \mathcal{U}(0,\tilde{\tau})$, $\tilde{\gamma} \in \mathrm{Tr}(\Sigma, \tilde{\eta})$, such that $\tilde{\gamma} : p \rightsquigarrow \hat{\gamma}(\tau)$. Then $q \in \mathcal{R}^\Sigma(\tilde{\tau} + T - \tau; p) \cap \mathcal{R}^\Sigma(T; p)$. So $\tilde{\tau} + T - \tau = T$, i.e. $\tilde{\tau} = \tau$. It is easy to see that $\tilde{\gamma} \in \mathcal{B}(\Sigma)$. So $\tilde{\gamma}$ *is an abnormal extremal*. Therefore, if we let $\mathbf{T}(\Sigma, \hat{u})$ denote the class of all trajectories that are concatenations of an abnormal extremal and a trajectory of for the constant control $\equiv \hat{u}$, we see that $\mathbf{T}(\Sigma, \hat{u})$ is sufficient for time-optimal control for Σ.

The above cannot be applied to Σ_{LT} because Σ_{LT} is not degenerate (since one can go from any p back to p in time 2π). However, if $\check{\Sigma}_{LT}$ is the *lifted system* —with state space $\mathbb{R}^3$— obtained by regarding θ as a true real number rather than as a real number modulo 2π, then $\check{\Sigma}_{LT}$ is degenerate. Suppose $\gamma \in \mathrm{Tr}(\Sigma_{LT}) \cap \mathcal{M}(\Sigma_{RS})$, $\tau_-(\gamma) = 0$, $\tau_+(\gamma) = T$. Then we can write $\gamma = \pi \circ \check{\gamma}$, where $\pi : \mathbb{R}^3 \to \mathbb{R}^2 \times S^1$ is the projection, and $\check{\gamma} \in \mathrm{Tr}(\check{\Sigma}_{LT})$. Then we can find $\check{\delta} \in \mathbf{T}(\Sigma_{LT}, 1)$ such that $\check{\delta}(0) = \check{\gamma}(0)$ and $\check{\delta}(T) = \check{\gamma}(T)$. If $\delta = \pi \circ \check{\delta}$, then $\delta : p \overset{\mathcal{T}}{\rightsquigarrow} q$, so $\delta \in \mathcal{M}(\Sigma_{RS})$.

When we apply the PMP to Σ_{RS} to study $\mathcal{M}(\Sigma_{RS})$, we find out (cf. [11]) that every $\gamma \in \mathcal{M}(\Sigma_{RS})$ is of one of two kinds, depending on whether a certain nonnegative constant κ does or does not vanish. When $\kappa \neq 0$, the PMP conditions, plus some extra geometric arguments, imply that γ is —or can be replaced by— a concatenation of at most five pieces, each of which is either a circle or a segment. However, when $\kappa = 0$, the PMP implies that $v \equiv 1$ or $v \equiv -1$, but yields no more information. On the other hand, if $v \equiv 1$ —the case $v \equiv -1$ is similar— then γ is actually in $\mathrm{Tr}(\Sigma_{LT})$, and so the geometric selection argument applies, and yields another $\delta \in \mathcal{M}(\Sigma_{RS})$, with the same initial and terminal points as γ, which is now a concatenation of an abnormal extremal δ_1 of Σ_{LT} and a $u = 1$ trajectory δ_2. The fact that δ_1 is an abnormal extremal gives very strong information, and implies that δ_1 is a concatenation of at most two circles. Since δ_2 is a circle, we see that, when $\kappa = 0$, γ can be replaced by a concatenation of three circles.

Combining all these considerations, one ends up proving that a certain family $\mathcal{F}$, consisting of concatenations of at most five C's (circles) and S's (segments), is sufficient. The elements of $\mathcal{F}$ actually satisfy further restrictions, e.g. CCCCC is not permitted, more than one S is not allowed, for a CCCC the times along the two inner C's must be equal, for a CCCSC the times along the second and third C must equal $\frac{\pi}{2}$, etc. (All this is done in detail in [11].) In particular, the elements of $\mathcal{F}$ that start at a fixed point p are parametrized by three continuous parameters plus a discrete parameter specifying the combinatorial type of the trajectory. (The class given in [11] consists of 46 three-parameter families.)

3.5 Subanalytic sets and Regularity of the Value Function

Now assume that M is a C^ω manifold. Then there are at least two important classes of subsets M that make intrinsic sense, and have nice "piecewise analyticity" properties, namely, the sets $SM(M)$, $SB(M)$ of *semianalytic* and *subanalytic* subsets of M. (By definition, a subset S of M is in $SM(N)$ if every $p \in M$ has a neighborhood U such that $S \cap U$ is a finite union of sets, each of which is defined by finitely many conditions $f(x) = 0$ or $f(x) > 0$, involving C^ω functions $f : U \to \mathbb{R}$. Then $S \in SB(M)$ if $S = f(\tilde{S})$ for some C^ω manifold N and some C^ω map $f : N \to M$ which is proper on the closure of $\tilde{S}$. In other words: semianalytic sets are locally defined by finite collections of analytic equalities and inequalities, and subanalytic sets are images of semianalytic sets under proper analytic maps. [5]

Following our general geometric philosophy, these classes of sets ought to be useful in control theory. To show that this is indeed so, observe that, for a complete system, the reachable sets are *images* of certain maps. (Indeed, let $\mathcal{U}_- = \cup\{\mathcal{U}(-T, 0) : T \geq 0\}$, $\mathcal{U}_-(T) = \cup\{\mathcal{U}(-t, 0) : 0 \leq t \leq T\}$. Define a map $\Phi_S^\Sigma : \mathcal{U}_- \times S \to M$ by $\Phi_S^\Sigma(\eta, p) = x_-(\gamma)$, where $\gamma \in \text{Tr}(\Sigma, \eta)$ is such that $x_+(\gamma) = p$. Then $\mathcal{C}^\Sigma(S) = \Phi_S^\Sigma(\mathcal{U} \times S)$, $\mathcal{C}^\Sigma(T; S) = \Phi_S^\Sigma(\mathcal{U}(-T, 0) \times S)$, and $\mathcal{C}^\Sigma(\leq T; S) = \Phi_S^\Sigma(\mathcal{U}_-(T) \times S)$. Similar identities —with Σ^- instead of Σ— hold for the reachable sets.) In addition, *the graph of the value function is a piece of the boundary of a controllable set.* Precisely, let Σ^a be the system with state space $M \times \mathbb{R}$, control space U, and dynamical equations $\dot{x} = f(x, u)$, $\dot{y} = -1$. (Think of y as "time to go.") Then (q, t) *is Σ^a-controllable to $(p, 0)$ if and only if q is controllable to p in time t.* Define the *lower boundary* $\partial_- A$ of a subset A of $M \times \mathbb{R}$ to be the set $\partial_- A = \{(q, t) \in A : (\forall s < t)(q, s) \notin A\}$. Then, if we let $S^a = S \times \{0\}$, and Σ is complete, *the set $\mathcal{C}^{\Sigma^a}(S^a)$ is closed in $M \times \mathbb{R}$, and its lower boundary $\partial_- \mathcal{C}^{\Sigma^a}(S^a)$ is precisely the graph $G(V_S^\Sigma)$ of the value function V_S^Σ.*

On the other hand, subanalytic sets are also, by definition, images. And one can prove that, if $S \in SB(M)$ and S is closed, then ∂S is subanalytic. Moreover, if M is actually a product $N \times \mathbb{R}$, and $S \subseteq N \times [0, \infty)$, then $\partial_- S$ is subanalytic in M. Now let us quote a property of subanalytic sets.

Theorem 2. *Let M be a C^ω manifold, and let S be a closed subanalytic subset of M. Let $\rho : S \to \mathbb{R}$ be a function whose graph $G(\rho)$ is a subanalytic subset of $M \times \mathbb{R}$. Then ρ is piecewise analytic, in the sense that there exists a ρ-locally finite partition $\mathcal{P}$ of S into connected, subanalytic embedded C^ω submanifolds of M such that the restriction $\rho\lceil P$ of ρ to each member P of $\mathcal{P}$ is of class C^ω.*

---

[5] If A and B are topological spaces, then a map f from A to B is *proper* if the inverse image of every compact subset of B is compact in A.

(A set $\mathcal{X}$ of subsets of M is ρ-*locally finite* if every compact subset of M on which ρ is bounded intersects finitely many members of $\mathcal{X}$.)

So controllable sets are are analogous to subanalytic sets in the sense that both are images. The lower boundary of a subanalytic set is subanalytic, and the lower boundary of a certain controllable set is the value function. And if the graph of a function is subanalytic then the function itself is piecewise analytic. One may hope to be able to combine all these facts, and prove that V_S^Σ is indeed piece-wise analytic for large classes of problems. However, subanalytic sets are images of semianalytic subsets of finite-dimensional manifolds under analytic maps, whereas $\mathcal{C}^\Sigma(S) = \Phi_S^\Sigma(\mathcal{U} \times S)$, and $\mathcal{U}$ is an infinite-dimensional function space. *Suppose, however, that we could replace $\mathcal{U}$ by a finite-dimensional object.* Then we would be much closer to proving subanalyticity of the graph of V_S^Σ. What we need is an "analytic finite-dimensional reduction" (AFDR), i.e. a collection $\mathcal{G} = \{\gamma_\alpha : \alpha \in A\}$ of trajectories, parametrized by points α in a closed subanalytic subset A of a finite-dimensional C^ω manifold N, and satisfying $\tau_+(\gamma_\alpha) = 0$, such that (i) Γ is STOC for Σ, (ii) the map $\alpha \to (x_-(\gamma_\alpha), x_+(\gamma_\alpha), \tau_-(\gamma_\alpha))$ is C^ω. We call Γ *proper* if the map $\mu_\Gamma : \alpha \to (x_-(\gamma_\alpha), \tau_-(\gamma_\alpha))$ is proper. If a proper AFDR Γ exists, and S is sub-analytic, then it is a rigorous theorem that $G(V_S^\Sigma)$ is subanalytic, and then V_S^Σ is piecewise analytic. (Proof: let $A_S = \{\alpha : x_+(\gamma_\alpha) \in S\}$. Then $A_S \in SB(N)$. Now let $\mathcal{C} = \mu_\Gamma(A_S)$. Then $\mathcal{C}$ is subanalytic, because μ_Γ is C^ω and proper on A. Moreover, one can easily verify that $G(V_S^\Sigma) = \partial_-\mathcal{C}$. So $G(V_S^\Sigma) \in SB(M \times \mathbb{R})$. Q.E.D.)

The above discussion shows that one can prove piecewise analyticity of the value function if one can find a proper AFDR Γ. It is now natural to ask whether the existence of such an AFDR is going to be an exceptional situation, or whether it is going to be true for large classes of C^ω systems. Examples have been given of systems where the value function is not subanalytic (cf. [7]), so we know that an AFDR need not always exist. On the other hand, it has been proved to exist for large classes of problems. We have already described one example in our analysis of the "Reeds-Shepp car." (The parameter manifold N is $\mathbb{R}^2 \times S^1 \times \hat{N}$, where $\hat{N}$ has 46 connected components $\hat{N}_j$, each one being a copy of $\mathbb{R}^3$. Each $\hat{N}_j$ corresponds to one of the combinatorial types of trajectories in the family $\mathcal{F}$. If we write $N_j = \mathbb{R}^2 \times S^1 \times \hat{N}_j$, then $A \cap N_j$ is the product of $\mathbb{R}^2 \times S^1$ times the nonnegative orthant $\mathbb{R}_+^3$ of $\mathbb{R}^3$. If $\alpha = (x_1, x_2, \theta, t) \in A_j$, so $t = (t_1, t_2, t_3) \in \mathbb{R}_+^3$, then γ_α is the trajectory of the corresponding type whose time parameters are t_1, t_2, t_3, with domain $[-T, 0]$, where $T = t_1 + t_2 + t_3$, and terminal condition $\gamma_\alpha(0) = (x_1, x_2, \theta)$.)

In general, one can find an AFDR whenever one can identify a finite family of analytic vector fields X_i, $i \in I$, possibly defined on other manifolds N_i endowed with analytic maps $\psi_i : N_i \to M$, such that there is a sufficient family $\mathcal{F}$ for our problem consisting of concatenations γ of a finite number $\sigma(\gamma)$ of pieces of the form $\psi_{i(j)} \circ \delta_j$, where δ_j is an integral curve of $X_{i(j)}$. The properness condition then amounts to requiring that the maps ψ_i be proper, and that there be local bounds on the number of switchings (i.e. for every compact $K \subseteq M$ and every $T > 0$ there is a ν such that, if $\gamma \in \mathcal{F}$, $T(\gamma) \leq T$, and $\gamma \subseteq K$, then $\sigma(\gamma) \leq \nu$).

An example of this that may be familiar to geometers is the case of minimum time control on a C^ω Riemannian manifold M. (The trajectories are arbitrary curves γ such that $\|\dot{\gamma}(t)\| \leq 1$. Of course, the Pontryagin extremals in this case are the geodesics, and they are projections of the integral curves of the geodesic flow, which is a vector field on the tangent bundle TM.) In this case, the properness condition follows *if the metric is complete.*

In many other cases (e.g. linear time-optimal control with polyhedral control constraints, general C^ω problems $\dot{x} = f(x) + ug(x)$, $|u| \leq 1$, in dimension two, general problems where the optimal controls are bang-bang) the structure of the optimal trajectories has been investigated, leading to the construction of a proper AFDR. Moreover, the existence of an AFDR also implies a stronger conclusion, namely, the existence of a *regular synthesis*, i.e., roughly, a piecewise analytic feedback. (The precise definition is analogous, but not identical, to that given by Boltyanski in [1].) At the moment, the study of properties of trajectories, from the point of view of trying to find nice sufficient families, and if possible AFDR's, is an active area in which many challenging questions (e.g.: is it always true for an analytic complete system with, say, a control set $U = [-1, 1]^m$, that every nondegerate minimizer[6] has at most a countable set of points of nonanalyticity?) still remain open.

References

1. V.G. Boltyanski: Sufficient conditions for optimality and the justification of the Dynamic Programming Principle. SIAM J. Control 4, pp. 326-361, 1966

2. R.W. Brockett: System Theory on group manifolds and coset spaces. SIAM J. Control 10, pp. 265-284, 1972

3. R. Hermann: On the accessibility problem in control theory. In: Int. Symp. Nonlinear Diff. Equations and Nonlinear Mechanics, J.P. LaSalle, S. Lefschetz Eds., , pp. 325-332. New York: Academic Press, 1963

4. A. Isidori: Nonlinear Control Systems: An Introduction. Berlin: Springer-Verlag, second ed., 1989

5. A.J. Krener: A generalization of Chow's Theorem and the bang-bang theorem to nonlinear control problems. SIAM J. Control12(1), pp. 43-51, 1974

6. C. Lobry: Contrôlabilité des systèmes non-linéaires. SIAM J. Control 8, pp. 573-605, 1978

7. S. Lojasiewicz Jr. and H.J. Sussmann: Some examples of reachable sets and optimal cost functions that fail to be subanalytic. S.I.A.M. J. Control and Optimization 23, No. 4, pp. 584-598, 1985

8. H. Nijmeijer and A.J. Van der Schaft: Nonlinear dynamical control systems. New York: Springer-Verlag, 1990

9. J.A. Reeds and L.A. Shepp: Optimal paths for a car that goes both forwards and backwards. Pacific J. Math. 145, pp. 367-393, 1990

10. H.J. Sussmann, ed.: Nonlinear Controllability and Optimal Control. New York: Marcel Dekker, 1990

11. H.J. Sussmann and G. Tang: "Shortest paths for the Reeds-Shepp car: a worked out example of the use of geometric techniques in nonlinear optimal control. Rutgers Center for Systems and Control Technical Report 91-10, September 1991

---

[6] A minimizer is *nondegenerate* if there is no other minimizer with the same initial and terminal points.

Coordinating vehicles in an automated highway

Pravin Varaiya[1]
Department of Electrical Engineering and Computer Sciences
University of California, Berkeley CA 94720

Abstract. The paper summarizes the design of an Automated Highway System (AHS). The design objective is to increase highway capacity. We assume the availability of certain elements: vehicles with appropriate sensors and actuators, highways with appropriate sensors, and the ability to communicate between vehicles and between a vehicle and the highway. The design specifies how these elements are configured and controlled, and how the 'intelligence' that carries out the control tasks is distributed among the vehicles and the highway infrastructure. One control task—the coordination of the movement of vehicles—is discussed in detail. The paper also presents a simulation suggesting that it is possible to increase highway capacity through automation.

1 Introduction

The paper summarizes design features of an Automated Highway System (AHS). The design objective is to increase highway capacity. We assume the availability of certain elements: vehicles with appropriate sensors and actuators, highways with appropriate sensors, and the ability to communicate between vehicles and between a vehicle and the highway. The design specifies how these elements are configured and controlled, and how the 'intelligence' that carries out the control tasks is distributed among the vehicles and the highway infrastructure.

The paper also presents a simulation of the AHS using SmartPath. SmartPath is a microsimulation: the system elements and the control policies are each individually modeled. Several elements and policies are parametrically specified. The user can change these parameters to understand how the AHS would perform in terms of highway capacity, traffic flow, and other performance measures of interest to transportation system planners and drivers.

The AHS design and work that implements aspects of the design are described in several PATH reports.[2] The overall design is summarized in §2. §3 explains how the task of coordinating the movement of several vehicles is carried out. §4 presents a simulation suggesting that it is possible to increase highway capacity through automation.

We now describe how you as a driver may experience the AHS. See Figure 1. To drive your car over a three-lane AHS, you enter from an on-ramp and safely join the traffic in lane 3—the rightmost lane. You announce your destination by voice or keyboard entry. Your vehicle's on-board computer communicates your destination

---

[1]Work supported by the PATH program, Institute of Transportation Studies, University of California, Berkeley, and NSF Grants ECS-911907 and IRI-9120074.
[2]See [1, 2, 3, 4] and the references therein.

to the roadside computer which assigns the lane number (1 or 2) that you should occupy for most of your trip. Suppose it is lane 1. The roadside computer also tells your vehicle at what point along lane 1 it should start changing lanes so that it can exit. We summarize these instructions by saying that the AHS assigns a *path* to your vehicle.

You then instruct your car's computer to take control. The computer will try to maintain a trajectory close to the assigned path. It begins by steering your car to change to lane 2, and then to lane 1. It will then keep your car in lane 1 until you are close to your exit. It then changes lane twice and re-enters lane 3. The computer then alerts you to take over control, and you then drive your car to the off-ramp. We refer to lane 3 as the *transition lane*, since cars on that lane may be driven manually or under automatic control; lanes 1 and 2 are *automated lanes*, since cars on these lanes are automatically controlled.

A major objective of the AHS is to increase highway capacity. This objective is achieved in part by organizing in platoons the traffic within each automated lane. A *platoon* is one or more vehicles traveling together as a group with relatively small spacing. Inter-platoon spacing is large.[3] For example, with an average platoon size of 15, intra-platoon distance of 2 m, inter-platoon distance of 60 m, vehicle length of 5 m, and speed of 72 km/h, the maximum flow through an automated lane is over 6,000 vehicles/hour—triple the flow achieved today.

In summary, the AHS tasks are to assign a lane to each vehicle, to steer it to its assigned lane, and to organize traffic in platoons in the automated lanes.

2   AHS control system architecture

The AHS tasks are carried out by the three-layer controller hierarchy of Figure 2. The implementation of the control system requires a communication system that supports the exchange of information between controllers in the vehicles and in the roadside. The control and communication systems are briefly described here.

The basic unit of automation is the *platoon*, which consists of one or more vehicles traveling together as a group with relatively small spacing. The first vehicle in the platoon is called a *leader*, the others are *followers*. A one-vehicle platoon is called a *free agent*. Thus at every moment of time, a vehicle under automatic control is either a leader, a follower, or a free agent, see Figure 3.

---

[3]Organizing traffic into tightly packed platoons with large inter-platoon spacing increases safety. Consider two vehicles, and suppose the first vehicle decelerates rapidly. If the following vehicle is very close it will collide but the relative speed on impact will be very small. If the following vehicle is far away, it can decelerate without colliding.

2.1 Control system

We discuss each layer of Figure 2 starting from the top. The link layer controllers are in the roadside; each vehicle has its own platoon and regulation layer controllers.

The *link layer* controllers are responsible for the smooth flow of traffic in each automated lane. There is one controller per highway section. A section is several kms in length, and its link layer controller sets the target platoon size—*optsize*—and a target platoon speed—*optspeed* for that section. These variables are based on macroscopic information about traffic flow, congestion, and incidents. A link layer design is proposed in [5].

The *platoon layer* controller of a vehicle determines which of three maneuvers the vehicle should execute, so that the vehicle trajectory is close to its assigned path, and so that its platoon size and speed are close to the target values designated by the link layer. The three maneuvers are illustrated in Figure 4. In *merge*, two platoons join to form one platoon. In *split*, one platoon separates at a designated position to form two platoons. In *change lane*, a free agent changes lane. Merge and split are initiated by a leader's platoon layer controller; change lane is initiated by a free agent's platoon layer controller. Followers do not initiate maneuvers; however, they may request their leader to initiate a split.

In order to carry out a maneuver safely, the platoon layer controller initiates a structured exchange of messages—a *protocol*—with the leaders of neighboring platoons. At the end of the exchange, the platoon layer secures agreement from those neighbors that the maneuver can be safely executed. Once agreement is reached, the platoon layer instructs the regulation layer to execute the maneuver. Thus a protocol coordinates the movement of neighboring vehicles to ensure safe maneuvers. The protocols are described in the next section.

The *regulation layer* of a vehicle implements at each instant of time one of five feedback laws selected by its platoon layer. When a vehicle is a follower the *follower law* maintains the required tight spacing with the vehicle in front of it in its platoon. When a leader is not engaged in any maneuver the *tracking law* keeps the target speed while maintaining a safe headway from the vehicle in front of it. The *merge law* causes a leader to join the platoon in front of it. The *split law* decelerates the appropriate vehicle in the platoon until it reaches a safe headway from the platoon in front it. Finally, the *change lane law* steers a free agent to the adjacent lane. Follower law designs are proposed in [6, 7, 8, 9].

The *physical layer* in Figure 2 refers to the vehicle dynamics. This layer receives steering, throttle and brake actuator commands from the regulation layer. It returns to the regulation layer information needed to implement the five feedback laws: its own vehicle's speed, acceleration, engine state, etc; its speed and distance relative to the vehicle in front of it; and so on.

In summary, the link layer assigns *optspeed* and *optsize*; the platoon layer selects which maneuvers to execute in order to follow the assigned path, coordinates that maneuver with neighbors, and maintains platoons; the regulation layer implements the maneuver selected by the platoon layer.

With this sketch of the AHS control system we can better describe how your vehicle is controlled. At any time, the vehicle is either a free agent, a leader or a follower. It enters lane 3 as a free agent. Its platoon layer negotiates the change lane protocol twice with the neighbors' platoon layer, at the end of which your vehicle is in lane 1. While in lane 1, its platoon layer attempts to merge with other vehicles to form platoons of size *optsize*; and it may alternate several times its role between follower and leader as vehicles join and leave its platoon. When the vehicle is near its exit, the platoon layer negotiates one or two split maneuvers at the end of which the vehicle is a free agent. It now negotiates two change lane maneuvers, re-enters lane 3, and returns control to you.

2.2 Communication system

Three kinds of communication capabilities are needed to implement the control system, see Figure 5. First, vehicles within a platoon need to exchange information required by their platoon and regulation layers. Second, leaders of neighboring platoons need to exchange protocol messages for the merge and change lane maneuvers. (No exchange is needed for split.) It is required only that such exchange be possible within a certain communication range, D_{comm}. Third, leaders need to receive the target variables from the link layer in the roadside. (The roadside-vehicle links are not shown in the figure.) We assume that these communication services are available with no error or delay.

3 Platoon layer

We describe the platoon layer protocols.[4] Each vehicle maintains the following 'state' information:

- ID of the vehicle
- Highway number of the vehicle
- Lane number of the vehicle
- Highway section number of the vehicle
- Position of the vehicle relative to the highway section
- Platoon ID, same as the ID of its leader
- Platoon *optsize* in the highway section
- Platoon *optspeed* in the highway section
- Position of vehicle in platoon; position 1 indicates leader
- Number of vehicles in platoon
- Vehicle speed
- Vehicle acceleration

---

[4]The report [3] presents a formal specification of the protocols described here. The specification is then verified for correctness. The language COSPAN is used for this purpose [10, 11].

- Flag indicating whether vehicle is engaged in maneuver (Busy flag)
- ID of tail (last) car in platoon
- ID of back car (the car behind) in platoon; this ID is 0 for tail car

ID is fixed when the vehicle enters the AHS. Highway number, lane number, and section number are updated as needed; *optsize*, *optspeed* are obtained from the link layer. Lane number changes after a lane change maneuver; platoon size and position of vehicle change after a merge or split maneuver. Vehicle speed and acceleration depend on the regulation layer. The leader sets the busy flag whenever it is engaged in a maneuver. The flag is used to ensure that a platoon is engaged in at most one maneuver at a time. This simplifies the platoon layer design.

The platoon layer controller is separated into two sub-layers. The upper, supervisor sub-layer determines which maneuver to execute, and instructs the lower sub-layer to carry out the appropriate protocol exchange. The design assumes that a message establishes a link giving the vehicle receiving the message access to the sender's state until the maneuver is complete.

3.1   Merge

The supervisor issues a merge instruction only if the vehicle is a leader in its assigned lane (and if it is not busy). Figure 6 shows the sequence of events that follow a merge instruction, and Figure 7 shows how the protocol works. B is the leader of the rear platoon which initiates merge, and A is the leader of the platoon in front of B.

B checks its platoon size. If it is smaller than *optsize*, B tries to locate a platoon in front of it and to merge with it. B's distance sensor has a certain maximum range, D_{range}, and it can locate a platoon in its lane within distance D_{range} from it. Suppose this happens. B then sends it a *request_merge* message. If the vehicle receiving the message is a follower, it forwards the message to its leader, namely A. A then checks its busy flag, and if that flag is not set, and if the size of A's and B's platoons combined does not exceed *optsize*, A sends an *ack_request_merge* message to B; otherwise it sends a *nack_request_merge*, which causes B to wait for some time and repeat its merge request.

Upon receiving *ack_request_merge*, B updates its state by changing the platoon ID to that of A, and sends a message to its followers to do the same. When this updating is complete, B's platoon layer controller instructs its regulation layer to execute the merge feedback law. That law causes B to reach a pre-specified distance from the tail car of A's platoon. During this time, the distance from A's platoon is continuously sensed, and the execution of the maneuver is aborted, and A is notified, if another vehicle has moved between the two platoons. (While B is accelerating, the rest of its platoon, under the follower feedback law, maintains platoon formation.) When B's regulation layer has completed the maneuver it returns control to its platoon layer, which transmits *comp_merge* to A. A then updates its state (the platoon size and tail car ID are changed), and sends a message to its followers to update their state. At the end of the update the two platoons are joined and the maneuver is complete.

3.2   Split

A supervisor issues a split instruction to its own vehicle only if it wishes to change lane. There are also cases when the leader tells a specific follower to split, either to accommodate a change lane by another vehicle, or because the platoon size exceeds *optsize*. There are two cases of split depending upon whether the leader or a follower wants to split. Figure 8 summarizes the event sequence for both cases, and Figures 9 and 10 illustrate how the protocol works.

If the leader A wishes to split, it sends *request_split* to A_2 (Figure 9). A_2 then updates its state (replacing its platoon ID by its own ID), and tells its followers to update their state. When A_2 receives *update_complete* from the tail, it sends *ack_request_split* to A and the latter breaks off, i.e. updates its own state to reflect the fact that it is now a one-car platoon. The maneuver is then complete. At this point A_2 is a leader, and it is not engaged in any maneuver. Its regulation layer therefore executes the tracking law, which causes it to decelerate until it is at a pre-specified distance, D_{safe}, from the platoon in front of it.

If a follower, say A_m, of A's platoon wishes to split, it sends *request_split* to A, see Figure 10. Upon receiving this message, A checks if its busy flag is set, and if it is not, it replies with *ack_request_split*, and instructs A_{m-1} to change its back car ID to 0, so that A_{m-1} is now the tail car of A's platoon. A_m updates its state (since it is now a leader), instructs its followers to update the state. When the tail car A_n has updated its state, it returns *update_complete* to A_m. A_m now instructs its regulation layer to execute the split feedback law, which causes A_m to decelerate until it is distance D_{safe} from A's platoon. When that distance is reached, A_m sends *split_comp* to A, and the maneuver is complete.

Recall that a vehicle can change lane only as a free agent. Therefore, if a vehicle within a platoon wishes to change lane, it must first become a free agent. This requires one split if the vehicle is first or last in the platoon, otherwise it requires two splits.

3.3   Change lane

A vehicle's supervisor initiates a change lane maneuver in accordance with the path assigned to it when it entered the AHS. If the vehicle is not a free agent, the supervisor initiates the required split(s) at the end of which it is a free agent.

Suppose A is a free agent in lane 1 and wishes to change to lane 2 (see Figure 4). It can do so only if there is adequate space in lane 2 and no vehicle in lanes 2 or 3 is planning to move into that space. The change lane protocol ensures this condition. It is assumed that A is equipped with sensors that determine the presence or absence of a vehicle within 30 meters from it in lane 2, and within 18 meters from it in lane 3 (see Figure 11). The vehicle can change lane under one of the following three conditions:

1. No vehicle is detected in lanes 2 and 3; A can move to lane 2.

2. No vehicle is detected in lane 2, but a vehicle is detected in lane 3 (vehicle C in Figure 4); A then requests that vehicle not to move into lane 2.

3. A platoon is detected in lane 2. A then conducts a protocol exchange with the platoon in the manner described below.

Figure 12 describes the sequence of events that must occur before A changes lane, and Figure 13 illustrates how the protocol works in the third case. (The two other cases are straightforward.)

Suppose A has detected vehicle B_m in lane 2. It sends *request_change_lane* to B_m which it forwards to its leader, B. If B is busy, it sends a *nack_request_change_lane* to A. If it is not busy, it returns *ack_request_change_lane*. At this point B determines how to create a space in lane 2 in order to accommodate A's change lane. B's decision is based on the location of A relative to B's platoon:

Case 1. A is alongside the front third of B's platoon; in this case B decelerates to create a space for A in front of B's platoon.

Case 2. A is alongside the rear third of B's platoon; in this case B asks A to decelerate and use the space behind B's platoon.

Case 3. A is alongside the middle third of B's platoon. B then decides to split its platoon at the appropriate vehicle (B_n in Figure 13 (case 3)). B_n performs a split. At the end of the split, space is created for A in front of B_n.

When space has been secured, A's platoon layer instructs its regulation layer to execute the change lane feedback law. During this execution, the regulation layer continuously senses its assigned space. If another vehicle has moved into that space, the maneuver is aborted and B is informed. After the maneuver is successful, A updates its state and informs B that the maneuver is complete.

4   Simulation example

This section presents a simple example using the program SmartPath [12]. The simulation time is 180 sec. The AHS has one automated lane, one transition lane, and three entrances. Entrance 1 is located at 0.5 km, entrance 2 is at 1.5 km, and entrance 3 is at 2.5 km from the beginning of the highway. (See Figure 14.)

A 'pulse' of 25 vehicles enters the automated lane every 2 seconds starting at time 0 until 60 seconds, corresponding to a flow of 1,800 vehicles/hour. The pattern is repeated at entrances 1, 2 and 3 except that vehicles enter starting at time 20 seconds, 60 seconds, and 100 seconds respectively. In all, 85 vehicles are created. All vehicles have an initial speed of 25 m/s which is also the value of *optspeed*. The value of *optsize* is 20.

The detection and communication ranges are $D_{range} = D_{comm} = 60$ m. The safe distance, D_{safe} is 20 m for a free agent and 40 m for other platoons. Lastly, intra-platoon spacing is 1 m.

Figure 15 displays the simulation results in the form of a time-distance diagram for each vehicle from the time it enters the automated lane. A vehicle in the transition lane gets displayed in the figure only after it has switched into the automated lane.

The first thing to observe is the process of platoon formation. The pulse of vehicles entering the automated lane starting at time 0 is unable to form platoons of size larger than two since two-car platoons become separated by a distance of 100 m, which is beyond D_{range}. By the time these vehicles have traveled 250 m, they have reached steady state.

Second, most of the vehicles which enter the entrance at 0.5 km have changed into the automated lane after traveling between 0.25 and 0.5 km along the transition lane, although one vehicle had to travel 0.75 km. These vehicles, together with those in the first pulse, form platoons of size up to five vehicles. Steady state is reached at distance 1.25 km, since platoons are separated by more than D_{safe}.

Third, vehicles which enter the entrance at 1.0 km and 1.5 km take more time to move into the automated lane, since the traffic flow in that lane is quite large and it takes more time to create space for the change lane maneuver. Nevertheless, a steady state is reached at distance 3.5 km. Platoon of size up to 15 are formed.

At around 180 seconds, the vehicles are in steady state and they occupy 1,200 m of the automated lane. This is a density of 85/1,200 vehicles/m. Since the vehicles are traveling at 25 m/s, this corresponds to a flow of 6,375 vehicles/hour. The platooning concept is key to this high throughput: in steady state, one finds closely spaced platoons separated by large gaps (of at least 60 m). The example illustrates how entrances should be organized in order to create 'tributaries' feeding the high capacity automated lane.

The large inter-platoon separation and the coordination facilitated by the change lane protocol account for the relative ease with which vehicles from the transition lane join the vehicles in the automated lane. This can be seen in Figure 16 which is a 'blowup' of a small portion of Figure 15. The figure shows how the change lane protocol works.

5 Conclusion

The design of the automated highway system presented here, together with the simulation, suggests that automation can provide significant increases in highway capacity. The technology presupposed by the design is available today either in commercial or prototype form. Thus the challenging task is to integrate these technologies into a working system. Parts of this integration have been demonstrated for example in [13, 14, 15, 16]. Beyond demonstrating the concept of an automated highway lie numerous problems concerning deployment.

References

[1] P. Varaiya and S. Shladover, "Sketch of an IVHS systems architecture," tech. rep., UCB-ITS-PRR-91-3, Institute of Transportation Studies, University of California, Berkeley, CA 94720, February 1991.

[2] S. Shladover, C. Desoer, J. Hedrick, M. Tomizuka, J. Walrand, W. Zhang, D. McMahon, H. Peng, S. Sheikholeslam, and N. McKeown, "Automated vehicle control developments in the PATH program," *IEEE Transactions on Vehicular Technology*, vol. 40, pp. 114–130, February 1991.

[3] A. Hsu, S. Sachs, F. Eskafi, and P. Varaiya, "The design of platoon maneuvers protocols for IVHS," tech. rep., UCB-ITS-PRR-91-6, Institute of Transporation Studies, University of California, Berkeley, CA 94720, April 1991.

[4] P. Varaiya, "Smart cars on smart roads: Problems of control," tech. rep., PATH Tech Memo 91-5, Institute of Transportation Studies, University of California, Berkeley, CA 94720, December 1991. To appear in *IEEE Transactions on Automatic Control*.

[5] U. Karaaslan, P. Varaiya, and J. Walrand, "Two proposals to improve freeway traffic flow," in *Proceedings of the 1991 American Control Conference*, (Boston, MA), pp. 2539–2544, June 26-28 1991.

[6] J. Hedrick, D. McMahon, V. Narendran, and D. Swaroop, "Longitudinal vehicle controller design for IVHS system," in *Proceedings of the 1991 American Control Conference*, (Boston, MA), pp. 3107–3112, June 26-28 1991.

[7] S. Sheikholeslam and C. A. Desoer, "Longitudinal control of a platoon of vehicles," in *Proceedings of the 1990 American Control Conference, Volume 1*, (San Diego, CA), pp. 291–296, June 1990.

[8] H. Peng and M. Tomizuka, "Preview control for vehicle lateral guidance in highway automation," in *Proceedings of the 1991 American Control Conference*, (Boston, MA), June 26-28 1991.

[9] F. Broqua, G. Lerner, V. Mauro, and E. Morello, "Cooperative driving: Basic concepts and a first assessment of "intelligent cruise control" strategies," in *Advanced Telematics in Road Guidance. Proceedings of the DRIVE Conference*, pp. 908–929, Elsevier, February 4-9 1991.

[10] Z. Har'El and R. P. Kurshan, "Software for analytical development of communications protocols," *AT&T Technical Journal*, pp. 45–59, January/February 1990.

[11] Z. Har'El and R. P. Kurshan, *COSPAN User's Guide*. AT&T Bell Laboratories, Murray Hill, NJ, 1987.

[12] F. Eskafi, D. Khorramabadi, and P. Varaiya, "SmartPath: Automatic Highway System Simulator." Preprint, Department of Electrical Engineering & Computer Sciences, University of California, Berkeley, June, 1992.

[13] K. Chang, W. Li, P. Devlin, A. Shaikhbahai, P. Varaiya, J. Hedrick, D. MacMahon, V. Narendran, and D. Swaroop, "Experimenation with a vehicle platoon control system," in *Proceedings of the Vehicle Navigation and Information Systems Conference*, (Dearborn, MI), pp. 1117–1124, October 20-23 1991.

[14] T. Hessburg, H. Peng, M. Tomizuka, W. Zhang, and E. Kamei, "An experimental study on lateral control of a vehicle," in *Proceedings of the 1991 American Control Conference*, (Boston, MA), June 26-28 1991.

[15] S. Tsugawa, H. Watanabe, and H. Fujii, "Super Smart Vehicle System – Its concept and preliminary works," in *Proceedings of the Vehicle Navigation and Information Systems Conference*, (Dearborn, MI), pp. 269–277, October 20-23 1991.

[16] F. Heintz and H. Winner, "A distributed controller system with a hierarchical structure for PROMETHEUS-functions," in *Proceedings of the ATA Conference, 'Vehicle Electronics Integration'*, (Torino, Italy), August 1991.

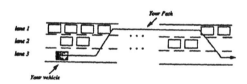

Figure 1: A path assigned by the AHS

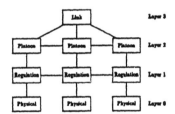

Figure 2: AHS control hierarchy

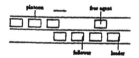

Figure 3: Platoons

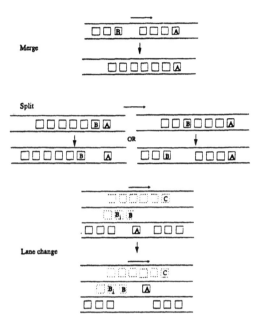

Figure 4: The three maneuvers

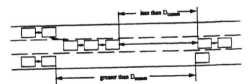

Figure 5: AHS communication system

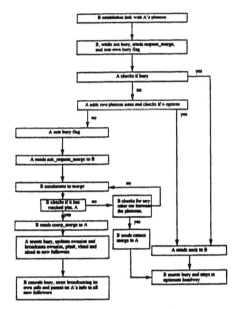

Figure 6: Sequence of events in merge

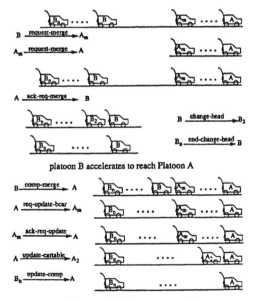

Figure 7: Merge protocol

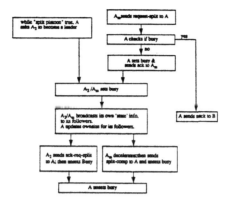

Figure 8: Sequence of events in split

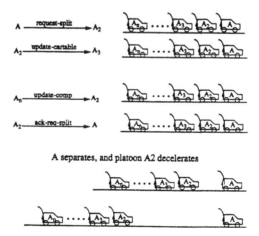

Figure 9: Split protocol: leader wants to break

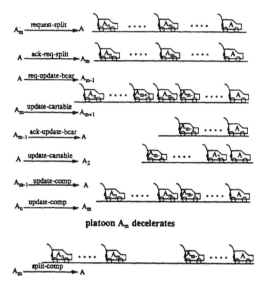

Figure 10: Split protocol: follower wants to break

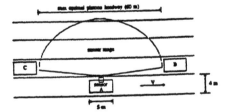

Figure 11: Sensors on vehicle

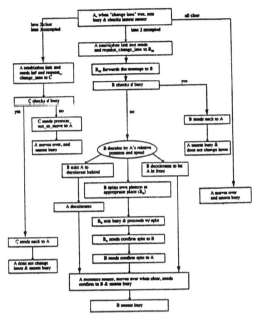

Figure 12: Sequence of events in change lane

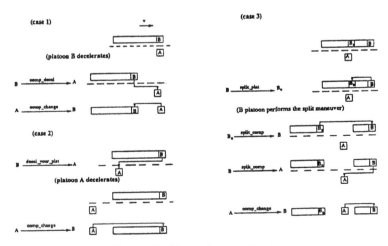

Figure 13: Change lane protocol

330

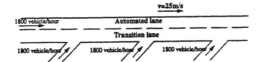

Figure 14: Highway configuration of example

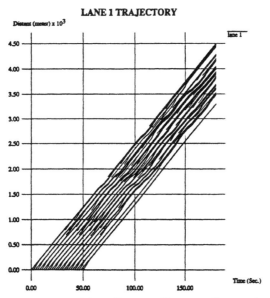

Figure 15: Time-distance diagram of example

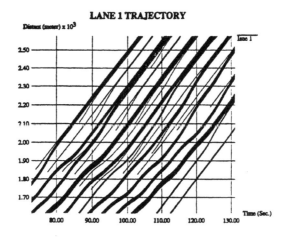

Figure 16: Blowup of portion of time-distance diagram

Opportunities and Challenges in Signal Processing and Analysis

Alan S. Willsky

Department of Electrical Engineering and Computer Science,
Massachusetts Institute of Technology, Cambridge, MA 02139, USA

Abstract. This paper provides an overview of the author's perspective on the numerous challenges and opportunities in signal and image processing. In particular we focus for the most part on problems and critical issues for problems of statistical processing of spatially-distributed data. In addition to pointing to several applications areas of some importance we also describe a view of the technical challenges and one perspective on how they can be met.

1 Introduction

For a variety of reasons—including significant advances in various sensing technologies, the possibility of using computational engines of stunning power, and the realization in an increasing array of scientific domains that signal and image processing represents a critical and frequently performance-limiting component of scientific inquiry and technological advancement—the field of signal and image processing has before it an unprecedented array of exciting opportunities and challenges. While there are certainly many such challenges involving the processing of time series, I will focus here on the broad variety of problems concerned with data distributed in space and, perhaps, in time as well.

A brief sampling of a small subset of the potential problems, I believe, makes clear the scale of the opportunity. First, there are applications in advanced manufacturing processes. For example, the growing of gallium–arsenide crystals [1] so as to realize their extraordinary electrical properties requires extremely careful monitoring and control both to detect crystal twinning quickly in order to avoid substantial losses of time and yield and to control crystal diameter to achieve the desired electrical properties without the waste caused by producing too large a crystal. The environment in which these crystals are grown, however, makes effective measurement difficult. In particular, it is possible to use a video camera to provide sequences of images on which such monitoring is based. However for a variety of reasons the quality of these images is extremely poor, making standard image processing techniques inapplicable. On the other hand, the very specific objectives of this image analysis involve extracting very few parameters— crystal radius, possible defects— and thus one would expect that an estimation-based approach that focuses on direct extraction of these parameters could yield the desired levels of performance.

Geophysical exploration represents another application area presenting a variety of challenges, ranging from the inversion of seismic or electomagnetic measurement data to the fusion of data sets corresponding to fundamentally different measurement modalities (EM, acoustic, nuclear,...) or corresponding to measurements at dramatically different scales ranging from high resolution, sparse data sets taken from boreholes to coarse resolution, broad coverage seismic data. Oceanography and in particular global ocean modeling [2] represents another domain with similar features and with perhaps even more importance to society because of the oceans' central role in heat exchange mechanisms whose understanding and evolution are critical to the assessment of global warming and global change. Oceanographers are confronted with the problem of inferring and tracking the properties of a medium of gargantuan extent, using a variety of data sources—ranging from point temperature and salinity measurements to satellite imaging to oceanacoustic tomography—of differing modalities, scales and irregular spatio-temporal sampling patterns.

And, of course, there are tremendous opportunities in the medical field. For example there is substantial interest in using a procedure involving very low radiation doses, known as cardiac perfusion imaging [3], to perform quantitative measurement of cardiac properties such as ejection fraction, *i.e.* the volumetric fraction of the left ventricular blood pool ejected during each cardiac cycle. While such a technique is far less dangerous than other methods, the quality of the cardiac images it produces is extremely low. However, once again the fact that one is interested in extracting only a single number strongly suggests the investigation of robust estimation methods focused on estimating that one parameter. At the other extreme, magnetic resonance imaging (MRI) with its incredible capabilities makes it possible to consider extremely complex image processing problems. For example there is considerable interest in exploring the use of sequential MRI images to track cardiac motion [4]. In particular cardiac motion in a healthy heart involves tension and strain through the cardiac muscle wall, while ischemic tissue and tumors move essentially as rigid bodies. Thus the tracking of motion fields in MRI images has considerable potential, especially when coupled with the MRI technique of tagging in which magnetic contrast is introduced by the introduction of magnetic "tags" or features.

This cursory sampling provides a glimpse at the opportunities and motivations for those of us involved in signal and image analysis. In the remainder of this paper I will provide a personal look at the technical challenges that must be met to take advantage of these opportunities.

2 Features of Problems Involving Spatially-Distributed Random Phenomena

There are several features of problems involving spatially-distributed phenomena that distinguish them and provide the source of the principal challenges in their solution. The first is that many if not all analysis and estimation problems involving spatially-distributed random phenomena have enormous complexity where this complexity manifests itself in two distinct ways. First there is the issue of the number of degrees of freedom to be extracted from the data. For example the tomographic reconstruction of a 512 x 512 image requires the extraction of more than $250,000$

unknowns. On the other hand typical high-resolution measuring systems produce on the order of 50,000 measurements, leaving a 200,000-dimensional nullspace! It is impressive that this level of data does in fact produce images of diagnostic quality. However, as we push the limits by reducing measurement quality or quantity, as is necessary or desirable in many contexts, the quality of images reconstructed using standard methods can degrade substantially or even catastrophically, and the reason is the overwhelming disparity between the number of degrees of freedom in the data and the number of degrees of freedom to be reconstructed. While mathematical physicists have dealt with such "ill-posed" problems for some time by various types of regularization, there seems to me to be a substantial opportunity for those of us in estimation and statistical signal processing to develop methods for the incorporation of prior knowledge, both about the phenomenon under study *and* about the objectives of the processing to be performed (e.g. as in estimating ejection fraction from cardiac perfusion imagery).

The second manifestation of complexity in spatial estimation problems is the potential for explosive computational demands. For example in going from 1–D signal processing to 2–D complexity does *not* go up by just a factor of 2. In particular sizes of data sets in 2–D depend upon the *square* of data array dimensions. Furthermore while complexity of a 1–D recursive filter depends only on filter order, *i.e.*, on the number of initial conditions to be stored, in 2–D it also depends on data array dimensions, since boundary, rather than initial, conditions are required. And if processing over time is required, complexity can appear to be prohibitive. For example, the tracking of motion in a 512 x 512 image sequence requires in principle a 2–D motion vector in each pixel, resulting in a 500,000-dimensional state model, but this number itself is dwarfed by global ocean modeling where models can involve 100,000,000 variables! Thus there is an overwhelming need for the development of estimation techniques that can take advantage of every bit of system structure in order to obtain algorithms of realistic complexity that are also well-matched to current and envisioned computer architectures.

A second class of distinguishing characteristics of spatial estimation problems is the nature of the physics characterizing both the phenomenon under study and the measurements on which the processing is to be based. For example the effects of gravitational anomalies are described by Laplace's equation; and Navier-Stokes equation plays a central role in the description of ocean dynamics. An important aspect of equations such as these is that they provide *spatially local* implicit specifications of the phenomena of interest. However in contrast to the temporally local specification of time series models such as state space descriptions, these spatial models are non-causal— *i.e.*, rather than having initial conditions and a natural notion of recursion, such spatial models typically have boundary conditions and *no* associated notion of causality. Given the fact that efficient recursive estimation procedures such as the Kalman filter are based on deducing a recursive filter structure from a causal description of the phenomenon under study and given the even more critical importance of efficiency for spatial problems, we see that there is a clear need for innovative approaches to take advantage of spatially local descriptions to develop efficient algorithms.

Similarly the physics of many measurement modalities for spatial phenomena lead to challenges very different from those arising with time series. In particular problems such as x-ray tomography, ultrasonics, seismic signal processing, and x-ray crystallography are characterized by the fact that the measurements, which are obtained by *probing* a medium, provide *non-local* information about the medium, leading to inverse problems which present substantial problems both in terms of controlling the degrees of freedom to be reconstructed by incorporating a priori information and in terms of developing computationally efficient algorithms capable of dealing with the mismatch in locality in the measurement and object domains.

A third important distinguishing feature of many spatial estimation problems is that often it is the *geometry* of regions in space about which we either have prior information or wish to extract information. For example in cardiac perfusion imaging we have both: that is, we have considerable prior information about the shape of the heart *and* the desired information — ejection fraction, location and size of infarcts — is *also* specified geometrically. Similar characteristics can be found in many applications — detecting occlusions or defects in nondestructive evaluation systems, low-dose tomographic tumor detection, mapping and tracking of the Gulf Stream, etc. For all such applications, by highlighting the geometric features of interest, it should be possible to focus limited or poor quality data and reduce significantly apparent problem ill-posedness and achieve levels of performance much greater than might be predicted based on a naive count of degrees of freedom.

Finally, another important characteristic of many spatial estimation problem involves the employment of multiple resolution concepts. In particular multiple resolution features can enter a spatial estimation processing problem in several distinct ways. First, the phenomenon understudy may have multiresolution features. For example, natural phenomena such as wave height distributions, vegetation patterns, terrain height, etc. are fractal or statistically self-similar in nature. Also, complex dynamic processes in the ocean lead to features of significance at a large number of scales. Secondly, whether the phenomenon of interest is multi-resolution or not, the *data* may be multi-resolution. For example a critical problem in oceanography is the assimilation of disparate sources of data such as localized measurements from ships, coarser resolution satellite data, and nonlocal oceanacoustic tomographic data. Finally, whether the phenomenon or the data are multi-resolution, the *algorithm* may be multi-resolution in order to deal with the issues of complexity described previously. In particular multi-resolution formulations provide an excellent framework for confronting the problem of dealing with large numbers of degrees of freedom. Specifically, multiresolution methods allow us to deal with resolution versus accuracy tradeoffs explicitly. In particular by producing estimates at multiple resolutions we can both maintain the accuracy of coarse resolution features which generally can be reconstructed with greater fidelity, while also allowing the estimation (albeit with reduced accuracy) of finer resolution features. Also, as with multigrid algorithms for the solution of partial differential equations, multiresolution algorithms offer the promise of substantial computational efficiencies, with coarse (and thus presumably simpler) solutions used to guide finer ones.

Each of the features we have described here has a significant implication for the design of estimation algorithm. In the next section we briefly describe several attempts to deal with and capitalize on some of these.

3 Estimation Problems for Spatially-Distributed Phenomena

Each of the issues raised in the preceding section leads to a variety of interesting and challenging estimation problems. Limitations of space preclude a discussion of the complete array of problems, and thus we focus here on some of the issues associated with models and efficient estimation for random fields. In particular, let us begin with a standard modeling and estimation framework for a random field x, whose statistics are specified implicitly through a model of the form

$$M x = w \tag{1}$$

where M is a spatially localized operator — $e.g.$, a difference or differential operator plus boundary conditions — and where there are at least two natural models for the driving noise w. In particular, one natural choice is that w is white noise, i.e. the covariance of w, $P_w = I$. For example in 1–D problems when M is lower bidiagonal this is precisely the form one would have for a causal state space model. More generally, this is the form assumed in so-called "boundary-value models" [5]. In this case, note that

$$M = P_x^{-1/2} \quad \text{(boundary-value model)} \tag{2}$$

The second choice is the one that leads to x being a Markov random field [6] with neighborhood structure inherited from the local structure of M, which in this case is assumed to be symmetric positive definite. Specifically in this case $P_w = M$ so that

$$M = P_x^{-1} \quad \text{(Markov model)} \tag{3}$$

In either case the key point is the explicit connection between covariance and spatial model.

Suppose we then consider the estimation of x based on the measurements

$$y = Cx = v \tag{4}$$

where C is assumed to act locally as well ($e.g.$, specifying point measurements), and P_v is diagonal (white measurement noise). In this case the optimal estimate is specified implicitly via the equation

$$(P_x^{-1} + C^T P_v^{-1} C)\hat{x} = C^T P_v^{-1} y \tag{5}$$

where $(P_x^{-1} + C^T P_v^{-1} C)$ operates locally. The problem, then is in how to implement the solution to (5) efficiently. For 1–D causal state space models, in which $(P_x^{-1} + C^T P_v^{-1} C)$ is (block) tridiagonal, there are several well-known solutions, one of which, the Rauch-Tung-Striebel algorithm, corresponds to Gaussian elimination from one end of the data interval to the other followed by back-substitution.

This idea can actually be generalized somewhat, and this in fact suggests a 2–D extension which is of potentially far greater significance [7]. Specifically for any 1–D boundary-value or Markov random field model, one can imagine using *radial* recursions, *i.e.,* rather than recursive processing from one end of the data interval to the other, we process radially outward from the center of the data interval out toward its boundaries, followed by a radially inward processing step. Moreover, if we break the data interval into segments, we can process outward in parallel in all of these, yielding at the end a decimated set of points corresponding to segment end points. These endpoints can then themselves be processed in the same way (i.e. radially outward, perhaps in several parallel pieces corresponding to partitioning of segment endpoints), resulting, perhaps after several nested steps in the elimination of all but the two overall endpoints. There then follows an analogous parallel, nested inward processing step.

The procedure just described, if taken to its ultimate limit of choosing initial segments of minimal size, is often referred to as "cyclic block reduction." The generalization just described not only leads to efficient algorithms for a class of noncausal processes and to a way to determine optimal partitioning and number of processors, but it also suggests an approach in 2-D.

In particular in 2-D we do *not* have the option of using the first algorithm just described – *i.e.,* processing from "one end" of the interval to the other. However, radial processing from the center of a 2-D data array certainly is an option. Note that this concept makes clear our earlier statement that complexity of algorithms in 2-D depends fundamentally on the dimension of the domain of interest. Specifically while a 1-D radial recursion involves recursively computing values at two endpoints of an expanding (or contracting) interval, its 2-D counterpart involves recursively computing values around the boundary of a radial region whose perimeter is proportional to the radius. Thus keeping the maximum radius of such a recursion within limits naturally suggests breaking the data array into sub-arrays of manageable size, using parallel radial recursions within each region, performing nested, parallel recursions to process the boundaries of these sub-arrays, followed by an analogous parallel, nested radially inward processing step.

Note that in 2-D the solution of the estimation equation (5) essentially corresponds to solving an elliptic partial differential equation, and thus any of the powerful methods for solving such problems could be used. The approach we have just described differs from standard methods (in particular it is *not* a standard domain decomposition method), and, moreover, the estimation interpretation of the problem being solved leads to approximations to the exact equations that yield substantial computational simplification with very little loss of performance in terms of error variances.

Finally, let us point out two extremely important complements to the preceding discussion. First of all, as mentioned in the previous sections, there are many problems in which we wish to track spatially-varying processes that evolve over time. In such a case we again encounter estimation equations as in [5], where x represents the one-step (temporally) predicted error field and y the temporal innovations. The problem in this case is that in general the inverse of the prediction error covariance P_x^{-1} or its square root are *not* local. The reason for this can be seen from the form of the temporal Riccati equation for the evolution of error covariance.

$$P(t+1|t) = AP(t|t)A^T + Q \qquad (6)$$

$$P^{-1}(t|t) = P^{-1}(t|t-1) + C^T P_v^{-1} C \tag{7}$$

where P_x in (5) equals $P^{-1}(t|t-1)$ for the incorporation of data at time t. In general the operators A, Q, C, and P_v are local, but such conditions do *not* maintain a local structure for P_x^{-1}. However, if we use the interpretation in eqs. (1) - (3) relating P_x^{-1} and a model M, we are led to the idea of *reduced-order modeling* of the error field. Several methods for doing this are described and applied with considerable success in [8]. One of the challenges in these methods is to do this without calculating the exact P_x or P_x^{-1} since for problems of interest these calculations are prohibitive in terms of operation counts and storage.

The last point to be made is that there is, in fact, a way in which truly recursive algorithms can be developed for spatial estimation problems. Specifically, as described in [9], it is possible to develop a very rich class of models for random fields that are described by recursive equations in *scale*. Roughly speaking, these models correspond to pyramidal representations of random fields, where at each scale we have an approximation of the field, where these approximations become more accurate as we move to finer scales. The result is that the structure of P_x is such that (5) can be solved *exactly* as in the Rauch-Tung -Striebel algorithm, but in this case the two sweeps correspond to a fine-to-coarse recursion followed by a coarse-to-fine sweep. In contrast to *all* known algorithms for Markov random fields, this approach leads to algorithms with constant complexity per pixel *independent* of *image size*.

An important question, then is: How rich is the class of random fields that can be modeled in this scale-recursive manner? As discussed in [9], there is a very simple way in which to realize processes with fractal characteristics in this framework. Moreover, it can be shown that any Markov random field can be approximated to an arbitrary degree of accuracy using scale-recursive algorithms. Furthermore, the gains in doing this can be substantial, leading to algorithms achieving orders of magnitude reductions in computational complexity, which can either be viewed as end results in themselves or as preconditioners for the solution of (5) when P_x corresponds, say, to a Markov random field.

4   Conclusions

In these brief remarks, I hope that I have given some feel for the scope of the opportunities, the nature of the challenges, and the possibilities for innovation in the field of estimation and statistical signal processing for spatially-distributed random phenomena. Taking advantage of these opportunities and meeting these challenges are by no means simple tasks, but the potential payoffs in terms of intellectual achievements and in terms of contributions to problems of considerable importance to society demand our spirited and whole-hearted response.

Acknowledgements

The research providing the basis for these remarks was supported in part by The Office of Naval Research under Grant N00014-91-J-1004, in part by the National

Science Foundation under Grant MIP–9015281, and in part by The Army Research Office under Grant DAAL03–92–G–0115.

References

[1] N.R. Sandell, D.P. Looze, and R.R. Tenney: Neural Networks Applied to Gallium-Arsenide Process Control, Alphatech TR-557, August 1992

[2] I. Fukumori, J. Benveniste, C. Wunsch, and D.B. Haidvogel: Assimilation of Sea Surface Topography into an Ocean Circulation Model Using a Steady-State Smoother. Journal of Physical Oceanography, to appear.

[3] J. Heo, G.A. Hermann, A.S. Iskandrian, A. Askenaseo, and B. Segal: New Myocardial Perfusion Imaging Agents: Description and Applications. American Heart Journal, Vol. 5, 1988, pp. 1111-1117

[4] E. Zeihouni, D. Parish, W. Rogers, A. Yang, and E. Shapiro: Human Heart: Tagging with MRI Imaging – A Method for Noninvasive Assessment of Myocardial Motion. Radiology, Vol. 169, 1988, pp. 59-63

[5] B.C. Levy, M.B. Adams, and A.S. Willsky: Solution and Linear Estimation of 2-D Nearest Neighbor Models. Proc. of the IEEE, Vol. 78, 1990.

[6] B.C. Levy: Noncausal Estimation for Markov Random Fields, Proc. Intern. Symposium MTNS-89, Vol. 1: Realization and Modelling in System Theory, M.A. Kaashoek, J.H. van Schuppen, and A. Ran, eds., Birkhauser-Verlag, Basel, 1990

[7] D. Taylor: Parallel Estimation on One and Two Dimensional Systems. Ph.D. thesis, M.I.T. Dept. of EECS, Feb. 1992

[8] T.M. Chin: A.S. Willsky and W.C. Karl: Sequential Filtering for Multi-Frame Visual Reconstruction. Signal Processing, to appear.

[9] M.R. Luettgen, W.C. Karl, and A.S. Willsky: Optical Flow Computation via Multiscale Regularization, submitted for publication.

NEURAL COMPUTING AND STOCHASTIC OPTIMIZATION

Eugene Wong

Office of Science and Technology Policy, the White House, and
University of California at Berkeley

1   Introduction

One of the promises of neural networks has always been their potential to have the kind of learning and general computing capabilities possessed by the central nervous system. To date, the potential of neural networks to learn has been extensively explored and the results are somewhat encouraging. There exist algorithms that can be used to systematically adjust the parameter of a neural network on the basis of sample inputs for which the desired response of the network is known. Under quite reasonable conditions, the parameters will converge to values such that the network will respond correctly not only to the known samples, but also for unknown inputs that are "similar" to the samples. Whether or not this is "true learning" is immaterial. These characteristics of neural networks render them potentially very useful systems for some classes of problems that do not lend themselves to efficient analytical or algorithmic solution. Viewing neural networks as computers, we might term the learning feature as "programming-by-example."

However, to justify applying the term "computer" to neural networks, some degree of generality is required. Here, the results are less encouraging. To date, the principal applications have been to pattern classification problems of one kind or another. For such problems, the lack of any underlying analytical models makes programming-by-example a particularly attractive way of designing the classifier. But examples of application not of this type are hard to come by.

The purpose of this paper is to examine a class of dynamical neural networks that can be used to find the global optimum for rather general functions. If this approach proves to be practical, then a rather large class of problems, from differential equations to digital communications, can be solved using such networks.

2   Stochastic Optimization

Let $E(x)$, $x \in S$, be a function (called the energy function) to be minimized over some space S. For our purposes, we shall take S to be either the unit cube $[0, 1]^n$ or $\{-1, 1\}^n$. Now, suppose that we can construct a stationary Markov process X_t, with discrete or continuous time, such that the equilibrium distribution of X_t is given by a density function

$$p(x) = \frac{1}{Z} e^{-\frac{1}{T}E(x)} , \quad x \in S \tag{2.1}$$

where

$$Z = \int_S e^{-\frac{1}{T}E(x)} dx \qquad (2.2)$$

or

$$Z = \sum_S e^{-\frac{1}{T}E(x)} \qquad (2.3)$$

according as whether X_t is continuous or discrete valued. The positive parameter T has the interpretation of temperature. For low temperature, $p(x)$ is sharply peaked at the local minima of $E(x)$. Intuitively, if we take a sequence of temperatures $\{T_k\}$ that decreases slowly enough so that X_t remains in equilibrium distribution, then as $T_k \to 0$, $X(t)$ should end up in the state corresponding to the global minimum of $E(x)$. Indeed, this situation can be made rigorous and for a suitable "cooling schedule" $\{T_k\}$ it can be proved that $X(t)$ will converge to the global minimum of $E(x)$, assuming that the global minimum is unique. The global minimization algorithm that results from this approach is known as *simulated annealing* [KIR83].

3 Dynamical Neural Nets

The states $x(t)$ of a Hopfield net [HOP82] are defined by a pair of equations

$$x_i(t) = g\left[u_i(t) \right] \qquad (3.1)$$

$$\frac{d\,u_i(t)}{dt} = -E_i\left[x(t) \right] \qquad (3.2)$$

where $E_i(x) = \frac{\partial}{\partial x_i} E(x)$. If g is a smooth increasing function, then in equilibrium $x(t)$ will be a local minimum of $E(x)$. This is because

$$\frac{d}{dt} E\left[x(t) \right] = -\sum_i E_i^2(x(t))g'\left[u_i(t) \right] \qquad (3.3)$$

so that $E(x(t))$ is never increased. In [WON91a] we show that (3.1) can be modified so that $x(t)$ is a stationary Markov process with an equilibrium density function given by (2.1). The modified version of (3.2) is given by a stochastic differential equation

$$d\,u_i(t) = -E_i\left[x(t) \right] dt + \sqrt{\frac{2T}{g'(u_i(t))}} \; dW_i(t) \qquad (3.4)$$

where $\{W_i(t)\}$ is a collection of independent Wiener processes. A popular choice for $g(\cdot)$ is

$$g(u) = \frac{1}{2}(1 + \tanh \frac{u}{a}) \qquad (3.5)$$

for which (3.4) reads

$$d\,u_i(t) = -E_i\left[x(t) \right] dt + 2\sqrt{aT} \; \cosh \frac{u_i(t)}{a} \; dW_i(t) \qquad (3.6)$$

Equation (3.4) can be implemented by injecting which Gaussian into a Hopfield net. We have called such a realization a *diffusion machine*.

4 Boltzmann Machines

For the discrete version it is convenient to take $E(x)$ to range over $x \in \{-1, 1\}^n$ and define

$$\Delta_i(x) = E(\bar{x}_i) - E(x) \tag{4.1}$$

where $\bar{x}_i$ denotes x with x_i replaced by $-x_i$. We have shown [WON91b] that a Markov chain $X(t)$ with an equilibrium distribution given by the Gibbs distribution

$$\text{Prob}(X(t)=x) = \frac{1}{Z} e^{-\frac{1}{T}E(x)} \tag{4.2}$$

can be constructed by injecting noise in a network and identifying $X_i(t)$ with the state at the ith node of the network. For convenience let t take integer values and assume that for each time change $t \rightarrow t+1$ only one node can change state, but that as $t \rightarrow \infty$ every node changes state infinitely often. Under these assumptions the construction can be described by a transition equation of the form

$$X_i(t+1) = X_i(t) \, \text{sgn} \, [\Delta_i(X(t)) - Z(t)] \quad \text{for some } i \tag{4.3}$$

$Z(t)$ is a continuous valued stochastic process with independent values at different t's (white noise). It turns out that Z_t cannot be Gaussian, but its density function must be of the form

$$p_Z(z) = -\frac{d}{dz} \left[e^{-\frac{z}{2T}} f(|z|) \right] \tag{4.4}$$

when f is any function that makes p_Z a probability density function. For example, taking

$$f(z) = e^{-\frac{z}{2T}}$$

yields

$$p_Z(z) = \frac{1}{T} e^{-\frac{z}{T}} 1(z)$$

where $1(\cdot)$ denotes the unit-step. We have called a neural network with states governed by (4.3) and (4.4) a *Boltzmann machine*.

5 Digital Receiver — An Example

A potentially important practical application of Boltzmann machines is as an optimum digital receiver. A somewhat simplified model of digital communication can be described as follows:

encoding: $\quad x \in \{-1, 1\}^n \rightarrow z(x) \in \{-1, 1\}^n$

modulation: $\quad z(x) \rightarrow \sum_k z_k(x) \delta(t - kt_0)$

transmission: $\quad \sum_k z_k(x)\delta(t-kt_0) \;\to\; \sum_k z_k(x)h(t-kt_0)+N(t) \;=\; y(t)$

receiver: $\qquad y(t) \to \hat{x} \quad$ best estimate of x

Under the assumption that the noise $N(t)$ is a white Gaussian noise, $\hat{x}$ is obtained by minimizing the function

$$E(x) = -\frac{1}{2}\int\left[\sum_k z_k(x)h(t-kt_0)\right]^2 dt + \int y(t)\sum_k z_k(x)h(t-kt_0)\,dt$$

In the uncoded case (i.e., $z_k(x)=x_k$), $E(x)$ takes on the form

$$E(x) = -\frac{1}{2}\sum_{i,y} W_{ij}\,x_i\,x_j + \sum_i \theta_i\,x_i$$

and (4.3) becomes

$$X_i(t+1) = \mathrm{sgn}\left[\sum_{j\neq i} w_{ij}X_j(t) - \frac{1}{2}Z(t)X_i(t) - \theta_i\right]$$

which can be implemented easily by a discrete time Hopfield net. In contrast, a conventional receiver would be made up of several stages of suboptimal operations.

For the encoded case, we need to compute $z(x)$ and $z(\bar{x}_i)$. This is interesting because to compute these we need the encoder, not the decoder. Therefore, we seem to have found a way of using the encoder to decode for arbitrary encoding schemes.

6 Conclusion

The potential of neural networks to find global optimum should be further explored. Their ability to do so using only local "gradient" information is surprising and can lead to very useful applications. Implementing an optimum receiver-decoder is a particularly interesting example.

References

[HOP82] J. J. Hopfield, "Neural networks and physical systems with emerging collective computational abilities," *Proc. National Academy of Sciences* 79 (1982) 2554-2558.

[KIR83] S. Kirkpatrick, C. D. Gelatt, Jr. and M. P. Vecchi, "Optimization by simulated annealing," *Science* 220 (1983) 671-680.

[WON91a] E. Wong, "Stochastic neural networks," *Algorithmica* 6 (1991) 466-478.

[WON91b] E. Wong, "Implementing Boltzmann machines," in *Stochastic Analysis*, E. Mayer-Wolf, E. Merzbach and A. Schwartz, eds., Academic Press, San Diego, 1991.

VI. Scientific Computing, Numerical Software, Aided-Engineering and Computer

Stabilization of Galerkin methods and applications to domain decomposition

C. Baiocchi*[†], F. Brezzi*[†], L.D. Marini[‡†]

* Università degli Studi, 27100 PAVIA (Italy)
[†] Istituto di Analisi Numerica del C.N.R., 27100 Pavia (Italy)
[‡] Università di Genova, 16132 Genova (Italy)

Abstract. We present an abstract stabilization method which covers previous concrete applications to advection–diffusion equations and to the Stokes equations for incompressible fluids. We then apply the method to stabilize domain decomposition formulations for elliptic problems. We obtain a method that allows the treatment of internal variables, interface variables and Lagrange multipliers (normal derivatives) by piecewise polynomials of arbitrary order.

Introduction

We present an abstract regularization result inspired essentially by previous regularization techniques introduced by Hughes and various other authors for advection-diffusion problems and for the Stokes equations for incompressible fluids (see [12], [11], [10] for surveys and references). To be more precise, the application of our abstract result to the Stokes equations leads to the method introduced by Douglas and Wang [9], while the application to advection-diffusion problems produces a variant of Galerkin least square methods studied in [11]. For a more general abstract setting which includes other regularization techniques, see [2]. If we apply our result to the Dirichlet problem (for linear elliptic equations) with Lagrange multipliers we obtain a variant of [3].

In this paper the use of this abstract theory for the macro-hybrid domain decomposition method of [6],[7] is investigated. We recall that the method of [6] produces a three-field formulation where the three unknowns represent the solution u of the original problem inside each macro-element, the normal derivative λ of u on the boundary of each macro-element, and the trace ψ of u at the interfaces. The application of our abstract theory to this method allows a great generality in the choice of discretizations for the three fields. For instance, piecewise polynomials of arbitrary (and independent) degree can be chosen for each variable, still preserving stability and optimal error bounds. Alternatively, different Galerkin methods (finite elements, spectral, Fourier, wavelets etc.) can be used in different macro-elements to obtain a variant of the mortar elements techniques of [4].

An outline of the paper is as follows. In Section 1, starting from an abstract variational formulation, we present a class of regularization techniques and prove stability and error bounds under reasonable assumptions. To help the reader, the Douglas-

Wang method for Stokes is used throughout this section to clarify the abstract objects we have to deal with. In Section 2 we recall the macro-hybrid formulation of [6] for domain decomposition methods. In Section 3 we briefly apply the results of Section 1 to the three-field formulation of Section 2 and we sketch the error bounds that can be obtained. We refer to [8] for a more detailed treatment.

1 An Abstract Result

Let $\mathcal{V}_1$ be a Hilbert space, and $\mathcal{A}_1(U,V)$ a bilinear form on $\mathcal{V}_1 \times \mathcal{V}_1$, which is continuous in the usual sense:

$$\exists M_1 > 0 \qquad \mathcal{A}_1(U,V) \leq M_1 \|U\|_1 \|V\|_1 . \qquad (1.1)$$

We assume that there exist two positive constants β_r and β_l such that for every W in $\mathcal{V}_1$ there exist V_r and V_l in $\mathcal{V}_1 - \{0\}$ with

$$\mathcal{A}_1(V_l, W) \geq \beta_l \|V_l\|_1 \|W\|_1 , \qquad (1.2)$$

$$\mathcal{A}_1(W, V_r) \geq \beta_r \|W\|_1 \|V_r\|_1 . \qquad (1.3)$$

It is well known that, with these assumptions, for every $f_1 \in \mathcal{V}_1'$ there exists a unique U_1 in $\mathcal{V}_1$ such that

$$\mathcal{A}_1(U_1, V) = < f_1, V > \quad \forall V \in \mathcal{V}_1 . \qquad (1.4)$$

Remark 1.1: A tipical example of the situation that we are going to face is given by the Stokes problem, which can be fit in our framework by setting, with obvious notation:

$$\begin{cases} \mathcal{V}_1 = \left(H_0^1(\Omega)\right)^2 \times \left(L^2(\Omega)/\mathbb{R}\right) \; ; \; U = (\underline{u}, p); V = (\underline{v}, q) \\ \mathcal{A}_1(U,V) = \left(\underline{\nabla}\,\underline{u}, \underline{\nabla}\,\underline{v}\right) - (\text{ div}\,\underline{v}, p) + (\text{ div}\,\underline{u}, q). \end{cases} \qquad (1.5)$$

The well–posedness of (1.4) follows from the inf–sup condition (see e.g. [5]) and cannot be deduced using Lax–Milgram theorem. ∎

Let now $\{\mathcal{V}_h\}_{h>0}$ be a sequence of finite dimensional subspaces of $\mathcal{V}_1$. It is well known that, in general, the problem of finding U_h^1 in $\mathcal{V}_h$ such that

$$\mathcal{A}_1\left(U_h^1, V_h\right) = < f_1, V_h > \qquad \forall V_h \in \mathcal{V}_h \qquad (1.6)$$

does not have a unique solution, unless discrete analogues of (1.2) and (1.3) hold. We present here an abstract regularization technique that allows to circumvent this problem. When applied to the Stokes problem our technique reproduces the Douglas–Wang method (see [9]); when applied to the domain decomposition formulation of [6] it gives rise, as we shall see, to a variant of [3]. Although this last application is our aim here, we shall keep track of the Stokes problem as a first illustration of the abstract theory. The main reason for that is that Stokes problem is much more familiar and also formally simpler.

First of all we assume that the bilinear form $\mathcal{A}_1(U, V)$ is non–negative. More precisely, we assume that there exist a seminorm $|\cdot|$ on $\mathcal{V}_1$ and a positive constant γ_1 such that

$$\mathcal{A}_1(V, V) > \gamma_1 |V|^2 \quad \forall V \in \mathcal{V}_1. \tag{1 7}$$

We also assume that

$$|V| \le \|V\|_1 \quad \forall V \in \mathcal{V}_1. \tag{1.8}$$

For the Stokes problem we clearly have $|V| = |(\underline{v}, q)| = \|\underline{\nabla}\,\underline{v}\|^2_{L^2(\Omega)}$.

We assume now that we are given a sequence $\{\mathcal{V}_2(h)\}_{h>0}$ of Hilbert spaces, with seminorms $|V|_{2,h}$ and norms $\|V\|_{2,h}$, such that $\mathcal{V}_h \subset \mathcal{V}_2(h) \hookrightarrow V_1$ and U_1 (solution of (1.4)) belongs to $\mathcal{V}_2(h)$ for every h; we also assume that

$$\|V_h\|_{2,h} \le M_c \|V_h\|_1 \quad \forall V_h \in \mathcal{V}_h \tag{1.9}$$

$$\|V_h\|^2_{2,h} \le c \left(|V_h|^2 + |V_h|^2_{2,h}\right) \quad \forall V_h \in \mathcal{V}_h \tag{1.10}$$

with M_e, c constants independent of h.

For the Stokes problem and for piecewise polynomial spaces $\mathcal{V}_h$, we can take

$$\|(\underline{v}, q)\|^2_{2,h} = \|\underline{\nabla}\,\underline{v}\|^2_{L^2} + \sum_{K \in T_h} h_K^2 \left\{ \|\Delta \underline{v}\|^2_{L^2(K)} + \|\underline{\nabla} q\|^2_{L^2(K)} \right\} \tag{1.11}$$

always with usual notation, and

$$|(\underline{v}, q)|^2_{2,h} = \sum_{K \in T_h} h_K^2 \| -\Delta \underline{v} + \underline{\nabla} q\|^2_{L^2(K)}. \tag{1.12}$$

We assume now that we are also given a bilinear form $\mathcal{A}_2(U, V)$ on $\mathcal{V}_2(h) \times \mathcal{V}_2(h)$ such that, for every W, V in $\mathcal{V}_2(h)$

$$\mathcal{A}_2(W, V) \le M_2 \|W\|_{2,h} \|V\|_{2,h} \tag{1.13}$$

$$\mathcal{A}_2(V, V) \ge \gamma_2 |V|^2_{2,h} \tag{1.14}$$

with positive constants M_2 and γ_2 independent of h. We set

$$< f_2, V >:= \mathcal{A}_2(U_1, V) \quad \forall V \in \mathcal{V}_2(h). \tag{1.15}$$

Note that (1.15) will not produce a reasonable right–hand side, unless it is effectively computable without knowing the solution U_1 of (1.4) explicitly. For instance, for Stokes problem, if $U_1 = (\underline{u}, p)$ and $-\Delta \underline{u} + \underline{\nabla} p = \underline{f}$, we can set

$$\mathcal{A}_2(U, V) = \sum_{K \in T_h} h_K^2 \left(-\Delta \underline{u} + \underline{\nabla} p, -\Delta \underline{v} + \underline{\nabla} q\right)_{L^2(K)} \tag{1.16}$$

so that

$$< f_2, V > = \sum h_K^2 \left(\underline{f}, -\Delta \underline{v} + \underline{\nabla} q \right)_{L^2(K)} \tag{1.17}$$

which is computable without explicit knowledge of the solution U_1.

We can now set $\mathcal{A} = \mathcal{A}_1 + \mathcal{A}_2$ and $f = f_1 + f_2$. It is pretty obvious that the problem

$$\begin{cases} \text{find } U_h \in \mathcal{V}_h \text{ such that} \\ \mathcal{A}\left(U_h, V_h\right) = < f, V_h > \quad \forall V_h \in \mathcal{V}_h \end{cases} \tag{1.18}$$

has a unique solution, since

$$\mathcal{A}(V_h, V_h) \geq \gamma_1 |V_h|^2 + \gamma_2 |V_h|_{2,h}^2 \geq \gamma \|V_h\|_{2,h}^2 \tag{1.19}$$

for every V_h in $\mathcal{V}_h$, from (1.7), (1.14) and (1.10).

On the other hand, it is also obvious that

$$\begin{aligned} \mathcal{A}(U_1, V_h) &= \mathcal{A}_1(U_1, V_h) + \mathcal{A}_2(U_1, V_h) \\ &= < f_1, V_h > + < f_2, V_h > = < f, V_h > \end{aligned} \tag{1.20}$$

for every V_h in $\mathcal{V}_h$, using (1.4), (1.15), and the definitions of $\mathcal{A}$ and f. It is still not clear whether U_h converges to U_1 (possibly with optimal rate) or not. For this we need some further assumptions. We assume therefore that there exists a linear operator $\pi_h : \mathcal{V}_1 \to \mathcal{V}_h$ and another seminorm, $|\cdot|_{*,h}$, on $\mathcal{V}_1$ such that, for every $W \in \mathcal{V}_1$ and $V_h \in \mathcal{V}_h$, we have

$$\mathcal{A}_1\left(W - \pi_h W, V_h\right) \leq M_l \left|W - \pi_h W\right|_{*,h} \left\|V_h\right\|_{2,h} \tag{1.21}$$

$$\mathcal{A}_2\left(V_h, W - \pi_h W\right) \leq M_r \left|W - \pi_h W\right|_{*,h} \left\|V_h\right\|_{2,h} \tag{1.22}$$

$$\left|W - \pi_h W\right|_{*,h} \leq M_* \|W\|_1 \tag{1.23}$$

$$\left\|\pi_h W\right\|_1 \leq M_p \|W\|_1 \tag{1.24}$$

with M_l, M_r, M_*, M_p constants independent of h.

In the case of Stokes problems, restricting ourselves, for the sake of simplicity, to finite element approximations with continuous pressures (but the case of discontinuous pressures can also be easily treated, following essentially [13]) we can take as π_h the usual projection (in $\mathcal{V}_1$) onto $\mathcal{V}_h$. It is easy to check that, in this case, for $V = (\underline{v}, q)$ we can take

$$|V|_{*,h}^2 = \|\underline{\nabla} \underline{v}\|_{L^2}^2 + h^{-2} \|\underline{v}\|_{L^2}^2 + \|p\|_{L^2/R}^2 \tag{1.25}$$

and (1.21)–(1.24) will hold. Notice also that, for $U_1 = (\underline{u}, p)$ smooth enough, the three quantities

$$\|U_1 - \pi_h U_1\|_1 \,, \quad \|U_1 - \pi_h U_1\|_{2,h} \,, \quad |U_1 - \pi_h U_1|_{*,h} \tag{1.26}$$

have the same order of magnitude (in powers of h), and correspond to optimal orders of accuracy.

We can now prove our two basic results.

Theorem 1.1: There exists a constant δ_1 such that, for all h we have

$$\|U_1 - U_h\|_{2,h} \leq \delta_1 \left(\|U_1 - \pi_h U_1\|_{2,h} + |U_1 - \pi_h U_1|_{\star,h} \right) . \tag{1.27}$$

Proof: We have

$$
\begin{aligned}
\gamma \|U_h - \pi_h U_1\|_{2,h}^2 \leq & \qquad (\text{use} (1.19)) & (1.28) \\
\leq \mathcal{A} (U_h - \pi_h U_1, \, U_h - \pi_h U_1) = & \qquad (\text{use} (1.18), (1.20)) \\
= \mathcal{A} (U_1 - \pi_h U_1, \, U_h - \pi_h U_1) \leq & \qquad (\text{use} (1.21),) \\
\leq M_l \, |U_1 - \pi_h U_1|_{\star,h} \, \|U_h - \pi_h U_1\|_{2,h}
\end{aligned}
$$

which easily implies

$$\|U_h - \pi_h U_1\|_{2,h} \leq (M_l/\gamma) \, |U_1 - \pi_h U_1|_{\star,h} \tag{1.29}$$

and the result follows by the triangle inequality. ∎

Theorem 1.2: There exists a constant δ_2 such that for all h we have

$$\|U_h - U_1\|_1 \leq \delta_2 \left(\|U_1 - \pi_h U_1\|_{2,h} + |U_1 - \pi_h U_1|_{\star,h} \right) . \tag{1.30}$$

Proof: We have from (1.3) that there exists V_r in $\mathcal{V}_1$ such that

$$\mathcal{A}_1 (U_h - \pi_h U_1, \, V_r) \geq \beta_r \, \|U_h - \pi_h U_1\|_1 \, \|V_r\|_1 . \tag{1.31}$$

Then we have

$$
\begin{aligned}
\beta_r \, \|V_r\|_1 \, \|U_h - \pi_h U_1\|_1 \leq \mathcal{A}_1 (U_h - \pi_h U_1, \, V_r) = & (\pm \pi_h V_r) & (1.32) \\
= \mathcal{A}_1 (U_h - \pi_h U_1, \, V_r - \pi_h V_r) + \mathcal{A}_1 (U_h - \pi_h U_1, \, \pi_h V_r) \leq & (\text{use} (1.22), (1.23)) \\
\leq M_r M_\star \, \|U_h - \pi_h U_1\|_{2,h} \, \|V_r\|_1 + \mathcal{A}_1 (U_h - \pi_h U_1, \, \pi_h V_r) = & (\pm \mathcal{A}_2) \\
= M_r M_\star \, \|U_h - \pi_h U_1\|_{2,h} \, \|V_r\|_1 + \mathcal{A} (U_h - \pi_h U_1, \, \pi_h V_r) - \\
- \mathcal{A}_2 (U_h - \pi_h U_1, \, \pi_h V_r) \leq & (\text{use} (1.18), (1.20) \text{ and } (1.13)) \\
\leq M_r M_\star \, \|U_h - \pi_h U_1\|_{2,h} \, \|V_r\|_1 + \mathcal{A} (U_1 - \pi_h U_1, \, \pi_h V_r) + \\
+ M_2 \, \|U_h - \pi_h U_1\|_{2,h} \, \|\pi_h V_r\|_{2,h} \leq & (\text{use } \mathcal{A} = \mathcal{A}_1 + \mathcal{A}_2, (1.21), (1.13)) \\
\leq M_r M_\star \, \|U_h - \pi_h U_1\|_{2,h} \, \|V_r\|_1 + M_l \, |U_1 - \pi_h U_1|_{\star,h} \, \|\pi_h V_r\|_{2,h} + \\
+ M_2 \, \|U_1 - \pi_h U_1\|_{2,h} \, \|\pi_h V_r\|_{2,h} + M_2 \, \|U_h - \pi_h U_1\|_{2,h} \, \|\pi_h V_r\|_{2,h} \leq \\
(\text{use } (1.9), (1.24)) \leq (M_r M_\star + M_2 M_e M_p) \, \|U_h - \pi_h U_1\|_{2,h} \, \|V_r\|_1 + \\
+ M_e M_l M_p \, |U_1 - \pi_h U_1|_{\star,h} \, \|V_r\|_1 + M_e M_2 M_p \, \|U_1 - \pi_h U_1\|_{2,h} \, \|V_r\|_1 ,
\end{aligned}
$$

from which

$$\| U_h - \pi_h U_1 \|_1 \leq C \big(\| U_h - \pi_h U_1 \|_{2,h} + | U_1 - \Pi_h U_1 |_{*,h} + \| U_1 - \pi_h U_1 \|_{2,h} \big) \quad (1.33)$$

and the result follows from (1.29) and (1.33). ∎

Remark 1.2: We notice that, for piecewise polynomial approximations of the Stokes problem, both (1.27) and (1.30) provide error estimates of optimal order (as it was already shown by [9] with a direct approach). In Section 3 we shall apply these abstract results to domain decomposition methods.

2 The continuous formulation for a domain decomposition method

Let us consider, for the sake of simplicity, a polygonal domain $\Omega \subset \mathbb{R}^2$ split into a finite number of polygonal subdomains Ω_k $(k = 1, .., N)$. Let

$$\Omega = \overline{\bigcup_k \overset{\circ}{\Omega_k}} \quad ; \quad \Gamma_k = \partial \Omega_k \quad ; \quad \Sigma = \bigcup_k \Gamma_k. \quad (2.1)$$

Let A be a linear elliptic operator of the form

$$Au = \sum_i \left\{ \sum_j \left(-\frac{\partial}{\partial x_j} \left(a_{ij}(x) \frac{\partial u}{\partial x_i} + b_j(x) u \right) + c_i(x) \frac{\partial u}{\partial x_i} \right\} + d(x) u. \quad (2.2)$$

We assume that the coefficients a_{ij}, b_j, c_i, d belong to $L^\infty(\Omega)$ and are smooth in each Ω_k, and we consider the bilinear forms associated with A in each Ω_k, that is,

$$for\ u, v \in H^1(\Omega_k):$$
$$a_k(u, v) := \int_{\Omega_k} \left\{ \sum_i \left(\sum_j \left(a_{ij} \frac{\partial u}{\partial x_i} \frac{\partial v}{\partial x_j} + b_j u \frac{\partial v}{\partial x_j} \right) + c_i \frac{\partial u}{\partial x_i} v \right) + d u v \right\} dx. \quad (2.3)$$

We also set, for $u, v \in \prod_k H^1(\Omega_k)$

$$a(u, v) := \sum_k a_k(u, v); \quad (2.4)$$

for the sake of simplicity we also assume that there exists a constant $\alpha > 0$ such that

$$a(v, v) \geq \alpha \| v \|_{H^1(\Omega)}^2 \qquad \forall v \in H_0^1(\Omega). \quad (2.5)$$

From now on we are going to use the following notation: $(.,.)$ will be the usual inner product in $L^2(\Omega)$; for $k = 1, ..., N$, $< .,. >_k$ will be the inner product in $L^2(\Gamma_k)$

(or, when necessary, the duality pairing between $H^{-\frac{1}{2}}(\Gamma_k)$ and $H^{\frac{1}{2}}(\Gamma_k)$). Let us now introduce the spaces that will be used in our formulation. For $k = 1, ..., N$ we set

$$\Upsilon_k := H^1(\Omega_k) \quad ; \quad M_k := H^{-\frac{1}{2}}(\Gamma_k). \tag{2.6}$$

We then define

$$\Upsilon := \prod_k \Upsilon_k \quad ; \quad M := \prod_k M_k, \tag{2.7}$$

and

$$\Phi := \{\varphi \in L^2(\Sigma) \; : \; \exists v \in H_0^1(\Omega) \text{ with } \varphi = v_{|\Sigma}\} \equiv H_0^1(\Omega)_{|\Sigma}, \tag{2.8}$$

with the obvious norms

$$\| v \|_\Upsilon^2 = \sum_k \|v^k\|^2_{H^1(\Omega_k)} \qquad (v \in \Upsilon; \; v = (v^1, ..., v^N)); \tag{2.9}$$

$$\| \mu \|_M^2 = \sum_k \|\mu^k\|^2_{H^{-\frac{1}{2}}(\Gamma_k)} \qquad (\mu \in M; \; \mu = (\mu^1, ..., \mu^N)); \tag{2.10}$$

$$\| \varphi \|_\Phi = \inf\{ \; |v|_{H^1(\Omega)} \; | \; v \in H_0^1(\Omega), \; v_{|\Sigma} = \varphi \}. \tag{2.11}$$

For every f, say, in $L^2(\Omega)$, we can now consider the following two problems:

$$\begin{cases} \text{find } w \in H_0^1(\Omega) \quad \text{such that} \\ a(w, v) = (f, v) \qquad \forall v \in H_0^1(\Omega) \end{cases} \tag{2.12}$$

and

$$\begin{cases} \text{find } u \in \Upsilon, \; \lambda \in M \text{ and } \psi \in \Phi \quad \text{such that} \\ \text{i)} \;\; a(u, v) - \sum_k < \lambda^k, v^k >_k = (f, v) \qquad \forall v \in \Upsilon \\ \text{ii)} \;\; \sum_k < \mu^k, \psi - u^k >_k = 0 \qquad \forall \mu \in M \\ \text{iii)} \;\; \sum_k < \lambda^k, \varphi >_k = 0 \qquad \forall \varphi \in \Phi. \end{cases} \tag{2.13}$$

Theorem 2.1: For every $f \in L^2(\Omega)$, both problems (2.12) and (2.13) have a unique solution. Moreover we have

$$u^k = w \qquad \text{in } \Omega_k \quad (k = 1, ..., N), \tag{2.14}$$

$$\lambda^k = \frac{\partial w}{\partial n_A^k} \qquad \text{on } \Gamma_k \quad (k = 1, ..., N), \tag{2.15}$$

$$\psi = w \qquad \text{on } \Sigma \tag{2.16}$$

where $\partial w/\partial n_A^k$ is the outward conormal derivative (of the restriction of w to Ω_k) with respect to the operator A.

Proof It follows from (2.5) that (2.12) has a unique solution w. Setting u, λ, ψ as in (2.14)–(2.16) it is easy to verify that this is a solution of (2.13). Hence, we only need to show that (2.13) cannot have two different solutions or, in other words, that $f = 0$ in (2.13) implies $u = 0$, $\lambda = 0$, $\psi = 0$. Let then $f = 0$; from (2.13;ii) we get $u^k = \psi$ on Γ_k for every k, and therefore the existence of a function $w \in H_0^1(\Omega)$ such that $\psi = w_{|\Sigma}$ and $u^k = w_{|\Omega_k}$. From (2.13;i) with $v = w$, and (2.13;iii) with $\varphi = w$ we have

$$a(w, w) = 0 \tag{2.17}$$

yielding $u = 0$ and $\psi = 0$. From (2.13;i) we have now

$$< \lambda^k, v >_k = 0 \qquad \forall v \in \Upsilon_k \qquad \forall k, \tag{2.18}$$

which easily gives $\lambda = 0$. ∎

It is very important, for applications to domain decomposition methods, to remark explicitly that the first two equations of (2.13) can be written as

$$\begin{cases} a_k(u^k, v^k) - < \lambda^k, v^k >_k = (f, v^k) & \forall v^k \in \Upsilon_k, \quad \forall k \\ < \mu^k, u^k >_k = < \psi, \mu^k >_k & \forall \mu^k \in M_k, \quad \forall k. \end{cases} \tag{2.19}$$

In particular, for all fixed k, assuming f and ψ as data, (2.19) is the variational formulation of the Dirichlet problem

$$\begin{cases} A u^k = f & \text{in } \Omega_k, \\ u^k = \psi & \text{on } \Gamma_k, \end{cases} \tag{2.20}$$

where the boundary condition is imposed by means of a Lagrange multiplier (that finally comes out to be $\lambda^k \equiv \partial u^k / \partial n_A^k$) as in Babuška [1]. Hence, for f and ψ given, the resolution of the first two equations of (2.13) amounts to the resolution of N independent Dirichlet problems.

3 Regularization of domain decomposition methods

We apply now the abstract technique of Section 1 to problem (2.13). For this, we have first to set it in the form (1.4). We define

$$\mathcal{V}_1 = \Upsilon \times M \times \Phi, \tag{3.1}$$

$$\begin{aligned} \mathcal{A}_1((u, \lambda, \psi), (v, \mu, \varphi)) &= a(u, v) - \sum_k < \lambda^k, v^k >_k \\ &+ \sum_k < \lambda^k, \varphi >_k + \sum_k < \mu^k, u^k >_k - \sum_k < \mu^k, \psi >_k \, . \end{aligned} \tag{3.2}$$

One can easily check that (1.1)-(1.3) hold true. Non–negativity (1.7) is trivial if we take

$$|(v, \mu, \varphi)|^2 := \sum_k \|\underline{\nabla} v\|^2_{L^2(\Omega_k)} \qquad (3.3)$$

(using (2.5)). Assume now that we are given finite dimensional subspaces $\mathcal{V}_h = \Upsilon_h \times M_h \times \Phi_h$. For the sake of simplicity we may think that we have a global decomposition $\mathcal{T}_h$ of Ω into finite elements ω (say, triangles), which is compatible with the macro-element subdivision (2.1) (in other words, for every ω in $\mathcal{T}_h$ and for every Ω_k, the symmetric difference $(\Omega_k \cup \omega) \setminus (\Omega_k \cap \omega)$ has zero measure). The decomposition $\mathcal{T}_h$ induces then, in a natural way, finite element decompositions of each Ω_k, of each Γ_k, and of Σ. For the sake of simplicity we shall write $\sum_{\omega(k)}$ and $\sum_{\sigma(k)}$ for the sum over those elements ω (resp. σ) belonging to Ω_k (resp. Γ_k). We shall also denote by h_ω and h_σ the diameter of ω and σ, respectively. As far as the degrees of the polynomials are concerned, we allow the maximum generality; the degree can also change from one macro-element to another. Since $\mathcal{V}_h \subset \mathcal{V}$, the functions v_h^k must be continuous in Ω_k, and φ_h must also be continuous on Σ.

Remark 3.1: Our assumptions on $\mathcal{V}_h$ are much more restrictive than necessary. In principle we can easily adapt these ideas to more general subspaces, even allowing different Galerkin methods (Fourier, spectral, wavelets etc.) from one Ω_k to another. However, as we shall see, the notation (more than the actual implementation) is already cumbersome in our simplified case, and would become too heavy in a more general one. ∎

From now on we shall often write U and V instead of (u, λ, ψ) and (v, μ, φ).

The bilinear form $\mathcal{A}_2(U, V)$ that we want to add to $\mathcal{A}_1(U, V)$ is the Fréchet derivative of the functional

$$J(V) = (1/2)|V|^2_{2,h} = \frac{1}{2} \sum_k \Big\{ \sum_{\omega(k)} h_\omega^2 \, \|A v^k\|^2_{L^2(\omega)} + $$
$$+ \sum_{\sigma(k)} (h_\sigma \, \|\mu^k - \partial v^k / \partial n_A^k\|^2_{L^2(\sigma)} + h_\sigma \, \|v^k - \varphi\|^2_{H^1(\sigma)}) \Big\}, \qquad (3.4)$$

(i.e., $\mathcal{A}_2(U, V)$ is the bilinear symmetric form associated with (3.4)). Note that (3.4) also defines the seminorm $|\cdot|_{2,h}$. The norm $\|\cdot\|_{2,h}$ can now be defined in a natural way as

$$\|V\|^2_{2,h} = |V|^2 + \sum_k \Big\{ \sum_{\omega(k)} h_\omega^2 \, \|A v^k\|^2_{L^2(\omega)} + $$
$$+ \sum_{\sigma(k)} (h_\sigma \, \|\mu^k\|^2_{L^2(\sigma)} + h_\sigma \, \|\partial v^k / \partial n_A^k\|^2_{L^2(\sigma)} + h_\sigma \, \|\varphi\|^2_{H^1(\sigma)}) \Big\}. \qquad (3.5)$$

The space $\mathcal{V}_2(h)$ will be defined accordingly (i.e., as the set of the V's in $\mathcal{V}_1$ such that (3.5) is finite). Note that (1.13)-(1.14) are trivial, while (1.9)-(1.10) can be proved (with arguments very similar to those in [9] and [3], for instance) by means of local inverse inequalities for piecewise polynomials. Note also that, if U_1 is the exact solution of (2.13), we easily have

$$A_2(U_1, V) = \sum_k \sum_{\omega(k)} h_\omega^2 (f, Av^k)_{L^2(\omega)} \tag{3.6}$$

which is easily computable.

We can now write problem (1.18), in the present application, in its expanded form:

find $(u_h, \lambda_h, \psi_h) \in \Upsilon_h \times M_h \times \Phi_h$ such that
$$\sum_k \{ a_k(u_h^k, v_h^k) - < \lambda_h^k, v_h^k >_k + \sum_{\omega(k)} h_\omega^2 (Au_h^k, Av_h^k)_{L^2(\omega)} + \tag{3.7}$$

$$- \sum_{\sigma(k)} h_\sigma [(\lambda_h^k - \partial u_h^k/\partial n_A^k, \partial v_h^k/\partial n_A^k)_{L^2(\sigma)} + (u_h^k - \psi_h, v_h^k)_{H^1(\sigma)}] \} =$$

$$= \sum_k \sum_{\omega(k)} (f, v_h^k + Av_h^k)_{L^2(\omega)} \qquad \forall v_h \in \Upsilon_h$$

$$\sum_k \{ < \mu_h^k, u_h^k - \psi_h >_k + \sum_{\sigma(k)} h_\sigma (\lambda_h^k - \partial u_h^k/\partial n_A^k, \mu_h^k)_{L^2(\sigma)} \} = 0 \quad \forall \mu_h \in M_h \tag{3.8}$$

$$\sum_k \left\{ < \lambda_h^k, \varphi_h >_k + \sum_{\sigma(k)} h_\sigma (u_h^k - \psi_h, \varphi_h)_{H^1(\sigma)} \right\} = 0 \qquad \forall \varphi_h \in \Phi_h. \tag{3.9}$$

Problem (3.7) – (3.9) has clearly a unique solution. We point out explicitly that the regularized formulation (3.7) – (3.9) is still well suited for parallel implementation. Indeed, for ψ_h and f given, the resolution of (3.7) – (3.8) amounts to the resolution of N independent problems, each of them being a Dirichlet problem with Lagrange multipliers treated with a variant of [3]. For studying the convergence of (3.7) – (3.9) we have to introduce a $|\cdot|_{*,h}$ norm. An easy computation shows that, by setting

$$|V|_{*,h}^2 = \|v\|_\Upsilon^2 + \sum_k \sum_{\sigma(k)} h_\sigma^{-1} \left(\|v^k\|_{L^2(\sigma)}^2 + \|\varphi\|_{L^2(\sigma)}^2 + \|\mu^k\|_{(H^1(\sigma))'}^2 \right) \tag{3.10}$$

(where $(H^1(\sigma))'$ is the dual space of $H^1(\sigma)$), properties (1.21) and (1.22) hold for any reasonable choice of $\pi_h : \mathcal{V}_1 \to \mathcal{V}_h$. Hence, we only need to choose π_h in such a way that (1.23), (1.24) hold and both $\|U_1 - \pi_h U_1\|_{2,h}$ and $|U_1 - \pi_h|_{*,h}$ provide estimates of optimal order. This can be done very easily in many ways. Let us see, for instance, what can then be deduced from, say, Theorem 1.2 as an estimate for the error. To fix the ideas, assume that we approximate u, λ, ψ with piecewise polynomials of degree r, s, t respectively. Clearly $r \geq 1$, $s \geq 0$, $t \geq 1$. If the solution (u, λ, ψ) is smooth enough we have the following estimate

$$\| \psi - \psi_h \|^2_{H^{1/2}(\Sigma)} + \sum_k \left(\| u^k - u^k_h \|^2_{H^1(\Omega_k)} + \| \lambda^k - \lambda^k_h \|^2_{H^{-1/2}(\Gamma_k)} \right) \leq (3.11)$$

$$\leq \delta \sum_k \left\{ \sum_{\omega(k)} h^{2r}_\omega \ \| u^k \|^2_{H^{r+1}(\omega)} + \sum_{\sigma(k)} (h^{2s+3}_\sigma \ \| \lambda^k \|^2_{H^{s+1}(\sigma)} + \right.$$

$$\left. + h^{2t+1}_\sigma \ \| \psi \|^2_{H^{t+1}(\sigma)}) \right\}$$

with δ constant independent of h.

References

1. I. Babuška: The finite element method with lagrangian multipliers, Numer. Math., 20, 179–192, 1973.

2. C. Baiocchi and F. Brezzi: in preparation.

3. H.J.C. Barbosa, T.J.R. Hughes: Boundary Lagrange multipliers in finite element methods: error analysis in natural norms, Numer. Math., 62, 1–16, 1992.

4. C. Bernardi, Y. Maday and A.T. Patera: A new nonconforming approach to domain decompositions: The mortar element method. In *Nonlinear Partial Differential Equations and their Applications* (H.Brezis-J.L.Lions eds.), Pitman and Wiley, 1989.

5. F. Brezzi and M. Fortin: *Mixed and hybrid finite element methods*, Springer Verlag, New York 1991.

6. F. Brezzi and L.D. Marini: Macro hybrid elements and domain decomposition methods. (To appear in *Proc. Colloque en l'honneur du 60ème anniversaire de Jean Cea*, Sophia-Antipolis, April 1992).

7. F. Brezzi and L.D. Marini: A three-field domain decomposition method. (To appear in *Proc. 6th International Conference on Domain Decomposition Methods in Science and Engineering*, Como, June 1992).

8. F. Brezzi and L.D. Marini: in preparation.

9. J. Douglas, jr. and J. Wang: An absolutely stabilized finite element method for the Stokes problem, Math. Comp., 52, 495–508, 1989.

10. L.P. Franca and S.L. Frey: Stabilized finite element methods: II. The incompressible Navier-Stokes equations, (to appear in Comput. Meths. Appl. Mech. Engrg.).

11. L.P. Franca, S.L. Frey and T.J.R. Hughes: Stabilized finite element methods: I. Application to the advective- diffusive model, Comput. Meths. Appl. Mech. Engrg., 95, 253–276, 1992.

12. L.P. Franca and T.J.R. Hughes: Two classes of mixed finite element methods, Comput. Meths. Appl. Mech. Engrg., 69, 89–129, 1988.

13. L.P. Franca and R. Stenberg: Error analysis of some Galerkin least square methods for the elasticity equations, SIAM J. Numer. Anal., 28, 1680–1697, 1991.

An Efficient Implementation of
the Spectral Partitioning Algorithm
on Connection Machine Systems

Zdenek Johan and Thomas J.R. Hughes

Division of Applied Mechanics, Stanford University
Stanford, CA 94305–4040

Abstract. A parallel implementation of the spectral partitioning algorithm is developed. A two-level parallelization is proposed to achieve maximum efficiency on massively parallel computers. Special features of the Connection Machine software such as scan operations and communication primitives are used to improve the efficiency of the algorithm. Decompositions of unstructured finite element meshes demonstrate the performance of this implementation.

1. Introduction

The spectral partitioning algorithm was proposed by Pothen *et al.* [10] as the basis for computing small vertex separators for sparse matrices. Simon [11] applied this algorithm to mesh decomposition and showed that spectral partitioning compared favorably with other decomposition techniques. Venkatakrishnan *et al.* [12] and Das *et al.* [3] used the spectral partitioning algorithm in conjunction with unstructured finite volume Euler codes on the Intel iPSC/860. The major drawback of the spectral partitioning algorithm is its high computing cost, as noted in [11]. It is often stated that a finite element mesh can be decomposed after it is generated, and the decomposition reused for the different calculations performed on that mesh. However, a new partitioning is to be obtained if adaptive mesh refinement is required. The mesh also has to be re-decomposed if the computer configuration (i.e., the number of processing nodes available to the user) is changed between two calculations. In order to avoid the mesh decomposition from becoming a significant computational bottleneck, an efficient parallel implementation of the spectral partitioning algorithm using the Fortran 90 language is developed.

2. Parallel Spectral Partitioning Algorithm

The first step is to define a good representation of the mesh element topology.

This is done through the rank-two array IEE of dimension $n_{\text{faces}} \times n_{\text{el}}$ which contains the list of elements sharing a face with a given element. n_{faces} is the number of element faces (e.g., $n_{\text{faces}} = 4$ for a tetrahedron and $n_{\text{faces}} = 6$ for a brick); and n_{el} is the number of elements. An element having a face on the mesh boundary has its corresponding entry set to zero. IEE is sometimes referred to as the *dual mesh connectivity array*. The purpose of the spectral partitioning algorithm is to generate a reordering of the elements P based on IEE such that n_{par} nicely shaped partitions of adjacent elements are obtained. These subdomains are then mapped to the n_{pn} processing nodes of the computer. The number of partitions is actually determined from the mapping strategy used by the massively parallel computer. In the case of the Connection Machine systems, a block decomposition is used: The $n_{\text{par}} - 1$ first partitions contain the same number of elements, the last partition having the remaining elements. This leads to having $\eta_{\text{el}} = \lceil n_{\text{el}}/n_{\text{pn}} \rceil$ elements in the first $n_{\text{par}} - 1$ partitions, with $n_{\text{par}} = \lceil n_{\text{el}}/\eta_{\text{el}} \rceil$ (Note: In the current release 1.1 of the run-time system on the CM-2/200 systems, n_{pn} has to be set to 4 times the number of processing nodes for the above mapping strategy to work. This restriction will be removed in release 2.1). Note that $n_{\text{par}} = n_{\text{pn}}$ for a sufficiently large number of elements.

The number of processing nodes is decomposed into a product of primes, viz.

$$n_{\text{pn}} = p_1 \times p_2 \times \ldots \times p_{N_{\text{iter}}} \tag{1}$$

In practice, n_{pn} is a power of two. However, future massively parallel computers may have a number of processing nodes not being a power of two. These future computers may also be able to keep working even if some processing nodes fail. Using the prime number decomposition (1) already makes the algorithm portable to these future configurations. The spectral partitioning algorithm is then applied recursively for N_{iter} iterations (i.e., the whole mesh is decomposed into p_1 partitions, each of which in turn is decomposed into p_2 partitions, and so on). The implementation of the algorithm is done such that all elements of the mesh are treated in parallel. It implies a two-level parallelization; one level on the partitions generated at a given stage of the recursive process and the other on the elements in each partition. This is to be compared with a serial implementation of the algorithm where not only the elements but also the partitions are processed sequentially. The number of calls to the partitioning algorithm is therefore reduced from $n_{\text{par}} - 1$ (in the sequential case) to at most $\lfloor \log_2(n_{\text{pn}}) \rfloor$. Moreover, there is no loss of performance during the recursive process since the Connection Machine system always processes the same number of data.

The array IEE is used to evaluate the Laplacian matrix L, defined as

$$L_{ij} = \begin{cases} 1, & \text{if elements } i \text{ and } j \text{ share a face;} \\ 0, & \text{otherwise.} \end{cases} \tag{2}$$

$$L_{ii} = -\sum_{\substack{j=1 \\ j \neq i}}^{n_{el}} L_{ij} \tag{3}$$

L is a negative semi-definite matrix. It can be easily shown that the eigenvector associated with the zero eigenvalue is $e = \{1, 1, \ldots, 1\}^T$. For a connected mesh, the zero eigenvalue has a multiplicity of one. The properties of the second largest eigenvalue (i.e., in absolute value, the smallest nonzero eigenvalue) and its associated eigenvector f have been studied by Fiedler [4, 5, 6]. He has shown that the ordering of f provides some information on the partitioning of the mesh. The vector f will be referred to as the *Fiedler vector*. In the parallel implementation of the partitioning algorithm, the second largest eigenvalue and the Fiedler vector are evaluated using a special version of the Lanczos algorithm [9]. The complete parallel spectral partitioning algorithm is presented in Box 1 and Box 2. Note that all array operations are performed component by component, as defined in the Fortran 90 language. For example, the component-wise calculation

$$r_i = u_i - \alpha_i v_i \tag{4}$$

actually reads

$$r_{ik} = u_{ik} - \alpha_{ik} v_{ik} \qquad k = 1, \ldots, n_{el} \tag{5}$$

The operator $(\cdot, \cdot)_d$ indicates a dot product on each partition defined by the partition delimiter d. Consider the case of two partitions:

$$\boldsymbol{u} = \begin{Bmatrix} u_1 \\ u_2 \\ \vdots \\ u_{p-1} \\ u_p \\ u_{p+1} \\ \vdots \\ u_{n_{el}} \end{Bmatrix}, \quad \boldsymbol{v} = \begin{Bmatrix} v_1 \\ v_2 \\ \vdots \\ v_{p-1} \\ v_p \\ v_{p+1} \\ \vdots \\ v_{n_{el}} \end{Bmatrix} \quad \text{and} \quad \boldsymbol{d} = \begin{Bmatrix} 1 \\ 0 \\ \vdots \\ 0 \\ 1 \\ 0 \\ \vdots \\ 0 \end{Bmatrix} \tag{6}$$

Then,

$$(u, v)_d = \left\{ \begin{array}{c} u_1v_1 + \ldots + u_{p-1}v_{p-1} \\ u_1v_1 + \ldots + u_{p-1}v_{p-1} \\ \vdots \\ u_1v_1 + \ldots + u_{p-1}v_{p-1} \\ u_pv_p + \ldots + u_{n_{el}}v_{n_{el}} \\ u_pv_p + \ldots + u_{n_{el}}v_{n_{el}} \\ \vdots \\ u_pv_p + \ldots + u_{n_{el}}v_{n_{el}} \end{array} \right\} \qquad (7)$$

This operation is actually performed in three steps:

i. First, a component-wise product of u and v is performed, i.e.,

$$u\,v = \left\{ \begin{array}{c} u_1v_1 \\ \vdots \\ u_{n_{el}}v_{n_{el}} \end{array} \right\} \qquad (8)$$

ii. A reversed scan-add operation, available from the CMF Utility Library, is then executed using d as the delimiter:

$$\text{scan-add}(u\,v; d) = \left\{ \begin{array}{c} u_1v_1 + u_2v_2 + \ldots + u_{p-1}v_{p-1} \\ u_2v_2 + \ldots + u_{p-1}v_{p-1} \\ \vdots \\ u_{p-1}v_{p-1} \\ u_pv_p + u_{p+1}v_{p+1} + \ldots + u_{n_{el}}v_{n_{el}} \\ u_{p+1}v_{p+1} + \ldots + u_{n_{el}}v_{n_{el}} \\ \vdots \\ u_{n_{el}}v_{n_{el}} \end{array} \right\} \qquad (9)$$

iii. Finally, a scan-copy operation is performed on the result of Step ii, leading to $(u, v)_d$. The scan operations are very efficient on the Connection Machine systems since they make use of special hardware.

The compact operator $\mathcal{C}_d(\cdot)$ extracts values from a given vector with d used as a mask. For example, if

$$u = \left\{ \begin{array}{c} u_1 \\ u_1 \\ \vdots \\ u_1 \\ u_2 \\ u_2 \\ \vdots \\ u_2 \end{array} \right\} \quad \text{and} \quad d = \left\{ \begin{array}{c} 1 \\ 0 \\ \vdots \\ 0 \\ 1 \\ 0 \\ \vdots \\ 0 \end{array} \right\} \qquad (10)$$

then,

$$\mathcal{C}_d(u) = \left\{ \begin{matrix} u_1 \\ u_2 \end{matrix} \right\} \tag{11}$$

This transformation is achieved using the PACK intrinsic Fortran 90 function. The inverse operator $\mathcal{C}_d^{-1}$ is implemented using the UNPACK intrinsic function followed by a scan-copy operation.

Box 1 - Parallel Spectral Partitioning Algorithm.

Given n_{el}, n_{pn} and IEE, proceed as follows:

(Calculate the number of elements per partition)
$\eta_{el} = \lceil n_{el}/n_{pn} \rceil$
(Decompose n_{pn} into a product of primes)
$n_{pn} = p_1 \times p_2 \times \ldots \times p_{N_{iter}}$
(Initialization)
$d = \{1, 0, \ldots, 0\}^T$ (partition delimiter)
$P = I_{n_{el}}$ (permutation mapping)
$\bar{n}_{par} = 1$ (current number of partitions)
$\bar{\eta}_{el} = \eta_{el} \, n_{pn}$ (current number of elements per partition)
(Loop over number of iterations)
$For \;\; n = 1, \ldots, N_{iter}$

     Form the Laplacian matrix L from IEE
     Calculate the Fiedler vector f (see Box 2)
     Update P using the reordering of f for each partition
     $\bar{\eta}_{el} = \bar{\eta}_{el}/p_n$
     $d_{i \times \bar{\eta}_{el} + 1} = 1 \qquad i = 0, 1, \ldots, \left\lfloor \dfrac{n_{el}-1}{\bar{\eta}_{el}} \right\rfloor$
     $\bar{n}_{par} = \displaystyle\sum_{i=1}^{n_{el}} d_i$
     Reorder IEE based on P
     Reset IEE for elements having a neighbor in a different partition
(End of loop over number of iterations)
Return

Box 2 - Calculation of the Fiedler vector.

Given L, d, $\bar{\eta}_{\text{el}}$, $\bar{n}_{\text{par}}$, N_{Lanczos} and $\varepsilon_{\text{Lanczos}}$, proceed as follows:

(Initialization)
$$e = \{1, 1, \ldots, 1\}^T$$
$$v_1 = \{1, 2, \ldots, \bar{\eta}_{\text{el}}, 1, 2, \ldots, \bar{\eta}_{\text{el}}, 1, \ldots\}^T$$
$$v_1 = v_1 - \frac{(v_1, e)_d}{(e, e)_d} e$$
$$v_1 = v_1 / (v_1, v_1)_d^{1/2}$$
$$u_1 = L\,v_1$$

(Loop over Lanczos iterations)
$For \quad i = 1, \ldots, N_{\text{Lanczos}}$

$\quad i_{\max} = i$

$\quad$ *(First part of Lanczos)*

$\quad \alpha_i = (u_i, v_i)_d$

$\quad r_i = u_i - \alpha_i v_i$

$\quad r_i = r_i - \dfrac{(r_i, e)_d}{(e, e)_d} e$

$\quad \beta_i = (r_i, r_i)_d^{1/2}$

$\quad$ *(Eigenvalue analysis)*

$\quad \bar{\alpha}_i = \mathcal{C}_d(\alpha_i) = \{\bar{\alpha}_{i,j}\}_{1 \leq j \leq \bar{n}_{\text{par}}}$

$\quad \bar{\beta}_i = \mathcal{C}_d(\beta_i) = \{\bar{\beta}_{i,j}\}_{1 \leq j \leq \bar{n}_{\text{par}}}$

$\quad$ Calculate the eigenvector $\zeta_j = \{\zeta_{k,j}\}_{1 \leq k \leq i}$ associated with

$\qquad$ the largest eigenvalue λ_j of

$$T_j = \begin{bmatrix} \bar{\alpha}_{1,j} & \bar{\beta}_{1,j} & & 0 \\ \bar{\beta}_{1,j} & \bar{\alpha}_{2,j} & \ddots & \\ & \ddots & \ddots & \bar{\beta}_{i-1,j} \\ 0 & & \bar{\beta}_{i-1,j} & \bar{\alpha}_{i,j} \end{bmatrix} \qquad j = 1, \ldots, \bar{n}_{\text{par}}$$

$\quad$ If accuracy of all λ_j's is within $[0, \varepsilon_{\text{Lanczos}}]$, **Exit** i loop

$\quad$ *(Second part of Lanczos)*

$\quad v_{i+1} = v_{i+1} / \beta_i$

$\quad u_{i+1} = L\,v_{i+1} - \beta_i v_i$

(End of loop over Lanczos iterations)
(Misconvergence treatment)
If $\lambda_j \geq 0$, $\{\zeta_{i,j}\}_{1 \leq i \leq i_{\max}} = 0 \qquad j = 1, \ldots, \bar{n}_{\text{par}}$

> (Calculate the Fiedler vector)
>
> $\bar{\zeta}_i = \{\zeta_{j,i}\}_{1 \le j \le \bar{n}_{\text{par}}} \qquad i = 1, \dots, i_{\max}$
>
> $$f = \sum_{i=i_{\max}}^{1} \mathcal{C}_d^{-1}(\bar{\zeta}_i)\, v_i$$
>
> (End)
>
> **Return**

The most crucial operations in the evaluation of the Fiedler vector are the matrix-vector products of the form $u = L\,v$. They have to be handled with special care to achieve good performance on the Connection Machine systems. The matrix-vector product $u = L\,v$ can be decomposed into two parts:

$$u_k = L_{kk}v_k + \sum_{\substack{l=1 \\ l \ne k}}^{n_{\text{el}}} L_{kl}v_l \qquad k = 1, \dots, n_{\text{el}} \tag{12}$$

The first term is simply a component-wise product between the vectors $\operatorname{diag}(L)$ and v and does not require any communication between processing nodes. Since $L_{kl} = 0$ or 1 for all $k \ne l$, the second term is actually a scatter operation. It can be rewritten

$$\sum_{\substack{l=1 \\ l \ne k}}^{n_{\text{el}}} L_{kl}v_l = \sum_{\substack{l=1 \\ \text{IEE}(l,k) \ne 0}}^{n_{\text{faces}}} v_{\text{IEE}(l,k)} \qquad k = 1, \dots, n_{\text{el}} \tag{13}$$

The scatter operation is achieved through the CMSSL (Connection Machine Scientific Software Library) [2] primitives `sparse_util_scatter_setup` and `sparse_util_scatter`. A mask is passed to these routines to allow the scatter only for the non-zero entries of IEE. The performance of these routines is given in [8] along with a description of the methodology implemented in the primitives.

The eigenvalue analysis performed during the Lanczos process is actually implemented on the front-end computer (or the control processor for a CM-5 system) for simplicity and maximum efficiency. The size of the data sets is indeed too small to out-balance the overhead associated with running on the processing nodes. Implementing that part of the algorithm on the front-end does not impede the overall performance because the time spent calculating the eigenvalues λ_j and the eigenvectors ζ_j is small compared to the array operations of the Lanczos algorithm.

A few additional remarks can be made about the evaluation of the Fiedler vector:

i. The first Lanczos vector v_1 is chosen such that information on the initial element ordering (or on the element reordering from the previous iteration of the recursive process) is passed to the Lanczos algorithm. Some mesh generators construct meshes in an orderly fashion which may help the Lanczos algorithm to converge faster.

ii. When experimenting with the parallel spectral partitioning algorithm, we have noticed that setting $N_{\text{Lanczos}} = 300$ and $\varepsilon_{\text{Lanczos}} = 10^{-4}$ yields nice mesh partitionings in a reasonable number of Lanczos iterations. These values are used for the numerical examples presented in the next section.

iii. If a partition is non-connected, i.e., the graph defined by the connectivity array IEE for that particular partition is non-connected, the zero eigenvalue of the Laplacian matrix associated with that partition has a multiplicity greater than 1. This leads to misconvergence of the Lanczos algorithm presented in Box 2. An easy way to cope with this potential problem is not to reorder the elements of the non-connected partitions. The latter will therefore be partitioned based on the ordering of the previous recursive iteration. This misconvergence could be avoided if orthogonalizations against e were performed for each connected block of the partitions independently of the others. This would mean defining a new delimiter d' for both the partitions and the connected blocks within each partition. The orthogonalization of a vector z against e would then read

$$z = z - \frac{(z, e)_{d'}}{(e, e)_{d'}} e \tag{14}$$

Unfortunately, no efficient technique for computing d' has been found yet, making this elegant treatment of misconvergence expensive to use on a massively parallel computer.

3. Partitioning Examples

3.1. Mesh Around a Double Ellipse

This example is a two-dimensional mesh around a space shuttle-like geometry made of two ellipses (see Figure 1). This mesh was used by Chalot and Hughes to perform high-speed inviscid chemically-reacting flow calculations [1]. Adaptive mesh refinement was applied in the bow shock region to better capture sharp gradients, creating possible difficulties for the partitioning process. The mesh has 8,307 nodes and 16,231 triangles. The parallel spectral partitioning algorithm was compiled using CMF version 1.1 and run in double precision on a 128-processing node CM-2 system under CMSS version 6.1. Separate calculations were made to decompose the mesh into 8, 16, 32, 64 and 128 partitions. The partitioning into 128 subdomains can be

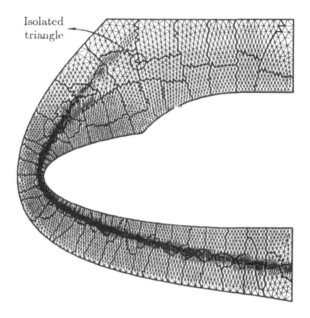

Figure 1. Mesh around a double ellipse. Decomposition into 128 partitions.

seen in Figure 1. One can note the high quality of the decomposition with nicely shaped partitions, even in the refined region.

Table 1 presents the statistics for the evaluation of the Fiedler vector at each iteration of the recursive process. The maximum number of Lanczos iterations allowed was reached during the decomposition into two subdomains. An explanation is the choice of the first Lanczos vector v_1 which led to a slow convergence of the Lanczos algorithm. However, the element reordering after the initial decomposition helped reduce the number of Lanczos iterations for the remainder of the recursive process. The second largest eigenvalue is always negative (as expected since the Laplacian matrix is negative semi-definite) except for the last iteration. This misconvergence indicates the generation of a non-connected partition, as defined in Section 2 (one can see an isolated triangle in the upper-left part of the mesh in Figure 1. This triangle is associated with the mesh partition into the bottom right of it). This phenomenon is well handled by the algorithm and has no negative effect on the quality of the decomposition. We have noticed that partitions have a tendency to become

Table 1. Mesh around a double ellipse. Lanczos convergence statistics for the generation of 128 partitions.

Recursion No. (n in Box 1)	No. of Lanczos iter. (i_{max} in Box 2)	$\min\limits_{1 \le j \le \bar{n}_{par}} \lambda_j$	$\max\limits_{1 \le j \le \bar{n}_{par}} \lambda_j$
1	300	-0.49×10^{-5}	-0.49×10^{-5}
2	134	-0.11×10^{-3}	-0.92×10^{-4}
3	135	-0.44×10^{-3}	-0.40×10^{-3}
4	113	-0.22×10^{-2}	-0.94×10^{-3}
5	115	-0.54×10^{-2}	-0.28×10^{-2}
6	102	-0.12×10^{-1}	-0.45×10^{-2}
7	79	-0.23×10^{-1}	0.29×10^{-5}

Table 2. Mesh around a double ellipse. Number of shared edges and nodes for several decompositions.

No. of domains	No. of shared edges	% total	No. of shared nodes	% total
8	188	0.8%	195	2.4%
16	381	1.6%	396	4.8%
32	752	3.1%	773	9.3%
64	1483	6.0%	1479	17.8%
128	2154	8.8%	2101	25.3%

Table 3. Mesh around a double ellipse. Elapsed and CM-busy times for several decompositions on a 128-processing node Connection Machine system CM-2.

No. of domains	Elapsed time	CM-busy time
8	52 s	47 s
16	62 s	55 s
32	73 s	64 s
64	89 s	73 s
128	96 s	79 s

non-connected when they contain a small number of elements. Table 2 contains the number of edges and nodes shared by two or more subdomains and the percentages relative to the total number of edges (equal to 24,537 for this example) and nodes (shared edges are darkened in Figure 1). The percentages remain acceptable even when the number of subdomains increases. This is another indication of the high quality of the decomposition. Finally, Table 3 presents the elapsed and CM-busy times for the different decompositions. The generation of 128 partitions is merely twice as expensive as the generation of 8 partitions. In addition, the overall time of 1 min 36 s spent to obtain the 128 subdomains is very reasonable. These timings show the effect of the two-level parallelization technique described in Section 2. The difference between elapsed time and CM-busy time is mainly caused by the eigenvalue analysis which is performed on the front-end computer.

3.2. Mesh Between Two Sphere Sections

This three-dimensional unstructured mesh demonstrates the efficiency of the parallel spectral partitioning algorithm for a large number of elements. The domain enclosed between two non-concentric sphere sections is discretized into 20,374 nodes and 107,416 tetrahedra (see Figure 2). The mesh was decomposed into 8, 16, 32, 64 and 128 partitions on a 512-processing node CM-2 running CMSS version 6.1. The decomposition into 16 subdomains is shown in Figure 3. The high quality of the decomposition is striking, the subdomains being very regular with "clean" boundaries.

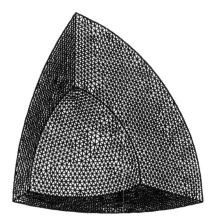

Figure 2. Mesh between two sphere sections. View of the surface mesh.

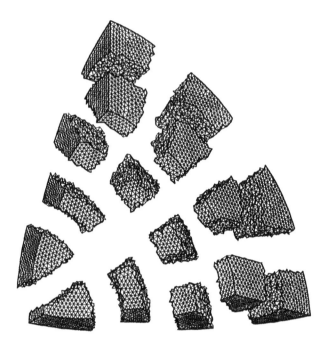

Figure 3. Decomposition into 16 partitions.

The Lanczos convergence statistics for the decomposition into 128 partitions are given in Table 4. As in the previous example, the maximum number of Lanczos iterations is reached during the first iteration of the recursion process but decreases afterwards. The subdomains are connected since the second largest eigenvalues are negative for all partitions. Table 5 contains the number of shared faces and nodes for each decomposition. The total number of faces equals 218,807. One can note that the number of shared nodes can become a substantial part of the total number of nodes when the number of partitions increases. For a given number of elements, the number of tetrahedra connected to a node can indeed be very large, causing the ratio between the boundary and interior nodes to be higher than for a hexahedral mesh or two-dimensional meshes. Finally, timings for each decomposition are given in Table 6. An elapsed time of 3 min 13 s to partition a 100,000+ element mesh into 128 subdomains is very acceptable.

Table 4. Mesh between two sphere sections. Lanczos convergence statistics for the generation of 128 partitions.

Recursion No. (n in Box 1)	No. of Lanczos iter. (i_{max} in Box 2)	$\displaystyle\min_{1\leq j\leq \bar{n}_{par}} \lambda_j$	$\displaystyle\max_{1\leq j\leq \bar{n}_{par}} \lambda_j$
1	300	-0.78×10^{-3}	-0.78×10^{-3}
2	165	-0.11×10^{-2}	-0.96×10^{-3}
3	206	-0.23×10^{-2}	-0.17×10^{-2}
4	192	-0.43×10^{-2}	-0.29×10^{-2}
5	150	-0.86×10^{-2}	-0.47×10^{-2}
6	145	-0.17×10^{-1}	-0.22×10^{-4}
7	116	-0.24×10^{-1}	-0.11×10^{-5}

Table 5. Mesh between two sphere sections. Number of shared faces and nodes for several decompositions.

No. of domains	No. of shared faces	% total	No. of shared nodes	% total
8	5186	2.4%	2735	13.4%
16	8005	3.7%	4095	20.1%
32	11553	5.3%	5747	28.2%
64	16055	7.3%	7721	37.9%
128	21502	9.8%	9827	48.2%

Table 6. Mesh between two sphere sections. Elapsed and CM-busy times for several decompositions on a 512-processing node Connection Machine system CM-2.

No. of domains	Elapsed time	CM-busy time
8	94 s	88 s
16	119 s	112 s
32	145 s	134 s
64	175 s	159 s
128	193 s	170 s

4. Conclusions

We have presented a parallel implementation of a mesh partitioning algorithm on the Connection Machine systems. Good performance is achieved through the use of communication primitives and special software features such as scans. This efficient mesh partitioning algorithm can now be used in conjunction with special mapping strategies to increase the speed of the gather/scatter operations needed in finite element applications, as described in [7]. Future work will focus on improved treatment of misconvergence of the Lanczos algorithm, and on the use of local subroutines to implement the eigenvalue analysis in a MIMD-style of programming.

Acknowledgements

The authors would like to express their appreciation to Horst D. Simon for providing them with his implementation of the spectral partitioning algorithm, and to Frédéric Chalot and James R. Stewart for generating the meshes. This research was supported by the NASA Langley Research Center, the Office of Naval Research and Dassault Aviation. Access to Connection Machine systems was provided by Thinking Machines Corporation and the Department of Geophysics at Stanford University.

References

1. F. Chalot and T.J.R. Hughes, "Analysis of hypersonic flows in thermochemical equilibrium by application of the Galerkin/least-squares formulation," *ICIAM 91: Proceedings of the International Conference for Industrial and Applied Mathematics*, ed. R.E. O'Malley, SIAM, 1992.

2. *CMSSL for CM Fortran, Version 2.2*, Thinking Machines Corporation, Cambridge, MA, 1991.

3. R. Das, D.J. Mavriplis, J. Saltz, S. Gupta and R. Ponnusamy, "The design and implementation of a parallel unstructured Euler solver using software primitives," *AIAA 30th Aerospace Sciences Meeting*, AIAA-92-0562, 1992.

4. M. Fiedler, "Algebraic connectivity of graphs," *Czechoslovak Mathematical Journal*, **23** (1973) 298–305.

5. M. Fiedler, "Eigenvectors of acyclic matrices," *Czechoslovak Mathematical Journal*, **25** (1975) 607–618.

6. M. Fiedler, "A property of eigenvectors of nonnegative symmetric matrices and its application to graph theory," *Czechoslovak Mathematical Journal*, **25** (1975) 610 633.

7. Z. Johan, "Data parallel finite element techniques for large-scale computational fluid dynamics," *Ph.D. Thesis*, Stanford University, 1992.

8. K.K. Mathur, "On the use of randomized address maps in unstructured three-dimensional finite element simulations," *Technical Report*, TMC-37/CS90-4, Thinking Machines Corporation, Cambridge, MA, 1990.

9. B.N. Parlett, H. Simon and L.M. Stringer, "On estimating the largest eigenvalue with the Lanzcos algorithm," *Mathematics of Computation*, **38** (1982) 153–165.

10. A. Pothen, H.D. Simon and K.-P. Liou, "Partitioning sparse matrices with eigenvectors of graphs," *SIAM Journal of Matrix Analysis and Applications*, **11** (1990) 430–452.

11. H.D. Simon, "Partitioning of unstructured problems for parallel processing," *Computing Systems in Engineering*, **2** (1991) 135–148.

12. V. Venkatakrishnan, H.D. Simon and T.J. Barth, "A MIMD implementation of a parallel Euler solver for unstructured grids," Report RNR-91-024, NASA Ames Research Center, 1991.

Lecture Notes in Computer Science

For information about Vols. 1–570
please contact your bookseller or Springer-Verlag

Vol. 610: F. von Martial, Coordinating Plans of Autonomous Agents. XII, 246 pages. 1992. (Subseries LNAI).

Vol. 611: M. P. Papazoglou, J. Zeleznikow (Eds.), The Next Generation of Information Systems: From Data to Knowledge. VIII, 310 pages. 1992. (Subseries LNAI).

Vol. 612: M. Tokoro, O. Nierstrasz, P. Wegner (Eds.), Object-Based Concurrent Computing. Proceedings, 1991. X, 265 pages. 1992.

Vol. 613: J. P. Myers, Jr., M. J. O'Donnell (Eds.), Constructivity in Computer Science. Proceedings, 1991. X, 247 pages. 1992.

Vol. 614: R. G. Herrtwich (Ed.), Network and Operating System Support for Digital Audio and Video. Proceedings, 1991. XII, 403 pages. 1992.

Vol. 615: O. Lehrmann Madsen (Ed.), ECOOP '92. European Conference on Object Oriented Programming. Proceedings. X, 426 pages. 1992.

Vol. 616: K. Jensen (Ed.), Application and Theory of Petri Nets 1992. Proceedings, 1992. VIII, 398 pages. 1992.

Vol. 617: V. Mařík, O. Štěpánková, R. Trappl (Eds.), Advanced Topics in Artificial Intelligence. Proceedings, 1992. IX, 484 pages. 1992. (Subseries LNAI).

Vol. 618: P. M. D. Gray, R. J. Lucas (Eds.), Advanced Database Systems. Proceedings, 1992. X, 260 pages. 1992.

Vol. 619: D. Pearce, H. Wansing (Eds.), Nonclassical Logics and Information Proceedings. Proceedings, 1990. VII, 171 pages. 1992. (Subseries LNAI).

Vol. 620: A. Nerode, M. Taitslin (Eds.), Logical Foundations of Computer Science - Tver '92. Proceedings. IX, 514 pages. 1992.

Vol. 621: O. Nurmi, E. Ukkonen (Eds.), Algorithm Theory - SWAT '92. Proceedings. VIII, 434 pages. 1992.

Vol. 622: F. Schmalhofer, G. Strube, Th. Wetter (Eds.), Contemporary Knowledge Engineering and Cognition. Proceedings, 1991. XII, 258 pages. 1992. (Subseries LNAI).

Vol. 623: W. Kuich (Ed.), Automata, Languages and Programming. Proceedings, 1992. XII, 721 pages. 1992.

Vol. 624: A. Voronkov (Ed.), Logic Programming and Automated Reasoning. Proceedings, 1992. XIV, 509 pages. 1992. (Subseries LNAI).

Vol. 625: W. Vogler, Modular Construction and Partial Order Semantics of Petri Nets. IX, 252 pages. 1992.

Vol. 626: E. Börger, G. Jäger, H. Kleine Büning, M. M . Richter (Eds.), Computer Science Logic. Proceedings, 1991. VIII, 428 pages. 1992.

Vol. 628: G. Vosselman, Relational Matching. IX, 190 pages. 1992.

Vol. 629: I. M. Havel, V. Koubek (Eds.), Mathematical Foundations of Computer Science 1992. Proceedings. IX, 521 pages. 1992.

Vol. 630: W. R. Cleaveland (Ed.), CONCUR '92. Proceedings. X, 580 pages. 1992.

Vol. 631: M. Bruynooghe, M. Wirsing (Eds.), Programming Language Implementation and Logic Programming. Proceedings, 1992. XI, 492 pages. 1992.

Vol. 632: H. Kirchner, G. Levi (Eds.), Algebraic and Logic Programming. Proceedings, 1992. IX, 457 pages. 1992.

Vol. 633: D. Pearce, G. Wagner (Eds.), Logics in AI. Proceedings. VIII, 410 pages. 1992. (Subseries LNAI).

Vol. 634: L. Bougé, M. Cosnard, Y. Robert, D. Trystram (Eds.), Parallel Processing: CONPAR 92 – VAPP V. Proceedings. XVII, 853 pages. 1992.

Vol. 635: J. C. Derniame (Ed.), Software Process Technology. Proceedings, 1992. VIII, 253 pages. 1992.

Vol. 636: G. Comyn, N. E. Fuchs, M. J. Ratcliffe (Eds.), Logic Programming in Action. Proceedings, 1992. X, 324 pages. 1992. (Subseries LNAI).

Vol. 637: Y. Bekkers, J. Cohen (Eds.), Memory Management. Proceedings, 1992. XI, 525 pages. 1992.

Vol. 639: A. U. Frank, I. Campari, U. Formentini (Eds.), Theories and Methods of Spatio-Temporal Reasoning in Geographic Space. Proceedings, 1992. XI, 431 pages. 1992.

Vol. 640: C. Sledge (Ed.), Software Engineering Education. Proceedings, 1992. X, 451 pages. 1992.

Vol. 641: U. Kastens, P. Pfahler (Eds.), Compiler Construction. Proceedings, 1992. VIII, 320 pages. 1992.

Vol. 642: K. P. Jantke (Ed.), Analogical and Inductive Inference. Proceedings, 1992. VIII, 319 pages. 1992. (Subseries LNAI).

Vol. 643: A. Habel, Hyperedge Replacement: Grammars and Languages. X, 214 pages. 1992.

Vol. 644: A. Apostolico, M. Crochemore, Z. Galil, U. Manber (Eds.), Combinatorial Pattern Matching. Proceedings, 1992. X, 287 pages. 1992.

Vol. 645: G. Pernul, A M. Tjoa (Eds.), Entity-Relationship Approach – ER '92. Proceedings, 1992. XI, 439 pages, 1992.

Vol. 646: J. Biskup, R. Hull (Eds.), Database Theory – ICDT '92. Proceedings, 1992. IX, 449 pages. 1992.

Vol. 647: A. Segall, S. Zaks (Eds.), Distributed Algorithms. X, 380 pages. 1992.

Vol. 648: Y. Deswarte, G. Eizenberg, J.-J. Quisquater (Eds.), Computer Security – ESORICS 92. Proceedings. XI, 451 pages. 1992.

Vol. 649: A. Pettorossi (Ed.), Meta-Programming in Logic. Proceedings, 1992. XII, 535 pages. 1992.

Vol. 650: T. Ibaraki, Y. Inagaki, K. Iwama, T. Nishizeki, M. Yamashita (Eds.), Algorithms and Computation. Proceedings, 1992. XI, 510 pages. 1992.

Vol. 652: R. Shyamasundar (Ed.), Foundations of Software Technology and Theoretical Computer Science. Proceedings, 1992. XIII, 405 pages. 1992.

Vol. 653: A. Bensoussan, J.-P. Verjus (Eds.), Future Tendencies in Computer Science, Control and Applied Mathematics. Proceedings, 1992. XV, 371 pages. 1992.

Vol. 654: A. Nakamura, M. Nivat, A. Saoudi, P. S. P. Wang, K. Inoue (Eds.), Prallel Image Analysis. Proceedings, 1992. VIII, 312 pages. 1992.